MY I'S:

ISMS

IGNORANCE

INTERRELATIONSHIPS

AND

INSIGHTS

CHARLIE SCHMIDTKE

Charleston, SC
www.PalmettoPublishing.com

My I's:

Copyright © 2020 by Charlie Schmidtke

All rights reserved

First Edition

Paperback ISBN: 978-1-64990-084-5
Hardcover: 978-1-64111-851-4
eBook: 978-1-64990-504-8

DEDICATION

To my Munchkins: May they understand part of their family's history.

Collette – the generational matriarch
Isabella – the drill queen
Jonah – reader *par excellence*
Alex – the careful creator
Liam – filled with energy and perception
Fiona – the quiet caretaker
Eliot – my duplicate
Elizabeth – a child of Hope

TABLE OF CONTENTS

Part VI: It's All about Love and Respect

INTRODUCTION TO MY REFLECTIONS

If you don't recount your family history, it will be lost.
Honor your own stories and tell them too.
The tales may not seem very important, but they are
what binds families and makes each of us who we are.

Madeline L'Engle

The mansion loomed in front of us: do we dare knock and go into a world quite different from our own? We had parked a couple of blocks away because there were no driveways and so many of the guests had probably already arrived and taken up the on- street spaces. Of course, we wouldn't have gone into a driveway anyway. We knew our place, and it wasn't high enough on the social scale to grab a prime location. Our apartment was not that far away, but I didn't want to walk in the heavy aired, August evening. I was nervous enough and didn't need the extra wetness that sweating from a walk would cause.

We had entered the strange and challenging world of New Orleans after venturing away from our white suburban, northern lifestyles. We had been married for just two weeks (22 and 21 year olds in 1968). I had started my graduate school classes at Tulane and Diane had started teaching second grade across the Mississippi in a highly transient area whose population primarily worked in a ship yard. We were flush with a new life and new marriage 1300 miles away from her hometown of Kenmore, New York and mine, Niagara Falls. We had graduated from our respective colleges in May and I had also received my commission in the Army. For some unknown reason I had been granted a graduate school deferment even though the Viet Nam war was in full swing and they certainly needed 2nd lieutenants in the MPs. Thankfully the Department of Defense extended my deferment the entire four years I needed to complete my Masters degree and all the PhD requirements (except for some corrections on my doctoral dissertation) in Philosophy. The adjustment to this new life of ours was a bit of a shock and we were still trying to adjust to the spoken and unspoken customs of this southern city.

We were living in the married apartments for Tulane University. A one-bedroom apartment doesn't quite explain our apartment's smallness. The kitchen was small enough to sit on the counter, which was adjacent to the living room. From that sitting position it was possible to open the fridge, wash the dishes and cook from the stove. We also, unfortunately, shared our living quarters with roaches. Per instructions we put masking tape on all crevices and openings around the sink and in the cupboards. Pest control came monthly, but all efforts were to no avail in an eight-story apartment complex in urban New Orleans. The roaches weren't all that apparent during the day but dare venture into the kitchen at night and turn on a light. The skittering sounds were alarming. Walking at night outside also brought the crunching sounds of larger, outdoor roaches meeting their doom. We lived there for three years and never completely adjusted to the intruders. Of course, if you look at it from their perspective, we were the intruders: they had been there long before we came and would remain regardless of all the control efforts.

Our adventure that evening to the party was early in our sojourn and we weren't familiar with the area. So we took the scrap paper with the address and drove down St. Charles looking for the intersecting side street. Even after we found the street and the mansion, we remained in the car for a moment to screw up our courage to venture forth. Diane was beautifully adorned in a dress and I had on a sport coat and tie that would just have to do for the evening. When we had gotten out of our car, we looked around and instantly knew we didn't belong. The surrounding houses were just as daunting as the one we faced but not as majestic as we found on Audubon (a gated street) a couple of blocks away. We were near St. Charles, a street of great character: Oak trees with Spanish moss, a Trolley system, and more mansions, one which was reportedly designed after Tara, of *Gone With the Wind* fame. I went around the car, opened Diane's door, clasped her hand and we meandered up the street to the walk leading to a new world. After a deep sigh we rang the bell and were greeted by a butler (I assume) well clad in his formal wear. Was the sport coat and dress sufficient? We walked into the room and confirmed we didn't belong.

We were attending the so-called casual start of the semester social at the Department Chairman's. The mansion was the product of his wife's wealthy inheritance. He was a prolific writer and had an established reputation in the Philosophy of Science. I later learned that his wife published his writings and her money probably had more to do with his position than his scholarship. We were fish out of water at this gathering with the multitude of servants, the formal conversations, the graduate students' attempts at profound dialogue in front of their professors, and the camaraderie we would never share in our four years. Other than the feelings of disorientation, the only other memory I have of that evening was being introduced to Professor Hamburg, a short, German professor who was completely full of his self-importance. He was making his way around the room pretending that he cared to meet all of the new students. That judgment may not have been accurate, but my own discomfort became projected onto others. Who would be interested in meeting me? However, my initial stereotyping of his self-importance was confirmed as I later learned that he was a world-renowned scholar of the German Philosopher, Immanuel Kant. He refused to teach any course on Kant at Tulane because the students did not speak or read fluent German. "Kant can only be taught in German; so you will have to get someone else with lower standards than mine to teach him, if you dare to bother!" (a quote another student shared with me the following week). As I introduced Diane, then me, he looked both of us over and stated: "She should be the student," nodding to Diane; and "you look like a football player", seeming to indicate that I was irrelevant. He pivoted and didn't bother to waste his time on us the rest of the evening.

This story has always struck me as an "aha" moment. I, a white male, was being stereotyped and this categorizing was not benign. It was only four years earlier that I had graduated from high school as a co-captain on our football team. My coach told me to forego a collegiate football career because I was injury prone. "Use your brains in school and you'll be better off," was his sage advice. Now my thick neck and stocky appearance led this German stranger to peg me as more brawn than brain and an unlikely candidate for his graduate program. The following year I successfully completed a course from him and am sure he had no recollection of our initial meeting. However, this brief encounter seems like a good place to start in sharing my journey in trying to understand and come to terms with the prejudices I have had, that I have witnessed and that I continue to experience in my life. These prejudices are cast within a larger framework of ignorance and the dynamics of interpersonal relationships that characterize my life and experiences.

This book is fundamentally a personal journey that includes my thoughts about my life and what I'll refer to as my "I's": isms, ignorance, interpersonal relationships and the insights I have had.

"Isms" – we've all encountered them, sometimes actively, sometimes passively. My stories will share the journey that a white male born in 1946 has had in coming to terms with the inevitable stereotyping that leads to common prejudices, feelings of bigotry, biases, attitudes towards others and discriminatory behavior in the areas of race, religion, gender, generations, and grieving. I will be interspersing my personal experiences with reflections in order to present my Life Review on the unwitting ways I have dehumanized others and what I have learned through the discriminating behaviors that have been a part of my actions/inactions or those of others in my life.

Ignorance -- Most of us go about our lives with a great deal of ignorance about the dynamics of interpersonal relationships, stereotyping, bigotry and discriminatory behavior. I believe my prejudices have been due to ignorance and a lack of awareness more than any malicious intent to degrade or injure another. By confronting my own ignorance, I have learned to recognize some of those inherent biases that I now believe are mired in a convenient white washing of serious barriers to respect based human relationships. We tend to bestow a distorted sense of self-worth upon ourselves (sometimes too positive; other times overly clouded.)

Interpersonal Relationships -- I also am reflecting upon the dynamics of the interpersonal relationships that are so important in forming the person I have become. The eyes on the cover are those of the most important women and people in my life: Diane and our daughters - Tara, Kris, Katie and Heidi. I see them as the transformational forces in my life. Although so many others have influenced me and changed who I am and what I believe, they, by far, are the foundation for this book. As I focus upon the "inter" dimension of interpersonal relationships (the connections between and among people) what they have taught me is deep and profound. I would not be who I am without them in my life.

Insight -- My journey through my "I's" of ignorance, isms, and interrelationships has led me to a crucial other "I": insight. This insight is a deep self-awareness that accepts internal honesty. My Life Review and self-reflections have opened up my eyes to chambers within my mind and heart that I had not understood nor contemplated before. The women of my life have ensured that I reflected and changed that which was disrespectful, ignorant, and misguided.

And my final I: "I," myself. This book is wholly personal, self-reflective and autobiographical. My stories are usually shared experiences or events. I am sure that those with whom I have shared those moments would provide different details or recall the events in ways that are different from what I have written. But isn't that the nature of collective memory? How often do we argue or become upset with the different recall of events? I hope my recall is clear enough for loved ones to accept my version of events. More importantly, however, is the meaning of the events. All who are involved will have some degree of shared meaning; yet it is quite evident that meanings will shift from person to person. I believe my journey has provided me with some insight into myself as well as the human condition. I apologize to all of those I have inadvertently (or blatantly) hurt or offended over my lifetime.

I continue to suffer from the "curse of the philosopher": that incessant need to question anything, to reflect upon just about everything and to seek answers where none may ever exist. One of the prevalent conflicts for me is between the social values that exist within the United States and what they now mean for me personally. I believe our personal values and the social values with which they are connected overlap and influence one another. Values are very dynamic, maybe even organic. As we go through life, our values change. Some of them may become more well-defined; others may slip away as less important. A crisis may help us discover what is most valuable in our life. Reflecting upon the habitual and mundane dimensions of our lives helps us to avoid holding on to immature ideas and values.

Social values and personal values are not always harmonious. Politics is a simple example about how personal needs and desires are not universally addressed politically. These conflicts can be as locally based as a school board's decision that adversely affects a particular family or group and as nationally based as immigration or health care policies. Values are neither completely singular nor independent; that is, no value really stands independently. Personal and social values interconnect in ways that may be overt and clear at times while they also may remain covert and below the surface of our consciousness.

The covert and overt nature of values can also be seen in our personal and societal embrace of prejudice. I tend to distinguish between covert forms of prejudices, stereotypes, bigotry, and discrimination and their more obvious overt forms. Everyone has covert types of prejudices whether he or she recognizes or accepts this fact or not. (The more common word in vogue today is "implicit", not covert; however, covert seems to capture my meanings throughout the book more effectively. Covert has a stronger connotation of being hidden or unknown – the essential elements for ignorance.) People may not believe or want to accept that these covert forms inhabit the recesses of our consciousness but they do. I am continually confronted with my own prejudices; this book attempts to understand them, confront them, and make sense of them. My hope is that my reflections will open the eyes of those people who say they have no prejudices or who have never discriminated against another person. Covert forms of prejudice and discrimination linger in one's psyche throughout life; often without our recognizing their existence. Social policies, educational programming, and political posturing seem to focus more on the overt forms or the extreme attitudes of these issues. That is as it should be.

But there is a real danger in overlooking the pervasive and chilling effects that attend to the more subtle forms of prejudice. For example, if you are a white woman who claims to have no prejudices but who becomes very uncomfortable in an elevator when a large, black male wearing a hoodie enters, then I believe you have a covert prejudice. Your response might be that any normal person would feel intimidated in that situation. Yet you are feeling a genuine form of prejudice. If you are white and hear footsteps at night in a parking garage and you turn to see three Latinos walking toward you, would you feel no concern for your safety? If you are a black male and a white policeman comes toward you without a smile on his face, would you feel uneasy and concerned for what might happen next? Do you dismiss people who have heavy foreign accents or use poor English or who have an affected way of speaking? Are you surprised to see a heavily tattooed biker being gentle and kind to a bratty child in a store? Are you uncomfortable in being asked for a handout by someone who is homeless? If all of these circumstances remain benign, I would categorize all of the feelings as covert forms of prejudice based on common experience and social stereotyping.

Overt forms of prejudice include refusal to allow someone entry into your life solely due to that person's color, religion, sexual orientation, gender, age, etc. Readily dismissing others or using disparaging language to categorize an individual or group are other forms of bigotry. Feelings of hatred and discrimination abound in our world; my thoughts will highlight the more routine and day-to-day dynamics that lead to our prejudices, our feelings of bigotry and our discriminatory behaviors. Little things may be the foundation for the big things in our life. A couple may start fighting over a big issue, but sooner or later the little things will intrude and maybe even take over the discussion. Attending to the little things (covert attitudes, e.g.) may be one of the more constructive approaches we can take as a society. Leaving them covert may only re-enforce overt behavior.

My distinction between overt and covert prejudices does not include the extreme forms of hatred found in such groups as the KKK, White Supremacists, or Neo-Nazis. The hatred and ignorance that is held by these groups is frightening. Their feelings of supremacy and self-importance are destructive forces in society. I will not directly address the issues of these hateful forms of bigotry. Other writers have much greater insight into the history, psychology, politics, and social dynamics of these groups. I have not really experienced these extreme feelings and attitudes, although I have been upset with news accounts of their continuing activities. History may mark 2017 as a seminal year in which America's moral compass was shattered as extreme groups and divisive politics tore our country into enclaves of mistrust and hatred. The erosion of healthy and positive interpersonal relationships and the preponderance of ignorance guised as truth are very chilling. Disregard for facts, truth, and intelligent discourse undermine our society's most basic human values. Maybe we need small steps, self-reflection and acceptance of our own ignorance to emerge out of these divisive moments. Maybe the accumulation of these small steps will lead to a giant leap for humanity.

This book is my small step. I have not been involved in any great movement or national activity. I have not made any significantly recognized contributions to improving race relations or addressing the myriad of prejudices that will be presented. In that sense I believe I am a normal and quite common representative of America. Reflecting upon and coming to terms with my prejudices and beliefs have brought so many of my values into focus. I have strengthened my belief in some and have disregarded others that I now deem as too superficial. Examining my prejudices and interpersonal relationships continues to be an awakening to the ignorance of my thoughts and feelings that have lain below the surface of my consciousness.

It is important to tell one's story and try to create meaning in one's life. I have been shaped by my experiences, my values, my prejudices and in turn I have shaped the world around me and the people whom I have encountered. This book is my attempt to make an ordinary life have greater significance.

This is my story.

PART I:

WHAT I'VE LEARNED ABOUT RACIAL PREJUDICE

CHAPTER 1
SOUTH CAROLINA

I have a dream that my four little children
will one day live in a nation where they will not be judged
by the color of their skin, but by the content of their character.

Martin Luther King, Jr.

They really were going to let me go -- for two weeks or more. At 13 this adventure was more than just exciting. It was an escape. I wouldn't have to babysit my bothersome brother, Billy (6 1/2 years younger), and I wouldn't have to fetch my dad's beer when he wasn't at the bars drinking (some nights that would take two trips, even though I had developed a way to carry eight bottles at a time). My father was always in his royal chair in the living room and the beer fridge was in the basement. It wasn't the distance; it was the language and behavior that emerged every night. No one would ever dare to disagree or challenge anything he ever said, especially when he was drinking. He was not a physically imposing man, maybe 5'8" and about 145 pounds. His demand for respect and domineering presence over my mom seemed to be factors in his control. I remember challenging him only once in my life. I was 16 and decided to hide his cigarettes. He had had part of a lung removed months before and was diagnosed with emphysema. The doctor told him to stop smoking and start walking. He followed neither admonition. So I put his cigarettes in my dresser draw under my underwear (the symbolism was intentional). When he couldn't find them he screamed at me, using his usual monikers (*dummkopf*, knucklehead and *dummer esel*). Of course I relented, retrieved the cigarettes, and threw them at his chest. I stormed out the door and went for a long walk. When I returned, nothing was ever said of the incident, and I never bothered to try to help him help himself ever again.

But back when I was 13, that adventure of going south loomed with promise. I did feel badly on the day of my departure, however. I was leaving my mom to have to cope with my sickly little brother and my over-demanding, drunken father, so the relief of getting away made me feel guilty yet somehow exhilarated. "Don't you want to wear the clip-on?" my worried mother asked. "Nah, I like this one," I held up a thin, grey and black striped tie. "The stripes go with the stripes on the pants, er... trousers." My older brother Paul (8 1/2 years older), who was going into the Navy's flight program and who had already served five years in the Naval Reserves, had drummed into my head that women wear pants and men wear trousers.

"Okay," she said. "That will look nice. But do you know how to tie it?"

"Yeah, Paul taught me. Watch!" I proceeded to deftly tie the thin piece of cloth only to find that it was a bit too long. Without missing a beat, I untied it and redid the knot, hoping that the desired length would magically appear this time; it did.

"And don't forget about those n...s!" she warned me for the umpteenth time. My mom and dad had drilled it into my head for at least a week that they would give me some of dad's hard-earned money and "those people" on the bus and in the depots would be out to steal it from me.

"Yes, Mom, I know. They will be trying to steal my wallet at every turn, so I have to be careful."

"More than careful! I'm telling you to keep that wallet in your coat's breast pocket and keep your hand on that wallet at all times - even when you're sitting alone."

"Come on, for Christ's sake, it's getting late," came the command from the other room: Smitty had summoned. So I grabbed my suitcase (a brown rectangle that contained a rather sparse variety of clothes) and headed for the car. At that age toiletries were not much of an issue: a hairbrush (not overly necessary given my crew cut), toothpaste and a toothbrush were sufficient. Looking back at my packing, I am now embarrassed because there were no books.

I was dressed better than ever, for me. I actually had my one pair of brown tie shoes on, a blue sports coat, grey trousers with an off shade of grey stripes, a white shirt and the tie. We drove to the station and had to wait forever for the bus (which was on time). I was instructed on how to protect the wallet a few times and dad made sure I had his instructions memorized: "When you reach Washington, DC look for the bus that says 'Florence.' Get on and it will take you where you want to go. Donny and his mom will be waiting for you."

I had been friends with Donny, or Murgy as I used to call him, since birth. We had been inseparable until he moved to Japan at the age of 5. He was a kindred spirit, despite (or maybe because of) our different personalities. He was the mischief maker, and I was easily swayed into his behaviors even though I tended toward being obedient and a rule follower. Despite being so young when he moved, my recollections of Murgy remain some of my favorite childhood memories.

One day I was sick in bed and he came over to play. Mom told him "no" because I was sick. Murgy proceeded to go home; get one of his play guns; return to our house; and smash a window with the gun. He reached in, opened the door and advanced toward my bedroom. Mom took him by the arm and marched him back to his home. I don't know what punishment he received. I don't actually remember this episode because I was in bed. My mom, of course, repeated it often over the years after his family had moved away. This is one of those memories that we all have of something we did not directly experience, yet we perceive it as a memory. These pseudo memories have been reinforced by the repeated telling of the stories and by our own adding of the direct experiences we have of the people involved.

One of the actual vivid memories of Murgy I have that has become a favorite story for my grandchildren, involves the two of us tormenting a neighborhood girl. The "witch" of our neighborhood (a trait that was bestowed upon her by children and adults alike) had three daughters. One of the girls was our age (four). Murgy and I often played Cowboys and Indians. We had the pistols, hats, feathers, bows and arrows, etc. to play the parts with our version of realism. So we donned our Indian headdresses, gathered some rope and each took a pair of scissors. We hung out in the open field across the house from the witch's home and waited. We weren't there long when the three girls came out. The two older ones left the youngest to play by herself in their front lawn. The older girls had headed to the playground not far away. Murgy and I saw our chance. We pounced. We grabbed the unsuspecting victim and tied her to the telephone pole in front of their house. We began to dance around her doing our version of a War Dance while we brandished the scissors above our heads. We decided that merely cutting her hair would suffice as our form of scalping. I now cringe at the thought of how completely influenced I had been with the television stereotypes of the 50s. I never remember reflecting on these attributions toward Native Americans when I was young: they were given to us as facts. The girl's horrified mother ran out of the house screaming "What do you two brats think you're doing? Untie her immediately!"

We sheepishly walked behind her and undid the knots. When the rope dropped, the girl ran to hide behind her mother. "You just stay here. I'm calling the police." Why we didn't run away, I'll never know. But she turned, marched into her house with her daughter tagging right behind her. We just stood there motionless and silent. She quickly returned and started ranting. "How could you two be so mean? What do you think you're doing? Don't your parents know how to raise you?" There was much more as she continued to give us a piece of her mind.

It wasn't very long before the police arrived. The only man in the car got out, and I saw Murgy's telltale smirk grace his face. He winked and I shrugged.

"Yes ma'am, I'll take care of these boys," said the policeman gruffly. "Get in the back seat, you two."

I sheepishly crept in beside Murgy, who was now grinning. I gave him a quizzical look and he smiled even more.

As we drove away Murgy said, "Hi, Grandpa. Can we go for ice cream?" "Of course, where do you want to go?"

Nothing more was ever said about our transgression -- not the best lesson for those who had terrorized an unsuspecting little girl.

I did have one misadventure that did not include Murgy directly, but was inspired by him. He and I were in awe of Superman and would "fly" around the yards saving poor terrorized adults from untold villains. We were becoming invincible as a dynamic duo. One day I decided to impress Murgy with my Superman powers. Along the walk in the front of our house was shattered glass. I put on my pretend cape (a towel since we didn't have costume capes), took off my sneakers and socks, and ran across the glass knowing that I was invincible. My plan was to do so and to challenge Murgy once I had proven to myself that I was capable of such a feat. I still remember the pain of my mom using tweezers to pick out the small pieces of glass from my feet.

"What were you thinking?" she plaintively asked.

"I was just being Superman," I winced. I can't be sure of any crying because my Superman memory would not allow for any such weakness. My adult brain now thinks otherwise. Mom just shook her head and I made sure Murgy never heard about my failure.

Later that summer, Mom and I went over to Murgy's house. Mom and Jane were like sisters and would often meet for coffee during the day.

Murgy took me out to the garage and showed me his wagon. A blanket was covering cookies, crackers, bottles of pop and potato chips.

"What's that?" I innocently asked.

"We're going to run away. These are our supplies."

We made a great show of walking past our unsuspecting mothers toward his bedroom. They smiled and returned to their conversation as we triumphantly entered his room and immediately closed the door.

"Here, help with this!" ordered Murgy. We pushed his dresser in front of the door to bar any entry from the outside. We then knocked the screen out of the window and jumped onto the lawn. After scampering around to the garage with great stealth we retrieved the wagon and put his pillow and blanket from his bedroom onto the other blanket storing our stash. We headed out on 84th Street and turned onto Lindbergh Ave. (the major street connecting our neighborhood to the outside world). About 3/4 of a mile down Lindbergh was a bridge that led to an area of LaSalle that was only partially developed in those days. It provided farmlands and open fields for the fearless adventurers. (Five years later my family would move into one of the neighborhoods created when developers bought the farms.) Our 5 year old legs were getting tired and we thought we had made a great escape and had travelled a long distance. We felt free and were making grand plans. As we stopped to have a snack, suddenly a car horn blared. Mac's angry face scowled from the car window. He demanded that his son and I return home immediately. We sheepishly put our cookies back into the wagon and retraced our steps. I don't remember what our punishment was; I just knew I hated the feeling of getting caught.

Shortly after our attempt to run away, Murgy did actually leave – he and his family relocated to Japan. His father was in the Air Force and, due to the Korean War, was being stationed there. Now, eight years later, my trip to visit him was an opportunity to reconnect with this boyhood soul-mate. The bus finally arrived.

Mom was busy giving me final instructions: "Do as you're told. And don't forget, you are NOT to call him Murgy anymore. Under any circumstances! His name is now Donny."

She had been preparing me for this change for a long time. I wasn't sure why, but I accepted it and never used the name Murgy again. My mom tried to kiss me, but I made sure it didn't land on any skin. I did say good-bye to Billy, but it was as nonchalant and un-feeling as I could make it. At that time my younger brother was just a nuisance: too young to do anything with and a constant annoyance because I was baby-sitting him more and more as mom refused to let dad go drinking alone. I never figured out why since she didn't drive and Dad never came home sober. Sometimes I would have to help him to bed when he fell into the front closet or linen closet or when he drove the car into a snow bank. Well, I was leaving all of that behind for a short while. Dad and I exchanged a formal hand shake. I got on the bus; waved good bye; and proceeded to stick my left hand into my breast pocket, determined to follow my mother's instructions to protect my wallet from "those people." Thankfully the jacket-makers hadn't sewn that pocket up the way they did the ones on the front of the coat. I never could figure out why they put a pocket into a jacket that was sewed up so you couldn't use it.

Hour after hour I played the usual travel games in my head and looked out the window. Surely profound thoughts were running through my head, but there is no glimmer of a recollection of anything that I thought on that entire trip. I don't remember anything about the ride to Washington, other than how uncomfortable it was to hold my wallet all the way. The DC bus depot was busy and a bit confusing. I got my suitcase from the driver and walked up and down the boarding area looking for the bus to Florence. Nothing. My first bus was on time and the next bus wasn't supposed to leave for another 45 minutes. I shouldn't worry because the other bus didn't have to be here yet. So I sat on a bench, leery of the other passengers, and checked out each bus as it arrived, making sure I carried my suitcase with me. I waited for about an hour and no bus to Florence was around. I finally screwed up the courage to ask a bus driver (even though he was black) if he could help me. "Son, where do you want to go?"

"Florence, South Carolina."

"Well, you missed the bus. You were supposed to take the Jacksonville bus that just left a little while ago."

How could this be? Smitty. Wrong? A black man was telling me that my dad made a mistake. I could barely compute the ramifications of this. But I quickly reasoned that I should trust the bus driver and not just sit here and wait for a bus to Florence. The driver had a cheery smile and said, "Tell you what. I'm headed to Richmond. It's on your way and better than sitting here. When we get to Richmond, I'll check to see what we can do about getting you to Florence. By the way, why were you waiting for a bus with a Florence sign on it?"

"My dad told me that and he's never wrong."

The bus driver chuckled, took my suitcase, stored it in the hold, and I proceeded to board into the unknown.

This memory of my dad's conviction of his own infallibility was played out years later: I was with my mom and dad at a Sportsman bar in LaSalle (a suburban area of Niagara Falls). My dad was arguing with the bartender (a friend and the manager of the Sportsman Club) over the date of the club's picnic. The bartender said it was Saturday and my dad informed him that it was Sunday. Joe became exasperated, walked around the bar to the club's entrance. He brought in the information poster and said: "See, it says Saturday." My dad's response: "Who wrote the wrong date on the poster?" He wasn't grinning; he was serious. Unfortunately, it took me a long time to recognize and understand the fallibility of my father.

When we arrived in Richmond, the driver took care of the other passengers, then grabbed my suitcase and told me to follow him.

"The angels are looking out for you, lad. Your bus had a gas tank problem and will be two hours late reaching Richmond. Sit by the window and make sure you look for the Jacksonville bus. Get on it and it will take you to Florence. This kind gentleman will tell the bus driver to inform you when it's time to board the Jacksonville bus. Good luck."

He extended his hand and for the first time in my conscious life I touched someone of another color. When I got on the bus I moved to my usual location (now that this was my third bus, I figured I was a pro) about two thirds of the way back and on the driver's side. My dad had informed me that that was the safer side of the bus because if we were going to be hit it would be on the other side, just like the death seat known as the front passenger seat. By now holding onto the wallet was getting tedious so I started to slouch a bit so my arm wouldn't get so tired. No one ever sat next to me, even though the bus was quite full. I remember arriving a couple of hours late and driving in the dark for the last hundred miles or so. When I stepped off the bus, Jane wrapped me in a huge hug (probably holding onto to me as if it were my mother she was squeezing - the two of them were two peas in a pod, as the husbands often said). When I freed myself from the maternal warmth I felt a tight, clenched hand wrap itself around my forearm.

"What's the matter with you?"

"Hi, to you too, Donny," I said in a more than perplexed tone. I was proud of knowing better than calling him Murgy; I wonder how much more agitated he would have been if I hadn't remembered my mom's instructions. "Get over here." He led me behind the bus and out of his mother's earshot (I guessed). "Why in hell were you sitting in the back of the bus with those n...s?" he snorted.

"Uh, ah, I, what?" came my totally incoherent response.

"Don't you know anything?"

It was 1959 and I knew nothing about Jim Crow or the laws that ruled the South. When I spent my summers in Kentucky there was no need to know the laws because we never encountered any of "them." My kin lived in rural areas and the small towns we shopped or drove through did not have a black population. The cemeteries we visited were white only. Now, however, I was in a different South with different laws and expectations That summer I learned a lot about the Jim Crow laws and for the first time began to think about racial prejudices. I saw the "Negro only" signs for drinking fountains and entrances. One day Donny and I were walking down a sidewalk in the town of Sumter where they were living. An old black man was coming in the other direction. When I started to drift back behind Donny, he grabbed my arm, "What's the matter with you?" (It was one of his favorite phrases for me that summer.) "They have to get out of the way; we don't move." Sure enough, the older man bowed, tipped his hat and slipped off the sidewalk and into the street so two 13-year-old white boys could pass. I didn't understand what was going on then, and for very different reasons I still don't understand now.

Donny had a clubhouse in the back of their property. It was a cool place for boys. He had three flags flying: American, Confederate and a skull and cross bones. We had meetings with other young teens whose fathers were also in the Air Force. Donny told me that his club was a junior KKK. I had no idea what that meant and still don't. One 13-year-old does not ask another 13-year-old to explain things. I was not about to look and act more stupid than I had already managed to appear from the day the bus arrived. I don't remember anything about the meetings other than hearing how stupid and animalistic "they" were. I didn't join in the conversations because I had nothing to offer. I lacked the knowledge and self-awareness to challenge their comments and was more intent upon being accepted than saying anything contradictory. I didn't believe what they were saying, but I didn't really understand why I disagreed. We did talk a lot about the Civil War and their refrain was that the South would rise again. I'm not sure they really knew what they were talking about, but it didn't matter. It was a rallying cry that they had heard and parroting it made them feel older and important.

One night we walked through the woods with bricks and stones. I didn't ask why we were doing this. They all seemed to know what was happening and where we were going; I just followed along. When we saw a clearing with some huts, they began to throw the bricks and stones at the huts. Not wanting to be noticed as being different, I threw my arsenal too, but I made sure none of the missiles hit any target. The display was clearly their way of proving something that I could not possibly figure out then. I didn't ask questions; didn't raise any objections; and didn't try to change anyone's mind because I didn't even know what my mind was thinking. If I really knew that their hatred and bigotry was injuring others (and themselves), would I have done or said anything differently? I honestly don't know.

I am ashamed of my cowardice that evening. Whatever prejudice I had that evening was certainly a juvenile attitude of not wanting to be different. I have outgrown that youthful ignorance, but it's hard to know whether I still have some residual elements of prejudice swirling in my sub-consciousness.

Later in life when Donny and I met, we never discussed this experience. Our conversations were sometimes soul searching and I am convinced that this juvenile behavior was just a passing phase in his life. As I have thought about my compliance with something that just felt wrong, I have wondered what I would have done if I were a young man in Nazi Germany. Wouldn't I have just followed along like the vast majority of the population? We may think we are truly individualistic in our thinking and behavior, yet, aren't we much more imbedded in our social context than we may realize?

Despite what I just shared with you, my memories of that summer do not revolve around the Jim Crow laws or my awakening to racism in my life. Most of the days were filled with the games and play of two 13 year old friends. I didn't stay with my friend for just two weeks; I was there for over seven weeks. His mom had talked my mom into letting me stay longer. The whole family was going to drive to Niagara Falls at the end of August and would drive me home. An entire summer with no familial responsibilities: it was a dream come true! Tuesday through Sunday Donny and I would go to the officer's club pool. Donny taught me how to swim, dive and enjoy the water for the first time in my life. From 5th grade to 12th grade I attended schools that had no swimming pools and, thus, no swimming instruction. The only grade in which I had swimming class was in 4th grade and I remember nothing of what happened. I do know that my only swimming stroke when I went to South Carolina was a doggy paddle. By the end of the summer I was doing the Australian crawl, back and side stokes. We would throw chestnuts in their shells into the water, watch them sink, then dive in the deep end to retrieve our treasure. Donny even encouraged me to swim with my eyes open under water! It took a while, but I felt an unusual freedom in being able to see where I was going and not just guess where the chestnuts were.

Diving was a real challenge for me. There was a low and a high board. I learned how to jackknife, canon ball, half preacher, a quasi swan dive and, eventually, do a full flip off the low board. There were far more failures than successes from the board, but the challenge was invigorating and Donny touted his expertise and advanced skills. I only tried one dive off the high board. It seemed to be a beautiful swan dive until I hit the water and instantly felt my waist and legs snap creating a peculiar "v" shaped body. I did manage to paddle to the edge of the pool and hoist myself up. It took quite a while for the pain in my midsection to settle down. No amount of teasing or "chicken" shouts would make me try that again. I would only jump from the high board after that. On Mondays when the pool was closed, we stayed home and played Monopoly. When we tired of the game, we retired to his room which housed his vast collection of soldiers, terrain, military vehicles, etc. We created elaborate battles with Donny always taking the lead. There were a few movies and outings with his parents. Mac supplied us with an arsenal of fireworks for the 4th of July. I thought we'd get into trouble when we'd throw baby fingers under the tires of cars driving down the street, but the military parents in those cars seemed to take it all in stride (even the police rover that drove by). Going to the Civil War site of Fort Sumter was a special treat and running on the ramparts and throughout the battle positions was far more interesting than learning any of the history that was available. Seeing the blocks and stages for selling slaves had no impact on me at that time. There was no personal connection or real empathy on my part

The Civil War became an intriguing period in history for me. In some ways it still is. I've visited many Civil War sites and in college my nickname was "Li'l Reb." Donny's dad taught me that the Civil War wasn't about slavery but about States Rights. I believed that into adulthood. I had favored the Rebel Cause from my earliest years because of my exposure to my southern relatives in Kentucky. My southern relatives seemed to ignore the fact that my dad was a Roman Catholic from Chicago, and I was his son. While I was in Kentucky, I was my mother's Southern Baptist boy with no Yankee roots. My grandma, uncles and aunts doted on me much more than they did my brothers (Paul wasn't around when I was in my more formative years and Billy had severe allergies and didn't run in the fields or help with the chores as I had). Neither of my brothers has returned to the farms nor kept our relatives so enmeshed in their lives as I have. Kentucky was a second home; one that I cherished more than the homes we had in the Falls. That summer in South Carolina only reinforced my preference for the South and The Cause. On the drive back north from South Carolina, I remember that Donny's parents took us on side trips to a number of Civil War battle fields, and years later when we were professionals Donny lived in Manassas (a fitting locale given our childhood).

Those early years of camaraderie with Donny cemented a friendship that would last despite our differences. Our contacts throughout adulthood were sporadic but had an intensity that comes with a deep-seated bond that needed no development or effort. Later in life I seemed to develop more leadership qualities and would stand on my own two feet. I no longer would blindly follow Donny's wild plans. In fact, once when I stayed with him when we were adults; he had a girl friend spending the night. He asked if I wanted him to fix me up with one of her friends. I said of course not; I was happily married. This was a basic disconnect between the two of us. He didn't understand why marriage should get in the way, and I couldn't imagine cheating on Diane. He was like his father, Mac. Fidelity never seemed important. I never met either of Donny's wives. Even though he and I had different moral compasses, we still had an unwritten bond of friendship. It was built upon our childhood and sealed during my visit. Looking back, that trip South has become an important stop in my journey of trying to understand the roots and expressions of my prejudices and biases, as well as trying to comprehend why I have consciously and unconsciously discriminated against others throughout my life.

But before I can reflect on prejudice and biases, I must first reflect on stereotyping. I have come to believe that stereotyping is inevitable. It is another form of categorizing. We place people or things into groups and provide labels so we can more easily manage our world. Stereotypes may have some element of truth or usefulness in them. For example, stereotyping is an essential ingredient in television, movies, theater, etc. We can readily identify with someone who exhibits a characteristic stereotype and become amused, startled or enraged when the stereotype becomes confirmed or gets flipped. Humor is really the shifting from what we expect to a twist that is unexpected. The result of the shift brings a smile, a chuckle or even laughter. Because of America's strong sense of justice, I see so many shows or movies revolving around the theme of justifiable revenge: good is supposed to triumph over bad or evil. Stereotypes help us identify the good and bad quite readily. Plot twists occur when the characters do not follow the expected behaviors of the initial stereotype. Thus, the stereotypes of the characters help move the plot along. In life Diane and I revel at the experiences when stereotypes get broken and are sometimes saddened when negative stereotypes become confirmed.

In 1993 I was on a medical delegation with People to People. It is a non-profit organization dedicated to Eisenhower's idea that governments cause wars and the best way to foster peace around the world is for the peoples of the world to meet, talk to one another and work together. The delegation lasted three weeks and we visited Moscow, St. Petersburg, Kiev, Prague and Berlin. I was the only non-physician in the group and was far more interested in the cultural aspects of our visits and briefings than the medical material. My unofficial task became one of debriefing the physicians on the bus or at informal gatherings. They made sure that I spent extra time with our translators. At the banquets we had at each city, I was positioned next to one of the city's top physicians or city officials. In Moscow we had a visit to the cardiology center for Russia. During the tour we had one male surgeon giving part of the tour. He looked as if he could play defense on the Russian hockey team and never spoke any English. Was I projecting a stereotype on him like Professor Hamburg had done to me at that cocktail party in New Orleans? His demeanor was stereotypically professional, unsmiling and curt. He seemed to glare at us and challenge us to try and disagree with anything he said. One of the American physicians and I nicknamed him Igor (reverting to a middle school mentality) and were glad when his portion of the tour was finished. Of course, that evening at the banquet he sat next to me. What was I going to do for the next 3-4 hours? The woman on my right was the Director of the Hospital and was more intent on talking to the cardiologist from the U.S. who was on her other side. Tentatively I smiled at Igor and offered to pour some wine. In unbroken English he said that he would teach me how to drink Russian style. Shocked, I asked why he didn't address us in English. His reply, "I wasn't confident in using the proper technical terms in English." Thus began one of the most memorable banquets of my life. We were soul-mates in many ways - loving literature, theater, our children, sports, gardening, and socially drinking. I learned the proper way to toast and consume beer, vodka and wine at the same meal. We looked at each other's pictures of our children; told story after story; and reveled in the beauty of two strangers breaking the walls of stereotypical judgments. I told him about my first impressions and he laughed. He told me I appeared stand-offish and arrogant (what he expected of an American physician).

On the negative side of stereotyping, though, I have encountered students whose behavior throughout a semester confirmed my first impressions. At the beginning of each course I would go around the class and ask students to tell me who they are, why they are in the course and what their expectations are. While they are doing so I make notes next to their names to help me remember who they are. I would not want many of them to see what I have written to identify them because the notations are sometimes quite unflattering (for example, mad scientist, brown nose type, flip flops, wild red hair, freckles, looks like Humpty Dumpty, etc.). In one class a male student was arrogantly pontificating about his wonderfulness. Next to his name I wrote: con artist. In the middle of the semester he turned in a paper that was blatantly plagiarized. When I confronted him he tried to talk me into feeling sorry for his heavy schedule. I told him that was irrelevant and the F would stick. He shrugged and walked away. He clearly was just trying to con his way through the course. Ugh. It is amazing how quickly we can make negative judgments from our first stereotypic impressions. I find it sad when they become confirmed

I disagree with those who think we can or that we even should eliminate stereotypes or stereotyping from our lives. First, it is socially impossible to do so. We need to order our lives and stereotyping helps us. We need labels, categories and groupings. The fundamental problem does not come from the process as much as it comes from what we do with that process. Second, not all stereotypes are bad or harmful. Third, what would happen with the entertainment business if this were ever successful? So the issue isn't eliminating stereotypes or even the conscious or unconscious process of stereotyping; rather, it is coming to terms with them. What do the stereotypes mean? Do they have any collective accuracy? How can we prevent stereotypes from negatively affecting the way we think about or relate to others? How can we make sure that we avoid attributing the stereotype's characteristics to individuals that we see, meet or read about? Can we avoid dehumanizing others in our stereotypes? How can we amend incorrect stereotypes?

In a sense, this is the basis for the current debates about profiling. When is it justified and when does it cross the line into harmful discrimination? How can we keep our judgments related to the individuality of the person we meet or see? How do we prevent ignorance from dominating the characteristics we attribute to our stereotypes? There are at least two types of stereotypes that can be very problematic: First, those that distort a group and provide harmful and/or inaccurate characteristics to the group. For example, blondes or Poles are dumb. Second, those that attribute characteristics of the group to an individual which are inaccurate or destructive. For example, my mom's insistence that blacks were out to steal my wallet. I remember looking at each man and woman that I encountered in the back of the buses from Washington, D.C. to Richmond and then from Richmond to Florence and wondering if he or she was the one my mom was warning me about. Or were all of them ready to pounce? Attributing these group characteristics to individuals compounds the problem significantly.

Until I was 27, I lived a white life. The two neighborhoods of my youth were completely white. There were no blacks in my elementary school or in my high school. My freshman year of college was in an all-white Roman Catholic Seminary, and I finished my four years of college at the Jesuit school in Buffalo, Canisius College. There was one black student in the school, but I never spoke to him or was ever in a class with him. In ROTC I attended a six week summer camp and did meet one black candidate, and we did work together for a couple of days during our field training exercise. My only real memory of him was that he had great rhythm and was designated by the cadre as being the one to provide cadence songs to our marching exercises. Did this experience enhance a covert stereotype about blacks that was buried in my sub-consciousness? He served as my map reader when I was the battalion commander for a day. We got lost in the woods, but I blamed myself, not him. As I reflect back on that experience I believe I just saw him as another candidate, not as a black candidate. Maybe subconsciously my philosophy training was beginning to look beyond the trivialities of stereotyping and recognizing the individuality that exists within each and every one of us. My memory of that summer is that all the instructors that I had were white and I returned back to campus with high honors in the program. I did not think about dealing with racial issues at all.

I went to graduate school at Tulane and again encountered no blacks in any of my classes and don't recall meeting or talking with any in the married student housing. The faculty were all white, males. There were, however, people of color from other countries attending or working at the University. We did not befriend any of them. Our friends were a Dutch couple we met in the dorms and women Diane met in teaching, or my brother's in-laws (Paul had married a woman from New Orleans and we became reconnected while we lived there). After graduate school, I served in the military for three months at Fort Gordon and again had no blacks in my class, nor did I have any contact with any in my reserve unit when I served for four years in Tonawanda, New York.

It wasn't until I started working at Canisius (when I was 27 years old) that I started to meet, talk, and socialize with people of color. During my administrative career, I hired three people of color (a female from England and two males from very different backgrounds from New York State). Thankfully my world has expanded and my contact with people of color has increased significantly since I turned 30, but my formative years were very lily white. One of my racket ball partners was a black man from the Financial Aid department. We became friends and I began to see how the world can be shaped by a person's color. The two men I hired while I was Dean became more than just work colleagues; they are true friends. I now know that no matter how friendly you may be that it is impossible to experience life from another person's perspective, regardless of your ability to empathize. Existentially I cannot experience the world as a woman or as black or as gay. I can try to understand our differences, but all my experience and understanding will run through the prism of a white, heterosexual male.

I'm not exactly sure when I started to realize that the n-word was pejorative and degrading. As a child it was the primary word I heard being used. Sometimes I heard the word Negro but in my mind they were interchangeable. There was no one moment that shifted my thinking or beliefs. Unlike Saul who was knocked off his horse on the way to Damascus, I had no divine intervention to wake me up to my prejudice and use of bigoted language. My evolution in attitude was more subtle and crept into my consciousness and language without me even becoming fully aware of the shifts. I can honestly say I do not know what I thought about people of color when I was growing up. Relationships with "them" didn't exist and so the question remained a moot point for me. There was no awareness of the racial struggles of the 40s, 50s and 60s in my world. In 1965 I registered as a sophomore at Canisius College, a Jesuit, urban institution. I was not an activist; instead, I was enmeshed in the existential struggles of a young man trying to open up to a world of ideas and a moral awareness of a world he had not encountered as a youth. The neighborhood around the college was predominantly black, but I had no real contact with the neighbors. Of course, I did not tell my parents that I freely walked the neighborhood (even at night) and thought nothing of it. They would have failed to understand why I had survived such an experience. For me it was just another middle class neighborhood and I had no car, so walking was my primary means of going from point a to point b. Strolling around at midnight to try and work through some philosophical conundrum was typical for me. Besides, my favorite college bar required a walk through the neighborhood. I never marched or picketed during those years but rather sat back and tried to understand why people said and did the things they did. Throughout my collegiate and graduate school career, I did not address the Civil Rights battles directly. I will discuss what I think are some of the social causes for stereotyping, prejudice and discrimination in the next chapter. For now here are some of my initial reflections on what I have learned about my racial prejudices.

No matter how open, friendly and welcoming I am to people of color, I still experience them as different from me. I do not think there really can be nor maybe even should be any movement toward complete color-blindness. A person's color should never define who he or she is, but it seems foolish to deny an elemental characteristic of who a person is. I am white. I will never have the experiences that my black friends have had. I will never be afraid of being incarcerated for anything to do with the War on Drugs. I do not fear being stopped by the police for walking or driving in the wrong neighborhood. Real Estate agents would welcome me as a client. I do not have the history of being a member of a race whose ancestors were uprooted from their native land. I can trace my ancestors back to Ireland, England, Germany and Eastern Europe and not run into a stone wall regarding the area of the continent that was the roots of my genetic heritage. How could I be color blind with these realities? The danger, of course, can emerge if this recognition of color difference leads to attitudes or behaviors that see or treat people of color with prejudice. Seeing color does not mean treating others differently based on their color. Color does not define character. Color's meaning is really only a social structure that consciously and subconsciously reflects attitudes and beliefs that generations of people have created.

It is possible that a person of any color can believe he or she is without any racial prejudice. I like the line from *Avenue Q:* "Everyone is a little bit prejudiced." This statement seems to be intuitively correct and I've never really discovered any counter experience or argument to discredit this assumption. If for no other reason, this belief acknowledges that all human beings stereotype others; as I said before, it is the way we order our social world. Becoming aware of prejudices and understanding what causes them is crucial for addressing the underlying ignorance we all have about interpersonal relationships. Ignorance plays a larger role in our lives than we sometimes wish to admit. Socrates proclaimed that acknowledging ignorance was the first step toward understanding. This book is about self-discovery and recognizing the covert feelings and ideas that linger in my heart and mind. Accepting my own ignorance gives me an opportunity to learn and grow. I believe this assumption can be applied generally to everyone. This is my belief and I'm not going to try and provide a formal defense of it. I merely ask each reader to ask him or herself whether he or she can discern ignorance and stereotyping in their lives. As a youth I was ignorant about racial issues and was unaware of the feelings and ideas I had. I have worked on my ignorance but am wise enough to realize that there is a lot I still do not know about me or about others to claim that I have no racial prejudices. We all have blind spots and it is difficult to address that with which we are unaware. I can only admit that I suspect that these blind spots exist in others.

One clear example of ignorance-based prejudice occurred early in my tenure as Dean of Continuing Studies. I was Dean for 11 years and was responsible for a wide variety of programming, some of which addressed cultural/racial understanding. I helped design and implement a Multicultural Office; served as an advisor to the Office's Director; assisted in the development of support services for students of color; and incorporated diversity components in a variety of courses that I taught. One year I even received the Canisius College Martin Luther King, Jr., award. One of the programmatic efforts I managed was providing non-credit business programs throughout Western New York. Faculty from the college provided the training and my staff promoted and marketed the offerings. We also identified areas of need and urged faculty to develop offerings to address that need. One year I decided to hire a young, African American, Kevin, to serve as the Director of the Program. I was criticized for doing so from a number of faculty and administrators. For me, hiring him seemed to be an important statement regarding who we, the college, should be to the business community. It was the 1980s and racial barriers needed to be addressed. Kevin was very successful in his job and I was very sad to see him leave for a better offer after a few years.

The incident that tugs at my conscience relates to a theme party Diane and I held. We have a reputation for having parties that have a theme or twist to them. One night we decided to have a *Gone With the Wind* party. The book and movie were important to us. When we first met, Diane was surprised to hear how much I loved the book and how much it meant to me. No male in Diane's experience loved this southern romance. After reading it I never knew anyone who loved it as much as I did until I met Diane. She and I met at a wedding and during the brunch after the ceremony we spent a lot of time talking about the book and what it meant to us. (We even named our first daughter Tara but pronounced her name differently from the plantation.) With my southern roots I readily identified with the rebel cause (something that was reinforced with my summer in South Carolina). When we decided to have a party, this theme was a no-brainer: it had been with us from the beginning of our relationship.

For this particular dinner party, we invited Kevin and his wife to our dinner, thinking nothing of the theme and any sensitivities they may have had to the blatant racism of the book and movie. The real kicker is that we dressed for the occasion and added the touch of hanging a Confederate flag on the outside of the house to welcome our guests to the Land of Cotton and Tara's Plantation. I gave no thought to the not-so-subtle significance that the flag had or that the idea of a plantation might mean. For me, they were just thematic details to enhance the evening. I was totally oblivious to the message that must have greeted Kevin and Wanda. He never said anything about the flag or going to a "plantation" and thanked us profusely for a wonderful evening and party. Looking back, however, I am horrified at my blind spot – at my lack of awareness of this blatant celebration of racist symbolism. People of color learn how to adapt to our white society. Everyone has limits, though, which necessitate saying or doing something about the unfairness or ignorance of others. Obviously my ignorance did not reach Kevin's limit of tolerance. This example is a great illustration of the inadvertent and covert racism that courses through our society. I mention this not to diminish the more egregious forms of racism but rather as an example of how pervasive ignorance is in trying to understand and address our prejudices.

Our preferences, prejudices, biases, etc. truly affect what and who we like or don't like. It is unrealistic to believe that we should like everyone and everything that everyone else does. Morality, social norms, personal and social values require that we develop and maintain behaviors that are ethical and/or socially acceptable. I do not believe I have to like baggy pants that droop below the belt line. I do not think that is a form of racial prejudice because this dress style is not racially restricted. This seems to be more a generational preference or personal style choice. If I were to exhibit "baggy rage" and verbally or physically attack someone who is dressed this way or if I made judgments about the person's character, then I have truly crossed the line. But preferences can and should not be eliminated from our lives. For example, likes and dislikes are very prevalent in sports at all levels. We may use the language of war and hate, but hopefully in our sane not fan moments we realize that we are merely dealing with preferences, not morally based actions. I am a Buffalo Bills fan and "hate" the Miami Dolphins, New York Jets and New England Patriots. Nothing can change my allegiance! I am proud to say that my daughters have inherited these "true" and "just" attitudes! I am saddened when fans get out of control and attack rivals or get into verbal or physical altercations that turn personal. Passion in sports can be a real powder keg. Racially based judgments about athletes are both overt and covert in our society. Shouting racial slurs at games or players using racial taunts are disgraceful. Stereotypes give way to pseudo-truth: white men can't jump, blacks don't swim, track is for black, shot put for whites, etc. The blurring of accuracy and prejudice abounds in people's minds and imagination. Again, I do not think it is wise to underestimate the impact of sports-based stereotypes, prejudices, and judgments. They consciously and subconsciously affect everyone to some degree in this country (even so-called non-fans).

Sports participation may or may not bridge the lines of prejudice. Inner city black teams playing suburban white teams may or may not shift players' attitudes or beliefs. One of the lessons that I taught in my cross cultural classes was the false notion that contact with people of other colors, other nationalities, or other ethnicities would lead to open acceptance and understanding. It was always possible that such contacts would only reinforce prior prejudices and stereotypic judgments. It was false to assume that the contact alone was sufficient. Attitude, willingness to open one's self to others, and a tolerance for difference are essential ingredients in shifting beliefs through contact. At workshops and in courses, I used a game called BaFa BaFa. Players were randomly put into two groups. After each group learned its cultural characteristics, I had representatives from each group visit the other. During the debriefings the students or participants were shocked at their behavior and how easy it is to prejudge others based on pre-set stereotypes. Each group accused the other of bigotry and prejudice without realizing that they themselves were exhibiting the characteristics they were attributing to the others. Cultural biases (especially racially based ones) run deep and sometimes silent in each one of us.

One last comment about race relates to a principle of harmony. I would hope that harmony would govern how we individually and collectively relate to others. As I reflect upon my life, harmony seems to be a very wise and equitable (aka fair) approach. It is not necessary to get people to agree on preferences, likes/dislikes, policies, laws, regulations, etc. As human beings we require a social order if we are to live together. This social order requires rules and regulations. Our political processes (from family relations, to church councils, to boards of education and to political bodies at all levels of society) clearly show discord and disagreement. It is unrealistic to believe that there are policies or programs that can be designed that will satisfy everyone and that would lead to universal agreement. Using a principle that achieves a level of harmony or balance is more useful and achievable than trying to identify a particular agenda that will yield agreement. Harmony in society will require an understanding of our prejudices and biases. Having balanced approaches to relationships will require trust and respect. Harmony and balance will necessitate that we replace discriminatory regulations with ones that are fair and just. I firmly believe in the principle of *In medio stat virtus* – loosely translated: "in the middle stands virtue". It is a call for moderation and an avoidance of extremes.

CHAPTER 2
GRAPPLING WITH MY RACISM

I refuse to accept the view that mankind is so tragically bound to the starless midnight of racism and war that the bright daybreak of peace and brotherhood can never become a reality... I believe that unarmed truth and unconditional love will have the final word.

Martin Luther King, Jr.

As we drove to Kentucky each year to visit my mom's family, my younger brother, Bill, and I would sit in the backseat with the usual bickering about who was infringing on each other's side of the seat. The distance was almost 800 miles, and when we were young, there were no superhighways. My dad's approach to traveling was to get from A to B as quickly as possible. We only needed to stop for gas because we could pack enough food into the car to last us the trip. It was always a very long, long day - no need to pay good money to stay in any motel, as my father used to claim. I always took it for granted that he would not get tired and that the sole purpose of a car trip was to just drive on and on until we reached our destination. We even had a "pee can" (a big, blue empty Maxwell House Coffee can) for my mom so we wouldn't have to make any stops other than for gas. If she couldn't make it to the next gas stop, dad would pull to the side of the road and she'd use the front and back passenger doors as a barrier. Being a mostly male car, we deemed this sufficient. I always took this phenomenon for granted while growing up. I assumed she brought toilet paper, but I honestly don't know if she did. I have no idea if this embarrassed her or if there were any unusual incidents along the way. It was just how we traveled.

As the miles rolled along, my brother and I would use the ornament on the hood of the car as our machine gun or rocket launcher. I don't remember playing games or reading anything other than comic books. I do remember the interminable length. And the heat. And I do remember Dad's advice: "Always trust the trucker – they'll always help you pass." I often wonder what he would think today if he were still alive and driving. One warning from my mom occurred each year. As we drove in our non-air-conditioned car through Cincinnati and were approaching the bridge to cross over into Covington, KY, my mother would say:

"Now roll up the windows. You know those n....s will try to pull you out of the car and steal what we have!"

Our retort: "But mom it's 1000 degrees out. Please let's keep the windows down."

"Absolutely not! They aren't to be trusted" was mom's unyielding reply to our pleas.

I could never figure out this line of thinking and still can't. For mom, Cincinnati was safe because it was white and Covington was dangerous because it was black. That was her plain and simple truth. My mom and our relatives in Kentucky were loving people; they were kind and giving. My perception of them is complex. I struggle, still, with the dissonance between the kindness and love they exhibited toward me and their total disregard of all individuals with dark skin. They never said they hated blacks. Yet there was only one word ever used to identify "them" – the "n" word. It was ubiquitous and a natural word for my kin (and as a child and youth, it was for me too). My relatives just seemed to assume black peoples' irrelevance. I'll never know my relatives' true feelings because it was a topic that never arose in all the years I visited and stayed with them. It was clear to me that they just naturally adopted the attitude that I experienced in South Carolina: blacks should stay in their place, and peace would remain as long as they did so. I spent time in Kentucky throughout the turbulent 60s and nothing was ever said about the riots, protests, sit-ins, overturning Jim Crow, etc. Those activities were not a part of their world and they did not seem to be affected -- at least not in my presence. After my summer in South Carolina and throughout my teen years, I became more and more confused how loving and kind people could have such ugly and universally hateful feelings, attitudes and language for people of color. Were my relatives entrenched in a social framework that was unreasonable, judgmental and ignorant? My dismay at the inconsistency of my family's, as well as American cultural attitudes has been reinforced many times in my life, and was a major influence in my decision to write this book. A central question for me, always, has been how to reconcile my evolving ideas, insights and reflections with the experiences I have had.

When I was a junior in college, I finally decided to major in philosophy (I had started with History as a freshman and changed to Sociology my sophomore year). When I graduated, I was commissioned a 2nd Lieutenant in the Army (MPs) with a BA in Philosophy and minors in Theology, English and Sociology. One of the Theology courses I tried to take in my senior year (1967-68) was from a Jesuit who other students told me was very liberal. The class was large due to his popularity. During the second week of classes, he informed all of us that we had to join him in picketing the showing of *Birth of a Nation*. Never having heard of the movie or knowing what the issue with the movie was I went to see it in order to form my own opinions.

My next class with this Jesuit professor was my last.

He began the class by ranting about the evil of the South's prejudice and discrimination. "This movie is an affront to all that is decent. The bigotry of the South is so evident in this film it should be banned. We must do something to eradicate Southern hatred of Negroes."

I raised my hand.

"Yes, young man." (I don't know if he ever learned the names of those who did not picket with him.)

"Father, I have lived in the North and in the South. I think you may have a distorted viewpoint."

"What are you saying?"

"In the South people are very clear about their prejudices. I saw the Jim Crow laws in action when I was 13 and stayed with a friend in Sumter, South Carolina."

"Exactly my point! What are you trying to say?"

"I believe bigotry and prejudice in the North is more problematic. In the South everyone knows about the discrimination and bigotry. Most people are honest about their dislike. But in the North we all deny any prejudice or discrimination. Northerners pretend they have no prejudices or biases because they may know someone who is a Negro and think that solves everything. I am convinced that the real danger is in the North."

"The real danger is your ignorant attitude. Get out of here. I don't want to hear anything as stupid as THAT spouted in my classroom." He screamed this and pointed to the door.

I picked up my books and quickly left the room. With a sense of self-righteous indignation, I stormed straight for the Theology chairman's room. I trusted the chairman and felt we had a decent relationship. He had taught classes I had been in and counseled me on how to interact with another teacher with whom I had tangled. The following year, he would be the Jesuit assigned to our floor in the dorm. And later, when I returned to Canisius as an administrator, he became a close friend and mentor. That day he told me to take a seat. After listening carefully to my indignant explanation, he said, "Charlie, drop the course."

"But I have a valid point!"

"Yes, but he won't listen. You've crossed a line for him. That will earn you an F."

"That's unfair."

"I know."

"Can't you do anything?"

Not for you and not for this semester."

"But aren't liberal thinkers supposed to be open to others' opinions?"

"Be careful with assumptions. First, whether he really is liberal and second, whether 'liberal' thinkers are really open to opposing ideas."

I left without losing my feeling of self-righteous indignation, even as I marched down to the Registrar's Office to withdraw from the course. Why couldn't I state what I thought was a legitimate point? Why couldn't the professor be reasonable? Eventually these questions melted into the category of just being rhetorical with no answer ever being given. This experience did teach me two life lessons that still affect my view of interpersonal relationships.

The **first** came as I thought about the bigotry displayed in the movie and my experience of the South and my southern relatives. The movie had scenes of the KKK being heroes and defenders of how America should look: white. They were defending their women's honor from the lecherous sub-human race. I began to realize that bigotry is deep-seated and all too often treated as the natural order of life. People who love me and people whom I love may actually hate other groups of people. The hatred makes no sense to me because it is really only based on a person's skin pigmentation. But society, history, power, etc. all seem to conspire to develop and sustain deep-seated bigotry and prejudices. As I thought about the movie and connected it to my relatives I was also taken back to my experience in South Carolina. When Donny and his friends met and talked about the inferiority of blacks was startling to me. I could picture the other kids as adults wearing the white hoods and riding on horses, just as in the movie. I'll always remember them saying, "#*+ ... N...s" as they hurled the bricks and stones at the huts of poor black people on the outskirts of town. I do believe (and fervently hope) Donny outgrew this racist attitude toward blacks, and I saw no signs of his adopting KKK attitudes in his adult life. But I can't say the same for the other guys who were present. I have never met or talked to any of them after that summer. Thirteen year old boys are still forming their consciences, but they still must be held accountable for their actions. I was complicit with them and am ashamed of my behavior. Maybe this experience began an awakening in me of the evil of racial hatred.

The hatred perpetrated by supremacist groups is dark and immoral. It denies the premise of human equality and proclaims a superiority that is dangerous and unhealthy. Believing that I am superior because of my race flies in the face of my Christian faith and makes no rational sense. How can pigmentation affect one's character, abilities, or worth as a person? Immanuel Kant said that we should treat all people as an end-in-themselves. His morality was based on this sense of equality and on the idea that we should never use or manipulate others for our advantage. In a sense we have a duty to respect others. I agree with him. And I now realize what I didn't understand when I was 13: by throwing bricks and stones and hurling racial epithets at the huts of poor, black people, we were perpetuating hatred and participating in a hate crime. I stand ashamed.

As I think back on my confrontation with the priest, I wish I had made the distinction between most Southerners and the hate groups of the KKK and White Supremacists. I think the distinction is important. Covert and overt bigotry and prejudice is corrosive and it may lie below the surface of our self-awareness. We may claim not to be racists, yet we are affected by either or both forms of prejudice. There is a big leap from this corrosive mentality to the vile and evil nature of hatred. Those who espouse such hatred have closed their minds to the inherent value of each and every person.

The **second** lesson I learned from my encounter with the *Birth of a Nation* classroom experience occurred the following spring semester. I proved the Theology Chairman's point that not all liberals may really be open to opposing viewpoints. I was taking a second philosophy course in the spring semester of my senior year from another avowed liberal. The two courses dealt with the history of philosophy and his emphasis was that this history revealed that the Liberal Arts open people's minds and make them into liberal thinkers. He characterized this liberal thinking as the gift philosophy had given to civilization. One way he proved his liberal approach to life was by organizing anti-war rallies on campus. In classes he talked about the importance of the liberal mind and its attitude toward openness and understanding. I decided to test this premise. One day I wore my army uniform to class (something that was required every Tuesday for everyone in the college's ROTC program). That was not the issue. I had worn the uniform every Tuesday and he and I had a cordial relationship throughout the fall semester. There weren't very many philosophy majors, so the Philosophy faculty were usually attentive to the majors. Occasionally I would talk to him after class about something he had raised. It felt as if we were developing a mutual respect for one another. That particular day I affixed to the uniform (and only for his class) a "Bomb Hanoi" button (a sentiment with which I did not agree but one I knew was antithetical to the professor's anti-war stance). Anti-war liberals condemned Nixon's bombing orders. On the other hand, the president's supporters were distributing the buttons all around the country to be a counter-protest sentiment. I was one of those who were anti-war, especially anti-Viet Nam war. I thought the bombing campaign was repugnant. However, I was in the ROTC and believed I had an obligation to our country to do my duty and serve our nation. Thus, I refused to join in any anti-war demonstrations. Even after I didn't join one of his fall protest demonstrations, the professor continued to talk to me after class. We maintained a respectful relationship.

The 60s were so confusing and conflicted and this dilemma was a constant part of my thoughts. During the class in which I wore the button, I saw him look in my direction – I could see that he had taken the bait – he saw the button. So how would he respond? If the liberal mind really was an open one, he would respect my right to wear this button. Actually I was hoping he would want to talk to me and ask me why I'd wear a button that seemed antithetical to the liberal philosophy he was espousing. It turned out that he refused to acknowledge my presence in his course for the rest of the semester. A few times I would encounter him in a hallway and he would not look in my direction or respond to any greeting I initiated either in the hallways or even before class. It would have been futile to try and talk to him after class or to confront him in his office; his body language and actions since that day made that abundantly clear. He had made up his mind and I was now one of the "others" – the war mongers – those who killed innocent people. Thus, he became an example for me about how the liberal mind can be as closed and unforgiving as the conservative one. Far right or far left: I seemed to have found a common bond between them: closed-mindedness. Their judgments were the only correct ones and those who opposed them were wrong. There even seemed to be an unwillingness to listen to the other side.

It was amazing to me that a little thing like wearing a button was sufficient to change a relationship. This self-proclaimed liberal thinker was judging me with a whole set of false assumptions. What might have happened if we had ever had a discussion about this incident? What could I have learned from him and what would he be willing to learn from me? I'm not comfortable with confrontation – maybe that's why I never bothered trying to pursue the matter further. Another rationalization for me came in the form of my belief that he was the teacher and, therefore, was more responsible for the break than I was. Regardless of culpability I began to learn that making assumptions about others can be very distorting and unjust. I have come to believe that judging someone as liberal or conservative is not necessarily very informative. The real issue related to prejudices is whether someone has or exhibits an open mind or whether the person is closed minded. Open-minded should not be equated with liberal and closed-minded is not just the purview of the conservative. Learning how to be open-minded and resisting making judgments based on distorted assumptions has remained an on-going process in my life.

A few years later I found myself teaching Religious Studies classes at an all white, private school in suburban New Orleans. I started doing so in my third year of grad school (starting a family and not just depending on Diane's income were primary motivators). That first year I taught "Church History", "Marriage", and a third course entitled "Poverty, Drugs, and Race Relations." The Christian Brothers were trying to expand their curriculum, and I was their first lay teacher. How do you teach poverty to rich, white suburbanites? One of my students was 16 and he already owned his own car, a motor boat and a couple of acres of property across the lake. Even more daunting was trying to teach race relations (it was 1970). The students knew that the 1968 riots were in the North and Los Angeles, so real race problems existed "there," not "here." They informed me that there were no problems in New Orleans because everyone "knew his place" – "no one was uppity here!" As I look back I shudder to think that I could even understand the issues well enough to try and provide any enlightenment to the students. My feeble attempt started by using the book <u>Black Like Me</u> as our text. I chose it because the setting was New Orleans and the author was a white man. My hope was that if I could reach anyone it would be through some type of identification-process with the author. As in most teaching circumstances, I have no clue whether or not I affected anyone's attitude or life in the class. It only lasted one quarter of the school year and I had three topics to cover. I do remember that it served as a catalyst for me to question the assumptions of being white in America and how little I could identify with people of color.

When I became Dean of Continuing Studies at Canisius, my responsibilities were quite wide and varied. As I have noted before, one year I proposed and worked very hard at developing and implementing a Multicultural Office and service programs for our students of color. The irony of having someone with my background of prejudice and ignorance about race relations create and institute the project still surprises me. The program began and continues to flourish despite the opposition and the rationale held by some faculty and high level administrators who thought that we really didn't need such a program because everyone is treated just the same. Do faculty really believe that there is equal treatment of students in their courses? Should they treat every student the same? Isn't fairness a much better principle to adopt? My working premise about covert prejudices is that we are not necessarily aware that we have blind spots about ourselves, our beliefs and our attitudes. Teachers may think they are fair, yet will subconsciously treat students of different races or genders differently. I remember talking to students of color while I was advising them. They shared their experiences about teachers who didn't even know that what they were saying was offensive and hurtful. One student, for example, told me that a teacher told her he was quite surprised that she could understand the material. "I didn't know your kind could do Calculus." This statement was a double whammy. Was he referring to her race or gender? Either way it was offensive and was reflecting covert prejudices at least.

We all have blind spots or wear blinders that prevent us from seeing everything about ourselves clearly. The problem with blinders is that we usually do not even realize that we are wearing them. I would hope that I treated all students fairly but I would be foolish to assume that I actually did so. I'm sure there were times when I was more lenient to some students and less so to others. I respected hard working students and may have given them some benefit of the doubt when it came to grading. Students whom I felt were ingenuously complimenting me or the course material were real irritations. It is hard to say how much of an impact my prejudices may have had in my courses. Did I treat black students with too much deference because I prejudged they had had poor experiences with other teachers? Over the years I have heard some very damning statements made by faculty who were quite prejudiced, racially and ethnically. "Why are we admitting poor blacks? They don't belong." Our blinders prevent us from seeing clearly what we believe and how we actually judge others. I pray my blinders are not that dark that I do not see the road blocks and the ignorance that dominate this world view.

As I have been grappling with racism in my life (my judgments and actions, as well as those of others) I have begun to reflect on a variety of experiences, issues and influences that have affected me directly and/or indirectly.

FIRST: SELF REFORMATION

As a teacher one of the strategies that I used in every class was to develop a character that I would use to provide a dramatic presentation. There were a number of reasons why I did so. Usually college courses focus on theories, research, general trends, categorical ideas, etc. I found it important to focus more on process and critical thinking than provide generalized information. My ethics classes included moral theories but also incorporated their applications. I wanted to apply moral thinking to cases, problems and contemporary issues within our society. My aging courses covered a wide range of sociological and psychological theories and research information. My cross-cultural classes dealt with general patterns of behavior, beliefs, and life styles. I was concerned that the focus on the general would overlook the importance of the individual. So I created characters that would take the theoretical and general and provide a "real" person that represented some of the lessons I felt were important to emphasize

One unique character I developed was Rev. John Newton, the author of the hymn <u>Amazing Grace</u>. I've presented this character in classes and in a couple of different churches. The presentation begins with someone – a student, a pastor, a family member – standing before the audience and announcing "Today we have with us a slave trader and an Anglican priest to share his story." Whatever the venue, I carefully walk to the pulpit or lectern wearing my academic robe over a black shirt with a Roman collar. The clothing isn't completely historically accurate, but my intent is to provide an image of a clergyman. I compensate for my weak British accent by lowering my voice, enunciating each word, speaking with precision and without Americanized idioms or phrases and projecting a sense of sincere authority. One essential ingredient for this presentation is having some type of a large screen so I can project performances of <u>Amazing Grace</u> taken from the PBS special Bill Moyers had produced in 1990. My performance begins with my Rev. Newton persona saying:

"It is difficult to come into a group of strangers and tell one's story with any assurance that what is said becomes that which is heard. But I have dedicated my life to preaching the Word of Christ and using my own wretchedness and sinful ways as a model for understanding the power and love and wonder of God and of Our Lord. Allow me to tell my story." My character goes on to provide an historical context for slave trading and informs the audience that only a fraction of the slaves ended up in the American colonies.

"In those days, there were about 100 vessels of all sorts involved in the African slave trade business sailing out of Liverpool. The standard qualifications for a captain of a slave trader included:

- A knowledge of and experience with the sea and sky
- An ability to control men and cargo.
- A background in being a mariner and merchant.
- A knowledge of merchandising in England, Africa and the Americas.
- A familiarity with the African and American coasts.
- An unscrupulous heart to take advantage of the human cargo we so wantonly used from the coast of West Africa.

"For 9 years I was a slave trader, working out of Liverpool and trading goods from England for slaves in Africa. These slaves I sold or traded for goods in America. My incentive was to raise enough profit to establish myself financially so I could marry my sweetheart. Her father required an established life financially, although he seemed to care little about how I acquired the funds, nor about the foul mouth that I carried with me."

I continue by sharing how a storm at sea began to change my attitude about life and about the cargo. I surmise that Newton's conversion was quite unlike St. Paul's dramatic shift on his way to Damascus. My character portrays his conversion as follows:

"No, for me the process was gradual. It was like the disciples on the Road to Emmaus. Christ's grace was working in my soul but I had not yet abandoned my sinful ways to follow his will and bidding. I had begun to realize that I was totally dependent upon Christ for all that I was and for all that I had. Yet I remained blind to who he was for still sometime. I stayed in the slave trade for years. I did begin to change, in some ways, however. I began to treat the slaves more humanely, but when I think back upon it, my humaneness was merely a rationalization to allow me to continue my wretched way of turning human beings into cargo and property. During those days, the hygiene and care of the slaves was quite poor. Many died and most arrived in poor health and, of course, in poor spirits. We never bothered to attend to their spirits, since they really were not much better than an animal, you know."

John Newton continues to provide historical context for the trade and reads some excerpts from his daily journal. He was married in 1751 and resigned his commission in 1754. He then began his studies and was ordained in the Anglican Church. Part of his ministry was not just being a vicar and parish priest in England; he also provided a weekly prayer group and in his later years he counseled William Wilberforce who was the primary abolitionist in Parliament. Reverend Newton provided Wilberforce with first hand information and helped guide him spiritually. Abolishing the slave trade was certainly a necessary condition for beginning to treat human beings as human beings; however, history has shown that abolition itself was not sufficient for eradicating prejudice and bigotry in society. My intent was to show how Newton realized that just stopping his slave trade career was not enough for receiving forgiveness for his actions. Helping Wilberforce became a means for seeking atonement. I continue with a passage from Newton's journal:

"With our ships, the great objective was to be full. The cargo of a vessel of 100 tons or a little more is calculated to purchase from 220 to 250 slaves. For the slaves lie in 2 rows, one above the other on each side of the ship, close to each other, like books upon a shelf. I have known them so close that the shelf would not easily contain 1 more. And I have known a white man sent down among the men to lay them in these rows to the greatest advantage, so that as little space as possible might be lost. I write from memory after an interval of more than 30 years, but at the same time, I believe many things which I saw, heard, and felt upon the coast of Africa are so deeply engraved in my memory that I can hardly forget or greatly mistake them. ... Think of the misery that was incurred upon humans who were wrestled from their land, their family, and their community. No one dared tell them what was happening. Think of the fear, the anguish, the dehumanization that occurred during their brutal voyage which would take about 2 months and cover over 3000 miles."

It is within this context that my character turns to his prayer group and the source for his inspiration for <u>Amazing Grace</u>. The hymn arose because of his slave trading experiences and grew out of the discussions and prayers of his group at his congregation in Olney. I then begin the process of shifting from an historical perspective to one that views singers and usages of his hymn. I take poetic license and pretend that Reverend Newton has seen the performances shown on the screen and I have him interject commentary for each one. This hymn, maybe even more than helping Wilberforce, gave him a sense of atonement. He begins:

"I continue to be struck at the beauty of this most humble of hymns. Is it the tune? Is it the words? Is it the singer or group? Or maybe, I have been the most fortunate of men to have allowed God's grace to work through me to give each of us a simple hymn and prayer that touches the innermost feelings of our faith. <u>Amazing Grace</u> is powerful because it does not try to be so. It is touching because it lacks the grandeur of a great masterpiece. It wrenches our souls because it was penned by a true wretch of a man who understood exactly the feelings that are captured in each word and phrase. It is also a hymn of irony because of the extensive use of my hymn in black congregations."

The examples I use include a clip of Jesse Norman (a black opera singer from England who is a Baptist), Judy Collins, Marion Williams (a black gospel singer), Johnny Cash with some inmates that Bill Moyers had interviewed and Shape Note singing in a southern congregation. I amended the script after 9/11to end with a jarring visual and auditory moment. My son-in-law, Joe, helped me to edit a CBS special on 9/11 and add a version of the hymn sung by Michael Crawford. The visual display starts with the towers standing tall on a bright sunny day. The planes crash, the buildings fall, the crowds flee in terror and the workers begin the grim task of working in the wreckage. The final scene is a procession of firemen during a funeral of "one of their own". All of these scenes appear with the hymn's haunting sounds carrying the images along. My Rev. Newton persona says the following as an introduction to this clip:

"There is a new meaning of fear and a new call for freedom that has emerged in your country since the tragedies of 9/11. That was a time for everyone to reconsider his/her meaning in life and to ponder what is truly important to him/her. I have been even more humbled by the role that my hymn has played in your grief and dismay. It has been a hymn for the all too many who were heroes or innocent victims in a day of ugly terrorism. I have heard it used at ground zero - at funerals - at memorial services - at civic gatherings. I am pleased that you do not take the separation of church and state too literally nor too explicitly. The human spirit requires a depth that only a religious consciousness can provide. I would like to share another version of my hymn with you. It is sung by Michael Crawford, a fellow Englishman and loyal Anglican believer. The visual effects are self-explanatory, but I would ask that you note the following in his version of <u>Amazing Grace</u>. It has a slave-like, rhythmic drum beat to it. The basic melody is from a southern harmony of the 18th century. This version is a favorite of mine because it seems to bring some of the wretchedness of the slaves and what I did to them to life. It rings out with the cry for freedom and justice that 9/11 seems to underscore."

The silence after this video is always thick with emotions, whether I perform this at a church, in a classroom, or in another venue at the college. This character allows me to examine the influence of racism in a man's life. Prejudice, bigotry and discrimination occur within a social context. Reverend John Newton was a product of his times and fell into the trap of adopting some of the social mores common for merchants in Britain at the time. He is an example of changing his beliefs, attitudes and prejudices: self-reformation. He did not remain trapped in his world of bigotry. His hymn is a lasting legacy of opening one's self to the humanity of all people and the power of God's grace. Maybe these chapters are another way for me to try and atone for the racism that has influenced me and led me to think and display actions that failed to respect my brothers and sisters of different colors.

SECOND: MELTING POT

The belief that America is a melting pot is a troubling view because it is neither descriptively accurate nor prescriptively desirable. **Descriptively:** Americans are not a blended mix of people who have adopted the same language, values, beliefs, religion and world view. A stir fry analogy seems to better describe the nature of America. We are a collective group of people who live within a society with laws, customs, mores and rules. These contextual characteristics are the wok but the contents of the stir fry is the diversity of races, religions, ethnic groups, immigrants (legal and illegal), generations, sexual orientations and genders. We do not blend into a homogeneous melting pot wherein our identities and individualities are lost. In essence we live together and hopefully accept the ideals for which America stands.

From a **prescriptive** viewpoint I do not believe we should adopt a melting pot model; rather an integration approach seems more desirable and reasonable. Integrating into society is a necessity for any chance of success, however that may be defined. Integrating people does not destroy their individuality, their differences, or their cherished histories. Immigrants need to learn the host language, laws and rules if they are to achieve any level of success or social advancement. It is not necessary for them to shed their native language or to stop teaching their children their native language and customs. Multi-lingualism is a strength, not a weakness. Europeans are far more prone to be multi-lingual while white Americans tend to be far less so. Teaching foreign languages in schools does not start early enough and has not been required long enough, and overseas opportunities have been too sporadic to eradicate this cultural deficit.

For European immigrants to America, the barriers they faced at integration were often less daunting than for Asian, Latino, or African immigrants. For example, German Americans were not put into internment camps as the Japanese were. Despite the terrible treatment of European immigrants in the late 1800s and early 1900s, the Irish, German, Polish and other European immigrants now see themselves as Americans. They believe they have assimilated and adopted the values of America. The difficulty for Non-Caucasian races and immigrant minorities (especially those who consider themselves Americans) is that the United States still has a perception, maybe a self-deception, that it is English language, white race, and Christian dominant. This is an illusion; it certainly is not a desirable one.

African-American integration is still a goal but far from a reality. The higher incarceration rates, poverty levels, and unequal employment opportunities are not a result of race; they are the result of historical prejudice, discrimination and bigotry. Caucasians often are not even aware of what "white privilege" means much less understanding how pervasive it really is. Buying homes, for example, is still not racially blind. One of the African American men who worked for me wanted to move. He and his wife were looking in a northern suburb of Buffalo. When they indicated a couple of houses they wanted to look at to their realtor, she told them that they really wouldn't be interested in those houses. She didn't take them to the areas that interested them and they realized that she did not want to be a part of helping a black family move into a white neighborhood. Truly integrated neighborhoods are still more an exception than the norm for all too many suburban areas. Whites may not even realize that this is an issue.

Black Lives Matter is a real call for recognizing the systematic racism that marginalizes far too many people of color. It is sad that too many people misconstrue the movement and feel as if there has to be White Lives Matter, or a Blue Lives Matter or All Lives Matter counter movements. Of course, all lives matter. That's not the point. The problem is that denying the legitimacy of Black Lives Matter only reinforces the alienation and marginalization of blacks. I'm reminded of the question: Why is the Holocaust still important; it happened so long ago? We must NEVER forget what one group of people can do to another, whether it is based on race, religion, politics, fear, terror, etc. All of us must continually be reminded of the atrocities to which too many people around the world turned a blind eye. That such hatred could be condoned or ignored is disgraceful. In like manner, whites should not condemn Black Lives Matter because they feel somehow victimized by reverse bigotry and discrimination. Of course there are individuals of any religion, race, or group who hate and detest members of other groups. That fact does not negate the legitimacy of such a movement as Black Lives Matter. If the movement loses its footing and becomes violent, then its members will need to undergo some soul searching. Let us not mistake individual vengeance for an injustice or an individual police brutality as representative of all whites, blacks or police officers. Police rightfully become indignant when all police are tarred by the injustices of a single officer (or even a small group of them). In like manner members of the Black Lives Matter movement should be equally indignant when their movement is condemned when someone gets violent during their protests.

Wanting to impose or prescribe that a melting pot is desirable may come from a conscious or subconscious need to have others adopt one's own point of view, values and/or beliefs. Wouldn't the world be better off if everyone thought or lived the way I do? A desire to have people melt into our own image and likeness may be understandable but not consistent with reality. I am concerned that those who adopt a melting pot model do so with an assumption or an expectation that everyone else in the model will believe or act "my" way. Which "my" way should be adopted? Who should determine the nature of the melting pot and how everyone should be mixed together? The assumption or expectation that the melting pot should be to my liking fails to see the uniqueness and difference that each one of us brings along on our journey through life. To expect everyone to speak like me, act like me and behave like me is unrealistic and actually leads to prejudice, discrimination and a weakening of our social fabric. One of America's greatest assets is its diversity and openness to alternative ways of viewing the world, solving problems, and improving life for all. Why should we try to eliminate these sources of strength? Shouldn't we try to improve our ways of tapping into our diversity and enhancing these abilities? Why should we demand that everyone talk and act like us, whoever the "us" is?

THIRD: CULTURAL INFLUENCES/LANGUAGE

As human beings, we are connected to others by laws, rules, norms, customs and mores. In addition, humanity is interconnected by actions and attitudes. Each action or inaction in our life creates ripples throughout all of humanity. Everything we do shifts the cosmic sands of life. The American belief that everyone has a right to do whatever he/she wishes as long as it does not affect anyone else is a myth. Life is continuous and interconnected and that includes human existence. Like the color spectrum, we each may have our own color, but our actions (or inactions) blend, mix and collide with the rest of the world. Whether we want to accept this fact or not, the truth is that humans are interdependent social beings. Our lives are interpenetrating waves and we have a responsibility as citizens of humanity and the world to respect and care for others. The very nature of social connectedness includes (a) the conscious and unconscious forces that influence who we are, as well as who we have been and will become, (b) what we think and believe, and (c) how we respond and act in life. These forces shape the way we think and feel.

Culture means more than just our national or racial identity; it is not just customs or ethnic heritage. It includes race, gender, generation, educational levels, sexual orientation, social class, ethnic background, where we live (nationally, regionally and locally) and religion. These cultural dimensions influence our values, attitudes, beliefs, and moral principles. The influences are interconnected, dynamic and overlap (that is, they are continuous). Sometimes they are apparent or overt; sometimes subtle; sometimes they are hidden or covert; and sometimes they are taken for granted or assumed to be true for all people. Certainly they are not always compatible or rationally organized. They mix and blend in ways that can leave us confused or living in a world of ambiguities. Sometimes they provide mixed messages, conflicted norms, and confusion for individuals and/or groups.

Some of the conflicts during my journey through my prejudices may be understood more clearly when we understand the characteristics and dynamics of these cultural influences. In a sense they apply to all the isms of my life. They provide a context and background for addressing the ignorance I have with respect to interpersonal relationships. In a sense they have helped me gain some insight into who I am, what I believe and what values affect my thoughts and actions.

One example of these influences in the United States relates to the generic forms of English that are spoken. Not only do we have varied accents around the country, but there are also gender, generational and work-related phrases and words that are quite distinctive. Each generation develops its own code words. Sometimes people from other generations can learn some of them. Using another generation's words can be humorous or can create discomfort in the conversation. An 80 year old man calling his friend "dude" for example seems cute or out of place. How many 90 year olds refer to hash tags in a conversation? Wouldn't a 5 year old calling his friends "colleagues" seem a bit strange? Are there really any 18 or 19 year old hippies anymore? The language of text messaging and smart phones is very different from the generations who used party lines or words for the beginning of their phone numbers (Butler 3-4951, for example). Of course everyone's language has been affected by computers. The level of sophistication with a computer and the frequency of use will alter the number of computer related words and phrases that become a part of the way we talk to each other (or, rather, connect electronically with one another).

One of the tasks of feeling included in a group is learning the language (words and non-verbal cues) that is a part of that group. Children start this process when they have secret words for their clubs or play groups. Effective orientations for schools, jobs, churches, volunteer agencies, etc. include the words, phrases and timing for accomplishing things. Usually, we take all of these activities for granted and do not consider the dynamics that are involved. In essence, that is one of the powers of culture at any level. We tend to take for granted or just assume that a particular way of doing something or a specific word or phrase is the natural way of doing things: everyone thinks or acts this way. I asked my students if they speak in the same fashion and use the same words and gestures with their friends, when they're in class, when they are with their parents or at a job. Of course, they all realized that the context changes the rules and the names or words they may use. The names we have for friends are usually not the names we would use in referring to relatives, especially parents or grand-parents, for example.

One of the simple topics I have used in courses or in workshops is looking at word associations. Black and white are perfect examples of the subconscious influences in our country. Our associations with white are often connected with purity, cleanliness, or Snow White. Black, on the other hand, connects with dirt, evil, or sin. The good guys are often white or ride white horses like the Lone Ranger. Lies that are acceptable are white lies while we would black ball someone who is undesirable. Darth Vader is all in black and we automatically understand the evil of Black Magic or the problems of being behind the eight ball. Souls are some-times portrayed as white while sins are the black spots that corrupt the soul's natural purity. White clouds may be pretty and yield images for our imaginations while black clouds bring rain, storms and a sense of fore-boding. It is naive to think that these connotations have no impact on people's subconscious view of the world. Like so much that deals with prejudices and bigotry, the conscious contours of hatred or discrimination are not necessarily the most influential causes for the way we feel, think or act. I wonder if basic ignorance, the lack of contact with people who were different and the subtle messages of language affected my loving rel-atives' views of other human beings. Was their bigotry the result of these forces? The power of language is significant in all of our lives. Sometimes language provides us with very subconscious messages that subtly reflect the attitude, values or beliefs of the dominant forces within a society. Language is only one dimension of a culture, but it is a readily recog-nizable example to illustrate the effects culture has on any social context.

FOURTH: DIFFERENCES IN THE REGIONAL CUL-TURES OF MY RELATIVES

Values differ within regional areas. This geographic context includes not only northeast, south, etc. dimensions, but also the differences that emerge from urban, suburban, rural areas, as well as the influences that may occur with weather conditions and types of terrain (mountainous, desert, plains, Great Lakes, etc.). Farmers, for example, from different regions of the country may have more in common with one another than their urban counterparts in their own region. Business people in New York City may have very little in common with the dairy farmers scattered throughout New York State. We can readily identify accents as regional markers. For example, as a child I noticed a tremendous difference in the lives of my extended family, some of whom lived in suburban Chicago, while others lived in rural, Western Kentucky. The pace of dialogues and the non-verbal dimensions of communication were quite different in the two regions. I remember my relatives in Chicago talked at the pace I was used to hearing in Niagara Falls. Talking with my uncles in Kentucky was quite different. I learned that there would be pauses, sometimes long ones. As a child I did not learn how to adapt very well, but by the time I was a teenager I began to fall into the same pace. Early in our marriage, Diane teased me about how my language changed when we would visit my relatives. I had learned how to adjust my pace of talking, to adopt different words to get my point across, and I even changed pronunciations of words when we were there. I don't ever remember doing so consciously.

I was also struck by the diversity of concerns and values that emerged from these different regions in my life. For example, my Chicago relatives have always been avid golfers and have belonged to country clubs for most of their adult lives. They are interested in fashion and current trends in society. They were business people. My Kentucky relatives, on the other hand, were interested in livestock, crops, and stretching their earnings as far as they could. They worked the land; used their hands; did not shun back breaking labor; and spoke with honesty and simplicity. *The Old Farmer's Almanac* dictated when to mate livestock, when to wean babies and when to get one's hair cut.

I also was struck by the vast difference between the daily routines. In Chicago, the big meal of the day was supper – usually around 5:00 or 6:00 PM. In Kentucky, the big meal was dinner, which we ate around noontime. As a child there was a world of difference for me between spending a weekend at my northern relatives' cottage in Wisconsin as contrasted to spending a week or more helping to feed the chickens, milk the cows, gather the eggs, cut tobacco, hoe the vegetable gardens, or run in the fields in Western Kentucky. In different ways I learned my racial and gender prejudices from both areas of influence. My northern dad had just as much disdain and disregard for people of color as my southern mom. Both taught me very clearly about the dominance of the male and the roles designed for the "little woman." It was my reflection on my relatives that prompted me to stand up in that theology class and muse that the insidiousness of northern bigotry is at least as problematic as southern prejudice and discrimination. I have not changed by opinion over the past 50 years.

FIFTH: MOTIVATING WITH INTELLIGENCE

Motivation is complex when it relates to racial issues. My inadvertent racial insensitivity by flying the Confederate flag is a good example of thoughtlessness. Just because I think I am not prejudiced or bigoted or discriminatory does not make by attitudes, actions or decisions just and right. The inadvertent, subconscious, and unintended covert forms of my prejudices truly give me pause. It is a primary motivator for writing these reflections. Is it not better for me to admit that I am blind to many of my values and beliefs than to assume that I know everything? If I have learned nothing else from my studies in Philosophy, it is that an unexamined life is not a good one. I only gain in wisdom when I recognize my own ignorance and accept that there is far more to learn than what I already know. I may feel strongly about many topics and issues, but it is important to realize that what I do not know about life and about myself is far broader than what I think I know. Accepting this fact is not really a sign of humility, rather it truly is a humbling feeling. I only wish shock jock radio hosts and pontificating people at parties and barbecues would think before spewing their venom and hateful messages. Too many conspiracy theories become based on misinformation or distorted "facts". The movement away from critical thinking and no longer relying on science and verifiable evidence is truly scary. Anti-intellectualism today seems to be rejecting the very act of using one's intelligence; I get the sense that there is an anti-intellect movement. Since our intellect is what distinguishes us as a species and since it is our basic evolutionary weapon for survival, such a movement would be a dangerous extreme. Humanity needs to continue to balance and utilize our common sense and our intellectual capacities. Prejudice and discrimination against facts, science, common sense and our intellect may be both overt (Facebook entries, for example) and covert (subconscious feelings, for example).

SIXTH: PERSONALITY

Ultimately, how a person responds to all of the influences in life and how he or she organizes these responses will have a profound impact upon his or her values, attitudes and beliefs, as well as how they become incorporated in any decision-making process or knee-jerk reaction. Our personality develops as we learn to negotiate the world. Some basic personality traits can be observed in infants, babies and young children, for example the outgoing and babbling baby or the quiet, shy one. Our personality shifts and emerges in varying ways throughout our life. Traumatic experiences can dramatically alter the way we feel or think about people, events, or our own actions.

The interactions among the other contextual influences in our life and our personality help form our dynamic character. Oftentimes our personality gets molded around the dominant influences in the different spheres in our life. Other times we may assert our uniqueness by acting in very individualistic ways following the contours of our personality.

Our personalities are complex webs, which may include what appear to be conflicting dimensions. For example, it is not unusual for someone to demonstrate introverted and extroverted tendencies that exhibit themselves in varying ways in different situations. I consider myself to be shy and introverted; yet I would guess there are people in my life who would be surprised at that self-assessment. Another confounding issue relates to the differing personalities within a family with more than one child. Siblings, even twins, exhibit very different traits and responses to situations. They may be living in the same family, but their personality becomes a major factor in identifying how and why they behave the way they do. Self awareness is the key for understanding who you are and why you behave the way you do. Prejudices and discriminations may find deep roots in someone who lacks even a basic sense of who he or she is.

One of the shortcomings of my reflections in this chapter is my preoccupation with racism as it relates to African Americans or Blacks. I have ignored Hispanic, Latino, Asian (East, West and Indian), and Native American. I sincerely apologize for doing so. My personal experience is very limited with Hispanics, Latinos and Native Americans. My experiences with Asians has been diverse and a bit more developed (traveling on professional delegations to China and Israel have had a tremendous impact upon me). The general concept of racism is comparable regardless of the group being targeted. Becoming aware of our own racism is crucial if we ever hope to achieve a civil and fair society.

PART II:

RELIGION:
THE BEST AND THE WORST MOTIVATORS

CHAPTER 3
MY JOURNEY OF FAITH

Just as a candle cannot burn without fire,
men cannot live without a spiritual life.

The Buddha

The drive was long and silent. Without Bill to annoy me or my mom's chatter, the miles rolled along with periods of blessed silence and periods of worried rumination. Since it was late August, the windows were rolled down so my dad's cigarette smoke would blow rather harmlessly out of the car. The smoke really didn't bother me too much then; my asthma had not surfaced in those days. Growing up I lived with my dad smoking three packs of Camels per day while my mom smoked two "healthy" packs of filtered cigarettes. After mom had complications while delivering me her physician prescribed smoking to calm her. There were no bans on smoking in my youth and a great deal of ignorance about smoking's damage pervaded society. Before my brother was born (when I was 6 ½) my folks would take me to bars and bowling alleys which were encased in a smoky haze. My mom taught me how to keep score for bowling by the time I was five and my prowess was rewarded by actually allowing me to keep score for one of mom's teams in league play. I can still feel the beer and smoke smell that seemed to seep into every pore of my body. Dad had a part of a lung removed during my junior year in high school and he and

I argued afterward about his need to follow the doctor's orders and stop smoking. Those arguments ALWAYS ended with the refrain: "I'm your father; you must respect what I say."

The trip that summer day, however, held no discussions or drama; the only interruptions in the silence were my navigational aids: "You'll be turning south onto route 15 in a few miles," for example. The response: "Yup."

I was in charge of the Trip Tik, the one essential (other than dad's smokes and mom's can for peeing) for all of our travels to Kentucky or Chicago. Bill still has the best line about the Triptik. On one of our trips to Kentucky, he was given the opportunity to hold the sacred text. He wasn't anticipating enough when he was supposed to give Dad the directions for the next turn. "So how far 'til I have to turn?" was the gruff query from the front seat. Bill's response: "It's a page and a half." Mom and I laughed; Dad did not.

My dad and I were now in Pennsylvania, headed for an 80-acre farm in Maryland. We only stopped for gas because Mom had packed us a lunch to eat while we drove. Stopping to eat or stretch our legs or turn off for a scenic view was not a part of any of our car trips. The purpose for driving was to get to the destination as quickly as possible (and do so relatively legally). Dad always tried to drive five miles-per-hour over the speed limit. In his mind, any faster was flirting with getting a ticket and any slower was a waste of time.

I was 18 for this drive and instead of going to Gannon University (and the possibility of the Naval Academy the following year) I was embarking on a new venture into the Oblates of St. Francis deSales Seminary. Mom was devastated that I would throw away my life. Her response, though, didn't quite match the deep misgivings she felt about my choice. She didn't plead for me to change my mind; she just cried a bit and said she hoped I'd be happy. But her reluctance to accept my choice was multi-layered, rooted in her Southern Baptist upbringing. She did not understand the rituals or many of the rules of the Roman Catholic Church: for example, having to eat fish on Friday as a form of fasting made no sense to her. I know she thought the idea of celibacy was an onerous distortion of human nature. One of her friends had a daughter a year younger than me. Mom was not too subtle over the years about me becoming interested in her. Going into the seminary was a waste to my mom because it would prevent me from having a natural loving relationship with a woman. Mom didn't ask me anything about my decision, but I'm sure she was confused because I had been going steady with a girl for seven months and then dumped her for the seminary. For mom, interpersonal relationships between men and women were just a simple fact of life. Why the church would create a rule for its priests to disobey this natural human drive was something she could never understand.

Another misgiving was more personal for her: she had depended upon me to be a confidante for her. In a sense she had groomed me to be an entertainer and the life of the party. She loved to laugh and socialize and she urged me to be happy and social. When I was 7 or 8 she enrolled me in dance lessons at a hotel ballroom downtown. I learned to foxtrot, waltz and jitter bug. At the end of the session we had a semi-formal dance which was a real torture for me. I had to dress up with a coat, tie and wear gloves. The boys had to ask girls to dance and I just fumbled my way through that experience. Another time we went to a show that had teenage girls doing the cancan. I was embarrassed and uncomfortable watching the girls acting in such a flamboyant manner. I noticed Mom watching me and encouraging me to enjoy the entertainment. Didn't she understand that this type of encouragement was not helpful for me at that age? Furthermore, even though I don't think she approved of the girls I dated in high school, at least she was relieved that I was doing so. The paradox may have been that no girl would be good enough for me to date, but not dating was unhealthy. No girl I dated would have passed muster except for mom's friend's daughter.

My dating history was pretty slim. From 5th grade through 8th grade I went to our parish school, Prince of Peace. There were about 10 boys and 8 girls in my class who were with me for all four years. A few classmates came and went, but for the most part we were a relatively homogeneous group. By 8th grade there were a couple of parties that I attended, a dance in Beverly's basement and a summer gathering at Mike and Marna's (the class twins). Because of my dance lessons, I thought I was a good dancer; the girls probably had a different opinion. Some of the kids at the twin's party went to the back of the yard to "make out", but that was way out of my league. I didn't go on any dates until my Junior Prom and this probably had mom worried. My second date was in the fall of my senior year (of course, after football season) to go to the class ring dance. I was the class President and was running the event so attending seemed mandatory. Mom shocked me when I turned 18 (January of my senior year). She threw a surprise party for my friends and their dates. She even invited the girl I would start going steady with a month later. Mom cleverly had me clean the basement for this party by telling me it was for the neighborhood adults (something they did regularly).

Thus, for Mom my entering the seminary was unnatural and she was afraid that I was throwing my life away because I was not living up to her image of what it takes to be happy. Besides, why would I leave a girlfriend to become celibate?

What she couldn't understand was that happiness was irrelevant in my decision. It was something I *had* to do. For the most part I was rather serious in my formative years. Of course I loved to laugh and have a good time, but there was an underlying sense of seriousness in my attitude toward life and people. After we moved to a new house when I was 10, I played with kids from my old neighborhood (about a mile away) or with my new friends at Prince of Peace. Rarely did I invite them to my home to do anything. Invariably I rode my bike to their houses or met at the playgrounds for baseball or football. I didn't allow myself to like the Beatles because in the mid-60s they seemed too light and trivial for me. Screaming girls was something I just could not understand. My serious side was embedded in a deep intensity to my character. I have always played sports with an intensity and passion. My father taught me to do everything in life correctly and well. Make no mistakes. Fix any problem. These became hallmarks of my masculinity, especially as a teen. Because I felt responsible for my mom's happiness and because I needed to protect her from my dad, I looked at life through a prism of duty and responsibility. As I have grown older and have the benefit of hindsight and perspective, I now realize that these attitudes were not healthy and probably were a distortion of reality. I *do* know my mom depended on me for serious discussions after a night of drinking. These talks began when I was about 13 or so. I don't remember many of the topics, just that I had a responsibility for listening and being her sounding board. My mom really didn't need my protection from dad. He was not physically abusive, although he probably was psychologically so by the time I was a teen. There was nothing I could do about his language or his demands so feeling responsible for fixing them was unrealistic.

By the time I was 11 or 12, I assumed the role of male parent for my brother Bill. Dad seemed to only make demands but didn't attend to the day-to-day discipline I felt was needed. One day, for example, while we were doing the dishes, Bill just left to go play with a friend before he finished drying. I told him to come back, but he laughed and took off. When he returned about an hour later, he said he would put the dishes away because they were dry now. I immediately went to the kitchen and rinsed all of the dishes again to make him dry them. He never skipped out on me again while we had that chore. I felt vindicated because I had taught him an adult lesson of discipline. This attitude, along with my sense of responsibility for my mom, caused me to feel a great deal of pressure - most of which was self imposed. Later in life I realized that the "had" I was feeling was not a calling, but an escape. I was running away from the pressures of my family and seeking quiet refuge from this world. I also had been groomed by nuns and priests since 5th grade (more of that later).

When we finally arrived at the seminary, my dad got my suitcase out of the trunk, shook my hand, and said good luck. He immediately got back in the car and headed home; he was going to make the 700+ mile round trip in one day and didn't see any need to waste time with good-byes to me or hellos to the priest waiting to welcome me to my new life. Dad didn't have anything to say on the way, so why say anything now? His initial response about my going to the seminary had been a little surprising to me, until I thought about it on the trip. "Why would you want to do something like that?" he had said. He was the Roman Catholic in the marriage. He was an usher at our parish and was raised Catholic by a devout mother and a converted father. They had adopted my father and his sister when the siblings were young. I think my dad liked ushering so he could stand in the back and not have to kneel down or say any of the responses during Mass. He was always a religious enigma to me. When I was 8 or 9 years old, he and I went to the monthly Monday night Novenas for nine straight months. When I was young, I would go with him to the noon Mass on Sunday which was the best time for him to recover from his drinking the night before. When I started serving as an altar boy (in fourth grade) I would walk to Mass and go without him, unless my assignment was the noon one (which was rare). So Dad and I did not attend Mass together anymore. I do remember that he would kneel with his rear end resting on the pew seat when he wasn't ushering. I vowed to never take that position and still do not to this day. He demanded that his boys be brought up Catholic and even agreed for me to attend Prince of Peace elementary school when we moved and I was going into 5th grade. When I was a junior in high school he had lung surgery and became disenchanted with the church. No priest visited him in the hospital or at home. He never went to church again and, typically, never said a word to any of us (other than blurt out an obscenity whenever something about the Catholic Church was mentioned on the television news). He lived for about 10 years after the surgery. Before his operation, I always thought that Dad was hedging his bets about the afterlife: have a clean slate when he died. The Novenas and weekly mass seemed to be the ticket he was seeking.

By the time I was going into the seminary he had recovered from his surgery that had occurred about 19 months before. By then his break from the church was complete. After driving me to my new vocation, Dad wasn't about to have a conversation with a priest and delay his return voyage. He must have come to terms with the afterlife in his own way. It was not something we would ever discuss; too bad, because I wish I had made the time to have this conversation with him. Whether he would have told me anything will always remain a mystery.

As I watched the car wend its way down the hilly drive, a smiling priest welcomed me to my new life. The next 10 months were pivotal in my spiritual, religious, and psychological development. For the first time, I felt free from the daily responsibility for raising my brother, caring for my mother, dealing with my father, and trying to go through my teen years with a sense of purpose and determination. Of course, these attitudes were self- imposed. My parents were more than capable of raising my brother (he was the third and they already had experience with Paul and me). Caring for my mother was both something I embraced and an expectation from mom. Now that I was in the Seminary, it was about my relationship with God and Jesus and what I would do with the rest of my life. The Franciscans tried to recruit me out of 8th grade, but my parents refused: the compromise was letting me attend the Catholic high school.

Looking back, it was easy to see why I fit the profile for having a vocation. From 4th grade through 8th grade, I was an altar boy and worked hard at doing everything correctly. By 6th grade I was missing classes 2 or 3 times a week to serve at funerals. I was overly obedient, worked hard, and did any of the extras that were expected of good Catholic boys of the day. (For example, on All Souls Day at lunch time I would enter and exit the church at least 15-20 times and say the appropriate number of prayers to release souls from Purgatory.) I served at the late Midnight Mass on Christmas Eve and at the Easter Vigil. I was very proud of learning all of the Latin responses during the mass and standing and kneeling at the right time and in the correct positions. I learned how to serve as the master of ceremonies at Solemn High Masses and always stood or knelt as if I had a board connecting my neck to my knees. My rule-following self made me a perfect candidate for being a patrol guard at school. We helped crossing the youngsters and got to wear a strap that went across our shoulder and was secured by a belt. The badge on the strap was a sign of authority. Of course, by 8th grade I was named the captain of the guard - something I had worked hard to achieve.

On that drive to the seminary, though, I wasn't so sure about this vocation. It wasn't that I was concerned about the vows I would take in 10 years (chastity, poverty and obedience); those I felt were just a matter of self-control, which was one of my strong suits. No, my concern was whether I would be good enough to fulfill the responsibility of being someone set apart from the rest of humanity. The nuns and priests had instilled the belief in me that the priesthood was a higher calling than just marriage. Of course, the church recognized being single as a legitimate form of living, but, at age 18, I couldn't imagine why anyone would opt for that way of life. Priesthood was serving God and humanity and marriage was for having children. Of what good was being single? All of these attitudes would dissolve over time, but they were clearly a part of my thoughts on that ride.

It didn't take long to get into the routine of my new world. Awake at 5 AM, meditate from 5:30 to 6:00, kneeling all the time; Mass at 6:00, breakfast at 7:00, chores from 8:00 – 9:00, classes began at 9:00. The faculty were affiliated with the Catholic University of America (located in Washington, DC) but all of our classes were on-site at the farm. We were allowed to talk only during recreational periods: 1:00 - 2:00 PM and 6:00 - 7:00 PM daily with the special time of 1:00 - 5:00 PM on Sunday.

Families could visit only during the Sunday recreational period. Parents and siblings who lived in Delaware or Philadelphia came often. My parents and Bill came only once. I don't remember what my folks and I talked about, but I do remember spending time with Bill. He had just received a bow and arrow and was anxious to show me his new-found skills. There was ample room on the farm, so we headed back to the barn areas and he proceeded to shoot to his heart's content. I falsely praised him for his skills. Later I confessed my sin of lying to my confessor.

My confessor was one of those people who comes in and out of life and had a profound, subconscious influence on me. He was my Latin teacher in high school but went to the Seminary to teach Latin there. It seemed natural for me to ask him to be my confessor in the Sem since we had had a positive relationship before. He was very disciplined, something that spoke to my personality, and was utterly fair and demanding. My Latin in those days was a strong suit for me. He was the primary reason.

Many years later when I was Dean at Canisius, one of my responsibilities was serving on the Advisory Board for a college program that offered degrees at Attica Correctional Facility. Canisius, Niagara and Daemon were the colleges sponsoring degrees and offering courses. One semester I even offered an introductory course in philosophy to a dozen inmates. Lo and behold at my first advisory meeting, I met the man who was appointed the curriculum director and student advisor for the program: it was Father Tom McHugh, my confessor/Latin teacher. We chatted after the meeting, and he told me that he had moved away from the Oblates and found this position to be his new calling. It was not surprising that one of the math teachers for the program was a former priest from my high school who had taught me Algebra. He and Tom had remained good friends. (Father McHugh became Tom to me during that time.) My last interaction with him was years later when he asked me to go to lunch. We had never done so before, but I felt honored that he had asked me to meet him. Toward the end of the meal, he informed me that he was dying of cancer and was going away. He wanted to say good-bye and wish me well in all of my life. I was stunned, touched, and incredulous. How could a pillar of strength in my life be saying that he was dying, that he would never be in my life ever again? He has always been a quiet model for me. I have given him too little credit for the lessons I learned from him. Work hard; be honest; be fair; don't take short cuts; and be true to yourself and your God. He asked that I let him go and I did. I never knew when or where he died. I just remember him in quiet moments of reflection.

In the seminary Tom was still Fr. McHugh. As I reflect upon those times when I went to confession with him, he exhibited the patience of Job. The trivial things I would use as sins must have been a bit amusing to him. For example, any time I talked while getting my haircut or when I confessed that I laughed when one of the seminarians slipped and fell. One of the key rules of the Seminary was that we were to remain silent except during the recreational periods. This silence included not being allowed to speak at meals, while studying or while doing our chores (especially the extended work times on Saturday morning). We could ask questions in our classes. I was always shocked that the second year student who cut hair would talk incessantly with anyone who was under his scissors or waiting patiently for his turn. His shop was open each Saturday to ensure we all looked "shorn for the Lord." Of course, I remember only nodding, smiling or laughing and only rarely joining in the conversations (which, of course, became fodder for my seeking repentance).

My first chore assignment at the Sem was ideal. I was teamed with a high school friend of mine who was a year older. The idea was to have the second year novices assist the first year postulants with their jobs. The postulants attended classes and lived in a large dormitory area. We each had a bed, a chair and a dresser in a large, open area. The communal showers and bathrooms were next to the dorm area. The novices did not attend college courses but spent the year discerning whether or not they truly had a vocation. They were given instructions about the order's founder, St. Francis deSales, and spent extra time in prayer and meditation. Each one of them had a separate room (which really was a concrete cell) and wore a cassock and collar. We postulants were looking forward to the summer ceremony when we would have our cassocks bestowed upon us.

Jack, the high school friend, and I were assigned to the boiler room for my first chore assignment. We got to clean out the soot and grime on a daily basis but Saturday was the real bonus for the job. On Saturday we got to clean all of the ashes and soot out of the boiler and transport them to the dump toward the back of the property. We had four hours to finish the job (and we, actually always Jack, got to drive an open bed truck to the dump!). It only took about three hours to complete our task, so we had an hour or so to kill out at the dump. There were two trees that were separated by the right distance for goal posts. In the dump were all of the discarded tin cans. Tin cans made great footballs, and Jack and I had weekly competitions. Jack instigated this defiance of the rules, but I readily enjoyed the naughtiness of our waywardness. (Yes, more fodder for Fr. McHugh to hear.) The dump was a large crater in the rolling hills of the farm. Three-fourths of the area around the dump was open (including the dirt path we used to drive our ashes to their final resting place); the other fourth was treed.

One Saturday evening in late October we were roused from our supper with an urgent cry of "FIRE in the woods!" There were about 80 students/ novices and about 5 priests and 2 brothers. We rushed to the barn and grabbed whatever tool was available; I got a pick axe. Some used the truck and tractor to haul water. We ran out to the fire and dug a trench and cleaned out the brush to contain the blaze. Thankfully, the wind was blowing the flames away from the woods and toward the open areas around the dump. About an hour into our fight, the local fire department arrived and took over. We were slightly amused when we heard the siren coming, then leaving, because the firemen missed the driveway in the dark (no lights were a subtle security measure, I guess). The next day Jack and I were reassigned to cleaning bathrooms; I was sent to the novices living quarters, and he went to the postulant area. No big surprise in that! The rector had to set an example of us to the others. Our dereliction of duty was the reason for losing what I felt was a great assignment. With the new task I decided to remake my attitude and considered that wielding a mop and a buffer to clean the floors was an ideal way to serve the Lord. Working in the boiler room was rather enjoyable and I liked teaming up with Jack. Kicking cans for making pretend field goals was just plain fun. After being admonished I realized that I wasn't in the Sem for enjoyment or fun. I was there to work, be serious, and determine if I was worthy of becoming a priest. Cleaning floors would allow me to refocus on this purpose.

Two experiences at the Sem remain vivid in my memory. Just after breakfast one October morning, I had about 20 minutes to continue praying and meditating outside before classes. To the west the full moon was still brilliant in the deep, rich blue of the evening sky that was grudgingly conceding its domain to daylight. To the east the yellows and oranges of a hopeful sky enveloped the horizon as a familiar dome was emerging. I stood transfixed between *Alpha* and *Omega*: was this new life my *Alpha*? If so, what was my *Omega*, my goal or purpose in life? The road ahead was clear: high school teacher, possibly an assistant in a parish. History was going to be my major and my current studies of America's past seemed to confirm that my choice was a wise one. Would I be up for the challenge? My Catholic roots seemed firm and the rules that governed my life seemed God given. That morning seemed to confirm in my mind that I had made the correct decision.

During Holy Week the following spring I had decided that Good Friday from noon to three (the traditionally accepted time of Jesus' crucifixion) was going to be a pivotal experience in my religious development; and, in a sense, it was. There was a small hedge around a figure of Jesus, the Sacred Heart, on the side of a hill near the driveway leading down to the road and the outside world. I had noticed that no one ever seemed to bother this area. It had become my little refuge for weeks. I had nestled into this little sanctuary with my copy of *Gone With the Wind* whenever I could find the time. Mom had given the book to me for my birthday. She never said anything but I'm sure she believed that my reading this great Southern romance was part of the reason I "came to my senses" the following summer and left the seminary. The novel truly had no impact on my decision (I think) but I would never have told her otherwise. For my Good Friday meditation I was going to spend the three hours with Jesus - no books, no notes, and a determination to keep my mind from wandering to the wide variety of venues it frequented. It was bright and very hot that afternoon (as the sun burnt face that looked back at me that night seemed to verify). Sweating and miserable was exactly how I wanted to feel. I would not remove the ants from my ankles or the flies that periodically landed on me. For three hours I kept my vigil. I started out sitting up but found myself laying on one side and resting my head on my hand. Unknowingly I had bent my elbow to provide a place for my head. I probably changed positions a few times, but I don't remember whether doing so was a conscious choice. I say this because I was relishing in the pain and discomfort of the conditions and would not have changed positions simply for comfort. I was intent upon using my imagination to relive each moment that led Jesus to His crucifixion and death. It was important that I suffer for Jesus as I tried to get some small measure of the torture he must have experienced when he was so unjustly nailed to the cross. I knew that my discomfort was minor compared to His suffering, but it was right and just that I endured some measure of pain.

I have always connected that afternoon to an experience I had when I was 13: My folks were out drinking, and I was baby-sitting my brother. He had gone to bed and instead of watching television I was sitting on the living room couch not wanting to have any distractions. Even at that age, I relished the quiet moments to be by myself with my own thoughts. That night I was trying to figure out what I would do if my parents were both killed by my dad's drunken driving. This was a common musing for me (from the time I was 11 when I started baby-sitting until the time I had escaped to the seminary). My dad always returned home drunk and my mom didn't drive. In front of me were the drawn curtains with mom's peacock designs on them. The windows were large and the curtains were floor to ceiling in height and probably 12-14 feet in length. As my thoughts poured into one another and my feelings became more disconnected, the curtains started to move. That was a bit startling because it was winter and the windows were closed and the furnace wasn't running. A figure with a beard emerged from the curtain and I felt the words "I am with you; do not fear." The figure was gone in an instant. The reason I say I "felt" the words was because the figure did not speak to me; I just felt His message as He appeared. I had not dozed off and knew that I was fully alert. Whether I was hallucinating or genuinely having a vision has always been irrelevant to me. The experience was real, and the message has been reassuring throughout my life. That Good Friday afternoon by Jesus' statue was my time to reconnect with my Savior. I felt that I did.

This reconnecting with Jesus brought a startling idea to me. Who was more important: the church or Jesus? I had been very dependent upon being good and following the rules of my faith. These rules were the means for the faithful to reach Jesus and secure salvation. But I began to wonder about whether or not the rules were starting to get in the way of my feeling a real connection to the Christ, my Messiah. This revelation was not a bolt of lightning or a singular moment of insight. It was more of a creeping awareness that began to unsettle me. The routine of the Sem didn't really bother me too much while I was attending classes and concentrating on successfully completing the courses. When the semester was over, however, we were given a one month vacation to go home. The contrasting life was a bit startling. We had been given strict instructions on what we could and could not do while home; for example, no alcohol of any kind, no dating, pray and meditate every day. Of course I followed these rules, but I began to wonder about whether or not this was the life for me. Two doubts crept into my consciousness:

1. Was I worthy enough to become a priest? 2. Is this really what Jesus and God wanted me to do with my life? The corollary feeling was whether or not my God-given talents were best suited for this calling. The first question was one that I had had from the day I entered the Sem. It was a doubt that would not go away. The other question became more of a preoccupation while I was home. To their credit, neither mom nor dad tried to change my mind about going back after my vacation. They probably understood my stubbornness better than I. There was only one evening when mom asked whether or not I was happy. I was upset with myself when I told her that the Sem was the best thing that ever happened to me and I was glad I was there and was looking forward to going back. In fact I wasn't.

I spent some time that summer thinking about the vows. Poverty was no problem at all. I had no drive to own stuff and money has never been a significant motivator in my life - ever. Celibacy wasn't a real issue then either. At Christmas time we had a week to go home. While we were home, my two high school classmates who were with me in the Sem and I were invited to a New Year's Eve party with a number of our former classmates. At the party two of us saw our high school girl friends with dates. Ugh. We only stayed for a short time and left, feeling sorry for ourselves. I can honestly say I felt jealous and sad but didn't believe that I needed to have a woman in my life. I had convinced myself that a priestly calling was far superior to the temptations of the flesh that a woman would bring into my life. During the summer vacation I did not revisit those feelings because I had worked hard at convincing myself that celibacy was not a barrier for me. Whether it was a sub-conscious factor for me leaving the Sem, I'll never know. The real problem for me revolved around obedience. At first I dismissed this issue because I had always been obedient. I was a rule follower because my father had instilled this attitude throughout my life.

71

At that time I was not rebellious and was not a risk taker -- those behaviors came during my years in college. Much of my free time was spent thinking about who I was and where I was going in life. It slowly dawned on me that I was responsible for whom I am and I had to make those decisions and not rely on others to give me answers to those questions. Guidance was one thing; surrendering my responsibility was quite another. In order to understand the progression of my thinking I have to make a diversion into the role that clock time played in my life then.

When I was very young, I was given a Mickey Mouse watch. It was a prized possession. One day on television I saw a commercial narrated by John Cameron Swayze. He was touting the wonders of a waterproof watch. So, of course, I wanted to make sure mine was just as good. I went into the bathroom, filled the basin and submerged poor Mickey. That was the last time his second hand ever moved. My father called me a numb-skull for being so stupid and I put that former treasure into the top drawer of my bureau. I have never worn a watch since and still don't. I pride myself in being punctual and have learned how to do so without having a watch on my wrist. The world is infected with time-pieces, so if you pay attention, you can always find out what time it is. As I was growing up, I didn't like the boundaries that clocks often seemed to set in the way we have to do things. I have never been a morning person, and as a student I hated having to get up, get ready and go to school at prescribed times. Of course such a system is necessary in our society, but later in life I began to appreciate those cultures that are not managed by clock-time. In the Sem I began to become irritated with the unyielding schedule and routine of life. Being told when to eat, for example, bothered me. The reason it did so was because that was such an important demand for my father. We had to have dinner on the table at 5:00 because he got home between 4:50 and 4:55 each night from work. I had wanted to have flexibility in this schedule but was powerless in having any effect on the routine. Thus, the Sem's rigid schedule was a subtle reminder that I had not completely escaped my home life. That fateful summer vacation provided me with the opportunity to think and pray, work and play at a different pace and with a different schedule. It slowly dawned on me that I was beginning to resent the schedule that told me what to do and when to do it. I wasn't having trouble with obeying the priests; I was having trouble fitting into their prefab structure of my life. I did return to the Sem after this vacation but decided a few weeks later to leave. This decision felt right. I was kidding myself and needed to take back my life and seek my purpose in living in another direction. My conscience would not allow me to stay in a world that I could not accept wholeheartedly. I was also becoming aware that my motives for being there were not pure. I wasn't there for a vocation; rather I was there to escape my family. I considered that self-centered and selfish.

So I went to the Rector to explain my decision. "Father," I said humbly. "I can't stay here anymore."

"Why not? You are a perfect candidate for us. Your behavior is excellent; your grades are very good; what can be the problem?"

Trying to formulate an answer that didn't sound whiny or insulting was difficult. "I'm really not worthy of being a priest."

He obviously had heard this excuse before. "Son, none of us is worthy of being Christ's representative on earth. You should never let that doubt deter you."

I tried again. "Father, I came here to get away from home. I didn't come here with good intentions." Good intentions were a key element in good behavior and I hoped that this reason would work.

He smiled and told me that God had called me here and it didn't matter what I thought my intentions were. God had made His plans for me. I remember thinking about his words and taking my time before giving him my final response. How in the world could this man look at me and say that he knew what God had planned for me? I knew his job was to run the place and make sure all of us became well trained candidates for the priesthood. But his job didn't necessarily include knowing what I needed and who I was. My response was simple.

"Father, I *have* to leave. I just cannot stay here anymore." I stopped trying to convince him of my decision.

"Charlie, you will be back in less than six months. You have a calling; you just need to see it for yourself. I will make arrangements for you to fly home tomorrow. Until then, do not say anything to anyone. I don't want you upsetting anyone." He shook my hand and I left the office with a great weight being lifted from my shoulders. Of course I obeyed his admonition, not even mentioning it to my two high school friends with whom I was very close.

The next morning was a Saturday. After Mass, meditation and breakfast, I remember packing my bag while the dorm area was empty (I was supposed to be at choir practice). As I was being escorted out by the back stair way, I did break away from my escort to stick my head into the choir room and say "Bye guys, good luck." I knew my two best friends were still there. They too left the seminary, but not after many more years for both of them. When I arrived home mom told me that the rector talked to her to explain I was coming home. He told her the same thing he had said to me, "he'll be back in six months. He belongs here."

My time in the seminary was pivotal in my spiritual development. My faith journey, however, started before that interlude in my life and has continued until today.

As I have reflected upon my faith journey I have become aware of an important distinction: inner and outer dimensions. The inner dimension is one's spiritual life, one's faith. The outer dimension is one's religion or group affiliation. After I left the seminary and enrolled at Canisius, one of my minors was Theology. By my junior year, my major was Philosophy. Issues of faith, belief and religious experience became somewhat of a preoccupation for me. I went into an Existentialist phase in my intellectual and emotional development. I devoured works by Kierkegaard,

Nietzsche, Camus, Sartre, Marcel, Ricoeur and made sure I took a seminar on Heidegger. Nietzsche's death of God story intrigued me. Not that I thought God was dead, but I pondered the madman's claim in the market place that mankind had killed God. The God of my childhood, the man with the beard who was paternal (loving and judgmental) and who had planned out all of life seemed to be too juvenile and not capable of being an idea that made any sense to me anymore. Maybe humans did make God in their own image and likeness and maybe that God was insufficient for dealing with the tragedies and problems of life. Having a divine plan put in place to answer the questions of death and injustice began to ring hollow for me. I had heard the so-called proofs for God's existence and read with relish Kierkegaard's admonition that if you have proof, you have no need for faith. Faith is a leap into the absurd, the unknown. That was now how I felt. I no longer felt any rational guarantee that God existed or that He/She cared for me. There really was no divine plan. Just like the child-hood game of Trust Me (wherein you fall backward and hope your friend catches you), I trusted that God loved me, even though I was now clueless about what that might really mean. I also began to accept the legitimacy of doubt. In so doing, I began to question a religion or church that asserted it had the one and only truth.

My inner journey of faith was beginning to come into conflict with the outer dimension: the religion(s) of my life. Faith as an inner dimension of spiritually is very personal. It is how I felt and how my thoughts connected my beliefs with these feelings. Spirituality and faith were how I directly connected with God and with Jesus. They spoke to my inner self. The outer dimension of religion started taking a back seat; it was becoming less important to me. After I returned home from the Sem, I did attend our parish church for Sunday mass, but I began to feel that the rituals were becoming sterile; there was something missing. A few weeks after leaving the Sem, I was enrolled at Canisius and through an unexpected meeting ended up rooming on campus. My folks had secured a bar-tending job for me, and I had purchased an old Dodge to drive to school (the college was about 20 miles from home). I was on campus a couple of weeks before classes started to talk to a priest about my status as a sophomore, which of my Sem courses would be accepted, and what would be expected of me to graduate. After leaving his office, I bumped into a high school acquaintance, Ted, who was a year older than I. When he heard that I was going to attend, he was adamant that I should room on campus and join the ROTC Drill Team. I had already been accepted into a Naval Flight reserve program and wasn't sure about making the switch from Navy to Army. It was blatantly obvious that I was following in my brother, Paul's, footsteps. Ted was not one of my favorite people from high school. We played one year together on the football team (my only contact with him). He was not a starter and I remember in practice he would always try to hurt me by going after my legs. I never liked dirty play or dirty players. So why I listened to him, I do not know. I told him about my parents' plans and he said that he could speak to them and change their minds. So I invited him to dinner and we sat around the dining room table with Ted giving his pitch to my unconvinced parents.

"Charlie will have more time to study and participate in activities. It will make his experience richer" was Ted's first argument.

Dad was not convinced. "Look, it will cost more. He'll have to pay for his room and will lose his bartending job."

Undaunted, Ted replied, "Look, he can sell the car and will save a lot of money on insurance, gas and auto repairs. Trying to drive to class during the winter is always iffy."

Dad looked at me. "What about the Navy?" he asked.

Before I could answer, Ted chimed in, "We have a great ROTC program. When he graduates, he will be a lieutenant and will only have to serve two years of active duty, not five."

Mom intervened, "What do *you* want to do?"

"I like the idea of becoming involved on campus. I don't think I want to make the military a career. So two years is better than five," was all I could think of saying. I was remembering how good it felt to be overly involved in high school my senior year. Just attending classes seemed to be missing the point of college. Although I had applied to the Naval Academy, my drive for flying had diminished in the Sem. I just pursued the Naval Flight Program out of some strange habit-- I really hadn't given it much thought; I just did it.

We continued to talk for a while, but it was clear what I wanted to do. Dad had always preached that when I was 18, I had to make my own decisions and live with the consequences. So I decided to follow Ted's advice and move to campus. This decision changed my life dramatically and introduced me to a world and to people who have redefined who I was and am today. This switch in lifestyle set the stage for me to eventually meet Diane and chart my course for my family life. It also became a crucial step in my religious development in life. I'm not sure if I would have had the time to turn to philosophy as a major or to have been free to think, read and write about who I was and what my faith would mean to me, if I had not lived on campus. The time it would have taken to work and drive to school and the dynamics of still living at home would have been real impediments for my intellectual and emotional development. I have often been struck by the apparent randomness of life when I recall this event. I did not like Ted, yet he had a dramatic impact on my life. What are the chances that I would just run into him, that I would listen to him and that my folks would believe him? I do not believe in coincidences so this randomness is either directed by God or by some strange, unknown power, by the peculiarities of life or by some unconscious force.

Another oddity with Ted occurred years later. I was working in the Alumni office as part of my internship (my first year as an administrator at Canisius). One of my duties was to be a staff liaison a couple of nights a week when alumni came in to make calls for our annual fund-raising drive. I would check the beer and drinks left in the fridge after each such session to determine if we needed to resupply. I began to notice that beer was unaccounted for. We didn't count how many bottles the alumni were drinking; rather we were just trying to keep inventory for making purchases from our budget. The Director and I tried to figure out the discrepancies but to no avail. About a month later I came in one morning and looked in the fridge. Sitting next to the beer were a pair of security guard gloves. How stupid could this guy be? His name was written on the gloves. Poor Ted was fired that day. I knew he was not above breaking rules, but I never guessed that he was the culprit until I saw his gloves. Yes, life does have strange twists.

For the three years I lived on campus, I rarely went to mass. On my breaks and during the summer months, I didn't bother attending mass and had no interest in our former parish. My ideas about religion were changing radically. I felt that the man-made rules of religion and the absolutes being promulgated by the Catholic Church were detrimental to my deeper feelings of faith. The church was getting in the way of my spirituality. I could not accept the church's position that the man-made rules of the religion were somehow God-given. One course experience exemplified this inner conflict for me.

During my junior year, a visiting professor from Germany was on campus to offer an Apologetics course. It was a traditional approach that defended church doctrine through reasoned arguments. I was questioning my outer self and the dimension that housed the church and religion. The professor read his notes in class and preferred not to answer any questions. The problem for me was that I had many, many questions and took the course in order to try and find some answers. He dismissed most of my concerns about the inherent irrationality of faith and the church's apparent presumption that reason could provide the answers its followers required: the rules and laws were guarantees for salvation. For a couple of classes I persisted in raising questions which he often refused to answer or dismissed as trivial matters. After one class, a few classmates came up to me and said that I should just shut up. "Take the damn notes and stop interrupting" was their admonition. Clearly they were taking the course to satisfy a requirement; I was taking it as part of my inner religious struggle. The professor required that all of us parrot his notes back to him on all tests and especially for the paper assignment he gave. His lack of dealing with critical thought and analysis of his topic was rather disturbing for me. My final paper was an anti-apologetics approach that defended the need to place church below faith; reason was to be considered secondary to one's trust in God. I even used a Charlie Brown strip to introduce my thesis. It is the only course for which I received a D. All the other students received As and Bs because they did what he wanted. He hated my paper and said it had no place in Catholic thought. The department chairman would not intervene because college faculty have almost complete authority in their courses. The chairman sympathized with my situation, but he said that I had to suffer the consequences of academic freedom for faculty. (A year later this same chairman had to listen to my complaints about the faculty member who kicked me out of class over our disagreement about racism.)

The conflict between my inner self and the meaning of faith in my life and the outer self being expressed in a religion continued to be waged in my mind. I began to defer to my inner self. Faith became more important than a religion or church, and I was having a great deal of difficulty in synchronizing these two dimensions. I had no trouble with the idea that churches and religions needed rules. Churches are social organizations and society requires rules, norms and mores. Without them our world would be chaotic. However, I was continuing to believe that the rules of the church were somehow disconnected with my faith. Synchronizing these two dimensions in life is important for leading a balanced and harmonious life. When the two dimensions are in conflict a person may experience serious stress or discomfort. Regardless of what my dad's inner faith was, after his lung surgery when no priest came to minister to him, his outer dimension became conflicted. He rejected that dimension because of his resentment. I have no idea whether or not he was able to resolve this conflict within his mind or not. My journey of faith after the Sem has been this struggle between my inner faith and the outer world of church and religion. My journey, of course, began with the strange combination I had as a child of living in both a Catholic and a Southern Baptist world. Were they the same world with different views or were they really two separate worlds? I still like that question for looking at life!

My childhood became the foundation for my values and beliefs. After my friend and soul-mate, Donny/Murgy, left when I was five, my behavior changed radically and I became a nauseatingly good kid: overly obedient, rule follower, and quick to please adults (with whom I could easily converse). Since my father was Roman Catholic, my mom agreed that while I was up north I would be raised according to the church's rules. For 13 of the summers before turning 18, I spent 1 to 8 weeks with my relatives in Kentucky. My Uncle James and Aunt Lona never had children and I became "adopted" as their son. Diane and I honeymooned in Western Kentucky and visited my relatives, spending a lot of time with James and Lona. Over the next 40 years I visited about 25-30 times and helped care for them, even though the trip was about 800 miles each way. Uncle James and Aunt Lona were devout Southern Baptists and I would attend their church at least once a week while I was there. (My summer in Sumter, South Carolina when I was 13 for 7+ weeks was with "unchurched" Presbyterians, whatever that might mean. I have no recollection of attending any service.) My Aunt Myrtle and Uncle Oral were not church goers but followed a Baptist ethic. While growing up, I heard a lot of sad and ugly denunciations of each branch of Christianity. Both sides of my family assured me of salvation if I followed their rules and guaranteed my damnation if I deviated into the sinfulness of any other form of religion, including the other church.

Before going any further, let me state that I am currently a confer-ence deacon and visioning minister in the Evangelical Lutheran Church in America (ELCA). A conference deacon is authorized to lead worship (both communion and non-communion services), preach and assist liturgically at funerals. So far I have led worship in 13 different congregations. It always amazes me how different each form of worship is among these par-ishes, even though they are all ELCA congregations. A visioning minister is a position I've created. The ELCA has adopted a model of providing transition teams for congregations after a pastor leaves. Our team consisted of a Pastor, a Programming Minister, a Pastoral Care Minister and me. All are part-time and some are volunteers. This model helps a parish as it tran-sitions from a full-time pastor into a joint parish model where two or more congregations share resources. As Visioning Minister I have been respon-sible for planning and leading our congregation into looking at alternative ways to provide ministry to our members and to the community. I helped our congregation develop a relationship with another congregation to share a pastor and provide him with a joint call. I have served on the Synod's Candidacy Committee, on the Conflict and Healing Committee, and am a member of the conference's transition table. There are a number of other roles I have had or now have: e.g., adult education teacher, co-convener of table talk, teen adviser and teacher, pre-marriage counselor (with Diane) and grief support minister. So I was raised Roman Catholic and Southern Baptist; married in a Methodist church; and now belong and serve in a Lutheran congregation. Reaching my current place in a religion was a rather circuitous route.

By the time I graduated from Canisius, I was no longer attending church and didn't have any problem putting what I considered artificial practices behind me. While we were in New Orleans, Diane and I did try connecting with worship services. We attended a Southern Methodist church, which proved to be something with which we were very uncomfort-able. We went to my brother's parish for Mass one Sunday. Diane became very upset during the Offertory. She couldn't understand why people were collecting money while the priest was praying at the altar. As a Methodist she wasn't familiar with a liturgically oriented worship service and wasn't comfortable with the rubrics (the methods and rules for worship) of the mass. We never returned. One of my graduate school classmates was a Jesuit priest attending Tulane for a Masters Degree. A few times during that first year we met with him and a few other classmates for an informal Eucharistic service in people's apartments. After he left we drifted away from any church attendance or even informal gathering. I began reading the bible on Sunday. Diane and I also have read the bible cover to cover out loud to each other. After graduate school and three months active duty at Fort Gordon (Augusta, Georgia) for MP training, I settled back home in Kenmore, New York. (Diane had moved into our apartment in Kenmore and didn't come with me to Georgia.) I was looking for a teaching position and Diane was caring for Tara. Diane became pregnant with our second child, Kristen, and I acquired an internship at Canisius. That was the beginning of my 35 years at the college. We decided to move to a house in 1973, and we are still living there. A year later our daughter, Katie, was born. I still wanted no part of a church, but we did attend Diane's former Methodist church and tried the Baptist church, which sponsored the preschool program our daughters were attending. Neither one helped me to synchronize my inner (faith) and outer (church/religion). One Sunday after going to church, Diane told me that Tara (age four) had asked why I didn't go to church with them. We had a long discussion about my feelings and our daughters' needs. We agreed that a church was an important social dimension in our children's upbringing. Churches provide a means to learn about moral decision-making and are an environment for learning about the bible and fellowship. It is a place to practice one's religion, not necessarily a venue for attending to one's faith. While Diane was in the hospital recovering from Katie's birth (in those days an overnight stay was routine), she connected with her roommate. They seemed to be on the same wave-length immediately. Michelle invited Diane to attend their parish. Diane suggested that we try going, even though she didn't think I could connect to a Lutheran church.

The first Sunday we attended something awoke in me. I had missed the liturgy (which actually means the work of the people). It was a way to worship and pray that was buried deep in my conscious self. The Lutheran liturgy is not that different from the Catholic mass. I had been studying Confucius at the time and his writing had prepared me for this experience. One of Confucius' views is that in order to achieve harmony and balance in life, humans need music and ritual. Music is a way to connect and feel unified. Ritual was necessary to identify roles and provide a social order that could guarantee peace. I had thought about the importance of ritual while simultaneously growing out of my Existentialist phase of development. Being and acting authentic was still important but that did not require dismissing all social structures, norms and behaviors. When I went to that first service I realized that I had really missed the Eucharist and that it was important to provide a social network for my daughters and for me. A new pastor came to the parish shortly after we arrived. He and his wife became, and still are, good friends of ours. He asked me to work with the teens who had completed the Confirmation program (usually 9th grade) and to be the moderator for the teen social programming. I agreed and did so for a long time. My classes were informal discussions and were used to subconsciously instill a comfort level with the church while allowing them to vent. I designed a service that the youth would run. The sermon was replaced with a chancel skit and all the readings and prayers were led by the youth. I wrote the skits and did take offs on movies or television programs, for example Mash, Star Trek, Wizard of Oz, a circus, and many more. After a year or so the pastor came over and told me that he was getting some pressure from the church council about me not being a member of the church while being responsible for the youth. He asked if I would consider joining. "As long as the church doesn't destroy my faith" was my cautious response.

Finally I found an opportunity to try and bring some balance and synchronization to my inner and outer selves. Over the past 40 years, this balance has remained because of important lessons I learned. First, there is a time to put away self-centered needs for the well-being of one's family. My girls needed me to grow up and accept the fact that religious participation was not just about me and my inner struggles. Second, as one matures, the answers of youth are never sufficient. I am saddened for those who never grow up in their faith or in their religion. When we are children we are given stories and lessons on morals that are appropriate for our age. The meanings to these stories need to mature and the norms we use for making moral judgments become more complex and difficult. If we try to live according to childish dictates, we will inevitably become disenchanted or live in a superficial bubble. We'll blame the church for answers that don't work or are unfulfilling; yet the problem is with us and our childish ways. Third, all churches are human oriented. The members may believe that God or Christ or any other religious figure that is their leader is the center of everything they do. The reality is that humans set the rules, make the laws, establish the services and interpret the bible (or other sacred texts). This human element should not be confused with being divine. Lastly, since any church is composed of humans, it will include all the short-comings and conflicts that people bring into any social setting. Churches will have disagreements, petty disputes, turf issues and sometimes even strife. People will come in and out of congregations and churches. I have come to believe that the disconnect from one's inner spiritual needs and the actions of the outer dimensions in a church can lead to crises in faith, or in people going from church to church, or for people abandoning any church altogether.

I have learned to accept the necessity of humanness in any church and to stop blaming God for its existence. I have become much more tolerant and open to the human short-comings in congregations. As I have served on the Conflict and Healing team for decades, I have seen so much unnecessary strife, heart-ache and pain. I often ask the rhetorical question, "Why do people hurt others?" That element of the human condition will forever haunt me. My personal journey of faith has now led me to more general concerns about faith and religion. Faith may be a personal matter but religion and churches are an outer manifestation of faith. Bringing the inner and outer dimensions of faith and religion into harmony is not always possible. The personal and social conflicts regarding faith and religion have and will continue to be part of the human condition.

CHAPTER 4
RELIGIOUS MISUNDERSTANDING
AND DISCORD

Faith is to believe what you do not see;
the reward of the faith is to see what you believe.

St. Augustine

I t had been sunny all day; the evening remained bright and the air was very warm. I was in a men's room stall of a restaurant in downtown Rochester, Minnesota, changing into my apostle's costume and preparing to enter onto a stage in an outdoor square. In a few minutes I would be introduced as Judas, Jesus' apostle from Kerioth. It was not my first performance of this biblical character, but it was the first time it was not associated with a church. My daughter, Kris, was working with the University of Minnesota at Rochester. One of her duties that year (2013) was to produce a weekly educational program available to the community. During the summer it was held (weather permitting) in an open air square that was surrounded by buildings that housed businesses, a shopping mall, and the University's campus. Kris had invited me to perform for an assemblage of people from the community who had been to other programs. The purpose for providing offerings in the summer in the square was to broaden the college's contact with the community. Since it was an outdoor venue, Kris told me to expect people to come and go and warned me that the chairs would be filled with people from all walks of life and with a wide range of educational backgrounds and interests. This crowd would be very different from any church group for whom I had pretended to be Judas.

I loved the challenge.

As I emerged from the bathroom stall and walked through the eating area, I decided not to make eye contact with the patrons who were not expecting an apostle to emerge from the men's room. An older man with sandals, a full length gown and covering cloak, and a head covering with cloth ties, was not a typical site for that setting. I walked outside toward the stairs to the platform that had been set up for the presentation, before realizing that the pre-program activities were going to run longer than I had hoped. So pretending I knew what to do, I mounted the steps and took a seat looking out at the sight before me. In the distance was a table with men providing information for their organization (I've already forgotten what it was). People were hustling from business to business; many may have been headed home for the day. There were also shoppers, some with bags filled with purchases, others going empty handed. Skate boarders were coming in from the street behind, expertly flipping their boards into their hands when they entered the square. I loved their respect for social norms. Behind me on the street I could hear the traffic and the cars stopping to unload family or friends, then speed off. There were buses and taxis, trucks and limos. The stage had a backdrop, so much of this commotion would not be in full view of the people sitting in front of me. For this performance I didn't even use index cards with notes to help me with the order of what I was going to say. I decided to just be Judas in the manner I had chosen to interpret the person and his actions.

While I sat there, I began to recall what an eventful year 2013 was becoming. It had started with my back surgery in January (the surgeon fused new bone to provide separation for my collapsed disc in L5). I started PT as quickly as I could but there were complications and other conditions associated with the surgery. (My sciatic nerve became inflamed and has remained a problem ever since. I needed hernia surgery which occurred the following year and bursitis in the hips complicated matters.) In late March Diane and I went to Disney World with Tara and her family. I was on a lot of medication and was very restricted on what rides I could enjoy. Watching three of our grandchildren become immersed in the fantasy and exhilaration of the different parks was compensation enough. By May Diane and I ventured to Rochester, Minnesota, to celebrate the birthdays of Kris' twins (Tara and Kris both have twins and a singleton!). At the end of June we spent time in Mayville with Tara, Katie and their families for a few days of family bonding. By July Diane and I were headed to Alaska for a seven-day cruise and three-day land adventure. Diane's sister, Donna and her husband Laurie, along with a friend of mine from Canisius and his wife, joined us. By August Kris met us in Mayville for a few days to have some family time. It was strange, but I flew to Rochester before she drove home and was alone in her place for a day before she returned. Two days later, I was performing for her program in front of at least 100 people.

Judas is a wonderful character for biblical interpretation and education. I started my monologue by providing a historical perspective of Judaism with an emphasis upon the Babylonian Captivity. I do so to provide a context for understanding what it meant to be Jewish for Jesus, His followers, and the other Jews of His day. I talked about the Assyrians scattering the Israelites (the northern part of Israel in the 8th century BCE). The Babylonians destroyed the temple and took Jewish leaders and many others into captivity in the 6th century BCE. This explanation leads to the development that Israel became separated into Galilee in the north, Samaria roughly through the middle, and Judea in the south. Judas goes on to explain who the Galileans and Judeans were in his day. This was an important distinction in understanding what happened because Jesus, Mary Magdalene and the other 11 apostles were Galileans; Judas was the only Judean. I try to set the stage for the humanity of the characters and the existence of prejudices and stereotyping that existed at that time. This entire historical account is cast in the eyes of Judas who reveals his preferences and prejudices.

"You see, Galilee was a place for revolutions" began my Judas as I started his version of history and what it all meant for his peers and him.

"There was too much Greek and Roman influence throughout the area. The Roman cities of Tiberius and Sepphoris were cesspools of depravity and corrupted everyone who had dealings in them. Jesus told me he had worked in Sepphoris with his father when he was young. He was appalled at the abuse of power and the subjugation of the poor. Maybe those days helped him to hone his message for the downtrodden and poor. For me there are a number of problems with Galilee:

1. The Galileans are racially impure because of the Assyrian invasion and the mingling of peoples.
2. Samaria and its heathen approach to Judaism isolates Galilee from the proper exercise of Judaism which is found in Judea.
3. Galilee had a separate governance system which always leads to problems.
4. The land is rich and the Sea of Galilee provides amble opportunities for wealth in the fishing trade. Such enterprises can always lead to corruption; especially when there are real gaps between the rich and the poor.
5. Galileans are backward and unsophisticated.
6. Their dialect is mockable.
7. Last, but not least, their practices are far too lax for living a good Jewish life. Their observance of ritual is improper; they are not consistent in their pilgrimages to the temple; they do not prepare food properly; they do not have adequate theological leaders; and they teach the Torah to their children incorrectly."

I use this part of his monologue to set the stage for the prejudices I assume to be a barrier between Judas and the other apostles. This barrier, which was reciprocally constructed, existed between him and the others from the very beginning of his call to follow Jesus. Why did he, then, follow this Galilean?

"He was charismatic and a great teacher and speaker. It was magical to be around him. My only real problem with him was that his head was in the clouds too often. He was too much of a dreamer and didn't seem to really grasp the true meaning of being the Messiah. From the very beginning, I believed he was the One, the Savior, and my job was to mold him into the true Jewish understanding of being our Messiah. Even though he was a wonderful Rabbi, I felt he was a bit too lenient with our laws and the dictates of the Torah."

I move on to John the Baptist and his influence on Jesus and many of the Galilean apostles who were following him before he sent them to follow Jesus. Judas rambles on about what it was like traveling around Galilee and having a pilgrimage to Jerusalem. His attitude is basically supportive of Jesus but wondering why he wasn't becoming the Messiah the Jews expected. I don't know if Judas was a Zealot, but I believe he shared their vision of the Messiah: a leader who would follow in the tradition of David and the other kings; a leader who would take up the sword in defense of Israel; a leader who would vanquish the Roman invaders and cleanse the Jewish leadership. I also have Judas give a brief rundown of his assessment of the other apostles; the reviews were not very positive. He probably trusted Thomas the most because both were very pragmatic and totally devoted to Jesus, not necessarily to the others. If you read the New Testament carefully with the perspective that Thomas and Judas are absolutely devoted to Jesus, you will see that time and again, they don't question Jesus, they just do what He says. Neither is really very trustful of the others, however. In fact, my characterization of Thomas dismisses the claim that he is The Doubter among the apostles. Thomas is not any more a doubter than any of the other apostles -- all of whom doubted Mary Magdalene on Easter morning. My Thomas character talks about the interpersonal relationships among the Apostles and reveals the conflicts and shortcomings that existed in the group. My assumption is that almost everyone has some doubt in his or her lifetime about God and his or her religion. We call Thomas the doubter, but in fact he is no different from any of the other apostles and is no different from any one of us. When Thomas returns and hears the apostles talking about seeing Jesus, I do not believe he doubted Jesus; rather he doubted the veracity of the other apostles. Jesus was trustworthy; they were not. In this sense Thomas and Judas had something in common: devoted to Jesus and discontent with their fellow apostles. Although Judas was a devoted follower, his attitude changed with what we call Palm Sunday. Here's how I played his inner conflict.

"Jesus was difficult to understand. His behavior was just strange. Here we are marching triumphantly into Jerusalem during Passover. The crowds are cheering; he is being exalted as the Messiah; he has a ready army at his disposal. And what does he do. Nothing! He does not call them to arms, which is exactly what he should have done. I liked his attack at the Temple. It was good to see that he had a backbone and justifiable anger. Those character traits are necessary for winning any conflict. Then he humiliates me by taking away my role of making arrangements for food and lodging. This was especially galling because we're talking about a Passover meal. What's even worse is that he turns the arrangements over to that hothead Peter and that simpering young kid, John."

Judas is just getting started at this point. Judas is not a betrayer. In my dramatic presentation, Judas was in charge of the finances for the group. As such it makes little sense to think that he betrayed Jesus for money. Why would he surrender the source of income if money really motivated him? Embezzling funds would have been easy for him. John even seems to indicate that Judas was doing just that. My characterization brushes that motivation aside. Disillusionment, more than greed, motivates Judas. He became disillusioned when Jesus didn't seem to want to lead a rebellion against the Romans. He decided to test Jesus' claim of being the Son of God and was shocked that Jesus was crucified. I try to humanize Judas and show him in a different light. I try to show Judas' motivation as being earnest and sincere. He truly believed that by testing Jesus the revolution would occur. He believed that Jesus would take up the sword like a Messiah. My character of Judas is shocked when Jesus seems to be defeated and cast into the trash heap of Jewish history.

"Yes I was hurt when Jesus had others make arrangements for the meal. I left because I believe Jesus and I had come to an understanding. I had to make something happen and Jesus wanted me to do so. When I led the Jewish leaders to him, I was shocked at a couple of things that happened. First he scolded Peter when Peter drew a sword and attacked a guard. Why was Jesus so opposed to the sword? That is how Israel became a nation. Jesus was a descendant of the most blood-thirsty of all our leaders, David. Then he meekly follows the Jewish leaders. In a whirlwind I see him judged, condemned, flogged and then see him staggering under that beam on the way to his crucifixion. It made no sense - no sense. I know he wanted me to release him to the supernatural world, but that would only be for his own sake. What about all of us who depended upon Him to be our Messiah?"

This comment is based on the Gnostic Gospel of Judas which asserts that both Jesus and Judas were Gnostics, that is, they believed in the supremacy of the supernatural realm and a person's call to get rid of the physical self that holds one's true self down. As Judas begins to finish his story I portray his character as changing his demeanor completely. Before he was self-assured, "right" and educating the crowd to his truth. In the end his basic love for the person, Jesus, comes through in utter remorse.

"Now that Jesus is dead I don't know if I misunderstood him all these years. Maybe he wasn't who I thought he was. In our private conversations I thought I understood what he wanted of me. But his death? Was I responsible for this? Did he use me? I don't know if I have any idea what has just happened. Was I merely a pawn in a great cosmic game? I know the apostles are clueless and will hate me forever. Maybe I will hate me forever?

I thought I was doing the right thing. How do we ever know if we are right when someone else is hurt? You know, I miss him. I loved him. I didn't think it would end this way. Will the apostles come to kill me? What will I do with my life now? Do I have a life? Can I live with a guilt I didn't ask for? What do I do?"

Judas bows his head and walks away.

I leave the ending open to the three causes for Judas' death that come to us from the bible and from the Gospel of Judas. The bible gives us two versions of Judas' death. First, he returns the money to the Jewish leaders; goes out and hangs himself; and the money is used to buy "Potter's Field". The second version is found in Acts when Peter explains that Judas purchased the field with the money he received and collapsed with his insides spewing out of him and onto the field. The Gospel of Judas asserts that a few of the apostles came and hung him. It is a mystery that will never be solved forensically, a story whose ending becomes entrenched in one's interpretation of ancient writings.

No one names a son Judas anymore because of the associations we have with the stereotype of Judas being an evil betrayer. I try to give an alternative view of who he may have been and what lessons we may learn from his behavior. In fact, aren't we all a little bit like Judas? We have our own expectations for other people and we want them to live up to these beliefs and expectations. At the end of the performance I allow for questions, which may be asked of either Judas or me. As I started answering questions and gratefully receiving some words of appreciation and support, I noticed a woman who had come upon the performance while she was walking out of a store. She stopped and began to pace along the outside of the seated area. As the questions went on I noticed that she was screwing up the nerve to ask something.

"Yes?" I indicated toward her.

"How could you be so sacrilegious? You are perverting the bible and you know it" was her impassioned condemnation. Ah. She was someone who takes the bible literally and allows for no interpretation, contextualizing or humanizing of biblical characters. My response was gentle:

"Ma'am, I'm an educator. My role today was to share one way of interpreting historical events, biblical stories, and the possible motivations of a human being."

"How dare you call the bible a book of stories? It is the absolute truth," she angrily retorted. I knew then that nothing I could say would matter. A couple of people in the audience perceived the same thing. One man came to my defense and when she started going after him, another woman asked a question to change the subject. Afterward I received warm comments that were supportive and appreciative.

That performance reinforced a strong belief I have: people can interpret their religion in very diverse ways while being quite unwilling to accept any other view than their own. I will not address the great issues of religious prejudice, conflicts and hatred because the topic is too vast, and I do not believe I have any authority to do so. Instead, I will continue to deal just with my own personal journey and how that journey applies to faith and religion in the world. I will focus mainly upon the Abrahamic faiths (Judaism, Christianity and Islam) in my life. The other religions and philosophies of the world have had an impact on me, but, again, the topic is too broad to delve into too deeply. Suffice it to say, I have been to China and studied and taught Taoism and Confucian Morality. Since the 1980s I have been doing Tai Chi daily. Diane takes yoga classes and Kris is an expert teacher in yoga. My admiration for the goodness in the Asian religions and philosophies is considerable. They have helped shape my world view and have opened me up to a respect for the faith, beliefs, values, and religious experiences of Hinduism, Buddhism, Confucian thought and Taoism. However, it is my experiences with the Abrahamic faiths that have primarily shaped my continually evolving views on religious thought.

All religions have prophets or saviors or leaders that open their followers to what God or a Supreme Being is offering. My faith says that grace is given freely to us by the Holy Spirit and my life should be guided by how I respond to this gift. Religions seem to take the message they have received and wrap this gift into a variety of packages: 1. a sacred text, 2. a theological view or system of beliefs, 3. doctrines, 4. rules and laws, and 5. churches/temples/synagogues/mosques.

1. SACRED TEXT

Although I have read the Upanishads, the Qur'an, the Book of Mormon, Confucian Analects, the *Tao Te Ching*, the *Bhagavad Gita*, and commentaries, I am going to restrict my comments to the Bible because that is a book I have studied throughout my adult life. I have taught bible studies and preached for decades at two congregations. My preaching has now expanded to serving as a substitute pastor throughout Western New York. Although I am not a biblical scholar and have far more ignorance about its lessons than I have knowledge to impart, I am more comfortable dealing with the sacred text with which I am most familiar.

Until I reached the seminary, I had little connection with the Bible in my Catholic settings; instead the focus was upon the catechism or religious instruction focusing upon what was right and wrong behavior. The nuns or priests told us what to believe and gave us instructions on how to live. We were instructed in the rules and correct practices for Catholics. If we believed and did what they said, then heaven awaited us for all eternity. From first through fourth grade, I attended public school and was released every Tuesday afternoon to receive catechism training at our parish (Prince of Peace). (For a country to claim to foster the separation of church and state, isn't it incongruous to release students from public school during the school day for religious instruction? In fact, isn't it incongruous that a religious wedding ceremony would be recognized by the state? The European model of requiring a civil ceremony even if the couple had a religious ceremony seems to make more sense if separation of church and state is an important value.) In Western New York there is a very large Roman Catholic population, and a great deal of leeway and deference is given to Roman Catholics, even though they often do not recognize this. Of course, similar favoritisms occur for Baptists in the South, Lutherans in the Midwest and Mormons in Utah, for example. I started to attend Catholic School in fifth grade and the nuns taught us right from wrong. I don't remember reading the bible in school, although we did hear bible stories. The Passion was a familiar section of the bible for all of us. Of course we heard the bible readings each Sunday in church, and I paid attention to them probably more than the average kid. When I was an altar boy, I felt a particular responsibility to pay attention. In high school in my senior year I became a reader at our weekly Mass. That's the only time I really remember spending time with the bible by myself when connected to my Catholic upbringing. I took my responsibility seriously and would practice the readings (always checking what went before and after in case that made a difference in how I was supposed to emphasize certain words or passages).

My first real experiences with the bible were in Kentucky: at Mount Mariah Primitive Baptist church and on Uncle Oral's knee. Uncle James and Aunt Lona would take me to church on Sunday mornings, and I would attend bible study with the other kids, then move on to worship afterward to hear the preacher explain what the bible means. My relatives had their bibles with them, and there were worn copies in the rack on the back of the pew in front of us. I heard the stories and endured the lengthy classes and the long-winded preacher focusing on damnation and hell fire (at least, that's what stuck in my mind). When I spent the night with Aunt Myrtle and Uncle Oral, we had a ritual in the evening. After collecting eggs, my uncle and I would retire to the front porch. Their farm was fronted by a highway, and they had a roadside stand and a small gasoline pump that operated until my uncle died. Uncle Oral would play his banjo or fiddle for a while then take out his bible. I would sit on his knee when I was small; later I would sit on the porch near his feet. He would read a passage; sometimes we'd talk about it. I have no recollection of any specific reading or any particular discussion, just the feeling that this was good. (I do wonder whether my favorite passages today may actually have been my uncle's favorites. I'll never really know – just another of life's mysteries hidden in the fog of memory.) Throughout my youth, the bible stories were literally true: I had no doubt that Adam and Eve heard a serpent tempt them; certainly Noah had an arduous ordeal during the deluge; and Charlton Heston in the film *The Ten Commandments* provided me with a visual image of exactly how the Jews escaped the Egyptians.

The seminary was my first awakening to the Truth that the bible is more than stories; in fact, the stories are merely the vehicle for the message. The Jesuits and other college professors in my religious studies and philosophy courses in college radically shifted my view and appreciation of the beauty of the bible. The stories are stories, but the deeper meaning is found in the messages of the beautiful prose and poetry of all the different writers. The Gospels were written in the context of oral history. The earliest followers of Jesus had no writings (other than the Jewish texts available to their area). What they did have were the shared stories that were passed on from mouth to mouth by the faithful. Throughout my teaching (collegiate, high school, and church classes for teens or for adults) the sacred texts have provided important material. After retirement I have been teaching biblical studies courses at my own church. Instead of trying to wash away the inconsistencies and contradictions that riddle the bible, my intent is to use the stories as the way to address the important lessons and messages that the authors intended (or maybe even ones they didn't realize that they were providing). I'm not sure that I can say with any assurance that I really understand their intention(s); however, I feel quite comfortable giving varying interpretations into what the passages may mean.

I have been preaching since the 1980s and over the years have enhanced my acting passion by creating biblical characters. Sometimes I've portrayed the characters during sermons while in other venues I have provided a longer dramatic presentation as noted above with Judas. The list also includes: Thomas, James (Jesus' brother), Paul, Abraham, Gamaliel (Paul's teacher), Pontius Pilate, John the Apostle, Aaron (a shepherd who was a child at the Christmas event and who encounters the blind man at the pool at Shiloam), a variety of Magi characters all with different story lines, and Joseph. I've also used the name of Aaron for a farmer living along the way from Nazareth to Jerusalem and as a childhood friend of Jesus while he lived in Nazareth. My approach is to show the characters in a real and human light. My intent in portraying these characters as I do is to try and place myself and the listeners into a real world of people struggling with life, belief, and doubts. These are people who are seeking love, assurance and hope. Writing and performing these characters have led me to conclude that a literal interpretation of the bible is very problematic.

Prejudice and misunderstanding arise in a few ways from taking the bible too literally. First there is a dangerous anti-intellectual and anti-science bias that emerges from literally accepting the creation story, for example. Science gives us the FACTS of evolution. Yes, there are theories of evolution. It is true that theories are not laws, which means they may be disputed or improved with more experimentation and evidence. In my studies, for example, I have read, discussed and written about such evolutionary theories as Darwin's, Lamarck's, Spencer's, Bergson's, and de Chardin's. Each theory has its advantages and its shortcomings; such is the fate of any theory. The problem I have with Intelligent Design or Creationists is that they are ignoring evolutionary facts and making the false claim that a theory is only a theory and so it can be ignored or disregarded. The bible is not science and its contents should not be taken in any scientific context. However, I do not believe that science is the only means for understanding the world, life and especially the meaning for being alive. Science is inadequate for understanding life's meaning and purpose. An example that I have often used relates to the rose. A botanist can study the rose and give us an explanation of how it works. The poet can help us marvel at its beauty. The nursery can give us beautiful displays and help us to stop and smell them. The marketing agent can have a field day for profits on Valentine's Day. Our youngest daughter used the rose as a symbol for strength and hope during her battle with leukemia. Each and every view is legitimate and valuable. They provide a perspective that gives us different meanings or views of a rose. Why should we draw the conclusion that there is one and only one way to understand the rose or the world for that matter? I have trouble with the bias of science, which rejects the humanistic or religious views of life, and I cannot accept the prejudices of a literal interpretation of the bible, which rejects science and intellectual analyses of historical events and characters.

Let me give an analysis of the creation story as an example. In Chapter One of Genesis, animals are created before human beings. In Chapter Two, Adam is created, then animals, then Eve. So which story is true: animals first or humans? It really doesn't matter because the account is not written scientifically or historically anyhow. Science clearly shows that creation could not have occurred over six 24-hour periods. A literal interpretation of the days of the bible takes away from the majesty and wonder of God's creation. Science provides us with a magnificent picture of this majesty. Why would we try to deny the richness and complexity that science gives? Why, on the other hand, would we ever believe that science can tell us about the meaning and purpose to be found in this creation? They are not questions that can be reduced to scientific inquiry. My meaning in life cannot be reduced to a mathematical formula. When we look up into the night sky we see the light of the stars that has been traveling for millions or billions of years and the geological formations of our earth reveal millions of years of history. Archeology has uncovered the richness of human evolution with discoveries of language, art, metal work, etc. for at least 300,000 years in the ancestors of homo sapiens. Denying a particular theory does not refute those facts. I wish science and religion would put away their prejudices and respect the different roles they can play in our lives.

2. THEOLOGY/PHILOSOPHY OF RELIGION.

When I was being raised in Niagara Falls, priests and nuns informed me that I belonged to the "one true faith": Roman Catholicism. If I followed the rules, confessed my sins and remained true to the Church, I was guaranteed eternal happiness. Of course I believed this, to a certain degree. My problem was I loved my Baptist relatives and they often seemed far more loving and Christian than some of the Catholics I encountered in the bars, stores, and schools in the North. Even more confusing was the message I received down South, which told me I needed to be "born again" to guarantee my salvation. I needed to examine my heart and allow grace to open me to the truth of the Baptist message: a literal use of the bible that provided a true guide for living. When I was older, they assured me the spirit would move me and the Lord would come into my life. I would be saved and I would continue to follow the truth the Lord professed. I was still too young to do so. How could both parts of my life be true when they clearly and unequivocally denounced the other side? The confusion reached its height when I was in the Seminary. I was being trained to profess Truth, which required turning my back on my relatives. I loved my mom and had a strained and difficult relationship with my father. I just could not conceive of any interpretation that put my father on a true path of salvation and my mother on a road to damnation. I had minimal contact with my Catholic relatives in Chicago. My grandparents were models of correct Catholic living, while my uncle, aunt and cousins were poor representatives of humble and faith-based living. My Kentucky relatives embodied love and care. They were living their biblical admonitions. What was I supposed to do? Whose way of life was a better model for me? In high school I had latched onto the teaching that non-Catholics could be saved through "Baptism by desire." As I understood the teaching then, it meant that good people of other faiths would be spared Hell because they really accepted Catholicism in their hearts even if they didn't realize it. I now consider that idea to be rather paternalistic and self-serving.

Beginning in college and throughout my life, my view of other religions became based in respect and sometimes even outright admiration. God could not condemn the faithful of all the world religions. Does God really command that one and only one way is the path to His or Her side? I have come to believe that for individuals, his or her belief in a particular religion as the true faith for him or her makes sense. For these people, they have found harmony in their inner self. Their faith and the outward manifestation of this faith in their religion work in synchronicity. The problem is in taking the next intellectual (or prejudicial) leap and making his or her religion required for all of humanity. Achieving a synchrony in one's life between faith and religion is great; but my synchronization should never be imposed on anyone else. No one has the right to claim that what makes sense for me must make sense for you.

I believe that Jesus is my Messiah and that the Holy Spirit gives me grace to lead a good and loving life. In no way does this belief need to be universalized; I do not need to make it a requirement for everyone or even anyone else. It would be far too conceited of me to think that my faith can be fulfilling for all human beings. It is for me; it does not need to be for others. I am more than willing to share what this faith means to me, but this sharing is an educational reflection for others to hear and do as they may. I hope my educational approach in sermons becomes helpful to those who are listening. I would like people to agree with me and I appreciate it when they thank me, but I have no desire to condemn anyone who objects, ignores, or dismisses what I say. If I am ever inspirational to someone else, that is a true gift and blessing; it is not something I would ever expect.

Why we believe what we do and how we live our faith are very complex issues. We are influenced on so many different levels that it is impossible for us to know all of the forces at work in our view of the world or in our set of beliefs. Besides, aren't we born into a context that defines and outlines many of the contours for our beliefs? Certainly our personality has significant influence upon how we integrate all of the social forces we encounter in life. I do not accept anyone's claim that he or she has the exclusive truth about God or the meaning of life. My conscience is my compass, and I should proclaim it as true in my life. To impose it on others just seems to be wrong. To condemn others because they do not agree with me is a terrible form of misunderstanding and discrimination. Implicit in much of what I have been saying above and what will become more explicitly expressed throughout the rest of the book is my rejection of extremes. The extremes of religion are and have been a significant cause for the hatred among peoples and a primary cause for justifying war. My concluding chapters focus upon respect and love. They should be the basis for people relating to one another. They require that other religious points of view or beliefs should not be condemned, trivialized or dismissed. Respect and tolerance should replace religiously based bigotry and discrimination. Love is universally accepted as good.

3. DOCTRINE.

Doctrine is the set of beliefs that a church develops over time. For the Abrahamic faiths, the founders were not involved in developing doctrine. Abraham, Mohammad, and Jesus were the teachers, founders, and the inspiration for their followers. Mohammad is unique among the three because he "wrote" the Qur'an. (Those outside Islam will attribute the Qur'an to him, although many inside the religion may attribute the writing to the Angel Gabriel who moved Mohammad's hand. Or ultimately Allah is the true author.) Regardless of this difference among the three founders, it was others who followed these men who became the architects for the doctrines that define the core of beliefs and the laws and regulations that govern the faithful. Doctrines can become the basis for misunderstandings and prejudices that lead to hatred and be the cause for war. Oftentimes the political structure for a religion becomes codified in its doctrine. The Reformation movement in Christianity led to wars and a great deal of bloodshed as the power and structure of the Roman Papacy was attacked.

The Reformation was a series of movements trying to address abuses that had arisen in the political and, for many, in the spiritual life of the Roman Catholic Church. The Church established the Inquisition as one means for reigning in the unrest. German princes used the Reformation as a justification for wrestling political gain from the Papacy and abusive bishops. The issues are so very complex and, again, I do not intend to go into an explanation for the causes and positions that were taken. My point is that in the name of religion, doctrines are established that become used by church leaders and dissidents or reformers to maintain the status quo or instigate change. Even though rational people recognize the inevitability of change, justifying the change and/or trying to implement it lead to challenges and opposition. The deep-seated divides that are created continually seem to burst into conflict over time. For example, even centuries after the Reformation we saw the violence between Catholics and Protestants in Northern Ireland in the 20th century. For Islam the warfare between the Sunni and Shia has played out in so many different ways and in a wide variety of times and places over the centuries. The current sectarian conflicts and wars throughout the Middle East are a testament to the never-ending use of doctrine to justify political ambitions.

The forces that have led to hatred, war and injustice in the name of religion have a history that is thousands of years in the making. In addition, the current level of killing in the name of one's religion may be unprecedented. The hatred is not just inter-religious, it is also intra-religious: meaning that the killing and warfare is occurring between religious groups as well as within religious groups. The wars between Christianity and Islam have been waged since the Crusades and the hatred between Protestant and Catholic sects as well as Sunni and Shia conflicts are notable intra-religious examples. Muslims and Jews, and Hindus and Muslims have committed atrocities against one another for over a millennium. The list of the injustices committed and endured in the name of religion and the "will of God" (regardless of the name ascribed to a supreme being) is unsettling. Those

Christians who condemn Judaism because "Jews killed Jesus" have missed the central message of peace and love that Jesus has given us. Religious justification for murder and the slaughter of innocent people may be the most heinous of human motivations. No religion is without blemish. The real cause, of course, is not the religion but the misuse of religion by those who are motivated by greed, power, or a desire for domination.

Understanding and/or using doctrine can be very tricky. Followers of a religion or sect may not understand their church's doctrine correctly. Individuals within a church may unjustly condemn actions or behaviors of others predicated upon a misunderstanding of their church's doctrine. Ignorance of doctrine also occurs for those outside of a religion. Condemning another's doctrine predicated on ignorance is an explicit form of stereotyping that can lead to overt prejudice and discrimination. Let me give a couple of examples. For many non-Muslims, the word *jihad* means that Muslims are justified in killing Infidels because they don't follow *Sharia* law. My studies have shown me that *jihad* has many meanings and going to war to kill non-believers is not one of them. Muslims, however, do have a call to bring all Infidels into a willingness to submit themselves to the will of Allah. This submission MUST be voluntary; no forced conversion makes any sense for the devout Muslim. For Christians, Christ gave the Great Commission: Go and baptize all people. Both religions call their followers to bring everyone into the fold. I do not believe that Christ or Mohammad had any intention of having their followers misinterpret this doctrine into justifying the killing of those who don't join the true faith. In fact, I don't believe that either one would condone condemning those who remain faithful to their own beliefs and faith and do not become followers of the other religion. My sense is that they are more concerned with their followers incorporating love and respect for others in their lives rather than condemning or even killing non-believers.

4. RULES AND LAWS.

The gist of my comments so far about religion revolves around the problem of extremes. For example, the extreme position of believing that one's church or faith is the only path to God or that one's church has the only true doctrines or the only true way of interpreting one's sacred text. Extreme positions tend to lead toward an intransigence that provides a motivation for categorizing and rejecting any opposition. Rules and laws help organize a religion; however, they can become very complex, problematic, and confusing. One problem for all religions is that their rules and laws may be misunderstood or misapplied, either by those within the religion as well as those outside the religion. For example, it was because of a church's rules that helped move me away from my Roman Catholic background and eventually become a member of the Evangelical Lutheran Church in America.

When Diane and I became engaged (three months after we met) we started to plan our wedding. She belonged to a Methodist church for her entire life and felt comfortable in her particular church. The pastor had a PhD in philosophy, and I noted that he smiled at me whenever I went to church with her. Later I found out that he was thrilled to have someone in the congregation who understood some of his more subtle and obscure philosophical references. This was during the stage of my journey of faith when I was attending Canisius. I no longer attended worship at my Catholic parish in Niagara Falls, and my faith had moved away from any particular church. I no longer felt compelled to ascribe to Catholicism or, in fact, to any denominational structure or church. I told Diane that it made sense that we get married in her church; it meant a lot to her and I felt no connection to any particular building. I did contact the Roman Catholic diocese to inquire how we should be married in such a way that I would still maintain my connection to my Catholic heritage. The Diocesan official told me that I could not make a request to be married in her church; the request had to come from Diane. When she did so, she was told that it would not be granted and that she should realize that getting married in her church would be wrong. I was furious and told her that we would forget about getting permission, and that we would just go forward with our plans. I did ask one of my philosophy teachers who was a Jesuit priest if he would co-officiate. I still had a lifelong urge to keep my ties with my childhood heritage. At first he said he could not do so because he would not be given permission by the diocese. It was against church law for him to disobey. He was campaigning against the church's teaching on contraception and did not want his participation in an unauthorized marriage to be an excuse for silencing him. We were thrilled when he showed up and assisted at our wedding despite disobeying the rules. A few years later he renounced his vows and married a nun.

Diane and I often become perplexed or even angry when we see church rules or laws (of any religious denomination or faith) become espoused as the Truth or as superior to any other form of belief. Diane's pet phrase is "are their laws any better than anyone else's? Aren't they just manmade anyway?" I agree. Rules and laws help codify one's beliefs. They are an outer manifestation of belief. Rules and laws are a significant source of conflict for people who are trying to synchronize their inner faith and its outer manifestation in a religion. I suspect just about everyone who is a member of a religion has had at least one such conflict in his or her life. Trying to resolve this tension often leads to what people may refer to as crises of faith. Religious thinkers and leaders over the centuries have provided us with brilliant insight into how we can or should relate to one another religiously or how we can try to relate to our God. Thus, I have a great respect for the structure that laws and rules can provide for us. However, I also can see how they become a barrier to following the most important values that a religion should espouse: love, hope, tolerance, respect, and faith. Laws and rules can divide people and provide for justifying condemnation and rejection. Some denominations, for example, use shunning as a way to punish a rule breaker. Again, the over-riding value I would like to see adopted is to assume that one's religious laws or rules should not be followed blindly and absolutely. They come from humans and can suffer from the fallibilities and short-sightedness that is a fundamental condition of being human. The key to synchronizing one's inner faith and outer religion is finding the balance between the guidance and wisdom that rules can provide and the fundamental values that are the hallmarks of any authentic religious faith. The connection one has within one's heart and soul with his or her Creator should always be the paramount value.

5. CHURCH.

The word "Church" is an ambiguous way for us to refer to either a building that people go to for religious purposes or to the group of people who use these buildings. It is not uncommon in Christian circles to say that the Church is really the people as a way to emphasize that the building isn't the most important dimension when referring to one's religious group. I will use the Christian reference to church, but I think that much of what I say may also refer to temples (Hindu, Buddhist or Jewish), synagogues or mosques. Churches are often most connected to the religious practices that occur within them, but the utilization of church property and/or buildings has had a long history of providing a wide range of activities beyond just religious. The most recognized is often education (or bingo) but the list can be quite extensive. The church Diane and I belong to has developed a Wellness Center ministry and we share our space with Building Partners (outside groups who use our facilities). A few years ago, the Center was developing with the guidance of a program director who also created a Respite Program for those suffering from dementia, especially Alzheimer's. It is run by volunteers who meet once per month to give a few hours of respite for care givers. Churches can also serve as sanctuaries for those who are fleeing from persecution or sources of sustenance through food pantries or kitchens.

Prejudices or misunderstandings that arise from religious differences, dislikes or ignorance often get translated into a church: "I would never step into that place because it is full of sinners." "My faith won't allow me to go into that church." "That Mosque is a place that sponsors terrorism." "It's a sin to go into that Temple." These are some of the examples of overt prejudice and/or discrimination that I have heard. Their interpretation of their faith's doctrine or rules gets morphed into these statements. Unfortunately the association of mosques with terrorism, the on-going terrorist activities throughout the world, and a heavy dose of ignorance and misunderstanding of the basic beliefs of Islam and the teachings from the Qur'an are sad consequences of 9/11. As a child and into my youth, I was told by priests and nuns that going into Protestant churches and attending their worship was sinful. Yet I spent my summers doing so with my Southern Baptist relatives. My mom rarely attended church away from Kentucky, although I did go with her to a Presbyterian church that was a block away from our home on Witkop Ave. I remember confessing my sin of attending her church a few times and feeling relief when all I had to do was say a few prayers and be reassured that I would go to heaven if I died that night. The only non-Catholic girl I ever dated became my wife. That has truly been a blessing and could never be construed as sinful.

It is natural for everyone to want to share that which they believe is true or right. In fact all religions urge their followers to do just that. As I mentioned above, for Christians, Jesus gave the Great Commission: Go and baptize all ...; and Mohammad says to bring all Infidels and have them submit to Allah. Being passionate about one's faith and trying to bring all non-believers into the fold makes a lot of sense. Condemning those who do not convert to your way of thinking is an extreme and regrettable form of discrimination and prejudice. Unfortunately, it also has become the root of hate, wars, and interpersonal conflict among friends and family. One of the fundamental problems I have with this hatred and prejudice is that all of the great founders of religions (the Buddha, Abraham, Jesus, Mohammad, etc.) do not foster an agenda of hate or exclusion.

Since this is my personal journey through life, I would like to finish this chapter with a few small examples of church-related problems that reflect smaller, maybe more covert types of prejudice that I have encountered.

Since the 1980s I have been involved in working with churches that are undergoing internal conflicts. It is very sad to see how members within a church can behave in hateful or destructive ways. One pastor asked me to come in and chair a congregational debate on whether to place the organ in the back of the church or near the front. The congregation was divided and passions ran high. She was afraid of being trapped in the middle of a no-win situation. I laid down basic rules for the discussion (all based on civility and respect) and allowed the topic to run its course. At the end I asked if everyone would accept the decision of the majority. Most, but not all, said they would do so.

Sexual misconduct by church officials (priests, pastors, ministers, rabbis, imams, etc.) or lay church leaders is another source of conflict that creates tremendous problems for churches. The scandals surrounding the Roman Catholic Church's crisis with priestly pedophilia has affected many congregations, even those who may not have directly experienced the abusiveness of a priest. Blaming a church for the behavior of an individual, even the church's leader, has always struck me as an unfair prejudice. When I was young, my aunt and uncle took me to Mount Mariah Primitive Baptist church. One summer, when I was 11 or 12, we started going to Zion's Cause. When I asked why, the question was always dismissed. I didn't learn the reason until I was about 20 and talking to my mom after she had been out drinking with my dad. She told me that the preacher man ran off with one of the women of the church. Uncle James and Aunt Lona could not abide the behavior and left the church because of its sinfulness. In fact, they would no longer even use the road that the church was on as a connecting short cut to a highway that had the nearest barbecue place and grocery store. It was better to drive an extra mile or so than put their souls in danger!

Sexual misconduct is a particularly heinous crime in any congregation. I was involved in working with a small, rural congregation that did not address the problem for 20 years. The pastor had sexually molested some boys 20 years before he repeated these assaults on more recent occasions. The guilt of ignoring the problem for so long, even when families who were friends and neighbors left the church, was deep and traumatic. Dealing with the confusion between a pedophile and a homosexual was another underlying problem for the members. Most, if not all, of the people with whom I talked about the pastor's behavior said that he was a homosexual and so being a pedophile could be expected. In their minds there was no difference. Homosexuality, for them, led to the abuse of young boys. Trying to convince them that homosexuality is a natural orientation and pedophilia is an abuse of power and a degenerate way of relating to children was rather unproductive. Their stereotypes and prejudices ran very deep. A woman and I ran a six-week program looking at the biblical interpretations related to homosexuality and the psychological forces involved in pedophilia. Despite our educational efforts, no one seemed to change his or her opinion or view. The inbred prejudices and hatred for homosexuals remained.

Churches are unique groups. Often they include members who may not otherwise interact or even care for one another. Churches in small communities may have another social dynamic because the members may be extended family members or long-time friends and neighbors. The beauty and blessing of churches occur when personality differences and covert prejudices and expectations people have are put aside in order to create a harmonious group of people sharing in their faith and living in the hope that the religion provides. I believe that the most powerful force in churches is the power of tolerance, acceptance and love shared by members and extended to visitors and guests. Churches can be the source of terrible prejudices and discrimination; they can also be the greatest source for overcoming these barriers to tolerance, acceptance and love. Diane and I are blessed to be in a congregation that is open and tolerant. They welcomed us when we were searching after deciding to leave our former congregation, having been active members for almost 30 years. We have found roles that nurture our need to participate in ministries that foster our inner faith.

Since the 1990s, most mainstream churches throughout Western New York (and probably throughout the United States) have had to deal with diminishing numbers of members and having to face the real prospects of closing or sharing ministries and resources with other churches. I have been saddened by the very prevalent attitude that the person's faith is connected to the building he or she calls his or her church. It is okay to merge or share resources with others as long as "my" church stays open: (even if the building is only used one day per week for most of the year). The Catholic Church has a political structure that allows bishops (or archbishops or cardinals) to close or merge churches within their jurisdiction. They can order closures and mergers because the rules and political structure is basically authoritarian. In most Protestant denominations, there is a more democratic process (Luther called it the Priesthood of All Believers). Only a congregation can decide whether to stay open or close. All too often, the need to keep a building going is the result of a few people who want to keep sitting in the pew that has been theirs for decades. Fear of change is a powerful inhibitor within life. Churches must deal with this dynamic on a daily basis.

As I have walked through my spiritual journey, I have reached a few conclusions about the prejudices and misunderstandings I have felt and that I have encountered. Sacred texts are important written documents that can inform and inspire the faithful. They are valuable means for inspiration, guidance, and comfort. Doctrines are intended to codify what followers should understand and believe. However, they can close people's minds and hearts to others even though the founders of all the great religions are calling for openness and love. Rules and laws are necessary to organize any group. They are essential for churches. All rules, however, are human based. The faithful of a religion may claim that the rules are divinely inspired or come directly from God. This may or not be true. What is true is that humans may have taken this inspiration and formulated the language that constitutes what the rules are. I am truly saddened when I see, experience, or hear about how people use their church's rules to exclude or condemn others. Punishment for rule breaking is the flip side for establishing any rule. I accept the need for punishment for those who break the rules (just ask my daughters). However, punishments should be commensurate with the crime. Finally, churches should be places for people to share their faith and embrace the beliefs that bind them together. Churches and congregations should help their members find a way to synchronize their inner faith with the outer dimension of the religion. I am continually examining my attitudes and behaviors related with my faith and church to uncover both the covert as well as the overt forms of prejudice and discrimination that exist. In essence religion or faith can be the cause of great prejudice, hatred and discrimination or it can be the greatest asset in a person's life for finding and sharing love, beauty and grace. I have come to believe that it is foolish to blindly accept whatever a church leader may say. Preaching and calls to faith must be placed into a context that filters away the prejudicial and discriminatory and fosters respect, love, peace and care for others. Religion and faith should empower people to promote love and goodness. Becoming aware of the barriers that religion and churches build to prevent this empowerment is a necessary step in addressing the ongoing prejudices in our lives. My faith journey has deeply changed the way I think, feel and live. I continue to try and synchronize my inner faith and my outer religion.

PART III:

ON GENDER AND BEING HUMAN: WHAT THE WOMEN IN MY LIFE TAUGHT ME ABOUT MYSELF

PART III

CHAPTER 5
RADICALLY CHANGING MY PERSPECTIVE

That's the thing about human life –
there's no control group,
no way to ever know how any of us,
would have turned out if any variables had been changed.
Elizabeth Gilbert

Diane was pushing hard and periodically straining while I was being the coach. "You can do it ... keep pushing ... you're doing great." I was bracing her back and eagerly awaiting our third child. Diane was delivering "naturally", as it was called then, and we were only moments away from delivery. Of course we did not know if the baby would be a boy or girl because in 1974, childbirth was quite different from today. Being in the delivery room was a thrill for me, especially since I missed that experience with my first child's birth.

Flashback to 1971, New Orleans: Tara, our first child, was about to be born in New Orleans. Diane's doctor there had a whole different approach to childbirth: put the woman out with drugs and put the father in a waiting room. I vividly remember that day. Diane and I had gone to her doctor's office for a weekly visit. She was late, meaning that the standard pregnancy timeframe was different from Tara's actual development. Our plan that day was to go to the doctor's and then take our friends, Peter and Tiny, to the airport so they could begin their return journey to their home in the Netherlands. Of course, the doctor had other plans.

When Diane came out of his office, she looked both apprehensive and excited. "The doctor says we shouldn't wait any longer. He's admitting me now and will induce labor shortly."

I was startled and instantly went into planning mode. "Great. Let's get you across the street. But then I better quickly run to let Peter and Tiny know we won't be taking them to the airport." The doctor's office was on one side of Napolean Ave. and Baptist Hospital was on the other side.

Diane nodded but was clearly more intent on what was about to happen to her, to the baby, to us and to our life. We slowly walked across the street; I had my arm around her waist. We didn't say much because we were in our own worlds. As soon as Diane was admitted and in a room, I quickly drove to our friends' apartment (5 minutes away) which was in the married student apartment complex of Tulane. Diane and I had lived next to them until just recently when we moved to a three bedroom apartment in anticipation of our about-to-be-expanded family. I dashed to the car, drove quickly and ran to the elevator. When I knocked on our friends' door, there was no answer. I wasn't sure where they were, so I quickly scrawled a note and slipped it under their door. When I returned to the hospital, the nurses were still settling Diane and told me to wait in the hall. I leaned against a wall with my mind swirling in many directions at once. I was getting excited, wondering what the next few hours might mean. In fact, what the rest of our life would be like.

A nurse emerged from Diane's room. "It's okay to go in now, but you will have to leave and go to the waiting room as soon as we give her the shots." The nurse was kind but very direct. I was taken aback because I had expected to be with Diane for much of the time before she went into delivery. That was not the case. Her doctor's approach was to sedate Diane and send me to a place removed from any contact, sight or sound of childbirth. I remember kissing Diane when I received the order to leave and saw excitement and a bit of anxiety in her eyes. Were those feelings really Diane's or was I projecting my own feelings onto her? The waiting room was a typical uncomfortable hospital area. The straight-back leather type chairs were merely functional and the magazines strewn around the tables were uninteresting to me. So what color were the chairs? Were they brown or yellow or red or orange? I stared at them for long periods and probably saw all of those colors over the next few hours, but there was no encoding of that information into my memory. I do remember calling my sister-in-law and letting her know about the delivery. There was the typical vending machine, but I was too cheap to consider buying anything. Besides, I have never liked coffee, in any context, and was too nervous to munch on anything. After about a half hour or so our friends from the Netherlands showed up.

"What.... Why are you here? You're supposed to be headed to NYC?"

They smiled, and Tiny gave me the traditional three kisses from cheek to cheek.

"We changed our plans. We couldn't miss this," Peter said with a smile.

So we waited and chatted about goodness knows what. It was probably only a couple of hours, but it seemed like an eternity. Sometime during that interval my brother, Paul, and his wife, Linda, came up and stayed with Peter, Tiny and me until we all saw our baby.

The first report I received about the delivery was when a nurse brought Tara into the waiting room to show her off. She was sleeping, and I assumed it was because the sedative they gave Diane also sedated Tara. The nurse slapped her on the foot saying, "Wake up little one; here's your daddy." I felt like slapping the nurse (paternal protection started at that instant). I was excited and thrilled that I was able to share that moment with Paul, Linda, and our friends who have remained a part of our lives ever since. Tiny, Peter and I went into her room. We were all smiles and thrilled to share the moment with Diane. The nurse had taken Tara back to the nursery almost immediately after she had slapped my little girl. There had been no chance of holding her at that time. When we entered the room, we saw that Diane was groggy. I kissed her and don't remember much of a response. I was excited while she was trying to return to reality. Diane has always had difficulty emerging from sedation. When Tiny said, "What a beautiful little girl!" Diane's memorable response was, "What do you think I'd have? A horse?"

Tiny pretended she wasn't phased by this uncharacteristically snide remark and continued to talk to Diane, who also muttered something about Tiny's poor playing in pinochle. I shuddered, and on the way to the car to take them to our apartment for the night I tried to explain Diane's response to them. They wanted me to ignore Diane's bizarre comments and proceeded to talk about other things. They spent the night with me and I took them to the airport the next day and proceeded to the hospital to see my girls.

Tara was the first of who would come to be known as "Charlie's Angels." Diane and Tara spent a couple of nights at Baptist Hospital (routine back then). After I visited on the second day, I decided to do something very uncharacteristic for me. I kissed Diane good-night, went to wave to Tara (isn't that really a rather silly thing to do?) and proceeded to walk a block to our favorite restaurant in those days: "Charlie's Steak House." The steaks were inexpensive but delicious. In honor of Peter and Tiny and the grand events of the past 24 hours I ordered a Heineken and privately toasted our friends, Diane, Tara and a life that brimmed with joy and possibilities. I still have the label that I carefully peeled off that bottle.

Fast forward two years to the birth of our second child, Kristen, who came to us with me involved and Diane conscious. We had gone to Lamaze classes, and I had learned how to be a coach. We brought tennis balls for me to apply to Diane's back when she was having contractions, and I was learning how to ignore some of Diane's comments and not take them too personally. She was amazing in her ability to deal with the pain of the contractions. It was exhilarating to be next to her and watch the professionals attend to her and to our little girl. Diane remained conscious through the entire delivery, and I learned that day that women are really stronger than men. I couldn't image doing what Diane did. That was truly humbling, but a significant moment of insight for me. Men are not necessarily stronger than women. So the contrast between the births of our first and second children was startling. Now, thirteen months later, we were back in the hospital with another doctor from the practice, but the dynamics were the same: Diane conscious and me being a foolish but excited coach

Before completing this story, I need to digress and expand on my childhood as it relates to my gender attitudes and prejudices. Before meeting Diane, my world and the gender roles defined within it were rather clearly demarcated. I was a very typical white male chauvinist brought up in the '50s. I have two brothers, no sisters. My high school years were spent in an all-male institution. I played football for three years, ran track the other year, and joined a wide range of activities. My freshman year in college was in a seminary. My next three years were at Canisius, which at the time had a female population of full-time students of less than one percent. My formative years were male-dominated and many experiences, major and minor, contributed to the formation of my view of gender roles.

Some particular anecdotes from my past stand out because of their impact on my perceptions of gender.

ANECDOTE ONE: LEARNING FROM CATS

Let's start with Belle Kitty and the long line of female cats that populated my childhood. Multi-colored Belle Kitty was a scourge to all who entered her space. She was mean and hateful. She would hiss at anyone who dared to invade her space when she was sitting on the back of our living room chair or couch. I saw her chase dogs out of our lawn. No one, and I mean no one, could pet her. My dad said she was as hateful as Grandma Pearl. I never agreed with this assessment since he and I had a very different relationship with Grandma Pearl. She was mom's mother and lived in

Kentucky, which I have indicated before was my safe space. Grandma and I had a special bond – she loved me but did not seem to like my dad very much. Back in Kentucky she wasn't a very pleasant person to anyone after her husband died (my mom was four at that time). I never saw her show any sign of affection to anyone but me and she always seemed cold to my dad. Was that my childhood prism or an objective assessment? I'll never know.

As I said Grandma Pearl and I had a close relationship and I never experienced her coldness. The bond was probably formed when I was born. My mom had serious complications in delivery and Grandma came to take care of Paul before my birth than Paul and me afterwards. I'm sure she fed and held me until mom came home, probably even afterwards. This bonding was a beautiful part of my life and I'll share other stories about her later. One family story that I was too young to see but had heard quite often while I was growing up relates to a day when Grandma was changing me. Unfortunately she did not cover my private parts and that was a real mistake. Apparently my waterworks spouted and hit her in the face. My dad roared with laughter and said "Was it salty?" My Grandma did not appreciate his attempt at humor. She picked up a kitchen knife and chased him around the room. Mom's telling of the story indicated that this was not done in jest. Mom's version included the fact that Grandma did not like dad's drinking, some of his language and his attitude (whatever that may have meant). I never asked mom to explain any of this to me; I just accepted the fact that dad and Grandma did not get along.

I do know that Belle Kitty was mean so I could not see how dad compared my loving Grandma to this terror of Witkop (our street name). One of his reasons may have been the fact that Grandma and Belle Kitty seemed to hit it off while Grandma stayed with us. Dad assumed that it was two peas in a pod getting along. I have no explanation for my Grandma's affinity to Belle Kitty since I can only piece the picture together from the stories I heard and my experience with each of the players. Belle Kitty managed to leave a lasting impression with people. One day I saw a neighborhood friend who was bald feel Belle Kitty's wrath. He dared to sit on her couch without permission and was instantly attacked on his domed top with out-stretched claws to make him move. Dogs knew enough to cross the street when entering our property. In those days cats and dogs roamed freely around neighborhoods. An indicator of Belle Kitty's reputation was the fact that even after she had died, dogs continued to cross the street and did not dare use our sidewalk.

Belle Kitty was the first in a long line of cats that my mother raised and upon whom she shed affection. I loved the cats that spanned my life with my parents. They took on unusual personalities: meanness in Belle Kitty; one who actually used our toilet by placing her feet across the seat for her elimination needs; poor Smokey was the dumbest and was often seen running into walls or getting tangled in the grapevines; Trixie was actually cuddly; Fluffy was lesbian - you get the picture. While I was living at home most of the cats were female. The one male cat had his days numbered when he began peeing on the bottom half of the television which was the sound system in those days. Belle Kitty taught me that females were diffi-cult to understand. However, this lesson became more complicated with the differing personalities in the cats that followed her. I began to learn that these differences were somewhat inexplicable. I could observe their behaviors but not necessarily predict what they would do in any given situation. Their intentionality was impenetrable. Was this a function of being female or just a part of differing personalities? Or was it rooted in my basic ignorance?

Belle Kitty was a stark contrast to my mom. The cat was dominant and unencumbered. Mom was somewhat passive and appeared all too submis-sive. As I grew older I began to discern how my childhood impressions of female behavior lacked insight and missed too many details. I didn't learn to see the subtleties of female behavior until my girls began growing up, and I started to try and be open to Diane and who she was. It has taken a lifetime for me to try and peel off the onion skins of what it means to be female and male. Mixing gender characteristics with personality dynamics is a wonderful lesson into what it means to be human. The cats were a child's entry into the differences personality makes in trying to understand people.

ANECDOTE TWO: BEING MOM'S CONFIDANTE

When I was young, we had milk delivered. The milkman was friendly and would have coffee with the women of the neighborhood periodically. This was a mid-morning ritual. One day when I was 3 or 4, I welcomed everyone to "Willie's Cathouse." The women laughed and I thought I was a real comic - obviously having no idea what I had said. My mother's birth name was Willie Udine, but she was always known as Wanda; her boys called her Willie as a loving way to tease her. Mom had trained me to listen to her, to be her confidante (beginning around 11 or 12), and to entertain her (and others). I don't remember singing on tables at my dad's favorite bar when I was 2 or 3, but apparently I was given quarters and applause for my performances. I do remember playing my accordion at my father's work picnic and winning a prize when I was 9 or 10. Dad worked at Hooker Chemical, so I brilliantly told people that I won a prize at the Hooker's picnic. As I was growing up, I began to learn the lesson that teasing can go too far and sometimes can become hurtful. I saw this in my dad when he thought he was being funny and I saw my mom's hurt looks. His teasing often focused on mom's gender (e.g. the silliness of being a woman) and her farm up-bringing (e.g. going bare foot in the fields).

"You really don't work for a living because I'm the real provider," was a sentiment of his that I heard. I remember him commenting on how women don't know anything important and it takes a man to get things right. As I grew into my role as confidante for Mom, I began to see that the world may have been divided into male and female with gender roles clearly defined. First Mom, then Diane, and subsequently my daughters have clarified this mistaken division. It is great to see the blurring of gender roles over the decades and the slow dismissal of prejudices and biases built on what men or women are "supposed to do" or how we are "supposed to act."

ANECDOTE THREE: HAVING GENDER ROLES DEFINED FOR ME

Obviously, as the only female in my childhood household, my mom was the greatest influence in my early perceptions of gender. My mom expected me to talk with adults and to make her laugh and be proud. I grew up thinking that was my role. My mom was the youngest of four children and was as spoiled as a girl raised on a farm could be. At age 19, she ran away from her rural roots with my father - a man from the North who was 14 years older than she. I know she regretted doing so.

One night when I was 14 or 15, my younger brother and I were at a bar with my folks. It wasn't, Fritz's, the bar we usually frequented for fish fries on Fridays. This was Louie's bar, and I was not used to the surroundings. Fritz's and Louie's were on the same street – but Fritz's bar was on the right as you entered from the front door while Louie's was on the left. Fritz's had a bowling machine and a bit more lighting, so the feeling was far more welcoming to me than this bar. I didn't recognize any of the patrons. Bill and I sat at a table, while Dad squatted on the stool at the bar and Mom flittered around laughing and joking with just about everyone. I was startled to hear my dad's voice rise above all the others and was dumbfounded by what I heard. First, dad was not a communicator and often drank in silence with a scowl on his face. Hearing his voice drowning out everyone else was a new experience. Second, the content of his outburst was horrifying: he was selling mom. "Buy me drinks and you can take her home for as long as you want!" These words slurred out of him and have stuck to me as yet another example of how I hated his drinking and his treatment of mom.

A little while later we returned home, with Dad driving while intoxicated. When we got home, Bill went to his room, and Mom and I put Dad to bed. As we did so, she asked me to stay up and talk with her. She was a mellow drunk; my dad was a nasty one. We chatted for hours. I don't remember what we talked about that night, but I do know that this was a routine for Mom and me. We had a number of chats after they came home from drinking; I felt as if I was Mom's confidante. I'll share more about this dimension of our relationship later.

Mom was an attractive woman who loved to party, laugh and socialize with others. Dad was the opposite. Our home was a male-dominant enclave. Dad worked, and since Mom stayed home, she didn't work. Dad provided for us, and we had to acknowledge our appreciation for all he did. We were to respect Mom and help her with chores because that was the right thing to do. Mom never drove and didn't even get a license until after Dad died. Although Dad complained when he had to drive her to the grocery store and shopping, he seemed to need to be in control. Friends helped her get her license within a few months after Dad's death, but as soon as she met Chet, her future husband, she never got behind the wheel again. Besides, her driving skills can best be described by the fact she is the only person I have ever heard of receiving a ticket for driving too slowly on a suburban street. Mom seemed quite comfortable taking the submissive role and remaining dependent upon her husbands and sometimes her sons. This attitude did not just relate to driving.

Dad seemed to make all the decisions and while he may have asked Mom, it didn't matter what she seemed to think. The roles in our house were consistent with what would be considered chauvinistic. Dad did the outside chores and after he had part of his lung removed, those tasks fell to my younger brother and me (our older brother had moved out by then). The males took down the screens in fall, cleaned them, put them away, cleaned the storm windows and then put them up. The reverse was done in spring. Dad took care of the car, and we painted the house. Dad fixed anything that broke. Of course we shoveled the snow. We mowed the lawn, raked the leaves in fall, and tended to the gardens.

Mom's role was to cook, clean the house, do the laundry, vacuum, dust and when we were small, take care of the boys. To respect our mom, we were given chores to help her: we kept our rooms clean, dusted and did the dishes after dinner. I vacuumed more than just my room during Saturday morning chores. She made our lunches for school and prepared the grocery list (to include cases of beer for dad and cigarettes for both of them). Since she didn't drive, we all had to go to the store when Paul wasn't around to watch us. After Paul went away to college, I started taking on the job of babysitting; I was 11. By the time I was 12 or 13, I also watched Bill when my folks went out drinking (2 or 3 nights a week). Of course we all routinely went out for a fish fry on Friday nights to Fritz's. We respected and loved our mom, but it was clear that her role was to take care of us and obey the wishes of her husband.

ANECDOTE FOUR: ACTING LIKE A MALE

My youth was traditional and chauvinistically based. I played pick-up sports, baseball and football predominantly. When I was 14 I finally was able to join a Babe Ruth baseball league. I never got to participate in Little League because teams practiced and played games too far away from our house (according to my parents). Besides, my father refused to drive me to any of the practices or games. My parents wouldn't let me ride my bike to that area either: "It's not safe; the traffic is too busy for you," was their joint refrain. The Babe Ruth league was closer to home. Beside the sponsor for the team was the brother-in-law of one of the tavern owners that my folks came to know in their travels to bars. That connection made it okay for me to play. I made the all-star team when I was 15 and hit the only home runs for our team that year. In high school I played football and became the defensive captain during my senior year. That responsibility taught me how to stay in control regardless of the situation. It was my job to make the correct reads on different plays and stop our opponents. I couldn't let emotions get in the way. Our coach told us not to see girls or go on dates during the season because it would sissify us. I obeyed and believed what he said. I made my debut on the varsity team the first day of scrimmaging in practice. Our star running back was loose and I tackled him in the open field (something no one imagined could happen). I grabbed and brought him down such that his knee landed in a "bad place". I did groan a bit and bent over for a second, but I made sure to show that I was a man and could take it. I smiled and returned to the huddle as if this injury was something I could take. This was part of my character formation even if I walked a little funny for awhile. In addition to what I learned from football my dad instilled in me that dominance was expected of males and I already knew that I couldn't cry ("or I'll give you something to cry about"), that I had to solve problems ("that's not right, do it again"), that I had to stay in control ("don't you dare talk to your mother that way") and that I had to do everything correctly ("no, numbskull, you do it this way"). I was compulsive, driven, and expected to follow the rules of proper male behavior (those norms and mores that boys learn from their dads and other men in their lives). Gender as I was growing up was clearly defined.

ANECDOTE FIVE: SAYING "I DO" CHANGED EVERYTHING

So I grew up in a male dominant world with few opportunities for understanding the differences between male and female attitudes and behavior. Attending an all-male high school and one year of seminary reinforced many of the gender stereotypes I encountered as a child. The three undergraduate years at Canisius furthered my male-oriented world. Although the college had started to admit co-eds, there were very few and I doubt I even talked to any of them. I also joined the ROTC Drill Team, which was a very close knit group of guys. We practiced up to 20 hours per week, travelled to drill meets around the country, and spent a lot of time socializing together. For the first year on the team, the squad leader of my marching unit, Ron, had a girl friend, Marsha, who didn't like all the extra time the team expected. Maybe she was also put off by the very distinctive male orientation of the team: be tough (a few scars from the bayonets don't mean anything); drink together (team and friendship bonding); shoot water balloons out of hotel windows (Piccadilly Hotel) or drop them on unsuspecting patrons going to a theater; pile furniture in an elevator (Dayton); play King of the Hill at midnight using a construction site (Cincinnati); "requisition" an American flag from 5th Avenue; etc. So Ron left after our sophomore year to become a member of the corps (the vast majority of ROTC cadets). At the time, Canisius did not have any building or facility for physical education, which was required by New York State for all college students at that time. Instead of physical education Canisius required all freshmen and sophomores to participate in ROTC. That lasted until a couple of years after I graduated when they opened the Physical Education Center.

After our sophomore year all students had the choice of whether to stay in ROTC or drop out. The vast majority did not continue in the program. Ron shocked the Drill Team when he decided that he would continue in ROTC but he would stop being a member of the Drill Team. Members of the Team teased Ron and gave him the cold shoulder; I didn't. I felt that Ron loved Marsha, and I secretly admired him for choosing love over "the guys." During those years my studies in philosophy challenged me to question most of the assumptions and beliefs I had held growing up. I began to rearrange priorities and values. Trying to understand the meaning of love was a singular preoccupation for me on an intellectual basis. The meaning of love became very real and existential for me with Diane. I will need to digress further to give the context for our relationship and its beginning.

I was glad that Ron was not afraid to make a choice that was not shared by our group. Not turning on Ron was the first sign in my past that testosterone was not the only prevailing element in my decision making. I began to think outside of my chauvinistic parameters. I never was macho, but I always saw myself as male (the meaning of which should become clear throughout the next chapter).

My accepting attitude may have been a primary reason for Ron asking me to stand up for him in his wedding (Nov. 18 of our senior year). We were sitting in a Philosophy class in late September. He was taking it as a requirement and I was using it as one of my major electives. The teacher was a visiting professor from the University of Buffalo. The course title was "Galileo, Bruno and Kepler." His request came out of the blue. "Charlie, would you stand up in my wedding?" My first thought was to tease him and ask whether I could sit during the ceremony. Puns were one of my trademarks in college (maybe even beyond). My next thought was "Doesn't he have any friends?" I felt we were good friends but not close enough for such a request. All of those thoughts transpired almost instantaneously because I quickly said "Sure." Later on I found out that I had to attend a rehearsal on Friday evening, November 17. On the 18th the wedding would be in the morning, followed by a ride in limos, a formal brunch for the wedding party, a respite at Marsha's house, and the reception at night. That weekend changed my life, my values, and my attitudes drastically.

I went to the rehearsal with another member of the Drill Team who also remained supportive of Ron and was the other usher. We arrived a bit early, and I was standing by the altar rail of the church. The middle aisle was long, and I turned to see two young women walking toward us. One I ignored; the other had a long orange winter coat, long hair, and was just stunningly beautiful. I was surprised at my gut reaction. Since the summer before my senior year, my roommate and I had been spending a lot of time together working out the details of new, very intricate and dangerous moves for our Team. I had become an avowed bachelor and he dubbed me the President of the Bachelor and Pun Club. We were the only members! I was going to try and date lots of females that semester (including my roommate's sister) which, of course, never happened. I was not really comfortable around meeting new women/girls and had none of the moves guys were supposed to have. One high school experience should prove the point. My best friend, Stan, and I went to a beach on Grand Island which was close to Niagara Falls. We decided we were going to try and "pick up" some girls. While we were swimming and nonchalantly looking around at prospects on the beach, we saw three girls sitting on a blanket. We mustered up our courage and ambled to them. "So, what are girls like you doing around here?" was my deft observation. We did sit down for awhile but left when it became clear we were not all that welcome. That was pretty much the end of my trying to pick up any stranger. Besides, as a teen and college student, I was too intense, earnest and self-conscious to think I could just go up and start talking to a strange female.

That evening at the rehearsal Diane walked down the aisle, and my gaze followed her the entire way. Marsha introduced us and told us that Diane and I would be standing up together. Later we found out that Marsha had planned this arrangement quite intentionally. After the rehearsal, we went to someone's basement for a "get together." I remember there was food and drink, and we stood around in small groups passing along pleasantries. I felt quite awkward but believed I didn't make a fool of myself. The next morning I donned the tuxedo and put on dark socks and tied my well-shined shoes. I mention the shoes because the wedding party and parents weren't sure what I would do. My reputation for always wearing sneakers was quite well founded. I only wore shoes when I had my army uniform on. All other times and for all other occasions I wore sneakers, even with the sport coat and tie that was mandatory for us to wear to classes. Marsha's father made a big deal about my shoes after the wedding. He may have thought he was teasing me; I took it as a badge of honor. Wearing sneakers was my way of being male, unique, rebellious, and, well, just me. It was my way of being authentic and real, important concepts for me. I didn't need boots in the rain or snow. I was tough. To this day I own and wear more sneakers than shoes (although I have found more stylish sneakers to wear to church these days). It has taken a long time for me to finally learn that many of my beliefs about fashion, clothes and footwear have nothing to do with gender. It's just about me.

I don't remember much about the wedding except walking Diane down the aisle after the ceremony. I tried to do so with class. Acting with class has always been a mantra for me. It relates to my sense of acting properly and sustaining a sense of dignity in situations that are formal or serious. We threw the rice and piled into the limos. I was sitting next to Diane and her friend Jan was with us. Jan and Diane were and remain very close friends. The ride was long because they needed to kill some time because we would be too early for the brunch reservations. At least that's what I thought was going on. During the drive Diane, Jan and I talked incessantly. I felt a real connection to Diane and the three of us decided that we would act with "couth" for the rest of the day and evening. During the brunch, Diane and I learned that we had quite a bit in common, including a love for *Gone With the Wind*. Neither of us had really met someone of the opposite gender with the affinity we had for the novel and movie. Our reasons were quite different. I believe for Diane it was the romance, relationships, and story. For me it was the connection with the South, the Cause, and my roots that led to my nickname of Li'l Reb. I made sure that I pulled out chairs for Diane and Jan, and we all ate quite properly and "couthly". After brunch we headed to Marsha's house. I was very intent upon watching as much of the UCLA vs. USC game as I could. For college football fans, this was one of The Games of the year in those days. As a diehard Buffalo Bills fan, I knew we would have the #1 pick in the draft the following spring and I wanted to see our top prospect, O. J. Simpson, play. The girls were aghast that we would be intent on watching the game on such a momentous day for Ron and Marsha, so they went into another room. My observation was stereotypic: guys like sports; girls get mushy for weddings.

The reception was a mixed blessing for me. I had already started falling for Diane and wanted to commandeer every dance with her. Such was not to be. I danced with Jan, Diane's sister, maybe her mother and somebody else. I didn't particularly like other guys dancing with her and was taken aback when one of them seemed to be going out of his way to flirt with her (and she seemed to be responding in kind). Where did this jealousy come from? It really was powerful though. During one of our dances I asked her to go with me to the Drill Team Dinner Dance. It was an annual, formal affair each year on Dec. 7. We wore our uniforms and the dates wore formal dresses. It was always on Dec. 7 because the college, at that time, always had Dec. 8th off for the Feast of the Immaculate Conception.

The dance was at the Niagara Falls Air Force base. Diane and I ate, danced and talked the night away. I was taken aback during the evening when there was one chair available while many of us were standing around. I offered it to Diane and she said I should sit and she would sit on my lap. Really? I don't ever remember that happening to me before. She was rather nonchalant and I was surprised. We even kissed once while we were dancing. I was on cloud 9. Maybe I should back up a moment. As I said the wedding was on Nov. 18 and the dance was on Dec. 7. In my own self-conscious way, I did not call Diane for about two weeks after the wedding. I wasn't sure if she felt anything for me and wasn't sure what to say anyhow. I felt much more confident in speaking to someone I could see rather than a voice coming to me over wires. (Although I must admit the telephone has **never** been my friend. Even today I'm not as enamored with my cell phone as everyone else seems to be with theirs.) Later on, I learned that Diane misinterpreted the delay, thinking I may not be as interested in her as she thought I may have been. After the Dinner Dance, though, we began to date if you can call it that. I did not have a car or very much money so we did not go out to eat or even to the movies very much. I did walk her home from her college (about 3 miles). I also walked to her house as much as I could. That too was about 3 miles from my dorm room to her home. I ratcheted up my courage and asked her to a Drill Team New Year's Eve party. I was staying at my home in Niagara Falls for the Christmas break from school so was able to borrow my dad's car for the party. That was a bona fide date, I guess. We arrived back to her place rather late and found out later her folks hadn't gotten home yet from their party. Umm – who were the night owls?

I remember one evening in mid-January. I had been to Diane's and we had spent the evening chatting and getting to know each other. On the walk back to my dorm room (it was cold and snowy) I smiled and actually skipped a short distance. "I'm going to marry her" wasn't just my thought; it became my plan. I waited until January 26th and gave one of the more foolish proposals known to western civilization. "I was thinking we could get married in August?!?" It was startling to her and typical of my social awkwardness with women. So my proposal came merely 6 1/2 weeks after our first date. But it made sense to me. She was the woman I wanted to spend my life with. There was no doubt or question in my mind; even with my training in Philosophy, I had no hesitation. Besides I was headed to graduate school. Tulane had accepted me, and it was 1300 miles from home. I knew I would have to study full-time and had no real means of income. I hadn't figured out what I actually was going to do because I was more pre-occupied with finishing college, serving on the Drill Team, and trying to cope with a love I had never experienced before. My vision was completely clouded and my obsessive planning had not fully emerged yet. Diane was finishing up an Education Degree with a concentration in English. She and her dad had connections and she was in line to get a full-time teaching position in the school district where she was living with her parents. Her response was practical; my so-called proposal was starry-eyed. She said that we should wait for a year. She could teach and I could study and we would have some money to support us. I guess she was saying yes to marrying and no to my half-baked idea of getting married in August. My plan had no tangible job for either of us. My thinking was that she would easily get a teaching position once we arrived in New Orleans, which would have been when their school systems were beginning classes. For the next couple of weeks we went round-and-round: Diane practical and making sense; me determined and driven (some may call it being stubborn). My usual response to her practicality was my own practicality. Since I had no income and would only have modest savings from the summer job that my friend, Ron, had lined up for me after graduation (sweeping floors in a windshield wiper factory), I could not afford to come home. "We wouldn't see each other while I was in school. Besides you know I would become so wrapped up in my studies that we would start drifting apart."

Long distance phone calls were rare in those days – besides the cost would have been prohibitive for me. That's what I said and believed. On February 14 I walked through a few inches of snow to go to her home. We began talking in her living room and she shifted our conversation to something she wanted to say.

"We have been going along two separate paths. I've decided to move onto your path. So, yes."

I was stunned. Was she saying what I hoped she was saying?

"Do you mean Yes, Yes?"

"Yes," she smiled.

We were engaged. I was so elated And thrilled And relieved. We smiled and hugged but decided not to tell our parents immediately. My great plan was to get married at the end of August rather than sooner because we couldn't afford anything other than living with our parents and working summer jobs to pay for our travel to New Orleans. (I gave no thought to preparations for a wedding. Don't they just happen was my only thought about such things.) The trip down south would also be our honeymoon, which eventually consisted of stops in Mansfield, Ohio, Elizabethtown, Kentucky and a stay in Western Kentucky near my relatives. Once we got to New Orleans, Diane could look for a teaching position: No problem. The issue now was telling our parents. We had to figure out how we were going to do so. Eventually we told both sets of parents on different occasions. For my folks we drove out to Niagara Falls and met them as they were returning from a bar. Mom was smiling; dad was drunk.

Their response was rather underwhelming and put a bit of a damper on our mood, but that was what I had expected. The announcement had come out of the blue for them since they didn't know much about our dating. The only inkling mom would have had that Diane was in my life was the day we met in downtown Buffalo. I don't remember some of the details, but the ones I do are vivid. Mom was very dressed up in a gown of some sort. It was in late December so she also had on her faux stole. She was going to a movie with a friend of the family. He was the owner of one of the bars my folks frequented. He had volunteered to give mom a social life while my dad sequestered himself in his chair. There was no doubt in my mind when dad died that he wanted to marry mom. I'm sure she broke his heart when she started dating Chet and threw her life into his control. So I introduced Diane to my mom that night and didn't clarify the nature of our relationship (of course this was only a few weeks after our first date and neither one of us knew at that time what the nature of our relationship was anyhow). I certainly didn't say much to my folks about our New Year's Eve date. I kept such things to myself. So that's all my folks knew ahead of time.

Telling Diane's parents was more carefully planned. I was over one evening; we sat in the kitchen planning; her folks were watching TV. After screwing up our courage and after drinking a bottle of orange pop, we walked into the living room and Diane went to the TV and turned it off.

"We have something to tell you," she started. Her dad slowly sat up (his head had been in her mom's lap). After we told them we were getting married, they seemed pleased and not completely stunned. As I learned over time, there is a great deal of difference about intra-family communication in a female dominant home as contrasted to my male dominant home. Her sister and parents had heard about me and there were probably more conversations than I would have ever imagined. Besides I had met Diane at the wedding which her sister and folks also attended. They had met me and probably saw the way I looked at her that evening. I picked Diane up for our first date wearing my army uniform and again met her family. I'm not sure how many evenings I spent with Diane during our courtship period, but in each case her family would have talked with me. My family was so different. I was living in the dorms and my folks only knew about our New Year's Eve date; and that was only because I asked for the car. I'm sure mom was curious, but I shared little about dating Diane (or anyone for that matter) and certainly would never have had a conversation with them about what I was thinking or even what my feelings were. Diane's folks would have had clues and would have overheard conversations (when I was there and when we talked on the phone). After we told her parents we were getting married we continued to tell them about our plans. They had fewer questions and challenges than I had expected. I did see concern, maybe some incredulity when we explained our timeline. The plan was based on love and hope. Diane's folks were practical but always supportive. Diane and her mom quickly went about making the arrangements and I followed along, helping with some of the details. So we were married on August 24, 1968 and the ceremony began at 7:00 PM. Our first daughter, Tara, would be born on August 24, 1971 at 7:00 PM exactly.

Surprisingly, the plan actually worked. I had no doubts; now as a father and grandfather, I can only cringe when I think of what Diane's parents and mine thought about such a plan. They must have thought we were crazy because, in a sense, we were. It may have been the best and worst of ideas; but it played out as I had imagined. (Did God smile or scratch His head?) We are still happily married!

Little did I know that marrying Diane would become the major factor in helping me shed many of my damaging chauvinistic ideas and feelings. The chapters in this section on Gender will include examples of my transformation. One of the key components in changing from living in a testosterone-dominant home to an estrogen-based family came with the birth of our daughters. Almost all of my friends expected our first child to be a son: how could Charlie have anything else? Our first two daughters, Tara and Kris, were born 25 months apart.

And now we have come full circle, back to the story with which I started this chapter: the birth of our third child, which was so radically different from Tara's birth in New Orleans. We were living in the Buffalo area and Diane's doctor thankfully embraced a more modern approach to childbirth. Our third child was coming 13 months after Kris, and I was excited and trying to put into practice the lessons we had learned the year before in Lamaze classes. As I was supporting Diane, I was looking down where the baby was soon to arrive. "Keep pushing. You can do it. Great. Breathe. Do you want the tennis balls?" These were some of my lame attempts at helping. The moment came, and I looked from my position of supporting Diane's back and saw the distinctive protrusion that was proof that I now had a son.

"Congratulations! It's a beautiful baby girl."

My first reaction was how could a physician not know the difference between a boy and a girl? When the nurses worked on Diane and congratulated us on our healthy little girl, I began to realize that what I had seen was the remainder of the umbilical, not a male organ. Quickly I became delighted and was relieved that Diane and Katie were doing just fine.

My male youth and early adult life were being overrun by a feminine culture that I still try to understand. Thus, we had three daughters three years apart. Our fourth came seven years after our third daughter was born. When we told people Diane was pregnant for a fourth time, a usual response was: "Well, Charlie, I guess you really want a son this time." My response: "No, not at all. I'm already overrun with females; one more won't change things."

I only told a couple of close friends that my real concern was with a baby boy having three older sisters. My image was that they would treat the poor boy as a doll and would overly feminize him. My gender stereotypes were still very entrenched in those days. Over time, with the help of the women in my life, I have become more attuned to these prejudices and biases. Over the years I have become more attuned to my feminine side (anima) also.

I think I experienced the emergence of my anima most acutely when Diane said we should go see the musical *Cats*. The experience was a moment of self-discovery and recognizing how much gender plays a role in the way we live and look at life. Diane has always loved musicals. I tolerated them then. I thought it was ridiculous to watch a show where two gangs ended up dancing on the street together; or when cowboys and farmers broke into song; or a former nun had children singing from the trees. The first time I saw *The Sound of Music*, I told my date that it should have ended at the wedding - that was long enough. But *Cats* changed me and my view of musicals forever. I can point to the exact song and the feelings I had for this transformation.

Having been brought up with cats, I marveled at the clever portrayal of feline personalities that T. S. Eliot had created and that Andrew Lloyd Webber and Tim Rice had set to music and dance. I had observed some of those feline characters while I was growing up. I found the music reinforcing the personalities and was enjoying a musical in a way I had never done before. Then Grizabella sang. She was the glamour cat seeking renewed purpose and acceptance. I gasped as I saw my mom and her life and my entanglement in all of Grizabella's feelings, trials, and challenges. It was the summer of 1985 and my mom was becoming more compromised almost daily with an illness that was robbing her of her ability to socialize and enjoy life (see Chapter 9 for details). Tears rolled down my cheek as the song "Memory" filled the theater. I felt a depth of emotion that I had never experienced before in any performance. The tears were for my mother, for me, for a life I wished she had had, and for a father I wished with whom I had had a better relationship. Since that day, musicals have had a significant impact on bringing out an emotional and artistic dimension in my life. Musicals and my own experiences in acting and performing (details will come later) have developed a Right Brain connection to my emotional self. I have come to see the value of balancing Yin and Yang in life, rather than allowing only one dimension to dominate my way of thinking or looking at the world.

As I have reminisced about how all of my girls have entered my life, I realize that marrying Diane and then having four daughters fundamentally changed my youthful conceptions of gender and what being male and female actually mean. Of course there are biological differences among the genders, but cultural and behavioral differences can be seen almost immediately. I think that the debate about whether gender is determined by nature or nurture seems to have created a false dichotomy. Our gender is both wired in our nature and influenced by our environment. For me, gender is one of the cultural factors in everyone's life: our gender matters.

When I taught, I would challenge my students with the idea that by improving the specificity of our language, we could enhance our understanding of gender. First I insisted on making a distinction between sex and gender. Sex meant physical contact and could be associated in a wide variety of behaviors and experiences. Sex was something we may do; it was not a biological classification. When filling out an application that asks for sex, I urged my students to be honest and say: sometimes, never, often, etc. Gender may include being male or female. Today sex refers to biological traits (genitalia, hormones, etc.) that differentiate between male and female. Gender relates to the cultural or societal attributes of people. These distinctions make a lot of sense to me. I hope I didn't confuse my students too much. Back in my teaching days, however, I would go on to tell students that we were not going to assume that there are only two genders. Gender is a continuum that may be defined as being male dominant at one end and female dominant at the other (realizing the definition of each was rather fluid and contingent upon context and perspective). Gay, lesbian, bisexual, non-binary fluid and transgender blend into the continuum and provide quite a rainbow of alternatives to the belief that there are only two genders. Our birth places us along this continuum and no one should ever have to fight to identify who s/he is. No one should be afraid to come out of a closet because no one should ever have to be in the closet in the first place. During our life, our gender continues to develop and takes on our own personal meaning.

CHAPTER 6
GENDER DIFFERENCES
AND THE HUMAN CONDITION

A woman's guess is much more accurate than a man's certainty.

Rudyard Kipling

I started writing this chapter during the Presidential election of 2016. After the Republican convention, a number of commentators stated their belief that the white male-dominated convention was trying to take the country back to a time in the '50s when all was grand, white, male dominant and ideal. As I reflect on my life, this mythical ideal of the '50s looms over my personal development. Over the decades following my youth I transformed the way I thought, felt and made decisions about gender. I now consider the notion that the '50s were somehow an ideal social time is mistaken and based upon misplaced conceptions of authentic social values.

My family was at the low end of the middle class; we lived in an older home when I was young, but at the age of 10, we moved to a new home in a suburban area of Niagara Falls. Our first home had a neighborhood filled with kids. We played continuously outside and invaded each other's lawns with impunity. Abutting the first house's back lawn was Bobby's back yard. The fence was made up of sections of two parallel, narrow logs notched into posts. They were perfect as horses or cars or whatever. Sliding between the parallel logs became a skill I enhanced over the years. My best move was to run and propel my body between the logs, then land, roll and stand on the other side without slowing down. Running through Bobby's yard led us to a circle that had no houses in the middle and was designated as our athletic field. Across the street was a playground with the requisite slides (one was short for sissies and the other was high for athletes), swings, a tee-ter-totter and a merry-go-round. Behind this playground was the Woods -- an ideal locale for imaginative boys to play. It had trees, bushes and tall weeds. There was one path leading into it from the playground. This path (a worn down entry) split about 1/3 of the way into our Woodland Wonderland. I seldom ventured to the other end of the Woods because we found our fort just before the path split. The fort was created by a couple of trees that had fallen in relatively parallel lines. The front of the fort was a tangle of branches and sticks that had been piled up to give us protection from our enemies. I don't know if any of us told our parents that we went into the Woods; I'm sure they knew and gave their tacit approval. None of the girls in the neighborhood ever went with us. They always stopped at the playground.

Our second home was in an area that was not as child play friendly as the first. Bill and I had friends, but the best places to go were down to the creek or to the nearby schools for their fields. Bill played by the creek far more than I did (probably because his best friend at the time lived in a house whose lawn abutted the creek). I found that I spent a lot of my playtime using my bike to travel to friends in other neighborhoods. One of the nearby schools was the exact location of the toxic dump ignominiously named Love Canal.

At the first home, I remember the parents chatting or drinking to-gether, smiling and having fun, but I don't remember very many large gatherings of families for parties or celebrations. One of the memorable moments of parental play came when our next door neighbor (Bob) chased my mom around the house with a garden hose. She squealed with laughter and feigned indignation. Bob followed her to a window and even sprayed into our screened porch that connected our living room with the garage. Despite that experience, this neighborhood seemed more children-driven than adult oriented (such is the assessment made by someone who hadn't yet reached 5th grade). Of course we all walked to 79th Street School (we were on Witkop and 84th).

When we moved to Moschel Court near 98th Street during the summer after my 4th grade, one of my neighborhood friends convinced me and then my parents that I should attend the private, Catholic school run by the parish in which we lived. I would automatically have friends and wouldn't have to deal with strangers; besides, "it was strict and taught religion all the time." Those words were for my parents, more than me. Although, that was the time in my life when I obeyed all orders, would never color outside the lines intentionally, and toed the line my folks set for me. As I think about it, that argument may have actually appealed to me too. My dad said that I could go as long as I walked (about a mile). He didn't want to have to pay for the bus.

When I petitioned to go to the private, all male Catholic High School four years later (with pressure from the nuns at school and the parish priests), he agreed to pay for the tuition, but again I had to walk. This time the distance was almost 3 miles (a very exciting experience during the winter snows and storms). I don't remember anyone ever giving me a car ride to school regardless of the weather. At our second home, the neighbor adults were more sociable. They started having monthly parties that rotated from house to house. In the summers, they were outside and in the winters in our basements. My dad finished the basement with a game room that had a bar, a dart board, a pool table, a half bath and a fridge. Children were not welcomed to the gatherings except at the yearly street party when the block was closed to traffic.

My childhood years were right out of the '50s family shows and I could readily identify with some of the television programs like "Leave It to Beaver" and "Father Knows Best". However, my dad's alcoholism and my mom's subconscious manner of creating a wedge between my dad and me were not reflected in the shows in those days. I learned about "triangu-larization" and what it meant much later in life. I may have felt the effects of this behavior, but I had no name or understanding of its dynamics while I was growing up. Maybe hidden beneath the veil of perfection of the families of the '50s were other types of dysfunction and disharmony. I shall leave that rumination to the reader.

I had no sisters so I had no direct experience to help me navigate the differences between boys and girls (male and female). Growing up during the 50s and 60s provided a social background that presented me with very stereotypic roles for the two genders. The following reflections and reminiscences will illustrate how my thinking was very stereotypical and superficial as I was growing up but how it slowly changed over time. Gender roles and identities have been shifting over the past 60 years and so have my attitudes and beliefs. I also have been thinking about whether my gender-oriented thinking really had anything to do with gender. It has taken time, but I'm now convinced that personality, up-bringing and personal preferences may explain differences far more accurately than attributing gender to my experiences. I'll explain these confusions in examples below.

As I consider the desire for some leaders who wish the United States could return to the '50s, I have come to realize that this is neither possible nor desirable. Women have become re-empowered since that time. I say re-empowered because women have always been leaders throughout history. Their primary roles may have seemed to be more subservient in the first half of the 20th century, but women really kept families together, worked in the factories during the wars, and continued to have influence in their communities. The second half of the last century saw women empower themselves by redefining their roles and what it meant to be a woman. This social force has not been universally accepted by men or even some women; nonetheless the shifts have occurred and the genie cannot be put back into the bottle. Nor should it be. A person's gender should not restrict opportunity nor define what social limits should be imposed. The stories that I use below are a way to walk through my life and illustrate how gender identity has shifted for me. In one sense these shifts reflect the broader social shifts that are quite recognizable within the United States. I hope my stories provide a way for you to assess your own feelings about gender differences in your life.

I learned fairly early in life that, yes, the male's job was to take care of the outside of the house: to mow, to care for the screens and to work on cars. My father tried to get me interested in working on the car. He had been successful with Paul but not with me. I'm sure part of it was that I didn't want to work with him. When I was young and helping him fix things, I was the gofer. He would bark out a tool, and I prayed that I knew what he was talking about. More than once I was called a knucklehead or *dummkopf* and I would sheepishly slink back to the toolbox hoping for divine revelation to guide my hand. I also found that I had no interest in cars or how they worked. When I was in 7th and 8th grade, I compensated for this weakness in my male-hood by making model cars and planes. A classmate had a great collection and encouraged me to make cool models. By the time we reached 9th grade, this connection was not strong enough for me to keep him in my inner circle of friends. I never have had a love for cars and making those models was not my passion, just a temporary way to make me feel male. That classmate was a good example for me of how people will come into and out of our lives for brief periods of time. He was one that never returned to my circle of friends even though we went to high school together. Our high school placed students into groups according to their academic skills. I was in the top group (Freshman 1), and he was in the last group (Freshman 3). Except for extracurricular activities or very close childhood friendships, this grouping often determined our social networks whether through making new friendships, keeping old buddies or losing prior ones. The daily routine and class assignments were oriented around the grouping assignments. After Diane and I married, her dad took me under his wing and taught me how to maintain my car. By then, necessity had kicked in and saving money became my motivator.

Another male outside task was the gardens. We tilled and planted and weeded. Mom's outside ventures were to hang clothes and help with the lighter chores of gardening: some weeding, planting and picking any vegetables. She would never edge the gardens or use a shovel for digging: it was okay for her to use a hand shovel to plant a flower. Mom's jobs were the indoor chores – dusting, vacuuming, dishes, cleaning, cooking, laundry, etc. To Dad's credit, he made us help mom with dishes, vacuuming, dusting, etc. He was adamant about respect: respecting him as the boss and breadwinner while respecting mom because she was our mother. Cooking was not necessary for us to learn, nor was the laundry. Dad relegated those tasks to mom and I never learned how to do laundry until mom gave me some lessons before I went to college. My only recollection of doing any laundry was the summer before going into the seminary. I was collecting my clothes from the washer and was going to hang them outside the way I saw mom do it. I instantly noticed that my tee shirts and briefs had changed color and realized that I had broken one of the two rules mom had tried to teach me. 1. Hot for towels and underwear only. 2. Don't mix whites with colored clothes. I have learned those two lessons well as an adult. The finer points still elude me.

One example of my cooking incompetence came when I was 11 or 12. Paul was having a party for some college friends, and it was a night for Mom and Dad to go out drinking. Paul wanted pizzas for the party, so Mom trained me on how to make her famous pizzas. She used the biscuits in the container that needed to be banged against a counter corner. I loved doing that for her because the pop was cool. That was not the problem. She had the sauce, pepperoni and cheese all ready for me. They were not the problem. She told me that all I had to do was roll out the biscuits, put the sauce, then cheese, then pepperoni on, place on a cooking tray and put in the oven for some designated temperature and heat. Almost none of those were the problem. Where the evening turned into a fiasco was when I decided to make the pizzas larger. My thought process: mom only rolls them out to "this" size; if I roll them out more, then the pizzas would be bigger and the guys would have more to eat. Having more to eat is always a good thing for real men. I guess I lacked the common sense to know that the diameter of the pieces did not actually increase the amount of pizza available. Of course the crust was now too thin for the time and temperature. Sauce, cheese and pepperoni on a crepe sized hockey puck is not a culinary masterpiece. Oh well, so cooking was/is not one of my talents, except for waffles (ask my grandchildren!).

Over the years with my own family, these roles of man works outside and woman works inside emerged and became redefined in very different ways. When my daughters were younger, they helped me in the gardens. I kept the roles rather gender driven. I dug up the weeds and they banged the dirt off and put the invaders in the bag. We all would plant but, of course, I was in charge. Diane and I would both water. I mowed the lawn and fertilized when necessary. Now I realize that those artificial roles should not have been so rigidly defined. When our youngest daughter died, gardening became a real escape for me. Our back yard is a testimony to my grief and a haven for me to see something tangible accomplished when I have been unable to do those things that a father is expected to do. I have always felt responsible for protecting my daughters, making sure their lives are safe, and that they have opportunities to be successful no matter which career road they choose to follow. In some ways I believe I have helped empower our daughters to become the incredibly successful mothers, wives, professionals and individuals that they are. Heidi's cancer was humbling and emasculating. I will deal with those issues and concerns about grieving in Part V.

Today, inside and outside are not as well defined for me as they were before. Diane does the cooking. Because of my incompetence I have imposed restrictions that Diane would readily lift if I showed any inclination to venture further than my current skill level. I often wash the dishes and clean the kitchen. We share in laundry duties (I can handle underwear, sheets and towels, but the colored stuff, pants and shirts are off limits.) The gardens in the front of our house are primarily Diane's. I help her with the preparing, planting, and weeding, but they are really hers. The backyard gardens are mine and the reverse is true. Diane helps me with the back, but the design and the majority of the work is mine. During my surgeries, she took over the mowing and trimming tasks. Although this may not be gender related (probably personality driven), our approaches to mowing are dramatically different. As I was growing up, my father made me mow the lawn in a particular way. For much of my youth, we had a hand-powered mower. Cutting in one direction was not sufficient. We HAD to mow in straight lines in one direction, then in straight lines in a perpendicular direction. There were no alternatives possible. This approach was most aggravating at our second home when the lawn at both sides of our house was rather narrow. I felt silly having to go back and forth when there was only about 6 feet between our house on one side and our neighbor's driveway on the other. Since Dad often watched me mow, I had to follow his instructions. When we finally got our first power mower, my father declared that there would be no short cuts permissible. Perpendicular mowing was still the only acceptable method. (I did cheat whenever I thought he stopped monitoring my task.) To this day I still mow in straight lines, curving only along the garden borders or around our peach tree in the front yard. The curving ceases as soon as straight lines can be etched into the grass. I refuse to double cut in a perpendicular fashion; I'm now the father and can decide what is right for our home. Diane, on the other hand, employs the full power of her right brain and takes the mower on a journey of discovery around the lawn. The indentations of the tire treads create patterns that I could never and would never try to emulate. In fact, no two mowings are alike. I have come to learn that my father's voice in my head is not the final arbiter of right and wrong, good way or bad way.

Mowing the lawn is a silly and simple example of a much more important lesson in my life. Difference is not only acceptable; it is preferable. Being me does not require that I behave like others because in many cases I cannot. (Just ask my grandchildren about my version of dancing.) I do not have to accept others' behavior that is immoral or illegal. But I do need to open up to the vast differences in style, taste, culture, etc. I no longer treat gender differences as one better than the other. Using comparative language can be demeaning and/or destructive. The stereotypical male drive to be bigger, stronger, or correct all the time now seems rather childish and sometimes downright silly. Mine does not have to be bigger than yours. I no longer have the need to be driven by this comparative monster. Comparative language or competitive juices are great for sports or games, as long as they don't go to extremes. I'll be coming back to this theme throughout this chapter.

My mom stayed home and never had an outside job. She made a number of crafts (jewelry, cigarette trays, and painted our curtains). As a child, I did encounter women who worked outside of the home, but I don't remember thinking much about this issue. My mom stayed home and wasn't that the norm? In a sense this may have been at the root of my dad's control over my mom. "I provide; you take care of the home and boys." It was an underlying assumption in our home: this was the way it should be. When Dad died, Mom thought about getting a job but started dating rather quickly and married before she had to work. She again stayed home after she remarried. Diane's mom stayed home to raise her daughters, but went to work at a local bank when they were older. She had worked in the financial office at J. C. Penny's in Winona, Minnesota, when she met Diane's dad. She was very good at both of her jobs, and I saw how important this competence was for her self-worth and self-identity. When I graduated from college and was accepted into the graduate program at Tulane, I did not receive a fellowship and did not have a Teaching Assistant position for my first year. Diane and I agreed that she would teach and support us as I pursued my

Masters, then Ph.D. In a sense this was a role reversal for me, but it didn't seem to register as that significant. I know my dad was perplexed: first that I would pursue degrees in philosophy ("What do you do with that?") and second that I wouldn't be the breadwinner when we got married. He had tried to instill in me that the man was in charge, made the money, made the decisions, and deserved the respect for such things.

Starting my third year of graduate school, I had completed all of my course work, competency exams and language requirements and, thus, did not need to be on campus every day. So I started teaching religion at a suburban high school and Diane continued working (her third year as a second grade teacher). During a couple of summers, both of us got jobs. One summer we ran a day camp for kids at a Presbyterian Church. It was six weeks long (three sessions of two weeks each). Another summer we worked for a YMCA. When she became pregnant, we agreed that if at all possible she would stay home and I would support us. I do not believe this decision was based on any preconceived idea I had about gender roles and working; rather it was based on our mutual value that one of us should be home with our children: having a PhD gave me more earning power than her BS degree. We felt that if she stayed home, she would be creating an environment that we wanted to provide for our daughters. I don't remember if it was a conscious consideration or just a sub-conscious one, but Diane was better with children than I was/am. It was not just her teaching skills; it was also her temperament and willingness to interrupt a task in order to attend to our daughters' needs or wants. I am more task-oriented and would tend to complete a task before spending time with my girls. This was especially true when I had to concentrate on trying to fix the car or attend to plumbing problems. I am convinced that we made the correct decision about Diane staying home. I believe there is a vast difference between those who believe women must stay home and raise the children (based on a model of control for the male) and those who believe a parent should stay home with his or her children. We adopted the latter model.

It is a value preference in how we as parents can structure and provide a supportive environment for child-rearing. I saw how my father had to control my mom, and I vowed to change that attitude in my life. If I hadn't, I wouldn't be married to Diane.

As a male I have become aware of my control drives and will illustrate them in the following pages; however, control is not the basis for our marriage or the dominant value in our family. Male control can become very destructive and not just for the man's partner. Having to be in control seems to diminish opportunities and narrow one's perspective. As my dad's alcoholism began to control his life, he began to control mom's life even more, which I believe contributed to her socializing and having fun with others. As a teen I have mentioned my late night conversations with her and as I reflect back on those nights I can see the destructiveness of male control. A male dominant relationship is out of balance and seems to be an extreme that diminishes everyone. Of course a female dominant relationship has its issues too. One of our neighborhood couples illustrated this point for me. The wife dominated everything so much that my folks often said "poor Richard!" Having a balanced and healthy life that minimizes extremes is a central theme for me as I try to understand human interrelationships. I am sure that my male dominant upbringing has crept into decisions I've made or actions I've taken (consciously and unconsciously).

"Stop crying or I'll give you something to cry about." Those words still ring in my ears long after the echoes of their uttering are gone. As boys, my brothers and I were taught that crying was for girls or sissies. It was okay for Mom to cry, not for us. Of course the crying was only the symptom; the real issue was keeping our emotions in check: self control was drummed into my head by my father and by the Catholic school training I experienced. It certainly was reinforced by the stoicism of my Kentucky farm relatives. By high school there was a strong emphasis upon controlling sexual drives: these were sinful and would diminish you somehow.

Our football coach reinforced this sentiment with his dictum of not being able to date during the football season.

I remember a public humiliation for me, which occurred in 8th grade. I was on the school's basketball team and during one of our games a teammate suddenly stopped and swung around with his elbows up. (This was the guy who had the great model car collection.) I didn't see this move in time, and my eye and his elbow collided in a jarring stoppage of my run up court. I screamed out in pain and actually cried for a brief moment. It was the shock and pain of it. But I was embarrassed and ashamed that I wasn't man enough to just take the hit and keep going. The only consolation was a beautiful black eye that gave me some status for a few days. Shiners on an eighth grade boy were true badges of courage. I told myself that this loss of control should never happen again. During my three years of high school football, I was injured quite often and was always willing to play hurt. I have a deformed little finger because I got it dislocated during a game and didn't want to miss a play, so I popped it back into place. This occurred numerous times afterward and I just kept popping it back until it became permanently restructured.

I mentioned in the last chapter how I made the high school football team and dealt with a very uncomfortable sensation. In addition to that experience I also dealt with water on my calves and three concussions (I think). One occurred when I was kicked in the face when tackling a runner from behind. The cleats went through my meager face bar (not a mask back then) and missed my eye, but I was completely disoriented when I stood up with cuts over and under the eye. I do remember staggering around until somebody guided me to the sidelines. Again I had a black eye as a badge of honor. This incident occurred on a Saturday (my folks' anniversary); by Monday I was back practicing fully. The other concussions occurred during more routine plays. In those days we just called it "getting dinged." Each time I went back into the game a few plays after being hit in the head. The coach asked me if I knew where I was. When I answered correctly, I assume, I went back in but don't remember anything else about either game. In addition to those incidents, I remember a game when I was headed down field on a kick-off to block one of the defenders. He was about 300 pounds and as my 160 pound frame launched for what I thought was a picture perfect block he swung his leg and kicked me full force in my ribs. I had the wind knocked out of me but didn't hear any cracks and saw no flag. Not wanting to show any weakness, I bounced up and grinned at him. For my last game of my career, I played with a broken clavicle. I adjusted the way I tackled and used the other shoulder. Thus, as a teen I bought into the male model of toughness: play hurt, don't cry, control emotions, be dominant in any situation, and always use your competitiveness to win. In differing ways I dealt with these attitudes over my life and believe they are now in a healthier balance.

My competitiveness was deeply instilled in my youth. It was reinforced in many ways especially through sports. One powerful, yet maybe subtle cause for my competitive attitude, came from playing cards with my father. I learned to play Pinochle when I was 5 or 6. By the time I was 7 or 8 I was being taught how to remember the cards being shown during the meld portion, thereby figuring out who had what cards and how they would play. By the time I was 10, I was playing with my father and our next door neighbor, Jake. I received 25 cents per week for an allowance. My father said I needed to learn about the cutthroat world, so he decided to include me in cutthroat Pinochle: three players, 25 cents into the kitty every time you are set, and 25 cents into the kitty if you lose. The winner took the kitty. The object is to reach 100 points and each time one player bids and got the three card kitty, the other two played against him: cutthroat. No one rooted or supported the other; everyone was out for himself. We played often and eventually I was holding my own. These games lasted for a few years. Jake may have taken a little pity on me because he hired me to mow and trim his lawn (a means for replenishing my Pinochle funds). There was little extraneous talking during the games. The men usually had beers; I had a pop when dad allowed it.

When Diane and I were in our graduate school apartment, we met our now lifelong friends from the Netherlands. As poor graduate students we looked for inexpensive ways to socialize. We would have each other over for dinner a couple times a week and we introduced each other to our country's cuisine and customs. We bought cheap tennis rackets and often played on the courts next to our apartment building. We also played cards. One thing we taught them was how to play Pinochle (they taught us a couple of Dutch games). Both Peter and Tiny were mathematicians and Peter was/is competitive like me. Diane saw my competitiveness very clearly then. Both Peter and I could determine with considerable certainty who had which cards. There are unwritten strategies for how to lay down the most effective cards during the play portion of each hand. We generally followed these strategies and were very compatible partners. Our wives, however, became real challenges for us. Not only because they would get better cards dealt to them more often than we desired, but even more so for their unorthodox style of play. It was difficult to determine what card they would play. More than once Peter and I scratched our heads over a hand and its outcome.

The worst example of my competitiveness came when Donna, Diane's sister, visited us in New Orleans. She was attending college in Oswego, New York and came to stay with us for about a week. One night we were playing cutthroat Pinochle. I was playing cutthroat and the sisters were playing for enjoyment. The contrast was very unsettling for them. I came across as rude and obnoxious without even realizing I was behaving in such a manner. I have tried to temper this competitive spirit, but it does sneak its head into life, sometimes, without warning. Again I believe balance makes more sense. Competitiveness in and of itself is not evil or wrong but when it goes to an extreme it is unhealthy for everyone involved. It certainly is a virtue in sporting events; it isn't in family relationships. I taught my daughters to be competitive while playing a wide variety of board and card games while they grew up. Diane often did not participate. Unlike some fathers, I did not let my girls win. I did, however, make sure I curbed my cutthroat drive. I was trying to find the balance between playing hard and playing for fun. I hope I instilled a healthy balance of competitiveness and fun in games with my girls.

In my adult years I have come to learn that I always play sports hard. I don't believe it is predicated on having to win as much as it is based on playing to the best of my abilities or to the fullest extent possible. I'm sure from the outside my behavior may be seen as wanting to win. It truly isn't. It's all about doing my best. Always. The clearest example of this is racquetball. During my tenure at Canisius, I played this routinely twice a week for decades. The players changed a bit over the years, but there was a core group for a long period of time. We all played hard and I consciously never kept score. I was there for the exercise and camaraderie. The sign of my aggressive style was the knee pads I had to wear to protect myself from diving and landing on the floor that was a frequent style of my play. I tried playing handball with one of the guys but almost knocked myself out one day when I ran into the wall. I was knocked backwards and ended on my back. I saw stars (maybe another concussion?). I decided that I would stick with racquetball because that wasn't a contact sport (except with the floor). Of course, sports and contact occurred years later in an unexpected fashion. Diane and I joined a couple's neighborhood bowling league. It didn't take long for the neighbors to start a betting poll on me. For no reason anyone could figure out and I could never predict or control, I would fall sometime during the three games. I always flew into the air, turned my body as I was off my feet and land squarely on my hands and knees without going over the foul line. I couldn't pull off that maneuver if I consciously tried to do so. The betting centered on which frame and which game my patented move would occur. Since it was such a random happening, it lent itself naturally for humor and betting. No one ever figured out how and why I did this. It only happened once a night and I still don't know how or why.

Over time I have learned that my competitive drive is not really defined by my gender, even though that was how my experience was defined in my youth and by my high school football coach. Competitiveness is not gender specific. I do believe that over-competitiveness is getting out of control in youth sports. I have umpired and coached softball and hardball. Early in my career at Canisius I wrote an article with a member of the Physical Education Department about the psychological abuse in youth sports. We were even on local radio shows discussing this topic. I was and remain convinced that youth (all ages before high school) should compete in sports but the leagues, coaches and parents should be emphasizing participation, fun and learning the game. Playing cutthroat, being driven only to win trophies, and only playing the best players is detrimental for a healthy approach to youth sports. High school seems to be an appropriate age to introduce competition as exclusive and talent driven. Handing out trophies and awards for every participant also seems to be an extreme. Encouragement is a virtue; derision and belittling the other team is not. Parents should not try to be living vicariously through their children. I have seen unbelievable cruelty and abuse by parents and coaches who scar children and implant an unhealthy stereotypic attitude toward sports and winning at all costs.

When I was working at the YMCA in New Orleans, one of my duties was to manage a basketball clinic for young boys and organize pick-up games at night. The usual suspects for the evening games included a couple of former college players, some former high school players and a father and son. The son was 16 and showed considerable talent but no drive or enthusiasm. I had two of his brothers in my clinic. Over time I learned a couple of things. First, the father had each son start a five days/week work-out regimen when they turned five. Each one was required to participate in at least three different sports, preferably football, basketball and baseball. He was preparing them to become college scholarship recipients in at least one of the sports. When I talked to the 16 year-old in private, I learned that he was already burnt out. He no longer liked sports and resented his father. This example was a motivator for me to emphasize the love of the game and the importance of sportsmanship over having to win being the primary motivator. Years later I taught an Ethics and Sportsmanship course in our graduate program for Sports Administration. I used this experience as an example for future coaches and athletic directors for the dangers that parents may create for their children. I applaud the parental exceptions and the coaches who share my vision of youth sports: opportunities to help children learn how to respect others while competing, who emphasize exercise and physical activity, and who bolster a child's sense of balance between learning how to compete and how to have fun. I still espouse a very throw back attitude: sportsmanship is a far more valuable lesson for youth to learn than winning.

As a young male I needed to be tough, build up muscles and show strength of character as well as being physically strong. Showing any type of vulnerability was anathema. This attitude became reinforced in my military training: always show strength, learn your vulnerabilities but never let them show or be seen. In a sense, this attitude has led me to deal with pain in unhealthy ways at times. In 2001 my then 28-year old daughter, Kris, gave me a weekend with her in Wellsboro, Pennsylvania. It was a way for us to share something we loved and to give me a break from my care giving for Heidi (see Chapter 10). Kris loved horses starting at a very young age; and we had had some interesting riding experiences throughout her life. For example, one of our family camping trips was to Prince Edward Island. While we were staying on the island we decided to go horseback riding one day. The adventure started out ominously but ended with a great experience for Kris and me. It started when the six of us, in our 8 passenger, red and white van, saw the sign for riding. It said to take the next right. Little did I know that I took the incorrect right turn. We began to proceed on a small island "road" which began to narrow, became a path and ended at a stream at the back of someone's property. As I backed up and turned around the girls shrieked and dove under the seats when they saw a car stop at the "road" and watch as we foreigners found our way off their property. We finally did find the proper stables. Heidi got to ride on a pony in the stable area with Diane as I went out with our older daughters on the trail. As we were finishing our ride, the guide asked if any of us were experienced. Kris immediately said that she was (she had taken lessons and really was adept). Of course, I also said I was because that's what I had to do. "OK, come back at 5:00. We take the horses out to the wooded area; then let them loose to run back to the barn so they can have some real exercise," said our guide. Kris was delighted. I summoned my usual: I can do this attitude. We had a wonderful time and the horses really did race back to the stable area. Kris could not have been more excited. I just held on to my horse's reins.

So, this weekend in Pennsylvania was supposed to be a special treat – another opportunity for us to create memories. It included a Friday night stay in Wellsboro with full day riding on Saturday, spending the night in a cabin in sleeping blankets with the others who were on the ride and a long Sunday morning ride. We had a delightful evening in Wellsboro and the portents for the weekend looked good. The problem was when we started the riding portion. The handler did not tighten my saddle securely. The horse I was on became spooked when a tree limb snapped (the crack sounded like a rifle shot). We were riding down the side of a hill so I was already leaning forward and the horse's head was down. At the sound of the crack the horse bucked and the loose saddle and I went over the horse's head. I landed on my back and side with the saddle next to me. I was hurt. The leaders immediately came to my assistance and asked if I needed to see some medical personnel. Instead of being intelligent and reasonable, my deep seated, "show no weakness male-hood" blurted out: "I'm okay, let's get going." Big mistake. They re-saddled the horse and I swung my leg over, trying to hide the grimace that accompanied the bolt of pain. Riding in this pain, lying on a wood floor in a sleeping bag, and roughing it for a day and a half was not smart. I did not see a doctor when I got home, principally because I was concerned with my youngest daughter's cancer. We had to focus on her, and I could live with a little discomfort. Today, I suffer from a variety of physical problems. I am sure that many of them are the result of my abuse of my body because of this toughness attitude caused by the male stereotypes that have driven me, consciously and sub-consciously throughout my life. The attitude of being always strong and tough certainly has physical consequences in life. It also has psychological ones, especially if the male remains unaware of his attitude and the con-sequent behaviors. Sometimes one has to endure pain; other times it is foolish to do so. On a battlefield dealing with pain can be the difference between life and death. Maybe casually riding with a daughter should not be such a time.

Living with five women has slowly had an awakening effect upon me (and not just about keeping the toilet seat down). When I taught cross cultural courses or components within other courses I emphasized to the students that the more they learned about other cultures the more they would become aware of their own American culture. Contact and knowl-edge about others should always have a clarifying impact on us. Learning about and encountering other cultures allow a person to see what cultural assumptions we have taken for granted. My doctoral dissertation was on a topic related to a French philosopher's (Henri Bergson) ideas about time. I love the topic of time and it is a wonderful tool for seeing cultural differ-ence. One topic that I would cover is Edward Hall's discussion of the mis-understanding between American Caucasians and the Hopi in the 1930s.

American engineers began a series of building projects on the Hopi res-ervation and needed some Hopi to help them with heavy duty work. The Americans were appalled at the laziness and unreliability of the Hopi. They didn't show up on time, would take breaks when they weren't scheduled and different men would show up each day. They couldn't rely on the men they had initially hired to do the work. Hall's study showed that the two cultures view and experience time differently. For Americans time is equated with the clock. We schedule our lives; often eating at the same time each day. Work days have scheduled break and lunch times. Tasks are often time connected; engineers will estimate the length of time it will take to do a task. The Hopi, on the other hand, have no clock time orientation. They eat when they are hungry, sleep or rest when they are tired, work when they have energy, and have a tribal sense of responsibility. The Hopi's commitment to the Americans was from the tribe, not from individuals. The Hopi saw no reason to report to work at a particular time and they had no sense that just certain men were responsible for the job. They did their tribal tasks and those who were available went to fulfill tribal responsibilities. They didn't understand why Americans would stop working when they weren't tired and wondered why they would work when they were too tired to do the job correctly. It is far more complex, but this explanation should make the point. Although I wanted my students to learn about Hopi culture, I always emphasized what they could learn about their own culture and what they assumed or took for granted in their view of life. I believed my students took away more self-awareness than they did learning the details of another culture.

As my wife and daughters affected me over the years, I have become aware of my maleness and some of the strengths, weaknesses, advantages and disadvantages that have characterized my life and attitude. My experience at *Cats* became a profound shift for me: I could cry and allow my inner feelings to come to the surface. My life with my women provided a constant dose that has helped me touch my creative, Right Brain self. A silly example will illustrate this shift. I am notoriously known for a complete lack of fashion sense. I am often sent back to the closet to get clothes that go together. "No Hon" or "No Dad" or "Those colors don't match" or "You don't wear casual and dressy together" etc. have been common refrains (even now). I've learned some basic principles but have to confess that I have never really been all that interested in what I wear. I never buy clothes for myself (except socks and underwear). This indifference has really never changed in my life. There have been occasions and times when I have tried to comply and pay attention. Certainly in the military and on the drill team, I was fastidious with my uniform and the polishing of my brass and boots. I would never go outside uncovered (not wearing a cap/hat). As I mentioned earlier, Diane and I met while standing up for mutual friends at a wedding. In the early years of our marriage and while the older girls were growing up, I attributed my fashion indifference to being male. Of course, I believed while I was young that gay individuals were very fashion conscious because that's what gay meant. Worrying about what clothes to wear was for sissies (another stereotypic sentiment that was drilled into my head from childhood). My associating fashion consciousness with gender made sense to me long into my adulthood. Slowly I began to realize that this association was more of a personality trait than a gender characteristic. Two of my sons-in-law have clearly shown me the fallacy in my stereotypes because of their clear sense of fashion.

One beautiful example of the influence my daughters have had on me comes with the experience I had with my youngest Heidi's "make-over day." It was during her battle with leukemia (see Chapter 10 for details). She said that she wanted Diane and me to go on a date and she wanted to make each of us over. She was passionate about the theater and had developed an acute fashion sense. She took me to have my hair styled (not too outlandishly). This is another area of great indifference to me. When we were first married we bought a kit so Diane could cut my hair. She hated doing so because she wasn't trained. I said it didn't matter; I just didn't want it to get too long. My unruly colic always annoyed her. Years later she finally rebelled and told me to go to a barber. I hated spending the money and still remain quite indifferent to my hair style (maybe others don't even see it as a style). My reason for getting a hair cut now is my dislike for long hair because it feels uncomfortable and wrong. I have no idea how to define wrong in this case. After the hair cut Heidi took me shopping: new shirt, trousers, tie and shoes. Diane was also refashioned but she didn't have very far to go. We got reservations for the evening and enjoyed a memorable night out looking stylish. I had learned much earlier that hair styles and fashion were important to the women in my life. I just have never shared the feeling or need to adjust my attitude to match theirs. This make-over day was a way for me to say to Heidi, and Diane, that I got it and accepted it, just don't expect me to change my indifference. I do think it is important to understand the difference that individual personalities or genders may have when it comes to such things as style and fashion. Certainly the stereotypes that follow a person's fashion sense can lead to real prejudices and even discrimination. In today's world clothing, piercings, tattoos, hairstyles, etc. can create chasms between people. It is easy to attach judgments on how someone looks. It is time for all of us to get beyond this superficial stereotyping.

When I was teaching high school in New Orleans (1970-72), I started a drug awareness program. Drug use and abuse was rather wide spread in the school, but the administration and faculty lived in a world of complete denial (so did most parents). It is impossible to know what effect the training and advising that I did may have had. I do know that one night I received a frantic call from a girlfriend of one of the young men who was involved with my training. He had overdosed and was passed out on his front lawn. I told her to take him to a "pumping station" - the horrid name given to a clinic that dealt with drug abuse/overdose. I spent the night with him and his recovery seemed to take a positive turn over the following months when I worked with him. Ironically his mother was the principal's secretary, and she threatened to sue me for not getting her permission (to save her son's life?). The principal interceded and she relented. It was in this environment that I learned that the majority of students were divided into three primary groups: jocks, pukes, and fruits.

Children and youth can be very cruel to one another. Bullying is certainly not new. Name calling, placing tags on others, and the effects that such behaviors can have scar children for a long time. Many of these scars may never become noticed or addressed in a healthy way. The scarring, however, occurs not just for the victims but also for the perpetrators. They are defining themselves and their relationships with others predicated on stereotypes and myths that are unhealthy, sometimes nasty, and always hurtful. In first grade I remember hearing kids chant to me: "fatty, fatty two by four can't get through a bathroom door." I have absolutely no recollection of my feelings or response to such taunts. One of the major victories of my youth came in fourth grade. At the end of the year we had a field day at the school that featured races as the culmination of the festivities. The high light was the 50-yard dash. Each grade level had two heats to determine the fastest in each of the classes. I won both heats and came up against one of the school's notorious bullies in the finals. He was fast and the in-crowd knew he would win. My class rallied behind me and cheered all the way. I have vivid recollections of this race (little else from that school year). He started out fast and had a quick lead. I heard the cheers and hit a gear I had never known existed. I pulled up to him about 2/3 of the way to the end line. He looked at me with disdain, but I just powered ahead and won. The cheers were a vindication for justice - the good guy had won. His illusion was shattered. Of course, this feeling of elation and sense of justice was probably just in my head but it has always stuck with me. It told me that I might be special and that I might accomplish important things in my life. It also reinforced my belief that there is justice in the world and good will overcome evil.

Back to the high school classifications I noted above: The school was all male and seemed to be dominated by chauvinistic attitudes and behaviors. Jocks ruled. That attitude has certainly remained with America over the decades. The football team was a perennial winner and the basketball team went to the state championship my second year of teaching. I found that I had special relationships with all three groups. First, the jocks. My first teaching experience involved a last period class of church history to 40 seniors, 35 of whom were members of the football team. After I held roll call on the first class, all 35 stood up and started to leave. I screamed "Where are you going?" The spokesman said that they always left after the prayer to get ready for practice and the teachers always let them go. Those teachers were Christian Brothers (I was the first lay religion teacher) and it shocked me to think that they would be so lax with religious education. So much for that stereotype, besides football rules in the South! I didn't pause in my response to the assembled mass, "Not me. Sit down!" They didn't know what to do but reluctantly sat down and figured that their coach would straighten me out. After class I marched down to the coach and told him that I wanted those boys in class every day and that the discipline of going to class was a valuable lesson for them. He smiled, shook my hand and said that he was impressed that someone with a spine had finally stopped this abuse.

That class was tumultuous for the entire term. The students hated being in class and gave me a hard time. One of the lesson blocks was putting Martin Luther on trial. Another was using the musical *Jesus Christ Superstar* to study early Christianity. I was trying to introduce some theatrics into this overly testosterone group. On the last day I came into class and saw a bottle of Wild Turkey and a thank you letter from the guys. I don't know whose idea it was, but they seemed to finally get what I was trying to teach them. They may not have learned one thing about Martin Luther or Catholic Church history, but they did learn a lesson about respect and discipline. As it turned out, I ended up serving as a timer for the track team for some of the home meets and played some pick-up basketball with the football players after school in the off season. I also played in the faculty vs. basketball team game each year. The year the team went to the state championship our star center's foot crashed onto mine under the basket (why I was there I can only blame on my competitive juices) and broke my toe. Of course, I did not leave the game and pretended it didn't hurt until the game was over. I never had any health care person look at it.

My relationship with the "pukes" revolved around the drug program that led me to know about pumping stations and where they were located. "Pukes" was the term used for the drug users, whether they were heavy abusers or recreationally oriented. I was affiliated with a city wide effort to teach high school students about drug use/abuse so they could go into middle schools to discourage those students from abusing drugs. In my mind the real benefit was for the high school students to learn about the realities of drugs and not just be influenced by what they were learning on the street. Some of the street myths were frightening. For example, peanut butter was a slang term for morphine at the time. A couple of cases of students actually melting peanut butter and using a syringe to inject it occurred in the city. One of my students liked to get high by tailgating buses on his moped to inhale the exhaust fumes. Another confessed that he "smoked somethin' " and beat up his girlfriend while high. He didn't know what got into him. Salad parties were scary occurrences. Students would raid their parents' medicine cabinets and bring pills with them. Everyone in attendance would drop their stash into a big bowl and party goers would help themselves to its contents throughout the night. The weed in New Orleans was always cut by using chopped up tennis balls or any other grass like substance to increase the profits of the sellers.

My relationship with the third group, the "fruits" needs some context. I have loved the theater since high school. In my senior year I was trying to run away from home while still living there. I was overextended in so many diverse programs: senior class president, football co-captain, editor of the year book, Honor Society president, reader at the masses, basketball announcer, co-lead in the senior play, class Salutatorian and member of the choir (a real joke). This jump into hyper drive away from home and alleged "big man on campus" started in my junior year. I had had a surprisingly good first year on the varsity football team. In January I decided to try out for the school's play: *No Time for Sergeants*. The lead was a hick and my southern roots had prepared me with an accent that no one else could match. The experience was transformative. I developed the confidence to speak in public, which I have done in a wide range of venues, styles, and topics ever since. It catapulted me into being popular because the play was a resounding success. I also learned how to ad lib and feel comfortable with going off book or script. One of the other characters and I had a scene that just included the two of us. We had a lot of fun during rehearsals making up dialogue. We drove the director crazy, but he saw an advantage in that some of our lines were actually funnier than the original script. He relented and told us that we could ad lib as long as we used the proper cue lines to bring in the other characters when our scene was finished. No rehearsal or performance was like any other. That confidence, too, has been a feature of my public speaking. When I preach, I almost always have a written sermon but will always ad lib and change what I say as I'm going along. I truly loved my first acting experience.

During my senior year I was the co-lead in *Charlie's Aunt*, a distinctly different play. My character had a scene in which I had to kiss a girl. This was quite an experience for me - being a rather prudish sort who was VERY inexperienced with girls. I remember during Chemistry class during my junior year receiving instructions from the guy who shared my lab table. He told me I was taking a very popular girl to the prom (she probably agreed because of my football and acting fame). He knew I was incompetent and tried to prepare me for how I was supposed to act. I really blew it because I decided to wear white socks with my tux and take off my shoes at the dance so I could be the hick character from the play for some of my friends' dates. They had convinced their dates that I really was from the South and they wanted to continue the ruse during the prom. I fell hook, line and sinker for the role.

"Golly girls, it sure is cold up 'ear", was my first gambit. My friends' dates giggled. One asked: "Have you seen the Falls?"

"No m'am, it's just been too dang cold."

"Did you know you can slide down the Falls," was a prepared line from one of my friends.

"Well, golly gee, that would just be a hoot," was my prepared reply. The banter continued in this vain for awhile. It did not go well for my friends when their dates learned that we had been conning them the whole time. I saw their displeasure in the parking lot as the prom ended. I don't know if any one of us would have opted out of the prank if we knew the outcomes. Needless to say, my date and I never went out again.

The play's director decided to enter a scene from our senior play in a high school theater competition for Western New York. The scene included me kissing the girl, proclaiming "I've done it; by George I've done it," then chasing another character off, then back onto the stage. At the competition all was going well until my Eton, starched collar snapped up when I made my proclamation. The timing was perfect even if it was unscripted. At that age I didn't catch the symbolism of the malfunction. I tried to tame the wayward board when running behind the scenes but to no avail. When I returned on stage I threw in the line: "This collar has become quite unseemly." I received a medal for my performance and remember one of the judges commenting that my composure with a costume malfunction was impressive.

During my senior year the play director came to me in December and asked me to join the choir. I told him that he had heard me sing in music class and I had a tin ear and a horrible singing voice. He said it didn't matter. He wanted me and a couple other football players to join the choir to take away the stigma it had to the student body. He said I was a leader in the school (which I honestly had never realized). If jocks and school leaders were singing, then it would be acceptable to other students. Before that time the priest had had a terrible time trying to recruit students to participate. At an all male school getting football players to participate fed into the strange notion that athletic ability equals acceptability and acceptability was somehow bestowed upon all who participated with the players. He added: "We're singing with the girls' choir at our performance and will have joint rehearsals." That was a worthwhile selling point! So my best friend, whose voice was comparably awful, and I joined. We made quite an impression during dress rehearsal. The guys were standing on bleachers. My friend and I didn't know how to actually sing the notes in front of us. Our skill was in being able to read music and know when we should be going up or down. Landing on the actual note wasn't the point - just heading our voices in the right direction was our goal. We would nudge each other to do so. During that fateful rehearsal we were nudging each other and singing what we thought might be near the prescribed notes. The problem was that in our eagerness to help each other we failed to watch the Director who had stopped the performance. Everyone else was silent. The laughter at our sour, off tone cattle sounds was so intense that a couple of my friends stumbled off the bleachers as they doubled over (as only high school guys can do when they diminish someone else who errs, especially in front of girls). For the performance my friend handed out programs and I was in charge of lighting. Sigh. But I did date one of the girls from the choir until I went to the Seminary. Thus, I was familiar with the arts/music/theater dynamics in high school.

In New Orleans the "fruits" were these guys. Ridiculed by the jocks and ignored by many of the pukes, they lived in an orbit unto themselves. Although the high school was noted for its athletic successes, the theater program was equally renowned; in fact, it had won statewide competitions over many years. The director was dynamic and organized three or four plays each year. During the spring semester of my first year at the school, the director came to me and asked if I would be willing to perform. He was intent upon blending faculty and students. The play was *Julius Caesar*. He wanted me to play Caesar, probably because I may have looked a bit like Julius in those days. I thought about it but decided to forego the invitation. I told him I was preparing for my Comprehensive Exams (18 hours of written torture) and starting to work on my dissertation, while also preparing my classes at the high school and coordinating the drug program. Of course, Diane was an important part of my life too. I said that I couldn't take the time to do so. I have thought back about that decision and wished I had tried to follow my heart and do what would have been a wonderful experience. I went to many of their performances and would look in on their rehearsals periodically. This group had a special place in my heart, especially when they performed *The Diary of Anne Frank*.

So I interacted with each of the groups at the school and, of course, ignored the stereotypes and labels that cast students into one of these pools. Each group had its preset views of the other groups, which became barriers among them. Some pukes were fruits, but not many. I remember that I wasn't startled at the naming of each of the groups. The words were the common parlance of the day and the stereotypes were almost socially prescribed. The pecking order was clear: jocks way on top, pukes on the bottom, with the fruits being deemed irrelevant. Bright students who would be called nerds today didn't belong anywhere. The jocks were in the gym, the pukes at the railroad tracks behind the school property and the fruits with the theater director. All the other students went in their own directions. I was struck by the power of the words used to name each of the groups. It horrified me then but didn't seem to faze the students. They accepted the tags as being accurate - even for themselves. The one lesson I learned from these experiences was the ability to diminish the power of labels over oneself. I may have been "fatty, fatty" in elementary school, but I won the big race in 4th grade. Labels are destructive when they eviscerate their target. When individuals fall for the labeling and then find themselves in a spiral of self-fulfilling behaviors the tragedy of prejudice becomes compounded. It is so important for people who are targets to find their own inner worth and not allow the labelers to have any power over them. This may be way too easy for me to say, however. The dynamics are so very complex. Shedding the slings of labeling is not easy, sometimes not even possible. What is true is that this practice is unjust. I have seen males who emphasize the athletic and demean the arts as some ritual dance to show power and dominance. It reminds me of the line from Shrek: "He must be compensating for something." Diminishing others to assert one's status is an all too common form of ignorance, prejudice and bigotry.

As I was going through these experiences when I was in high school and, then, while teaching high school, so many of the behaviors were associated with being male. Playing sports, especially football, was a male enterprise. Diane told me she was a tomboy growing up – loving to play ball with the boys in the neighborhood. I never really had that experience – a girl playing sports with me – until Diane and I used to play catch, then tennis together. Realizing that sport was not just male dominated slowly began to dawn on me. By the time my daughters were born I became intent upon them playing sports and following in Diane's footsteps. When I coached them in softball it was imperative that we found teams that emphasized sportsmanship and not cutthroat competitiveness. My teaching experience in New Orleans created another shift in my attitude toward adolescence. As a teen I entwined being male with playing football. The participation enhanced my gender and made be a better male. My dad and my coaches in baseball and football re-enforced those beliefs. I began to see through those mythical beliefs in the seminary and had it finally debunked when I taught students whose gender would never be defined by sports participation. It may sound strange to hear today but for me I had to learn how to unbundle maleness and sports.

Another form of male chauvinism for me arose with my youthful belief that risky behavior was for males who were daredevils. As a youth I was very cautious and not known for being much of a risk taker. During college I moved away from my "follow the rules, be completely obedient, shy kid" to someone who was willing to take chances and risks. Without going into details, let me just say that in addition to marching on a drill team with dangerous moves involving bayonets, I jumped trains, climbed water towers, teased a polar bear in the zoo while sitting in his cave above his head, climbed to the top of the dome at the college and placed a beret on the top of the cross, scaled the walls of school buildings -- you get the picture. At the time it was a way for me to be myself - which really translated into proving to myself that I was a real man. Risk-taking behavior was almost an expectation for males of my generation. Of course, gender equality has led to the idea that risk-taking behavior is okay for anyone now. When I was growing up, females were to be protected and be safe. I remember feeling that one of my most sacred duties to my daughters was to protect them and keep them safe. When I found out one of my daughters had been raped, I was devastated. That was followed by our youngest daughter's diagnosis of leukemia, her struggle and death. Dealing with these failures as a male and as a father was/is visceral. I still have not fully come to terms with the depth that these experiences have had. They have scrambled my self-worth and value as a person. Cerebrally and cognitively I can discuss and determine some of the effects these experiences have meant to me. Emotionally and sub-consciously I will probably never know. Even though the stereotype of danger being okay for males while females are to remain safe has diminished in meaning and importance, the underlying premise probably still remains. Fathers still feel they should protect and keep their families safe. This does not mean mothers do not have these feelings too, but they may come from a different place. How we define and provide safety and protection can be vastly different. I leave the analysis of this issue to the reader. I will share two experiences as examples.

My brother-in-law and I took some of our children camping to Watkins Glen State Park. We did so in 1984 and again a few years later in 1987. The first trip included my 13, 11, and 10 year olds and Laurie brought his 10 year old. One of the highlights was stream walking. We found a waterfalls that led to a stream which ran through some back woods. At the beginning of the stream, there were rocks and drops as the water made its way into the wooded area. Laurie and I believed that we were balancing the risk/safety factors correctly. We wanted the kids to feel the thrill of a bit of danger in negotiating the climb down the rocks with the water running gently in some places while going more swiftly in different areas. We handed the kids down in the steeper areas. We protected them and kept them safe, while giving them an adventure. The second trip included my 16, 14 and 13 year olds and he added an 11 year old along with his 13 year old. Again we navigated the stream walk, although this time the run off was a little faster, making the assistance down the rocks a bit tricky. I noticed that my 16 and 14 year olds were having no part of needing assistance and would negotiate the rocks just fine on their own.

One story from this excursion needs to be shared. My 14 year-old and Laurie's 13 year-old were preoccupied with looking good, meaning their puffed hair needed far too much attention. Our two daughters were spending too much time in the facilities to do whatever teen girls do to make their hair behave in unnatural ways. It became quite annoying for the rest of us who were out for nature, camping, hiking, swimming, etc. Laurie and I decided to teach them a lesson. We took scissors and asked two of our other daughters if we could cut a small bit of their hair. We gathered a rope and one of us kept it hidden. (Maybe I was returning to my earlier experience with my friend, Donny.) When the preeners returned, we told them that the rest of us had decided to play a game. To start they had to stand at the nearby tree with their backs against the trunk and they needed to close their eyes tightly. When they complied, Laurie and I took the rope and bound them to the tree. We took out scissors and pretended to cut their hair: snipping at their hair and brandishing the results. The girls were horrified and screamed. When they settled down we explained what we had done and told them that this trip was not about grooming, it was about bonding and enjoying nature. They were very compliant the rest of the time. Afterwards the kids went about getting ready for our next adventure and a couple of older people ambled across the road. I had noticed that they were watching our antics. Wondering if they were going to be judgmental, Laurie and I were duly amused when they proclaimed

"That was the funniest thing we've seen in a campsite in a long time."

The second experience occurred in 1983 when Diane and I took the girls on a big camping adventure. I had a sabbatical for the spring semester so I could take an extended vacation that summer. We had a pop-up camper that became a home away from home as we traveled around the country and Canada. In addition to this trip out West and our camping in Watkins Glen, we also ventured to Disney World, Amish country near Lancaster, PA and to Prince Edward Island - twice. For our big adventure we started by visiting my relatives in Kentucky, then headed west for Rocky Mountain National Park, on to The Tetons, next was Yellowstone, then Mount Rushmore, on to visit Diane's relatives in Minnesota before heading home. We probably got a little too close to one bison, but otherwise we were pretty safe. One day, however, things did not go as planned.

While we were in Rocky Mountain National Park at Camp Estes, I had read the maps and decided we would have an adventure hike. Our daughters were 12, 10, 9 and 2. In one area of the park Dream Lake was an inland oasis away from most tourists. We could park in the lot that was on the same level as the lake, hike to it, have a rustic lunch, continue hiking to the side of the mountain and take the trail down to another parking lot that would provide a bus back up to our van. All was well. We had our back pack with food and provisions and I carried Heidi, the 2 year old, on my back. We marched to the lake enjoying the bright sunshine and beauty of the landscape. Our lunch was rather delightful: sharing stories and eating in the great outdoors. When we got to the trail that would head down the side of the mountain, I said "We are the Schmidtke Van Trapp Family. Let's sing." I don't think my exuberance was fully shared. Our 9 year old was fearful of the height, and Diane said that she would take care of her on the serpentine trail. It was narrow, a bit muddy and filled with rocks and stones. That was only the setting. What happened next turned a safe and fun hike down a trail into quite an adventure. Out of nowhere a hail storm blew in. The clouds were black and the lightning loud. The rain and hail beat relentlessly for our descent (at least 1/2 mile). We told our oldest daughters to go first so we could watch them and Diane managed to hold and help a terrified 9 year old. Heidi immediately went to sleep on my back - that was her defense mechanism throughout her childhood. We made it to the bottom but there was no bus in sight. A newly married couple in a VW pulled up and offered us a ride. How the six of us with our back packs and drenched clothing crammed into their little bug I'll never know. We learned the value of helping strangers that day. When we got back to the campsite we realized that we had kept the screening down from the windows because it was sunny and warm when we left. What a lesson for all of us.

This experience helped me sort through the ideas and feelings related to planning and being spontaneous. As I was growing up I identified planning and being prepared with being male. I learned or received this attitude from my dad (always plan and be precise) and the boy scouts (always be prepared). Mom seemed to be more spontaneous; so such ways of doing things were feminine in my childhood. Slowly the silliness of this belief has washed away. One of the women who has been our friend for many years at both of our Lutheran churches shares my birthday. We are both rather Type A planners and detail/task oriented. If I was writing this book 50 years ago, I would have had planning and spontaneity listed as a gender dichotomy; thankfully I have gotten beyond that superficial stereotyping. But the lessons of planning and spontaneity are woven into my life's experiences.

I am an inveterate planner. My family either grins or groans when I start looking ahead months or years in advance. Diane will mention that we should do "x" and I'll start mentally running through details and plans. My family now realizes I can't help myself. This trip to the mountain and encountering the hail storm is a good example of my planning. I had it all arranged and thought I had figured out each detail. God laughed. First I didn't anticipate a hail storm and then I didn't count on the rain at the camp site while we were gone. In the first instance we adapted and shifted what we were doing to cope with circumstances. In the second we just had to deal with the consequences. I always expect that something unexpected will happen and try to even prepare for the unforeseen. Maybe a good example is Tara's wedding. We helped plan and prepare for her special day. I had my computer list of all possible items to be attended to. I also had prepared an emergency kit for the day. My daughters made fun of the kit which included screwdrivers, hammer, wire, the ever present paper clips, duct tape, etc. As it turned out at the church Tara needed long-nosed pliers to fix something on her dress. Subsequently, the other girls didn't argue with my handy kit being available for their weddings. So I don't expect that things will go as planned but that doesn't stop me from planning. I also try to learn from the mistakes that I make in planning. For example, we always closed our camper screens when we left after that day.

Diane is much more attuned to finding serendipity in life and in events. She is more in touch with her feelings and the world than I am. Our last trip in the United States with our Dutch friends had a theme of serendipity. We toured NYC for a few days together before heading to New York's wine country and roaming around the Finger Lakes. I always plan where we're going to stay each night but we readily shift our plans during the days as something unexpected may arise or we just feel like doing A rather than B or C. This trip was a good example of trying to find a healthy balance between planning and being open to the spontaneous. We even found a street sign Serendipity on a country road outside of Ithaca. On our return to our rooms we made sure to stop and take a picture. I actually took my first selfie with it. In college being spontaneous for me was associated with risk taking. My college roommate and I were exploring different dimensions in what it meant to be alive. We were both driven by doing what was right and planning everything in great detail. But we encouraged each other to find a different sense of being alive - being spontaneous/taking a risk. One example for us was jumping trains, climbing to the top of the cars and jumping from one car to the next. I realized how risky this behavior was one night when he got on the train before me. He was 5 or 6 cars ahead and we were jumping cars to meet. It was always easier to jump from car to car when you were going from the front of the train to the back. Those jumps had the advantage of the direction and momentum of the train to make the distance shorter. On this particular night (we only jumped after dark) I saw an overpass coming toward us. I was signaling to Boo to get down. At first he didn't understand until I dove to my stomach and he realized he needed to do so also. As we went under the overpass I realized that what we were doing was really, really dangerous. But it was exhilarating.

The riskiness became even more apparent one night when I jumped the train by myself. I just needed a ride. As I rode along I was looking for a landing area that was less rocky than where we often disembarked. Up ahead I saw a ledge along the side of the tracks at an overpass and wondered if I could roll onto it. That would be new, different, and tricky. I took too long to decide and the opportunity was lost – or was it. A few days later I was walking past the so-called ledge. When I looked down toward the tracks I saw that the ledge was really a cluster of bushes. In the dark it looked solid; in the light of day it was a hazard and would have impaled me if I had tried my great idea. I realized I had averted disaster but smiled at the daring nature of my crazy idea. And isn't that the point of taking risks? There is a thrill; a touching of something deep inside of us that makes us feel more alive than when we are going about the routines of our life. Planning and spontaneity have nothing to do with gender but are connected to social mores, a person's upbringing and family dynamics and, of course, one's personality.

In the 50s risk taking may have had somewhat of a gender overtone but even then there were notable exceptions: e.g. Amelia Earhart. I have been keenly aware of my overly planning nature and truly try to be more spontaneous and intuitive in my experiences and outlook. Planning my spontaneity is always an option! I am aware of my overly analytic/cerebral nature whenever I go through my Tai Chi form. It requires incredible focus and attention for me to merely breathe and empty my mind while my body goes through the movements. If I can muster 1 - 2 minutes of meditative stillness, that is an achievement. I can be halfway through my 15 minute form and realize that I have been planning something or making a list, or discussing a topic with myself, writing something, etc. before I realize that I am supposed to let all of that go. It just isn't easy for me to do so.

Diane and I have learned to respect and accept our differences. These differences are strengths for each one of us. Planning and spontaneity may belong to the passage in Ecclesiastes: A time for peace, a time for war; a time for death, a time for birth; maybe also a time to plan and a time to be spontaneous. Of course being spontaneous does not mean risk-taking. That is just how I began to learn the importance of these dimensions in being fully human. There are extreme behaviors that don't allow some planner/type A people to open up to the spontaneous or to taking a risk; likewise there are some free-spirited people who do not want to be encumbered with plans or details. The diversity and combinations of attitudes and behaviors in this regard are endless. What I have learned is that gender is not really the defining characteristic when it comes to risk-taking and life seems more fully meaningful when people are open to the diversity and beauty of planning **and** spontaneity; of risk-taking **and** being safe and cautious. There truly is a time for everything under the sun!

As boys, my brothers and I wrestled and loved to watch wrestling. Too often on Saturday morning (actually close to noon) mom would send us in to wrestle with dad in their bed before he got up. The stale beer and liquor smell along with the cigarette odor always made me a bit nauseous, which in turn led me to dread this ritual. I was thankful when I became too big to continue this subtle form of torture. Rough housing was a staple in my childhood. I remember boxing with Billy, the next-door neighbor at our first home. He had the gloves, and we pretended to be the great fighters of the day. All of the boys had pistols and we played Cowboys and Indians for hours. At night in our first neighborhood all of the kids, boys and girls, joined in such games as Kick the Can, Red Rover, Red Rover or Tag. I don't remember encountering tomboys in my childhood. Girls played the evening games, but none of them played football or baseball with the guys.

One Christmas my brothers and I received typical boy gifts: rocket launcher, bow and arrow, rifles with rubberized bullets, etc. We split into two teams: Paul and dad positioned in the living room vs. Bill and me in the bedrooms down the hallway. It was Christmas morning and World War III had commenced. We were enjoying the kills and wounds (although there were never-ending arguments about whether we were actually killed or not). Our poor mom was trying to get dressed and needed to go from her bedroom to the bathroom crossing the hallway all too often. We were merciless and did not heed her calls for a truce. Finally she demanded that we stop because we had to go to church. It always fascinated me that the Southern Baptist was intent on getting to the Catholic mass on time when my dad seemed rather indifferent (and this from a man who was always otherwise punctual to a fault). When she emerged from the bedroom at our reluctant truce, she asked "What do you think of my dress?" I knew she was very proud of the bright red addition to her wardrobe. She and dad had spent some time shopping and she was excited when she brought the box home. My deft response: "Well, at least it fits." Clearly I had a long way to go in speaking to women!

My parents taught me manners and how to be polite and treat women with respect. The manners I learned had a distinctive maleness to them. For example, there never was any notion that the boys had to put the toilet seat down when we were finished. That concept never entered my consciousness until Diane and I were married. We opened doors for mom because that was how we showed respect. I try to do so for Diane as often as possible. It has been instilled since childhood: it's what guys do to be polite. We are living in a society in which our norms are becoming so radically redefined that there really is no social balance or acceptance of what is right or wrong, just or unjust, or even polite or rude. I now know that these issues really have nothing to do with gender – they really revolve around common human decency.

My dad demanded obedience, not just from his boys, but also from his wife. He was the boss and what he said was law: no ifs, ands or buts. When I was growing up I had a tendency to think that the man could make demands and the woman should obey. Dad, as the man, was in charge and mom, as the woman, was supposed to obey. There was no opportunity to question the authority or to ask why such and such was being demanded. "Because I said so" was not an uncommon retort from my dad. Maybe my repressed desire to ask why led me to pursue philosophy when I was away from my father. I loved the questioning, ideas, and pursuit of truth and wisdom that philosophy engendered. Maybe Dad's disdain for my major solidified my choice. No way to know for sure. This idea that obeying and demanding were gender based became reinforced in Kentucky. My aunts obeyed their husbands. I remember when I was working with Uncle James and Aunt Lona on their wills, it was clear she did not agree with his decisions. She did not think that all of the nephews and nieces should receive an equal share of their estate, but she kept her silence. After Uncle James died, she cleverly changed some of his intent. She kept the equal distribution, except that she had sold her farm and put the proceeds in a CD in my name. She told me she was not disobeying Uncle James since he had offered the farm to me. She said she was just doing what he intended. My Grandma was a special case. Although she was a woman, she was also the matriarch - the parent. Her sons and daughters deferred to her, but she never really made any important decisions when we were around. Once she decided to move with my mom to live with her daughter (my Aunt Myrtle and Uncle Oral), she seemed to relinquish her need to decide. She worked the soil, sewed and tried to help Aunt Myrtle keep her house clean (which never seemed to materialize).

I have seen male dominance occur in many different venues over my life time. A very sad example occurred at a Remembrance Service for those who have experienced the death of a child. Each year hundreds of people gather in a Greek Orthodox Church in Buffalo. At the service a parent is asked to speak and share some thoughts about his or her experience and grief. It is a time to share the story of our deceased child. One year a Greek man was chosen. He brought his wife up with him and made sure that she stood behind him. He fumbled and rambled. She tried to assist with his notes, but he was rude and condescending to her. It became a spectacle that totally detracted from the somber evening we had attended over the years. As he droned on I thought about my own journey away from the need to be in control in our marriage. I know it has crept into my life un-wittingly, but I do not believe it has ever surfaced as a need or a demand for Diane to obey me. That has never been a dynamic in our love or marriage.

We did not subject our daughters to this belief of male dominance that I saw in my parents. I never really thought that a woman should obey me anyhow. But I do know that my ideas shifted about obedience in the seminary. My biggest problem with remaining there and becoming a priest related to obedience. As I noted in Chapter 3, I could not abide being told when to pray, when to eat, when to speak, etc. The obedience was suffocating. My military training taught me the importance of chain of command and the almost absolute need to obey orders. In that context I did not question a command and followed the orders that I was given. But that was a military context, and as I became an adult I became aware that context shifts the way we think and behave. I always obeyed my parents: that dictum seemed to be respectful, morally sound and biblically based. There was a difference between asymmetrical relationships and those more equally based. By that I mean, parents and children do not have equal standing. Parents who try to be friends and treat their growing children as equals are making a mistake. It is misplaced and fails to provide a societal structuring necessary for respect to grow. A marriage, however, is not asymmetrical - husbands and wives or partners must always share a mutual love and respect. Adult children may still feel a sense of asymmetry even when obedience is no longer part of the relationship. A sense of friendship and shared attitudes are healthy additions to the relationship. A parallel attitude comes from adult friends of our daughters who still refer to us as Mr. or Mrs. There were some friends of my parents to whom I could never use their first names; others, however, were on a first name basis once I became comfortable with it.

As I studied for my philosophy courses and began to think about the relationships between men and women, I rejected any basis for this belief that one person automatically deserves to be obeyed based on gender. The biblical passages that seem to justify it occur within contexts of mutual respect, not unilateral female obedience. Isn't this just another example of literal vs. contextual readings of the bible? The literalists might reach the conclusion that the man is in charge and the woman should obey. Clearly that was the basis for my Southern Baptist relatives. I think for my dad it merely had to do with control and was just assumed to be the correct way of behaving. Those who read the bible contextually will reach a very different conclusion. Men are to be respected AND they are to respect their wives. Diane and I usually make joint decisions (for bigger items that is). It would be silly to check each other's opinion on every purchase or decision. Sometimes we just defer to the other's strong preference or expertise. I have become sensitive to the underlying assumption in this belief: the one in charge has power and the obedient one cedes this power to the other. For men there may be nothing worse than being or feeling emasculated. Sometimes this experience is unjustified, unhealthy and wrong. However, if emasculated means ceding power away from the man and shifting the relationship onto a more equal footing, then it's the man who has to change his ideas about who he is and how he should treat others. Besides the stereotype that says women are really in charge does have an element of truth to it. I now realize that my mom probably had a lot more to say about how our home was run and what we were going to do than I realized when I was growing up.

I wish human relationships were not so embroiled in power dynamics. Nietzsche claimed that power was the defining characteristic of being human. The "overman" or "superman" (an *Ubermensch*) was a model of power and dominance. The Nazis misused his philosophy to justify a male-dominant, German first nationalism that proved disastrous for the world. On an interpersonal level adopting the idea or belief of male dominance and female obedience is inherently destructive. This abuse of power is all too common in our world. It may be male harassment or parental sexual abuse. It may have the form of teacher, priest, pastor or minister who takes advantage of the person for whom he or she should have care and respect. It occurs all too often in the workplace. Somehow we need to restore a sense of balance and respect in all human relationships. Power should not be the defining dimension in any interpersonal relationship.

Years ago I wrote an article for the *Buffalo News'* "My View" column. It was a reflection of straight lines and curves in my life. Living with five women taught me how my gender differences with them were reflected in my overly straightforward ways of doing things as contrasted with their more curved approach to life. In the context of this book this analogy seems quite apt. I tend to focus my attention when I am pursuing a task. Typically I'll focus on one task at a time. I learned my lesson about my ability to multi-task in Prince Edward Island. We were getting ready to leave after camping on the Island. The girls wanted to visit the home of Lucy Maude Montgomery and see the inspiration for their beloved books about *Anne of Green Gables* (that's Anne with an "e"!). I was preparing the van, changing the oil, packing the camper, etc. All was well until we hit the highway and at 50 MPH, the hood slammed into the windshield, shattering it. I had closed the hood but not enough to latch it completely. A friendly islander led us to a garage where they fixed the windshield quickly and efficiently. I was very upset with myself: how could I be so careless; how could I endanger my family; how could I not do the simplest of tasks? You get the picture.

Since then I have tried to stay focused on tasks, even more so than before. In that sense I am what is called Monochronic: doing one thing at a time and primarily focusing on the task. Diane is far more Polychronic: doing many things at a time and focusing more on people and diverting attention to them. She would readily interrupt anything she was doing to take care of, play with or read to the girls. She still starts a number of projects almost simultaneously. My phrase was, "Don't bother me now." Hers was "What do you need?" Those responses seemed rather gender oriented to me. Diane's world has curves, twists and turns. She loves spontaneity and looking for the serendipity in life. I plan my spontaneity. We have a mutual respect for one another and have learned over time that neither approach is wholly right or wholly wrong. Each one has advantages and disadvantages. I am habitually planning and looking ahead. Diane is far more capable of *Carpe Diem*. These differences address our habitual behaviors and basic attitude toward life. They do not describe the way we may go about making important or ethical decisions. That is far more complex. Fundamentally, however, our attitude is built upon respect and accepting the difference in our ways of looking at life and addressing tasks. Over time I have learned that planning is not male and spontaneity is not female. Gender distinctions are irrelevant.

Language is an example of our habits. As a youth I was exposed to using the "n" word in any reference to anyone with dark skin (not just blacks). For my parents and my Kentucky relatives, it was a habitual way of speaking and was done without any pre-thinking. It just came out. They learned it when they grew up, and they passed it along to me. I do not know when my language shifted and I broke this habitual way of speaking. It is clear that there are people who are quite unaware of the consequences of using this word. There are others who use it quite intentionally - sometimes for attention, sometimes for an effect, and sometimes out of hate. Part of the Political Correctness movement is an understanding of the consequences of one's speech and a desire to eliminate the consequences of speech that are hurtful and destructive. Words matter. I have been combing through my vocabulary over the last few decades to try and cull out the language that I may have taken for granted but which clearly reflects my covert prejudices whether racial, gender, or religious. A language that incorporates respect for others would go a long way in creating positive relationships among and between people. I do find myself having inappropriate words come to my mind when I see someone from another culture or when I see behavior that I have found offensive. I'm still taken aback when women curse like sailors (an interesting stereotype that sailors are male). As I think about such things it reminds me of the distinction that is so important. Our feelings are what we feel. It doesn't make sense to deny the existence of the feelings or even the attitudes that may emerge from those feelings. One of the least helpful phrases in our language is, "Don't feel that way." Denying the legitimacy of what someone is feeling is an affront to him or her. From the outside, it may seem illegitimate to feel a certain way or to respond to a situation in a particular fashion. Rejecting that response is usually not helpful. Helping the person to see the situation in a different way may be helpful. I know after Heidi died, I resented people telling me I shouldn't feel sad because she wouldn't want me to feel that way. Wrong. That was how I felt. The more I have thought about this topic the more I am convinced of the legitimacy of these feelings. The issue is not the feelings but what I do with them or how I live my life. Allowing these feelings to dictate all of my behavior or succumbing to a crippling depression would be unhealthy and destructive. Denying one's feelings is counterproductive. Learning how to cope with them is maturity and healthy.

Let me finish this section with a couple of observations. There is a common stereotype that men who gray as they age look more dignified while women just look older. This stereotype certainly benefits the salon and dying industries. Although this may seem benign, I believe that it relates to the underlying male agenda of expecting beauty in women and artificially defining what that beauty may be. One of my daughters suffered from anorexia and I became all too aware of the problems of body imaging in the United States (see Chapter 15). Teenage girls and women in general have to deal with this pervasive force in America and throughout the world. Men also have a need to look muscular, trim and fit. These forces place an unhealthy burden onto young girls and boys and women and men generally. If this observation is not readily apparent to you, please do some soul searching to discover the prejudices and stereotypes surrounding body image that pervade too much of our society and maybe your own life.

I am amused when I see other men sitting on benches in the Mall or outside stores around the world. I have applauded the bar entitled "Men's Waiting Room" in a shopping area. Diane often tells me to stay home when she is going shopping; rarely do I object. We reflect the stereotype that women shop and men wait. Unless it is a sports store or at Christmas, I go to buy; Diane will shop. Although this difference is not universal, it is extremely pervasive and easily recognizable. I have also noted a difference between my brother-in-law and I and our wives when it comes to talking on the phone. If we have to talk to each other, it won't last long. (Using the verb "have to talk" should be a clue regarding our phone usuage.) We get to the point and get off. Texts are short and infrequent. Our wives, on the other hand, talk, chat, and go into details that sometimes I don't see a need to share. Over the years my brother-in-law and I have an understanding. When either of our wives says that it is time to leave, we sit down and wait for what will inevitably be another 30 minutes of talking. We have even marveled with the phenomenon that we could spend, for example, a Christmas day together and the wives would call each other for some reason that night. Diane does not understand my infrequent calls to my brothers. She feels a need for me to make much more frequent contact than I feel necessary. How universal these phenomena are, I don't know; they certainly are a part of gender difference in my life.

There are a wide variety of other differences, but this chapter is not intended to be an exhaustive study on the differences with the genders. Obviously my focus has contradicted my opening premise. I asserted that we should not just focus upon the two genders of male and female, but rather we should see the continuum that exists along the line of having male represented on one side and female on the other. After making that claim I have continued my discussion revolving around male and female as the only two definitive genders. The reason for doing so is simple. On my journey of becoming aware of who I am, I clearly started in a worldview that had only two genders. My own growth has taken me through this prism of male/female. Today, my worldview is a bit more developed and broad minded. It has taken decades and experiences I could never have imagined as a youth to shift my ideas and beliefs. I cannot speak for the gay, lesbian or transgender populations with respect to gender identity. I really have no basis for making claims about the prejudices that they have experienced or that they themselves have. Sexual orientation is a different topic than gender identity. The first is based on who we are; the second relates to how we may relate to others. We do not have a choice in determining either our gender or our sexual orientation. We do have a choice on how we behave and the attitude we may take regarding our gender or sexual orientation. I see the topics as distinct yet related.

PART IV:

ON GENERATIONS

CHAPTER 7
INTERGENERATIONAL RELATIONSHIPS

It is up to us to live up to the legacy that was left for us,
and to leave a legacy that is worthy of our children
and of future generations.

Christine Gregoire

Here we were packed into the car for another excursion to Kentucky. Although the travel down to my Shangri-La was routine (a road side stop for mom to pee, food packed away to eat in the car, only stopping for gas and closing our windows when crossing into Covington from Cincinnati), this time there were some differences. Bill, now 8, got to navigate the oft-travelled route with the Trip Tik (and delivered his famous quote: "it's only a page and a half", when he was asked how much further to Columbus, Ohio); Dad told me to pack a couple of pairs of jeans, which made no sense; and I was more eager than usual to return to a familiar South after having spent the previous summer in a confusing but wonderful sojourn in South Carolina.

This summer was distinctively different because my grandma Pearl was going to move into a trailer on Uncle James' and Aunt Lona's (pronounced Low-Knee) farm after living with Uncle Oral and Aunt Myrtle since her husband died 38 years earlier. Grandma Pearl had five children – Myrtle,

Elmer, James, my mom (Willie Eudine but everyone called her Wanda), and a daughter Pauline who died at eight months. My mom was only four when her father died, so she also lived with Aunt Myrtle (21 years older) and Uncle Oral, their daughter Myra Ellis (pronounced Mar-Alice), and Grandma Pearl.

Mom grew up on a farm that was one of my more entertaining places to stay. I took it for granted that three generations lived together for decades on that farm, probably because it only seemed as if there were two. Myra Ellis and Mom acted like sisters (since they were only two years apart) while my Aunt Myrtle seemed more like my mom's other mother. Mom was called the spoiled baby by her brothers -- something I heard most often by her brother, James. My Uncle Elmer and his wife, Marie, had moved to Delaware for a job with Jolly Green Giant when I was young. Mom's two brothers were very protective of her, but they teased her mercilessly. She was afraid of snakes and worms and the boys would chase her around with wriggling critters. I heard these stories when we visited and the siblings recounted childhood escapades. One of mom's favorites was the day she and Myra Ellis climbed up a tree to throw apples at a boy from a nearby farm who was delivering the newspaper. James and Elmer had a different favorite story. As they tell it mom went to the outhouse while they were down by Kentucky Lake swimming. James and Elmer had some rope and wove it around the outhouse, locking Mom inside. Her cries for release received laughter and shouts of "how's it goin' in thar?"

Mom told me that Myrtle and Oral were her disciplinarians because Grandma Pearl ceded that responsibility when they moved to the farm. I have concluded this was true from the stories I heard that Grandma changed when my Grandfather died. She became quiet, almost reclusive at times, withdrawn emotionally, and outwardly bitter and unfriendly, even to family. No one but me seemed to pay attention to Grandma Pearl. My mom spent some time with her mother, but I don't ever remember seeing them laugh at something together. Mom smoked and hid that fact from her mother because she knew Grandma Pearl would not approve. Grandma accepted the fact that men smoked (my dad, Uncle James, Uncle Elmer, and Uncle Oral had his famous pipe). She did not condone women smoking for a reason I never knew or even thought to ask why. I don't understand how mom really thought her secret was well kept. I'm sure Grandma Pearl had the usual smelling capacity of any normal person and mom's cigarette smoking odor would be a telltale sign for Grandma. But I guess we all live with some deceits that we believe others have never discovered.

My grandchildren revel in Aunt Myrtle stories - most of which center around her cooking and attempts at cleaning. When she was in her 70s and Diane and I were visiting, she told me that she was living with old folks in the county during the winter to cook and clean for them. Doing so lowered her cost for heating. The first year she did so was just after the plumbing went indoors. She didn't realize that some level of heat was required for the pipes. Thus my Uncle James had the privilege of replacing her burst pipes in the bathroom (which used to be a bedroom for my folks when we visited and stayed on that farm). By the time she had plumbing installed, none of us were staying with her. I have found it to be ironic that when the plumbing was a two-hole outhouse in the back yard, we would stay. But by the time the plumbing went indoors, my folks never visited again (Dad for health reasons and Mom because there was no one to drive her down). I thought that Aunt Myrtle's living with older people and cooking and cleaning for them were devious ways to reduce the social security payrolls in the county. As a young child, I thought nothing of staying there or of eating the meals placed before us. Now, at age 14, I was beginning to realize that something was amiss. As an adult I rarely availed myself of her culinary creations and never considered spending the night. The excuses we used were often masterfully crafted to avoid hurt feelings.

A few examples of her cooking exploits are in order. Mashed potatoes did not include the milk and butter that was common in most homes; no, for Aunt Myrtle it made more sense to mash the potatoes in the water in which they were cooked. Of course she would never bother taking the time to mash the potatoes into some semblance of smooth or creamy (since no dairy ever entered her chunks of spuds). Gray, lumpy, semi-mashed potatoes went well with the grayish gravy that covered the entire plate that my Uncle Oral would assemble from the food that was made available to him. I never remember seeing Uncle Oral with any teeth, so maybe mixing everything together and covering it with gravy made gumming the food easier. For me the visual effect was quite memorable. The skillet on the stove was never cleaned. The drippings and grease/lard/etc. that remained after depositing meat in Myrtle's magic pan mingled to form a deep and useful source for frying. She would wrap fruit in a doughy concoction and let them swim in the skillet's mixture to produce her proudly made pies. Dunking for burgers is the only way to describe the patties of mostly bread crumbs and bits of ground beef also carefully dropped into the bubbling mixture. Chicken was one meat that we commonly saw on the table. My recollection was that the chicken was usually breaded (sort of) and intro-duced to Myrtle's favorite method of preparing food: float the meat in her skillet! The taste of chicken prepared in her oil, grease and lard mixture was unique and not a gastric delight. I never equated collecting eggs from the hens in the chicken coup with the fried bird sitting on the table. One day the connection began to dawn on me when I woke up to see three chickens running around the alleged back yard without any heads. Grape juice was made by mashing a few grapes in a sieve, then pouring water over them into a glass. Uncle Oral's lack of teeth was passed on to his daughter. One time when we visited the farm and saw Myra Ellis (who was in her 40s), we saw her proudly displaying three - two on top (one at a right angle) and one on bottom. Could the cooking have been a contributor?

Sleeping on a feather bed may sound rustic, but Aunt Myrtle's feathers also included chicken feet to provide bulk. The thin cloth holding the innards together didn't prevent being poked by the sharp feather points or claws from the feet. Have you ever lain down to be engulfed by cloth that had feather quills sticking into your sides? I'm sure she washed the cloth - even though saying this does not guarantee that it was so. I can attest to the fact that the quilt did have a smell that can only be described as: indescribable. As a child I slept in the room behind the kitchen receiving its fragrance emanating from the delights that only that kitchen could produce. The view from the window above the bed looked out to a magnificent view of the two-hole outhouse that was distinctive for their farm. There were times when I was young that Uncle Oral and I would go in tandem for a "sit down." He would read the Montgomery Ward Catalog to me before we used it for other purposes. There is a family folk legend about the time when a couple had stopped at the country store my relatives kept along the roadside. They asked to use the outhouse and the man was standing outside waiting for his wife. A three year old Charlie Ray (my southern family's name for me, pronounced Cha-le-RAY) went up and informed him that he didn't have to wait because there were two holes inside.

I never really noticed the lack of dusting or cleaning in the house until later in life when Diane and I went to visit (starting on our honeymoon). One April years later we were headed to visit friends in Nashville with our three oldest daughters (still young at the time). Since it was a bit chilly outside, Aunt Myrtle invited us in. It took about 30 seconds for our girl's clean, white socks to become polka dotted with fleas. Her cats were allowed to run the farm yet stay inside whenever they wanted. Bringing the outdoors inside was habitual for them. I was surprised to see that my aunt had a phone. No such contraption had been there when I was growing up. Diane was even more surprised when she took the phone from me and was confronted with particles of corn and other aged foodstuffs caked on the mouth piece. Of course that surprise was not as startling as the summer when we visited with our daughters and ventured to stay awhile. The porch chairs were a bit dangerous because Aunt Myrtle was becoming incontinent. We knew that was the case because of the condition of the pads that were fermenting on the seats. The surprise came when she asked, "Char-le-Ray, do you want a Billy Beer?" Really? She had beer on the premises. She lived in a dry county; so was the adjacent county. I didn't bother asking where she got it or when such a liquid became available in her home. "Love to" was my feeble reply. "It's in the kitchin". Sure enough her refrigerator had a six-pack with one can already consumed. Adulthood certainly brings revelations about older generations. It is unfortunate that I did not inquire about this behavioral change (or was it really a change?). I assumed it was a change because I don't ever recall seeing such drinks in her frig ever before. Her grandson, however, just told me that she routinely kept a case under her bed. But aren't assumptions something which pervades family relations. If we do not make a conscious effort to listen to the stories of the older generation(s), so much gets lost. How often do we regret not asking questions of the older generations? Also many of the details we may want to know are just not items that normally enter into conversations. Maybe this book is fundamentally a way to make sure my grandchildren know a little bit more of who I was/am from the inside. I applaud all the efforts being made for oral histories among our veterans. Oral histories should not just be limited to them, however. My daughters reveled in listening to Diane's mom tell her stories about childhood, courtship and the life she lived in Winona, Minnesota. Intergenerational sharing is an important glue for any society.

As a young child I found Aunt Myrtle and Uncle Oral's farm to be magical. There was a mound about 100 yards from the house that became a world of war, travel, and mystery for me. Tending to the chickens was something I enjoyed doing every morning and evening. I never thought to count them to see if any had shifted from laying eggs to providing us with a dinner. They had a yard around the house with no grass, just tufts of something green in various spots. The area was predominantly matted down dirt with a few mossy areas scattered for a splash of color. Along the highway extending from the store to the apple orchard was a grassy patch about the size of a football field. That's where the mound was located. On the other side of the house there was a ravine (aka ditch) with a rickety bridge. I had defeated untold enemies over the years on that "last stand" for the brave and courageous. The island on the other side of the bridge was froth with danger, but I always seemed to overcome each challenge. Of course I didn't venture into the Apple Orchard alone because Uncle Oral told me about the snakes out there. Yes, I inherited mom's hatred and fear of snakes. The fear wasn't just for the dangerous chicken snakes or black racers; no, it also even included the garden variety.

When I was much older and he was dead, I began to realize that the real reason Uncle Oral didn't want me to venture into the back fields was his fear that I might fall into the still that he had dug underground. It wasn't until 2015 that the people of that county finally approved the sale of alcohol. Living in a dry county can lead to various and sundry ways for satisfying one's thirst. I was never told about his clandestine distilling but firmly believe that my uncle was supplying the county with apple-based moonshine throughout the 1940s, 50s and into the 60s. I vividly recall one day when I was delivering mail with him. (That was the only job I ever knew that my uncle had, other than farming apples and selling things in the store that no one ever seemed to buy.) We drove in very back country roads, most were dirt, although one was all stones. It was on that road that we stopped nowhere near any farm. He told me to stay in the car, which I dutifully did. I looked in the rear view and saw him open the trunk (getting the "mail" out). Men were wandering to the car from many directions. As was the custom of the area, their gait was slow; some were spitting out tobacco; and most had a big smile for my uncle. They seemed to linger for awhile and left with their "mail". It never dawned on me then that the "mail" was in brown bags, not envelopes or packages. My treat for waiting patiently was a visit to the post office and getting to cancel letters that he was putting into his bag for the second leg of our delivery route. The postman was a tall and friendly sort. As I think back on that memory it was clear that he was delivering his moonshine and he was protecting me from knowing about it. Certainly my Southern Baptist relatives would never have revealed such a sin to me while he was alive or even after he passed away (if they even knew).

Five miles down the highway was the farm where I would spend the most time throughout my life. Uncle James and Aunt Lona provided a completely alternative rural experience. Everything was clean in the house (although the outhouse did have spiders and the seat was rough - Uncle Oral's was nice and smooth). The meals were very good and utterly predictable. As a child I never noticed that we were served the same food for dinner (the main meal around 1 PM) and supper (six-ish) each day we were there. Desserts would change (ranging from chocolate pie to a blueberry cobbler that was short on berries and heavy on sugar). The meals would sometimes have biscuits, other times corn bread. For as long as I can remember those meals always included barbecue, pressured cooked green beans with bacon, lima beans, corn (either on the cob or creamy buttered), slaw, "tamaters" and mashed "pataters" (white, smooth and with butter and milk). They had a large, well-mown lawn on the sides and front around the house and a barn/silo area behind their one acre vegetable garden. Beyond the barn area were four fenced fields that rotated crops while Uncle James was young (tobacco, feed corn and hay). As he got older the fields produced only hay for his livestock - usually cattle - and the unneeded was sold to other farmers. Shucking the feed corn for the cattle when I was young hurt my suburban hands, but I never said a word: a real man never complains. When I was a child they had a few milk cows - my favorite was Popeye because she was the one I could readily milk (the others seemed too scary for me). In my childhood brilliance I figured that Popeye was a male because of his (her?) name and because he/she was kind to me while the female cows were not. As you will hear later, Popeye was the only creature that caused my grandma Pearl to discipline me.

This farm was my oasis and the source of comfort and self-renewal throughout my life, until Aunt Lona had to move into a nursing home after her stroke (when I was 52). I cared for her at a distance and remember viv-idly my last time roaming the fields of my youthful dreams and adventure. It was a difficult pill to swallow. As a child the freedom to wander through the fields and turn them into whatever my imagination could concoct was truly special. I don't remember encountering any snakes on their farm and have no explanation why not. As an adult, the fields became a balm. Since Uncle James and Aunt Lona had no children, I was their son and I believe they felt that my daughters were their grandchildren. They truly adopted and loved Diane. One memory sticks in my mind (and heart). Uncle James took me for a stroll and we spoke at his pace, sometimes resting a foot on a fence. Rarely did we make eye contact and sharing feelings was taboo - there was never a need to articulate what we knew in our hearts. That afternoon he gazed around his homestead and asked if I wanted it when they died. It was stated matter-of-factly but with the slightest catch in his throat. I paused longer than the usual pace. It was important to let him know with non-verbals how important I took his question. What was I going to say? I told him how honored I would be to live there and how much the farm meant to me (not venturing into my love for him). My out was that there would be no job for me in the area and I wanted to continue to use my PhD for the purpose God gave me. This line of thought was the only way I felt that he would understand why I would never move Diane and my family there. He smiled and said that if I ever changed my mind the land and all that came with it was mine.

I helped both of them with their wills and telling them what language to use with the lawyers when they had it finalized. When Uncle James died years later, my aunt made all the preparations for her own death. I worked with her and her attorney to make sure everything was in order. As farmers they experienced life and death on the farm (chickens, roosters, pigs, hors-es, cats and cattle) and saw death as a basic part of life. When I returned the following summer, she presented me with a framed picture of the farm house taken from a crop duster. It was large (2 feet by 3 feet). She said that any money she received when she sold the property and buildings would go into a CD for me. It was a touching moment when she gave me the framed photo. In her mind she was fulfilling her husband's promise to me. I was deeply moved and felt the depth that familial love can give without ever saying a word. Burying both of them was an unusual type of grief; almost like burying another set of parents.

In addition to them no longer being a part of my life, losing the land was painful. It reminded me of the scene from *Gone With the Wind* when Scarlett's father told her that the land was the bedrock for one's purpose in life. Later there is the iconic scene where Scarlett holds dirt from the land in her hand with a fiery sky in the background. She then proclaims that she will never be poor again. That image always reminds me of my relatives' love for their land and their hard work to maintain what they owned and stave off poverty. Their farms always had a magical hold over me when I visited. I know Diane and our girls loved Aunt Lona and Uncle James and they enjoyed being spoiled when we visited. Aunt Lona always bought the sugary cereals that were never in our cupboards. For me there was a depth and comfort just being in that place. I felt a strange connectedness with the fields, barn, paths, and crops: all of it. I always felt as if I belonged there; I had a sense of being home and having purpose and worth. This piece of land and the people who were there helped me to see that there is beauty and purpose in life. All it takes is to be open to its self-affirming energy. Purpose is something to be discovered and something we can create. Diane and our daughters understand how important this place has been for me, but they cannot feel its depth because no one can ever really feel as another person. We can share feelings but their contours and wrinkles in our being will forever be unique.

My feeling for Aunt Myrtle and Uncle Oral's farm is quite different, yet still profound. It was a different home and has more specific sources for my feelings. Uncle James and Aunt Lona's is contextual; Uncle Oral and Aunt Myrtle's is specific. That's the only way I can describe the difference.

In both places my love and feeling at home begin with my relatives. I have had a special bond with each and every one of them. Uncle Oral died when I was a teen, yet he has remained in my memory as a living relative, that is, someone who has and continues to touch me and be a source of who I believe I am as a person. The farms, themselves, are what's different for me. I now realize this. James and Lona's farm is contextual because it's the totality of the place that brings me into a sense of worth and purpose. When Uncle James offered the farm to me, I sensed this totality. It all really was mine from childhood. I wandered and roamed and each part of the farm fit into a sense of place and purpose for me. For example, behind the house was a washroom. It housed the hot water tank and freezer. During the winter the clothes were hung in that room. It always was our shower facility. The bathroom, once the plumbing went indoors, had no shower, just a bathtub. So as a very young child I was given a bath in the washroom's laundry tub. As I grew up, the shower was the only option. I don't ever remember taking a bath indoors.

Since their water was supplied by the well in their yard, they had to be very careful about putting any paper in the toilet. So the little wastebasket became the depository for any toilet paper being used for our normal bodily eliminations. The washroom's shower consisted of a nozzle at the end of a hose attached to the wall and located above a drain in the floor. The towels remained the same throughout my lifetime. They were blue and thin. In hot summer days trying to get dry with even two of these undersized pieces of cloth never seemed to work for me. Outside of the washroom was a glider for relaxation. Like each of the structures on the farm, this house was a part of the larger picture. I felt a synchrony with every part of this farm - they meshed into a whole that remained magical until it was sold away to a neighbor.

Uncle Oral and Aunt Myrtle's farm had and still has a very different feel. There really was no wholeness for me. The apple orchard was out of bounds and there was no sense of a synchronized way of life. Everything was piecemeal. As an adult I began to understand one of the reasons for this feeling: Aunt Myrtle. She was a "nervous Nelly". She would scamper from place to place. At meals she rarely stayed seated while we ate; she was constantly getting up to do something. As a child I never paid attention, I just accepted the fact that Aunt Myrtle was always on the move. As an adult I looked back and wondered what she ever accomplished with all of her activity. This farm had specific spots that meant something to me. I've already noted the little hill, ditch and outhouse. The garage was close to the house but out of bounds for some reason (storehouse for moonshine?). The well and porch were almost sacred places for me because that is where I bonded with Uncle Oral the most (the outhouse doesn't count!). I marveled at my uncle's deft dropping and raising the bucket to get the best tasting water I've ever had. I stood and watched the pail splash the water and I knew I would get the first ladle full. The porch was the sacred area when my uncle read the bible to me or when he played his fiddle or banjo or when I just sat on his lap to talk about life. These were particular spots that mattered to me. The current transformation of the farm is another story.

Myra Ellis' son, Keith, inherited the farm when his mother died. He had left his mother and step-father as a young man to find his fortunes out west. He started in Colorado then headed to Los Angeles. He worked as a puppeteer, took acting classes and had some small parts in television and the movies. He told me about being in acting classes with Angelina Jolie for two years. In one session they were instructed to smear dog food on each other's cheeks and lick it off. I didn't ask any questions - what is there possibly to say with that information? When Keith was growing up his parents would take trips and stop at road side attractions. He loved the tackiness he saw. Over time he and his mother amassed a large number of collectible items: figures, train sets and all that goes to enhance a train running around a track, pictures, lunch boxes, small toys of all kinds, etc. After inheriting the farm he moved his family back to Western Kentucky to fulfill a childhood dream. He was going to convert the farm into Apple Valley Hillbilly Garden and Toyland. I understand the Hillbilly and Toyland monikers; I fail to see the garden part of the title. He has used his creative juices and love of puns to transform this lazy piece of property into a roadside attraction with very bizarre areas. Some examples: mattresses hanging in trees, a lawn mower cemetery (for the machines he destroyed while trying to clean out the property), a non-petting zoo, an area with old toilets placed in a circle - he calls it Thronehenge - a display of soup cans in the shape of Kansas with a ruby slipper on a branch ("we're not in Cansas, Dorothy"), and much more. He has converted the garage into a display of trains and toys that is so packed that there is only a small path to navigate around the floor to ceiling display. The old Country Store that his grandfather had is now a small museum. He's also adopted a hillbilly persona to promote his attraction.

In 2017 we had a family vacation to Papa's (my) roots. Tara and family (living in Mayville, New York) and Kris and her family (living in Rochester, Minnesota) joined up with us for a night in Louisville. The next day we toured Churchill Downs then headed as a convoy to a rental house on the shores of Kentucky Lake. Katie and her family (living in Ho-Ho-Kus, New Jersey) flew to Nashville, rented a car and met us at the rental. It was a great facility for kids and adults and was located conveniently for me to share some of the food and sights of my childhood. In many ways it was a great vacation for all of us. The cousins love their time together, regardless of place, and the adults have bonds that find their base in the love Diane and I have for one another and our deep love for our daughters and their/ our families. Everyone got a taste of the barbeque and catfish that I had experienced growing up – although no restaurant could compare to either Aunt Lona's and for very different reasons Aunt Myrtle's cooking. I'll refrain from going into lengthy detail of the trip; rather I'd like to share one sadness for me.

I could not share any sense of what these farms meant to me with my Munchkins (grandchildren). Uncle James and Aunt Lona's farm now belongs to strangers. We stopped at a road near the house and barn area. We were able to see part of the farm at a distance but how does this provide any sense of the feelings I had and how could this view put any meat on the bones to my stories? We needed to walk around on the land itself, but such was not possible. The sons-in-law and Munchkins got a partial visual to help them place the stories into a real place, but my story telling is never good enough to translate what this place meant to me.

The jaw-dropping experience, however, occurred at Hill Billy Gardens. What an experience for all of us. The driveway is a small, stoned semicircle so it is easy to drive in, then out without having to back onto the highway. We had to wait for the geese and other animals to move so we could park. Some of the grandchildren, I heard, did get out of the van but quickly retreated back to its safety. Others wandered a little. A couple had seen Keith bolting scantily clad across the yard. I started to walk around and was getting ready to gather the 8 grandchildren and 2 sons-in-law into a tour group so I could start showing them the farm and describe what it used to be. Unfortunately that never happened. Keith cornered me and wanted to give me a one-on-one tour so he could tell me his puns and what he'd done. (He may not have even recognized me at first.) I'm more of a "smiler" than "laugher", so he kept repeating himself thinking that I didn't understand his pun because I wasn't laughing as he expected. I kept trying to reassure him that I did get the point. As he walked me around I found my mind running in two parallel tracks. The first was taking furtive glances at my family and wishing I could be telling them my stories. The second was walking back in my memories to those moments that ring deep in my consciousness. It was a bit jarring because of the dramatic transformation from the lazy childhood haven of years long past.

The grandchildren who ventured out did go through the Toyland but they could never have any sense of my experience as a child. Additionally, and very sadly, youth from the surrounding area had poured oil down the well when Aunt Myrtle was older and living alone. No longer would that wonderful, fresh water ever be available. Talk about a graphic experience to re-enforce the dictum: "you can't go back again". The house was in even worse shape than when Aunt Myrtle tried to keep it up. We heard that one of Keith's feet went through the kitchen floor while washing dishes. It was sad to see them having to struggle so much to make a living while trying to follow a dream. It is impossible to know exactly what the Munchkins felt about what they saw. They didn't provide me with very many details when I asked them about it later. It was a good example that we all know so well: my memories have a depth and density that cannot be fully shared with anyone else. No matter how much we may try, my experiences will always be uniquely mine and yours, yours. The beauty of life is in sharing as much as we can while respecting the gaps that separate me from you. My daughters had direct experiences of the farms and have their own stories to tell. In the end this trip was great because we all created new memories in an old place. It was capped off with a two night stay in Nashville where there was no significant history. We created family experiences in new places that brought laughter and joy to all of us.

Whenever I visited Uncle James and Aunt Lona's farm, there were two gastric rituals that went beyond the normal mealtime fare. Watermelons were inexpensive in the area and Uncle James made sure we had an ample supply whenever we visited. Diane was taken aback the first time she was given a slice of watermelon from Uncle James. The melons were long, not the roundish types. His idea of cutting pieces had always been to divide the melon into four equal parts with each person receiving 1/4. My brothers and I walked around the yard spitting the seeds as far as we could muster. I remember teaching our daughters to do the same. In addition to the water melon, often when we visited Uncle James would bring out the ice cream maker. There was no variation in what was made: Vanilla. Nothing was ever added and no change was ever even considered. As a young boy I thought turning the handle to mix the ingredients would be easy. Uncle James and my dad made it look that way. I was a bit embarrassed when

I couldn't repeat their speed and length of time for turning the crank. As with the watermelon, the portions were large. Catching fireflies was an evening adventure that started when I was young. Diane and I were happy to pass that ritual along to our daughters.

As I was growing up, rides on the tractor with Uncle James were exciting, especially when his eyes would sparkle and he'd utter his unique laugh (somehow managing to have his tongue and teeth produce a hissing sound). One summer (when I was 12) I tried to show off to my younger brother, Bill. He had been fishing in the pond by the barn. That was truly a fool's errand. The pond was small and had a couple of shiners, at most a minuscule sunfish available. But the only outdoor activity Bill would attempt as a child was fishing. So I would take charge and waste time while he cast for his undersized prize. One day, after an excruciating 10 or 15 minutes (patience was not a virtue for me then), I asked him if he wanted a ride.

"Do you know how to drive the tractor?" he inquired worriedly.

"Of course, I've seen Uncle James dozens of times."

Watching is not always the best teacher, especially when the usual driver rides the clutch incessantly, thus making it rather difficult to use. I opened the doors to the barn, mounted the seat and reassured Bill that all was well as he hopped onto the back frame. The tractor lurched forward and was headed straight for the pond. No problem, I'll just turn to avoid following gravity's call to end up in the muddy, reedy water. Well, the wheel wasn't turning for some reason so all I had to do was just apply the brake. Again, that was much easier in theory than in practice for a suburban novice. I can't remember exerting that much pressure with my feet ever in my life. We did stop in time and Bill asked if that was the end of the ride. Since I was no longer confident about steering the stubborn machine and my masculine pride would not allow me to admit any deficiency, I merely told him that he looked too bored and that was all we were going to do. After my deceit I had to work feverishly to get that tractor back into the barn in roughly the same position we had found it. That was a triumph I could never share with anyone.

As an adult I would wander through my childhood fields of dreams and would always come away refreshed, regardless of what life was pitching our way. Diane and I honeymooned nearby, staying at a Holiday Inn for five days near these farms. Ostensibly Uncle James and Aunt Lona gave us this stay as their wedding present, claiming they got a deal since she worked as a cleaning woman there. As we got older, we began to realize that our parents probably talked to them about doing so (maybe even paying the bill). We never asked them – another one of those little family secrets that never got revealed. Our plan was to camp and sleep (having purchased a pup tent ahead of time) in the Land-between-the-Lakes (a large wild life area created by the Tennessee Valley Authority by damming up two rivers). We were in love and thought that would be romantic, or at least I did. At that time the camp sites were very primitive (no water and outhouses at some distance from the camp sites); I'm sure the experience would have been a disaster. We were far too young and immature to realize what we were getting into. Thankfully our parents were a bit wiser.

To illustrate how naive we were, a short side story is in order. We had very little money and were depending on the cash we received from the wedding to pay for our move to New Orleans. The trip down was our honeymoon. The stop in Kentucky made sense to me since I deeply wanted to share this part of my life with my new bride. Since the trip down was really our move to New Orleans we had packed all of our possessions into our used Ford Fairlane. Diane's dad told me that the load was too much for our shocks, and I assured him I would take care of it when we got to New Orleans. We were leaving the day after we got married. On the day of our wedding in the morning, I was playing golf with a friend, Diane went to a friend's wedding, and her dad installed new shocks in our car. Our parents had to be very concerned because we weren't.

Back to our honeymoon: we spent a day with Uncle James and Aunt Lona who were thrilled to show Diane around the Land-Between-the-Lakes even though we had been taking almost daily adventures throughout this 170,000 acre recreational area. After the tour with them we went to the barn on their farm and Uncle James asked if I wanted to ride Red, a younger horse he had recently acquired. Of course I had to show off in front of my new bride. After almost being bucked into the barbed, electrified fence, I did trot the horse for a short distance and happily dismounted with my pride intact. Uncle James grinned and hissed his giggle of approval having pulled a fast one on me. Then Diane when for a short ride too. Uncle James' prank: The horse hadn't been broken. Our day with them ended with a barbeque dinner and the menu I described before.

Kentucky was truly an intergenerational experience for me. One summer I did meet another cousin who lived in Paducah (25 miles from the farms). We played for a couple of days, but that was the only time I interacted with a peer. Everything else was with people of older generations. Fishing and spending some time with Bill didn't count. His asthma and his dislike for becoming sweaty kept him indoors most of the time: besides Banty Roosters chased him around and terrified him.

My relationship with Grandma Pearl was unique and quite special. I was a jewel in her eye. She adored me and we would do simple things together: work on patches for a quilt, shell peas, shuck corn, sit on the porch. She rarely spoke but seemed to relish in my constant prattle. As a child I was comfortable speaking with adults, whether neighbors, adults at the bars we would frequent, or relatives. Grandma just listened and rarely commented. Only once did she ever scold me. I was five and we were visiting her and Uncle Oral and Aunt Myrtle. Uncle James had charged me that summer with milking Popeye at 5 PM every day. Since it was going on 5:00 I asked my folks to get me back in time for my chore, but they kept ignoring my request: "Go out and play." When I checked the clock for the umpteenth time, and it was almost 5:00, I started heading down the highway (two lanes with high speeds, truck traffic, and no real shoulder). My thinking was that I might be a little late, but it only took about five minutes to drive from farm to farm (5 miles apart). At five years old, I hadn't conquered the relationship between speed of a car going 60 and the pace of a child walking. Grandma saw me headed away from the farm and ran after me. She screamed, "Cha-le-RAY! You stop right now!" When I turned around she catapulted toward me at a speed I had never seen from her. One hand held up her black dress so it didn't cause her to stumble and with the other she grabbed my arm, turned me around, then gave me a sharp slap on my backside as I stood motionless. "Don't you ever do that agin! Do you hear me?" I was shocked that Grandma would spank me and could just muster a nodding of my head. Needless to say, Popeye did not feel my hands that evening.

In the summer of 1960, I was 14 and life was changing. On the drive down, my mom said that we would be moving Grandma from Aunt Myrtle's to a trailer next to James and Lona because her mom was starting to become forgetful – "hardening of the arteries" was the family's diagnosis. As we talked, I learned things about Grandma that were a bit surprising. Mom said that she was a stern and sometimes unpleasant woman with whom no one liked to spend much time; there also were times when Grandma didn't want to be around others either. My dad reinforced this message when he repeated the story of Grandma changing my diaper which led to her chasing him with a knife. Dad claimed that the chase was not in jest but in an earnest attempt to hurt him. Whether true or not, my mom indicated that I was the only person she had ever met that Grandma liked to spend time doing things and with whom Grandma would listen to what was being said.

I thought Dad was crazy when he told me to bring a couple of pairs of jeans for this trip. Kentucky summers were hot and one pair for going into the deep grasses in the fields was always sufficient. However, this wasn't the first time that I rolled my eyes with demands he made of me. When we first moved into our new house when I was 10 and Bill was still 3, I had to water the unpaved street in front of our house to settle the dust down so Bill's asthma wouldn't become overly problematic. I also had to paint our gutters with vinegar because dad said that was the best primer. Neither of these activities were my favorites when I was trying to adjust to a new neighborhood. I thanked him, however, in my mind that summer when I was on top of that shiny grey trailer cleaning it to my dad's specifications. That was certainly one of the top five hottest jobs of my entire life and the extra pair of jeans was deeply appreciated (unfortunately for our relationship I never thanked him). After cleaning the trailer we moved Grandma into her new home. She really didn't say anything in my presence about it. When I was eavesdropping on my parents and other relatives, I heard that she thought it was foolish and that she could manage just fine where she was. I chatted away with her in the trailer when we were alone, and I didn't notice any difference in her.

The following winter mom received a letter from Grandma saying that she didn't know those strangers who were in the house next to her trailer. She no longer seemed to recognize my uncle and aunt, yet she could write to her youngest daughter. We didn't go to Kentucky that summer rather we went to Wisconsin to visit Pops, my paternal grandfather, at his cottage. It was a family get-a-way from the bustle of Chicago for Pops and my aunt and her family. We hadn't been back to Chicago since my grandma, Nana, had died on Good Friday, 1957. Dad said he wanted to do so before something happened to Pops. Ironically it was my dad's health and the estrangement with his sister (details later) that prevented us from ever returning to Chicago or Wisconsin.

The following summer it was back to Kentucky as usual. We weren't staying long because we were on our way to New Iberia, Louisiana, to see my brother, Paul, receive his Wings at his Naval Flight graduation ceremony. When we arrived at Uncle James and Aunt Lona's, we were quickly escorted into their home and were told of Grandma's condition. They turned to me with sad eyes and said "Cha-le-RAY, Grandma Pearl won't know who you are. She doesn't know who anyone is and can't remember anything - even her youth or husband."

I went alone to the trailer and noticed the others lingering behind. I knocked on the door. When she opened it I heard, "Well I'll be, Cha-le-RAY won't you come in and have some lemonade with me." I turned, smiled, and entered the trailer. She got out pictures we had often looked at together and we talked about family. The only difference I noticed was that she was far chattier than I had remembered. She was also becoming feeble. She had always been thin, but now the veins in her arms and her chicken neck were very pronounced. Her movements were slow and strained. The rest of the family was astounded - for some reason I was not.

Life's twists provide us with blessings and pain. I never would have imagined that that would be the last time I would ever see her or talk to her again. One of the most important lessons that maturity can give us is the danger of taking health, family, friends, or anything, for that matter, for granted. Aging does not guarantee maturity, but when it arrives it is truly a blessing. My last experience with my Grandma Pearl came during the summer after my sophomore year of college. One day I was walking with a girl friend around her neighborhood. When we returned to her family's home, she asked if I wanted a sandwich. Never one to turn down food I said sure. When she returned to the living room, she found me in a fetal position on her couch.

"What's the matter?" with concern in her voice.

"My grandma just died. I have to go." I immediately got up and took off for home. All I remember of the experience is that my stomach had suddenly knotted up, crippling me. I managed to crawl to the couch and curl up. I was conscious of nothing. I heard no voices; had no thoughts; sensed nothing else but the tightness in my whole torso. I hadn't even thought of my grandma until my girl friend asked her question. I did not intend to say the words I did; they just came out of my mouth. My dad had actually let me drive the family car to visit her (she lived about 20 miles from my home). On the drive home I reminisced about my grandma. As soon as I got in the house my dad yelled "For Christ's sake, where have you been? Your grandmother just died and I have to get down there. Your mother just called." (I don't remember how long mom was with her mother before the call.) I was working that summer and couldn't afford to lose any time or wages, so my dad drove down by himself and I was charged with taking care of Bill. I will never forget that last and enduring connection with my Grandma Pearl.

The generations that were old during the 1930s, 40s and even 50s seemed more resigned to their lot in life and were generally less active than they had been earlier in their lives. The WW II generation seemed to begin the shift in old age, as they became more active in retirement and became more interested in senior villages, senior housing, senior discounts and blue light specials. The Baby Boom Generations will extend this redefinition of old age in ways that may not even be imaginable yet. There are three primary reasons for this: improved health, extended years of retirement, and the dynamics of the Baby Boom Generations.

As a member of the Boomers I have gone through the significant redefinitions of society that these generations have created. It is a misnomer to refer to the Baby Boom Generation in a singular way. The dates for the Boomers range from 1946 to 1964. That 18 year span really covers three different generations and should be understood as three different cohorts. These generations have been redefining social structures and activities from the very beginning. First they caused significant shifts in education; then in the workplace; and now as they begin swelling the ranks of retirement, they are having a profound impact on what retirement means and about what lifestyles for older people entail. Retirement and being an older person today has a greater image of activity and engagement in life than it did 50 years ago.

Each generation has very distinctive markers and attitudes. It seems to start early. Ask teachers in elementary and secondary schools and they will tell you that each class year has distinctive traits, some more tolerable than others. Wars and attitudes towards war help define generational attitudes. WWII produced an overwhelming support of the war and of our GIs. Our service personnel returned to people who supported them and cheered their service. Unfortunately, as a country and as a medical profession, we underserved their mental challenges and failed to address the terrible toll that PTSD imposed upon so many people (service personnel and their families). The generational conflict over war became exposed during Viet Nam. We truly were a country divided and for the most part the older generation could not abide the protests to the war by the youth. What was even more challenging were the awful attitudes that emerged toward our military personnel.

One personal experience explains the conflicting mores of the Viet Nam generation. Before he married Diane's sister and became our brother-in-law, Laurie was a close friend of mine from college. We had become close while performing for our nationally recognized drill team. We were commissioned upon our graduation. I went to graduate school and he went to active duty. I never had to go to Viet Nam; he did. I have always admired his service and have always respected our military personnel. Laurie was stationed in Georgia while we lived in New Orleans and he visited us a few times (even leaving for Viet Nam from New Orleans). On one such occasion Diane couldn't help herself; she set him up on a date with one of her fellow teachers. It was during Mardi Gras season, so the four of us went down to see one of the parades in downtown New Orleans. That night at the parade, I became ashamed of America. I think we took the trolley down St. Charles so we didn't have to try and find a parking place if we drove. Mardi Gras season lasts for a couple of weeks and has at least one nightly parade downtown, meaning it goes down part of Canal Street and St. Charles. The length and directions of the parades vary from

Krewe to Krewe. Each parade has a theme and the floats and trucks can be either sparsely decorated or have elaborate designs along with stunning costumes. Members of the Krewe design and decorate the floats and then ride in their creations throwing trinkets or doubloons to the throngs along the parade route. Each Krewe has its own type of doubloon and during our four years in New Orleans we collected a wide variety of these doubloons, especially the most prized gold ones. Beads were a common item to throw. It is not uncommon to come away with pounds of beads from a more popular parade. Krewe members may also throw other trinkets such as plastic animals, squirt guns, or anything they think will add joviality to the parade and experience.

That night we gathered along the parade route and the three of us showed Laurie how to raise his hands and yell "throw me something miss!" The trick is for men to make eye contact with a female or for females to connect with males on the float so the flirting will end up with a prize - doubloon or trinket thrown into the outstretched hands. If someone doesn't catch the prize, a free-for-all can be expected as anyone nearby will try to retrieve whatever had fallen free. Sometimes revelers would toss a handful of trinkets or doubloons and send them out into the masses without any particular target in mind. As Laurie began to follow the rules a peculiar phenomenon began to emerge. People on the floats would start yelling at him - "baby killer", "monster", etc. They seemed to be blaming him for the war when he was only doing his duty to protect those who were yelling at him. They also made it clear when they threw trinkets at his head; they weren't tossing their treats; they were aiming them and sending them toward Laurie as if they were missiles intent upon hurting, not rewarding their target. The war divided people into opposing camps: for the war, against it, willing to serve but not liking it, serving because it was one's duty, and a number of other permutations. One significant impact was a general lack of respect for our military personnel. That attitude bothered me. I was opposed to the war but would have gone to Nam if I had been ordered to do so. Thankfully, I never had to go into combat. Laurie and so many others did. They deserved our respect then and they still do today. Now we seem to have a generation that has learned how to oppose a war, decided upon by politicians and military commanders, while respecting and supporting those who defend us. Why should we blame those who do their duty while not holding accountable the others who make the decisions to fight?

There are many generational markers: music, clothing, taste in food and the arts readily come to mind. I remember a colleague of mind at Canisius telling me about a student who asked her, "Did you know that Paul McCartney was in a band before Wings?" We both groaned and laughed. Another defining characteristic for generations relates to significant national events. Everyone in my generation knows what he or she was doing when we heard about JFK's assassination. I was on a bus with my high school football team. We had come within one point of winning our league championship and our coach was rewarding us with a trip to Detroit. We left on Friday, November 22, from school and were going to spend the night in Detroit; the next day we were headed to the Michigan vs. Ohio State game. We were all excited and many were sharing the usual male testosterone that emerges on a bus with teenagers. We stopped at customs at the Lewiston-Queenston Bridge. (We were taking the route through Canada to get to Detroit.) The agent told our coach that Kennedy had shot himself in the foot on a hunting trip in Texas. That is the only thing we heard until we reached Detroit. I remember some of the guys making far too many jokes about JFK and his ineptitude. Kennedy had become my first political hero. As a Catholic boy of 14, I followed the presidential race and wanted Kennedy to win and show the world that Catholics could be leaders. The debate with Nixon is something I watched with a great deal of interest and, like so many others, I knew Kennedy had won the hearts of America against the more seasoned politician. When we arrived in Detroit, I was duly shocked when I got off the bus and saw the headline on the paper at the newsstand going into the hotel: "Kennedy Assassinated." It was rather surreal. The coach and the team seemed to slough the tragedy off and adopted a typical male attitude: we've come this far, let's enjoy ourselves and the game the next day. So the next morning we drove to the stadium in Ann Arbor only to find out the game was cancelled. The prevailing attitude was disappointment, others were resentful. I was one of those who were disappointed about the game, but my respect for the President overrode my initial selfish response. Of course the game should be cancelled; it would be far too disrespectful in the wake of this tragedy. Our coach took us to a restaurant before we headed home and we had a back room all to ourselves. We ordered steaks and the coach handed out cigars after the meal. The male ego and hormones were being assuaged. When we got home, I spent as much time as I could in front of the television watching the coverage of the assassination and then of the funeral. I still see JFK's son, John, saluting the casket. That event was a marker for my generation: truly Camelot was shattered and our world changed forever.

Of course 9/11 impacted all of us. I do believe that our responses may be contoured by our generations. For my generation it was another horrible tragedy that the country experienced. I expect that those who were teens on 9/11 will forever remember what they were doing and where they were when they first heard. In like manner, what was the generational impact upon the children who were in school and glued to the class room television only to see the Challenger explode? That was another generational defining moment. Around these moments, attitudes and beliefs become formed, changed, solidified or shattered. One's personality will create deviations from the norms of the cohort for that generation but collectively generations and our society become shifted. America still has not recovered from the hatred unleashed on 9/11 - some justified, some not. That event certainly has unveiled covert and overt prejudices and discrimination. Far too many people have fallen prey to false images of Islam. Those who were teens during 9/11 have a formative trauma that will wittingly or unwittingly define them for the rest of their lives. The number of men and women who volunteered to protect our freedoms increased significantly and respect for their service has reached its appropriate level of recognition.

One of the more famous intergenerational quotes goes something like this: "The children now love luxury. They have bad manners, contempt for authority and show disrespect for elders." This quote is attributed to Socrates, which makes it over 2400 years old. Some things never change, including the stereotyping and images which generations have for one another. The WWII generation becomes exasperated at the younger generations for wearing hats indoors or backwards. Social changes may shift generational relevance. The younger generations have to tutor older generations on how to use smart phones or other technological devices. Older generations want to talk to younger people, while the youth prefer tweeting, texting, snap chatting or just remaining glued to their devices. This shift from interpersonal connectedness to the intermediary connections of social media is profound. Older generations have historically wanted to share their knowledge and wisdom with younger generations. It is not uncommon for children to reject their parents' teachings or admonitions (especially during the delightful teenage years). Sometimes the youth shift their attitude when they become adults or parents themselves. "Oh my gosh, I sound just like my mother or father!" This proclamation is not uncommon. The notion of a generation gap has become a cliché, which is rooted in reality. Grandparents, especially those who do not have to raise grandchildren, may be an exception to the rule that the younger generation doesn't pay attention to the older generations. There is a common stereotype that intergenerational respect often skips a generation. Grandchildren and grandparents may get along better than children and their parents. I love being a grandparent (papa) because I am not responsible for my munchkins. I can enjoy them, talk with them, tell stories, go for walks, read together, go to movies, play games on land or in a pool, etc. We try to get the whole family together twice a year (Christmas or Easter) and during the summer. It is great to have the three generations enjoy each other's company. When Diane's parents and aunt were still alive, there were times of four generational activities. The only tiffs among the children are with siblings; the cousins have great relationships. I know I treated my uncles and aunts in Kentucky in a very different way from my parents. I probably never realized they were the same generation. Uncle Oral and Aunt Myrtle seemed more like my Grandma Pearl, and I viewed them as an older, respected generation - not my parents' age. Uncle James and Aunt Lona were singular since they had no children and treated me as a king. It was easy to listen to them and relate to their experiences. My relatives in Chicago were not a real part of my life.

Generational issues and discussions may be even more generalized than the other topics I have been addressing in this book. Deviations and exceptions are rather common. My brothers and I actually represent three different generations Paul is almost 15 years older than Bill. Paul is not a member of the Boomers and I was born the year people assign as the beginning of the Boomers. Bill is 6 ½ years younger than me and is part of the second grouping of the Boomers. Compounding the age and cohort differences we actually experienced a different father, even though he was the same man. Our relationships were quite different and we have very few common experiences among the three of us. As the middle son I can relate to each brother in a different way when considering who our father was and what we may or may not have learned from him. My older brother relished in the mechanical things and the carpentry he learned from Dad. Dad was more active and his drinking was more social when Paul was around. I know Paul learned to love and respect the discipline Dad meted out to him during Paul's challenging youthful years. I used to consider Dad's parental teachings and practices to be those things I would avoid as a parent. He became an alcoholic as I was a teen and I felt I needed to protect my mom from him. My younger brother received more parental guidance from my mom's second husband than from our father. Bill's memory of dad is a drunk who did nothing but sit in a chair, smoke and give orders.

I have thought a lot about the educational role of older generations and have been thinking about legacy issues myself. One definition of legacy is that it is "something transmitted by or received from an ancestor or predecessor". That something has a wide berth of meanings. You can make your own lists. What have you learned? What do you remember? Which memories are cherished and which are painful? The issue remains that generations define themselves and others in ways that follow the contours and collective experiences of their cohort. As with all other groupings, we set up categories and attribute values or judgments predicated on stereotypes that have emerged from our collective experiences. As with all stereotyping there are elements of truth in them and there are dangers in attributing those collective assessments to individuals. My life has evolved and changed from being the youngest generation, through middle, now to an older generation. I am no longer the adored grandchild, but I do hope I'm becoming a loved and respected Papa.

CHAPTER 8
AGING'S REALITIES AND MYTHS

The great thing about getting older is that
You don't lose all the other ages.

Madeline L'Engle

The walk was by now a familiar one. Off the elevator and out through the doorway leading toward Tulane's campus. The laundry was on the right and almost always full of people from around the world. Our apartment was in the married housing unit at one end of the campus. My route took me past the old Sugar Bowl - an icon of New Orleans that is now long gone. I had been to Green Wave and Saints football games there. It was the site for Super Bowl IV, and I could have gotten a ticket for $15 but decided that was too expensive for us. Since the stadium had no parking lots, on game day or night the neighborhoods became overrun with cars looking for a place. Buses would line up next to the stadium to drop off fans. Tulane's campus is narrow and long. In the late '60s and early '70s most of the buildings were old, stone testaments to a staid, elite bastion for learning. They had slowly sunk into the ground so that you had to walk down a few steps to get to the first floor. The large, stone staircase going into the oldest building located on St. Charles led directly onto the second floor. At one end of the campus was Claiborne, the street on which our apartment was located. At the other end was St. Charles

Ave. with its trolley cars and beautiful houses and mansions. Across the avenue from the campus was Audubon Park with its majestic oaks and Spanish Moss. Loyola New Orleans, a Jesuit college, was along part of one of the long sides of the campus, while neighborhoods completed that side and the opposite long side. My walk took me past the library, a frequent destination for my research. My dissertation is now housed in some dusty corner of the building. At first our dissertations were placed on the shelves available for any and all to read. A common challenge was to put a $1 bill somewhere inside the dissertation to see if it was still there when the author checked out his or her book a year or so after publication. I never expected to be back to the library once I'd graduated so I never bothered to waste the money. I couldn't imagine anyone would have been interested in "Bergson's Meaning of Continuity" anyhow.

After making a right on Willow, then a left on Broad St., I would approach the old, old home of my mentor, Professor Lee. Most people affectionately referred to him as Old Man Lee, because his son, Donald, also taught in the Philosophy Department. Often a graduate assistant would greet me at the door and then disappear while I spent the hour or hour and one half with this wise man. His wife was always a peripheral character to the home. I don't ever remember talking to her or of hearing Old Man Lee talk about her or any experience he ever had with her. Only about 30 to 40 percent of our time together focused upon my thesis or dissertation. The rest of the time was his reminiscences of his career and people with whom he had taught or those who taught him. He regaled in John Dewey's boring lectures. "Dewey just sat there, staring at a corner where the wall and ceiling met. He would drone on and on shelling out brilliant gems for us to gather," he said with a smile. He also shared his views of tangential but very intriguing philosophical theories or controversies. For example one day we agreed that elementary education in the United States was suffering because Aesop's fables were no longer a part of the curriculum.

Old Man Lee was a logician and specialized in symbolic logic - a requirement for all graduate students in the department. I struggled at first because I never had an undergraduate course in traditional logic and his course assumed a basic understanding of logical thinking. That was not my only deficiency in my undergraduate preparation for my graduate degrees. I also had not taken any Greek or Medieval Philosophy courses, which were also a prerequisite for some of the courses I had to take. My 13 undergraduate philosophy courses were filled with what I felt like taking - those topics that appealed to my authentic self. At Tulane I probably spent 80+ hours a week not only doing my assignments and readings but trying to catch up with material I should have had in my undergraduate courses. My college advisor allowed me to take the courses I wanted rather than the courses I needed to take. This was a lesson I used as an advisor in my career at Canisius: allow students to follow their passion for study but guide them in the selection of courses. Determine what their next goal was and tailor the courses to help fulfill that goal. If a student is undecided, then keep the course work diverse and cover as many areas as reasonable.

Old Man Lee and I were an unusual combination. During my first year I had to take a full load of courses each semester and begin to decide upon a thesis for my Masters Degree. Satisfying my language requirement has always amused Diane. I had to demonstrate proficiency in two languages. French was not a problem (two years of high school and two years of collegiate course work were sufficient). I decided that my Latin wasn't up to speed and German seemed out of my reach, so I opted for Spanish - besides Diane seemed to be an expert for me. Over about a six-week period, I took out some Spanish books written by philosophers (not the easiest reads). Diane helped me with the translations, along with a dictionary. I assumed that my French grammar would be satisfactory for the Spanish. I decided to take the proficiency exam quickly to see how far I had to go to satisfy the requirement. When I received the test results, Diane and I laughed because I had passed with plenty of room to spare. Whew.

My deliberations for a topic for my thesis focused upon two philosophers: Henri Bergson and Soren Kierkegaard. I had studied Kierkegaard
extensively in college and had read almost all of his works. The only problem I saw was my feeling that I may be too attached to his ideas and may
lack the objectivity or distance needed for defending a particular topic and
theme. I had been introduced to Bergson's ideas in my first semester at
Tulane. His concepts of creative evolution and time, along with his methodology of combining the intellect with intuition were very appealing. I
decided to focus on Bergson's meaning of intuition. When I presented
the idea to the department chairman, he suggested that I work with Old
Man Lee. The chairman said the problem I would have in trying to defend
Bergson's methodology of using intuition would come from faculty who
did not accept this methodology. I would confront stiff opposition from
those faculty assigned to read, critique and challenge me during my oral
defense. He was wise in saying that Old Man Lee would be perfect because Old Man Lee was a logician who did not believe there was any such
thing as intuition. If I could write and defend a paper with him, then the
hurdle with any other professor at Tulane would be minimal. He thought
intuition was folly but he did not discount my desire to try and prove that
intuition had a place in intellectual discourse. He kept me intellectually
honest and rigorous; something I tried to impart to my students throughout my teaching career.

I started working with Old Man Lee that summer and by the following
April I was ready to defend my thesis. The day of my defense, before Lee
and two other faculty, proved to be a bit of an adventure. One of the faculty members assigned to the team had read my thesis and provided critical
comments that I addressed in my revisions. My defense was scheduled
for 10 AM (the year was 1970). Old Man Lee and I were the only ones
to show up. The other two were involved in the campus demonstration
against the Viet Nam war. After about an hour, one of them did show up
and Old Man Lee decided that was sufficient. I received my Masters that

May. Since I had decided to stay with Bergson for my doctoral dissertation, I asked Old Man Lee to remain as my advisor. He readily agreed and we spent two more years working together. There were a couple of bumps along the way.

During my first semester at Tulane I took a course entitled "American Philosophy" taught by Andrew Reck. He was a noted scholar in the field. I received A's in my oral presentations, but when he returned my final paper assignment he gave me a "U" and wrote at the end that I should consider leaving the program because my writing was so poor. He assigned me a B for the course (considered to be a very low grade). I remember looking at his comment and walking out of the classroom building and crossing St. Charles to wander through Audubon Park. I found a swing and spent quite some time pondering what to do. Eventually I realized that writing was one of Diane's many strengths and, therefore, my deficiencies could be remedied. I never spoke to Dr. Reck about his comments, knowing that I would not have to take another course from him. After I received my Masters, however, Dr. Reck was named the department chairman. I hoped that wouldn't be a problem. When I went to him to get permission for Old Man Lee to be my dissertation advisor, he threw me a curve.

"Of course, Professor Lee would love to work with you. He told me so himself. However, he is having difficulties with his eyes and may lose his sight. So it is possible that he may not be able to work with you for the entire time you will need to complete the dissertation. Usually you, the candidate, would select the other members of your review team, but in this case I am going to appoint myself as the co-advisor in case he is incapacitated."

My stomach lurched and I felt a sense of doom overtake me. Of course I nodded and said that would be great. I moved ahead very warily knowing that I had to work with a man who thought I should leave his program. Despite this underlying concern for the next two years, I wrote, submitted chapters and met with Old Man Lee regularly. By the end of May, 1972 I was not finished with all of the revisions that were made on my 300+ page dissertation. Old Man Lee indicated that I was on the right track, but revisions were necessary in many of the chapters. The challenge I encountered was a call to military service that would begin on July 1st. I had to report for advanced training for the Military Police at Fort Gordon, Georgia. Old Man Lee assured me that we had been working together for three years, and we could readily complete the process via the mail. I reported to Fort Gordon on July 1 and left on Sept. 30. While I was undergoing Military Police training I was revising my dissertation to address the concerns and comments made by Professor Lee and one other faculty member. It took me another two months after my training when I returned home to Diane and Tara to finish the edits.

By the following February I was ready to type up the final version and submit it to the department. In April I had to go to Tulane to defend the dissertation in front of the entire Philosophy Department plus one outside expert knowledgeable about my theme. They selected a man from France who was an international scholar in Bergson. I was very nervous walking into the room. The faculty wore their academic regalia and I sat at the head of the long table with Old Man Lee at the other end. For two hours I was peppered with questions. One exchange was very taxing. Young Lee, the old man's son, was an expert in the philosophy of science. I had taken him for a course during my first year and was invited to his house to witness Neil Armstrong take the first steps on the moon. During the defense there was no evidence of the amiability he had shown me years earlier. He was direct, unrelenting and challenging the basic methodology I was using. I had expected him to challenge my chapter critiquing Einstein, but he passed over that. After almost 15-20 minutes Dr. Reck chimed in and chided Young Lee.

"That's enough Donald. He has stated his position and provided his defense. Just because you don't agree with his premise is not a sufficient reason for continuing this line of inquiry. Let's move on."

I was stunned. The man who told me I should leave the program was now coming to my defense. The expert from France asked a few questions but I did not find them too difficult to answer. Hopefully, I wasn't deluding myself. After the inquisition was completed, I was asked to leave the room and wait in the hall. That was a long wait (a totally subjective assessment). I kept revisiting questions and my answers. The non-verbals were of no assistance in determining what the faculty were thinking. It never dawned on me that much of the time they may have been zoned out of the conversation. This was my life and involved years of research, study, drafting, dealing with critiques, etc. How could they not be as invested as I was in the topic? Finally Old Man Lee emerged with a smile on his face and came over and congratulated me. The next person was Dr. Reck who smiled and said, "I'm glad you proved me wrong." Whoa - he hadn't forgotten. Old Man Lee and I remained in touch for a number of years. He sent me articles he had published and he assisted me in getting an article published a year later. As is so often the case in life, we corresponded less and less over the following years. I do not know when he died; I had let my life and commitments get in the way; another important person in my life now gone without me knowing where or when. I did care; it's just that I took him for granted and didn't bother to take the time to reconnect with him.

When I was an Assistant Dean in the late 1970s I worked with a colleague to develop and implement a Gerontology Program for Canisius. In addition to my administrative responsibilities, I became intrigued with the study and research on aging. My doctoral dissertation dealt with the meaning of continuity related to the philosophy of time espoused by Henri Bergson. At the center of my research was the topic of change and time. As I dealt with aging issues related to this new program it struck me that aging is really a temporal concept or phenomenon. I began to research this thought (and/or phenomenon) and found very few people even bothered with applying any philosophy of time to aging. I've written a couple of articles and given a number of talks on the subject. A couple of my papers included a model for looking at time and aging from an unconventional perspective. I developed a course entitled "Time and the Human Condition" which applied different philosophies of time to cultural studies and aging. Later I developed an Honors version of this course that allowed me to expand the philosophies being covered. My premise was if we studied three (later four) differing philosophies of time and applied them to aging, we would get different ways of looking at aging. Briefly:

Theory 1 (Aristotle). Time is an objective medium within which events occur. Time is linear (running from birth to death) which allows us to measure this medium. Clocks become useful tools for reading these measurements. Time is on-going (never stops), objective (independent of any person) and homogeneous (one measured minute is just like any other). In a sense it does not change, but it does cause events to change. With this theory, aging is a numerical process that happens to us. We can measure it and we can feel the pressure of time moving from our past to our future. Age happens to us and it is inexorable. Age causes decay and increases declines over time. We have to struggle to slow this inevitable process down. Basically we are living in time.

Theory 2 (Augustine). Time is subjective and a part of our consciousness. It is coming at us: time flows from the future to the past. We may perceive three times but only one really exists: the present. The past is our memory that exists in the present. The future is our anticipation, which also exists in the present. Our language proves this case because the present tense is the only one that exists; the other tenses are dependent upon the present. Aging is subjective: we are as old as we feel is a common cliché for this theory. Aging is not causal. Aging is related to maturity and wisdom. Who we are relates to our souls and our mind, and we have the opportunity for gaining wisdom. Aging should not be seen as a decline or decay; rather it is filled with hope and the development of wisdom. Maturity is more important than numbers. Basically time is in us.

Theory 3 (Bergson). Time is a creative, evolving process of consciousness. It entails our memories and our hopes. Who we are is a creative blending of all the dimensions in our lives. An objective view of time is only a measurement. This measurement is distorting and misleading. I often used the following example to explain the issue: if we use a ruler to measure the height of a person, there are three elements that are necessary for doing so: a ruler, a unit of measurement, and the person being measured. When applied to time, we have the clock as the ruler; hours, minutes, etc. as the units; and time itself as what is being measured. Trying to understand what time means becomes the issue. One real deficiency in thinking about time is when we reduce the meaning of time to its measurement. They are quite different. The meaning of time is much more than understanding the way it may be measured or the characteristics of this measurement. In this view, aging is a creative and dynamic process that includes ebbs and flows. It is neither objective nor subjective; in a sense it is both. We experience increased vulnerability (our bodies may have to deal with conditions that are problematic, although we can do things to cope with or ameliorate these conditions). We also have opportunities that are continually becoming present to us. We have options and choices. We may mature, learn and develop wisdom; all of which are dependent upon our life styles, background, choices and the impact of all the contextual dimensions within our lives. Basically time is an evolving and ever-changing flow of consciousness.

The more I delved into what aging meant the more exposed I became to the issues revolving around ageism in society. Ageism is usually based on societal ignorance and stereotypes. As with all stereotypes we may see examples that may seem to confirm the stereotype, for example, slow drivers, especially those whose heads are hidden by the head rest on the seat. Of course when we pull next to the driver and see that it is a short teenager, we may either smile at our rash judgment or just ignore what could be a lesson for us about stereotyping. Our language plays into our stereotypes and the meaning we attribute to aging. In one of my aging courses I asked the students to immediately write down the words they associate with: old man, age, elderly, and old woman. Their responses usually fell within two categories: one with positive connotations, the other negative. Typically they wrote down: wise, mature, respected or senile, declining, vulnerable, out of touch (or out of date), incompetent, over-the-hill, etc. I'm sure you could readily add to the list. As I mentioned with respect to the racial connotations of the words black and white, the connotations that we have for these words must have some impact upon the way we view those who fit into our stereotypes. I tried showing the students that the negative stereotypes of decline and decay in aging fit into Aristotle's view: we live in time; it pushes us along; and we decline as we go. Augustine's view is more positive – wisdom can be discovered as opportunities come toward us. For me Bergson's view provided a means to avoid either view: too negative or too positive. Change is inevitable in life and we have opportunities to learn from our experiences or those opportunities may be lost.

Years ago the stereotype of nursing homes was that they were a way to get rid of a burden or ease the lives of those saddled with the responsibility of caring for an old person. There have been significant changes in attitude and approaches in institutional care for our "elderly" population, yet the feelings of guilt for institutionalizing a loved one persists. I had this experience with my Aunt Lona. She had worked at a nursing home not far from her farm. It was located near Possum Trot, Kentucky. I had been there once years before to visit my aunt's sister. My impression was not positive. When I talked to Aunt Lona about what to do if something happened to her, she was adamant. "Char–la–Ray, there is no way you can care for me, and I don't want to go north where you live. Just put me in the home. I'll be fine." Her generation was and continues to be preoccupied with not being a burden to a younger generation. Diane's mom was almost obsessed with this feeling and had difficulty with living with one daughter and imposing on the other for transportation and care. I remember telling her that she should reconsider the way she thinks. I wish I had the opportunity to share experiences with my mom. She's been gone since 1986. I told my mother-in-law that her daughters still had the opportunity I was denied. She should relish in giving them the time and experience of sharing her stories and of creating new memories. Her grandchildren and great-grandchildren were given a wonderful gift of her presence, love and care. Those connections are not a burden.

The nursing home for my aunt had three hallways with different levels of care. One was for those who had dementia; another for those who were physically dependent; the third was for those who were mobile (including wheelchair patients). It was a sad place to visit and seemed to embody many of the negative stereotypes of nursing homes: tiled floors, bored residents, pre-occupied staff members, and overly medicated people in wheel chairs. I had one significant frustration with almost all of the personnel who worked there. They seemed to assume that my aunt's aphasia (caused by the stroke) meant that she wasn't "all there" anymore. However, she was still aware and connected to the world and to others. She just couldn't get the right words while trying to communicate. I noticed a slow deterioration of her condition over time. I was convinced that it was largely exacerbated by caregivers who stereotyped her behavior and treated her accordingly. Since she couldn't speak properly or use the correct words, she was seen as incompetent. The care givers seemed to assume that all she needed was to be fed and given her meds because she couldn't engage with other people. All they had to do was insure that she was clean and docile. In the last couple of years of her life, my aunt began to behave in a hostile fashion, especially to anyone who had the misfortune of becoming her roommate. Throughout her life she was a gentle and kind human being. But that person seemed to have become lost. She was replaced by a caustic, nasty woman. Eventually they just stopped assigning anyone to room with her. One time when I was visiting I asked what happened to her roommate. I was able to decipher her answers to my probing questions.

She said that the last one was just plain stupid. The daily frustration of pigeon-holing someone and treating him or her in ways that are demeaning and degrading is just too much. Respect requires more than just patting someone on the shoulder and calling her Sweetie or Honey.

When I left administration and began teaching full time, I expanded the Gerontology Program and developed more courses in aging in a variety of departments. My administrative career spanned 17 years; full-time teaching lasted 18 years. Regardless of the administrative position I held, I tried to teach a course each semester. I felt it was important for me to keep myself engaged in the primary purpose of higher education: teaching. Besides, it has always been my calling. While I was Dean in addition to offering the Time course on a regular basis, I developed and started offering "Ethics and Human Services". It became a requirement in Gerontology and a major elective in Psychology and in Sociology. Thus, I ended up teaching at least one course a year for all 35 years at Canisius. When I was transitioning from administration to the faculty I had a sabbatical devoted to curriculum development (which included a 10 day course in Hawaii addressing intercultural education and a 3 week delegation to Moscow, St. Petersburg, Kiev, Prague and Berlin dedicated to Medical Care for the Elderly). I began teaching our basic aging course by myself (having team taught it for a few years), took over an English course developed by a friend and former teacher, and designed new courses in psychology, sociology, philosophy, communication studies and anthropology. Those courses were added to the Ethics and to the Time courses I already was regularly offering. I had given papers at a state-wide association for aging and two different national associations while I was in administration. After I began teaching full-time, I had the time to become very active in the national association dedicated to development and improvement of programs in aging: The Association for Gerontology in Higher Education (AGHE). This activity included running two national conferences, one in Boston and the other in Philadelphia. These activities opened up a number of opportunities for me to learn about aging.

One semester while I was still in administration I was awarded a sabbatical and a friend of mine at Syracuse, who was the chairman of their All Gerontology Center, appointed me as a Visiting Associate. I commuted from home, while sometimes staying with my sister-in-law and brother-in-law and their family who were living in the Syracuse area at the time. I took some courses, visited with faculty throughout the University to assist my friend in expanding the interest in teaching aging to other faculty, co-authored a paper, and talked with a colleague in the Sociology Department about an aging game. We discussed some of its outlines and I finished developing the board game on my own over the following year. I have used it in classes and for a couple of workshops. The game intentionally places the players into stereotyped roles in life and assumes some basic categorizations to illustrate social dynamics. Players are born into a socio-economic class with a gender and race that usually is not their own. A white middle class male student, for example, may play the game as a lower class Asian woman or an upper class African American male or a middle class Native American woman. All players proceed through childhood by answering questions based on Eric Erickson's stages of life. (Eric Erickson provided stages that we go through in our life. His stages included late life transitions and were not just restricted to childhood or adolescent development.) The responses to those questions are converted into Maslow's Needs. (Abraham Maslow said we have five basic needs that we must address in our life: Esteem, Belonging, Physical, Security and Friendship.) Each player acquires or loses chips that simulate attending to or failing to address these essential needs in life. Players also acquire or lose stress depending upon the decisions they make throughout the game. Too much stress could lead to life- altering consequences, including a fatal heart attack. Not attending to Maslow's needs definitely impacted what a player was able to do or not to do.

I named the game "Decisions." Once players have finished their childhood, they start making decisions and proceed at their own pace. They roll dice and move along life's path and are given decision cards at each stop. They may choose from two or three options; however, some options are closed based on their life situation. For example, lower class African Americans are restricted in their housing options. As players proceed through life, they are required to make decisions about major stages in life: college, work/career, marriage, and housing. At these junctions they stop and follow the instructions for each stage. All players earn or lose money along the way. Pay scales are skewed depending on race and gender: White and Asian males earn the most, while the other categories can only earn a percentage of what these males can earn. For example, African American females and Native American females have pay scales that are reduced by 50%. All players go through mid-life and late life transitions. Everyone is required to retire (unless they have experienced an early death). The end of the game is Life Review and the players have a list of questions they must address. Instructions for different stages in life are only to be read when they reach that stage - life doesn't give us a guidebook ahead of time. The purpose of the game is to create an opportunity for students to live an entire life and reflect upon what they could and could not do. The aim is to simulate one's psychological development and the impact of the consequences of their decisions. The game provides for some individual decision-making but also includes forces that are beyond one's control. The game blatantly exposes the injustices and inequities in our society. Most students feel the brunt of the inequities at some time during their lives, while others may sail through life and can call their lives successful by the stereotypical standards the students discuss at the end.

Social stereotypes are built into the game to encourage a discussion about the impact they play in our lives. All players see the consequences of stereotyping and discriminatory practices in society. One important lesson I've included in the game is developing friendships in life. I have a brief paragraph explaining the rules for friendship (basically there are none). At the beginning I briefly mention the instructions but leave the students or players to make friendships or not. Few students end up having friendships during the game. Some may not bother reading these rules and just ignore it. Some are so intent on getting things right or getting through life or getting to the next stage that they don't bother befriending other players. Players may marry a fictional character or someone else in the game. If they marry another player, they are required to make major decisions with their spouses. Those players are typically the only ones who usually engage in any meaningful way with other players. There is bantering and laughter, but for the most part players are rather task-oriented and oblivious of what is going on around them .

I introduce homosexuality by making it one of the cards players may pick during their way through life. All of a sudden they have to deal with this realization. I wanted students to have to confront what this lifestyle would mean but did not include it from birth. Maybe my covert prejudice was closing my eyes when I was designing the game in the early 90s. I have never seriously looked into having it published in any format. If I were to do so, I would change that element and make sure that sexual diversity is built into the options for an individual's identity at the very beginning. The game is best played with a group of 10-15 players. One last note: I am the Shogun. That means that I make overarching decisions that occur: whether people can buy certain houses; how divorces will be managed; and walking them through the childhood questions. I have also outlined how to shift the entire playing of the game by introducing major societal events: 9/11, recessions, natural catastrophe, pandemics, etc. The game plays well and achieves its purposes. It makes for a good simulation for a basic course on aging. It always provides for detailed discussions in classes after the game is played. The paper assignments are designed to make students reflect upon the meaning of aging and the impact society has on individuals.

Americans make a fundamental mistake if they assume that older people are inevitably either in decline or wise. There is a danger in either stereotype: overly positive or overly negative. Seeing aging as constant decay or proceeding along a line of decline or leading to social disengagement is overly detrimental to older people. Such a view can create self-fulfilling prophecies for seniors. On the other hand, thinking that getting old is easy and everything is just grand is similarly distorting of reality. Growing old isn't easy! Being old is never a guarantee for wisdom either. I return to the constant theme in this book and say that balance should be our guide. My life has had tremendous blessings but has not been without its trials. I revel in my retirement: visiting my daughters and their husbands, grandchildren, travel (especially with our Dutch friends), time with Diane, ministry work in the church and the opportunity of writing this book are true blessings. Medical issues including surgeries and chronic conditions are real impediments. Truly life is a balance and any stereotype which puts aging in a too positive or a too negative a light is doing a disservice. Those extremes suffer from prejudices that can have a profound impact on people. Aging should not be modeled either as being illderly or wellderly. It is neither **and** both. (By the way: words such as elderly and senior are not welcomed! It was difficult for me to use them.)

I included this chapter within a section on generations because that is how I have always framed aging. We age within a generation and that generation has a profound impact on how we age, how we approach aging, and on how others look at us. Our prejudices, stereotypes and behaviors toward aging are inevitably linked to our generational cohorts. Societal attitudes toward aging and how younger generations treat their elders reveal a great deal about the values of that society. I am impressed with the Chinese who refer to their nursing homes as Homes of Respect. For the Chinese, aging and intergenerational relationships are centered upon the value of respect: respect one's own aging processes and respect those who are older than you. Confucian morality is predicated upon intergenerational reciprocity with very strict admonitions for attending to one's elders. "Do not do unto others what you do not wish done unto you" is one of his formulations for love, the basic value in his moral code. For him a society that is based upon reciprocal respect and motivated by love would be a good and healthy society. In addition to Confucian moral teachings, the Chinese have practiced ancestor worship for millennia. Mao tried to undermine these codes and principles during the Cultural Revolution, but the people did not forget Confucian thinking or honoring their ancestors. As China industrializes its economy and becomes a world leader, Confucian values are becoming challenged and eroded by the governing institutions. How well the people maintain these values will be an interpersonal and intergenerational conflict that is rarely discussed or maybe even noticed. The soul of China has been Daoistic and Confucian. Ancestor worship, Christianity and Buddhism have left their marks in recognizable and in some very subtle ways. Will China lose its soul as it modernizes? Has it already done so? How have traditional values affected modern family relationships? How has and how will the one child per family policy remodel China's intergenerational relationships? Even though the policy is no longer enforced the effects will continue to ripple in unforeseen ways.

In the early '80s I was on a delegation to China (visiting Shanghai, Beijing, Dalian, Wuxi and Hangzhou). We visited hospitals and saw traditional Chinese medical practices at work. We also visited Homes of Respect. I was struck by the Chinese reverence for elders. Deference was always given to those who had grey hair in our delegation. The Judeo-Christian practice of honoring one's parents paled compared to the societal practices in China. Today, there seems to be a resurgence of their traditional values. The Chinese are trying to blend industrial and economic progress with their traditional values rooted in Daoism, Confucian morality, ancestor worship and Buddhism. These traditional values place one's elders in a preeminent role for everyone.

In Dalian I gave a paper contrasting Chinese and American values about aging. I did so to address, indirectly, some institutional problems the Chinese were beginning to face as they, like us, were experiencing a declining work force and an expanding retired population. In China, however, the prevailing attitude has been deferential and demonstrated reverence for older people. A Chinese morality story explains the issue. A young man was married and had one son. He and his wife were poor. As was the custom they cared for the man's elderly mother. Their poverty became so severe that they had to make a decision about eliminating one person from the household. So the man took his son into the woods with a shovel. As he began digging the hole for his son's grave, he unearthed a pot of gold. His respect for his mother became a reward for his proper values in life. I used this story to contrast with a comparable American parable. A mother bird is carrying her baby bird. Another bird asked the mother, "Will your son carry you when you are old?" "No," she responded. "He will carry his baby just as I have taught him."

I used these contrasting stories in my courses to illustrate the different values that exist within the cultural contexts of the countries. America is a youth-based culture and older people are sometimes dealt with in a "throw away" manner. Of course, this attitude is undergoing tremendous shifts as we are becoming an aging society. However, I have been in far too many nursing or retirement homes that have residents who are rarely seen by relatives. When I had to sign the papers to have my Aunt Lona put in the nursing home of her choice, I felt real guilt. I visited once or twice a year. What appalled me was the fact that her nieces, nephews and grand-niece who lived nearby never visited her, EVER. Once her home and belongings were distributed, they no longer had an interest in her. As a society we have a focus upon youth because they are our future and America is predominantly a future oriented culture.

I also served on a delegation that went to Moscow, St. Petersburg, Kiev, Prague and Berlin. The cultural attitudes toward aging in Russia and the

Ukraine were quite depressing. I was the only non-physician in the group and was tasked with understanding cultural issues while the physicians focused on medical matters. I was involved in the sessions for the physicians but made sure I spent extra time by talking with people from all walks of life and especially with the translators. I was trying to get an understanding of their views and values. All of us were appalled by the medical practices we saw at the hospitals in Russia and the Ukraine. The medical practices were outdated, the facilities were dark and poorly equipped, and the staff were inadequately trained (including nurses, physicians and aides). The most telling experiences for me, however, came at the nursing homes. As I talked to residents, there was almost a universal attitude that they were dumped into the homes and were just waiting to die. Being old was cruel because there was nothing else for them to do but live out the days, months and years that their bodies provided. It was startling.

In my courses I used a continuum of social values toward the older members of society. Russia was on the one end with a truly fatalistic attitude that embraced a sense of decline and decay for aged people. China was on the other side with a positive sense of respect and service for older people. America was in the middle. I gave my students contrasting examples from Russia and China. One involved me talking with residents in Russia who had experienced the siege of St. Petersburg during WW II. They had undergone the most horrific experiences imaginable. Those people told me that they had accomplished enough in their lives and now it was time to sit and wait to die. In contrast I talked with four women in a Home of Respect in Beijing. They were life-long friends. They decided to move into the Home because it offered so much for them, including good health care. When I came into their room they were playing MahJong (a game they played very often). They were smiling and extremely pleasant. In Russia the only smiles I saw were ones of melancholy or resignation.

Aging is not just a physiological process; it is not just about our bodies. Aging is psychological, social and spiritual. We are involved in interconnected layers that combine and sometimes clash throughout our life. Who we are cannot be reduced to one part of our life or to one role that we assume. I am not just a father, or grandfather, uncle or brother, deacon or worship leader, neighbor or friend. I am not just a product of 70+ years of living. My journey through life is a complex rainbow of people, experiences, contextual spheres of influence, hopes and dreams, sorrows and tears, and so much more.

Canisius has a number of study abroad programs. One of the features of the program calls for a faculty member to meet the students for a week in the foreign country before their semester begins and to teach them a concentrated course during that week. The course requires an introduction to the city including guided tours. It also allows the students to reduce their course load for the semester, thus giving them ample opportunity to explore and better understand the other country. I mentioned my experience in London and this course earlier. There are a few other details in that experience that relate to the topic of aging. The course I offered was entitled "Psychological Development throughout the Life Course." One of my requirements was for the students to adopt a grandparent from the neighborhood around the campus. For the basic aging course that I offered at Canisius, I required my students to undertake an oral history for two people over the age of 70. (I shudder to think that I am now old enough to be one of their subjects.) We spent time during the first class to go over the protocol that served as the outline for their interviews. I helped them with techniques for interviewing and even discussed the little details necessary for being successful (for example, bringing and using a notebook, getting permission to share their stories, having extra pens available, bringing tissues, etc.). In London I decided that instead of interviewing two people and contrasting the responses, the students had an opportunity of establishing a semester-long relationship with someone in the University's neighborhood. The coordinator from the University did some research for me and provided the students with a list of names, addresses and phone numbers from which they could select their grandparent. Part of their final assignment was to write an analysis of their interviews and relationship and utilize the material from the course as the subject matter of their analysis.

One anecdote will illustrate the success of the venture from my perspective. A student from Philadelphia adopted a widow. After his initial meeting, he decided to visit her almost weekly. They developed a close relationship and he told me how much he learned about England, London and being a widow. When he graduated from the college, a year later, she sent him a sweater that she had knitted. He decided to take his diploma to London to show her and to thank her. What a beautiful intergenerational and intercultural exchange.

At the end of the week the students held a going-away party for me at a nearby pub. We laughed and talked about some of the events of the week: those they liked and those that were less interesting. They loved the "Jack the Ripper" tour we experienced one evening. The various museums received mixed reviews. I taught them how to negotiate The Tubes (subway system) and what to expect at some of the more noted London areas: Soho and Covent Gardens, for example. They also were fascinated by the *Les Mis* experience. One night I took them to a London Theater. I selected *Les Mis* for a number of reasons, one of which related to my use of characters from musicals in my courses. I talked about my portrayal of Rev. John Newton in my chapter on racism and my performance of Judas in a chapter on religion. I had a number of different characters in my aging courses. In my time and aging classes, for example, I wrote a script for the character, Raoul, from *Phantom of the Opera*. The opera begins with Raoul as an old man sitting in a wheel chair at an auction that was selling memorabilia from the Paris Opera House. I projected this character as that of an old man, in a wheelchair, suffering from Parkinson's disease (a testimony to my mom). The musical is basically a love triangle occurring during operatic rehearsals and performances. The Phantom is entranced with Christine's voice (she was a member of the dance chorus). He disliked the operatic lead and managed to secure a lead for Christine. The Phantom was a recluse (having received ugly scars on his face in his youth) who found his creative release in the opera and dictated what could and could not be done in "his" opera house. He secretly gave Christine vocal lessons and he believed she loved him. Raoul is a wealthy patron of the house and was a childhood friend of Christine. When he sees her at her debut he is smitten. The opera weaves a story of the Phantom's quest for Christine's love, only to be rejected. She and Raoul become engaged, which infuriates the Phantom and leads to deadly confrontations. My performance features Raoul talking about his relationships with Christine and the Phantom. It was designed as a life review and I incorporated music from the musical. The lesson was focused upon how a person deals with regret in his life. My interpretation and projection of Raoul as an old man included some guilt about the way he treated the Phantom. He sees that his passions of youth blinded him to the person behind the mask. My portrayal is a monologue directed at the audience (there is no "fourth wall" between me and the audience). Here is one of the observations that my character makes:

"Let me ask each one of you: who among you has not been rejected by others and been made to feel like a fool. Our world is full of the selfishness of people who belittle others and walk over others in order to seek personal gain and power. Each one of us, I'm sure, has become a victim of physical, mental or emotional abuse or ridicule. Do not delude yourself - these travesties may have been blatant or they have been just a subtle assault; nonetheless you have felt at least one of their blows. So in that sense we are all a bit of a phantom: we all don masks to hide our pain. The tragedy is for those of us who are never able to take the mask off or to find someone willing to share our inner hurts, our inner pain, our deepest fears. I see so many people donning masks: the old, the poor, the lonely, and those who are considered to be different, unwanted, disadvantaged or down trodden."

Later on my character turns inward to examine his own motivations driven by a self-centeredness that he says is something we all share. He is talking about how he drove the Phantom away from his love of Christine. Here is what he/I says:

"I crashed into his lair and called him a tormentor and the angel of darkness. I helped drive him back into the abyss to which society had condemned him. Instead of reaching out to try and understand his pain, I inflicted more. You know, I believe, that's why you and I are alike at times. We don't always follow a call for love; instead we follow our own desires and passions - we continue to populate the world with masks and unfortunately keep others feeling lonely and rejected. Why do people persist in hurting other people? Why do we not listen to the cries of others? Why do we remain silent when someone else is hurting? I believe that there is within each one of us a terrible specter of selfishness that causes pain and harm to others. I believe that each one of us uses a phantom's mask to cover up our own ugliness and wretchedness."

The students were required to write a letter to my character reflecting on what they heard and how it applied to the course and to their own lives. Reading the letters gave me a chance to judge the effectiveness of the course's lessons and how attuned the students were to the character. Having read hundreds of such letters over the years, I believe that this artistic element helped make the general material become humanized. I have been struck by the insights the students seemed to garner from the performance and believed that it was a valuable learning tool. I always put it in the context of realizing that when we deal with people in general terms we tend to lose their individuality. My teaching helped me learn how my stereotyping in my own life always ran the danger of missing the person in front of me. The danger is seeing only the surface and losing the inner essence of a person. That is true when walking by a homeless man, a foreigner, someone of another color, the heavily tattooed girl, etc. I tried to help my students learn that same lesson: be careful about your judgments and first impressions.

I also developed the character of Marius from *Les Mis*.

For my course in London I had the unique opportunity of having my students go to the theater and see the character of Marius as a young man. The next day I performed my version of Marius as an old man. Thus my students could examine the psychological development of a person over his lifetime. My intent was qualitative and artistic. At the theater they saw a young man dealing with the conflicts in his life. The next day they saw him as an old man (with a severe arthritic condition) undergoing a life review. Again songs from the musical helped me to bring emotion and power to the character. Marius' character is dealing with survivor guilt since his comrades died at the barricade while he was saved. He also misjudged people and came to realize the errors of his poorly founded judgments. One lesson was how powerful guilt can be. What can we do in our lives that can mitigate these sweeping feelings? How can we adjust our judgments and views of others to minimize the regrets and remorse that we may have to bear? Can we open our eyes and take the blinders off so that we do not allow our prejudices, biases and stereotypes to lead to discriminatory behaviors against others? Can we discover our own ignorance of interpersonal relationships and our misunderstanding of others? Marius sings "Empty Chairs at Empty Tables" as he reflects upon the loss of his friends and his guilt for surviving. Here is a passage from my character's monologue after the song has been played:

"My grief resides with me still. I have lived a life of joy, because I have lived it with my love, with my Cossette. But this life's meaning, its existence, comes upon the shoulders of those who suffered so much - those who died before me. I ask myself, was it worth it? Was their sacrifice worth my joy? Is it ever worth it for young people to shed their blood for ideas, or for power, or for the whims of leaders and rulers who may never care whether they have lived or not? The longer I live, the answers become fewer and fewer. When I was young, I knew the truth; I knew what was right. Today, I am confused and I see so many conflicting lines of thought become tangled and knotted before me. I am thankful for the beauty and goodness in my life and I am saddened by the misery - not my own, but that of others. ... For those of us who are old, we must see through these illusions and try to capture a measure of wisdom and an inner quietude."

I'm not sure the students knew what to do with the contrasting experiences. I believe most of them enjoyed the theater and seeing a great performance on a London stage. My performance, however, was a stark contrast: there was no theater setting, no orchestra, no cast, no ambiance, just the stark reality of a classroom and a teacher trying to provide a lesson in a rather unorthodox manner. At the end of course party, the students and I had an honest exchange about our experiences.

"You know, doc, we didn't really get much out of that performance of yours," came a sentiment from one student which was re-enforced with a number of nods in agreement.

"Was it the character or the message?" I asked.

"Huh?" was a general sense of confusion.

"Was my acting a problem?" This was my first question to tease out the distinction and help them reflect upon the experience. Of course the setting was in a pub and everyone either had a pint, a glass of wine, or something stronger in a glass. They looked around at each other and said, "No, you were actually good." I wasn't sure whether this was genuine or one of those white lies we all tell to save someone's feelings.

I continued the lesson: "Was the setting too sterile? You know being in a classroom rather than a theater."

"Yeah, that didn't help." I could sense they were searching for something and didn't really know what it was.

"But what about the message Marius was trying to share?"

"Well we talked about it in class. Wasn't it guilt?" a response that was more of a pleading question hoping to land on the right answer.

"Guilt was only part of his review," I began. "The point of the performance is to make you rethink your ideas about what it means to age. You saw Marius age in front of your eyes. What did you learn about the change from his youth to his old age?" I let the question hang. The bartender interrupted and asked who was ready for another pint. I let the discussion die until the next day when I was saying good-bye.

"Don't forget that you will continue to interview your grandparent. I want you to put together the course material and tell me how your experience of the young and old Marius and your relationship with your grandparent impacts on the topics of the course."

Their final assignments showed a different assessment of the Marius experience. Whether they were trying to butter me up or whether they really discussed the lessons and reached different conclusions, I'll never know. Almost all of them compared or contrasted the idea of Marius' feelings of guilt and experiences their adopted grandparent shared with them. They also seemed to draw some lessons from Marius' life review that reflected on their own struggle with meaning and purpose in their lives. One student contrasted Marius' relationship with father figures and his own difficulties with his father. Another student spent time talking about the bonds of friendship Marius had established at the barricade. He had lost a childhood friend and felt Marius' pain. That's what I was hoping they would see: connection and the importance of relationships. Maybe the experiment was more successful than I originally thought.

One humorous question arose at the party before we started discussing Marius. "Uh, why did we see you on the corner every morning doing something?" asked one of the students. Clearly he had never seen Tai Chi before. The apartment building that housed the students was in a neighborhood of Northern London. I spent the week in one of the rooms in their building. Each January morning I would go out and go through my Tai Chi form wearing a coat and brimmed hat (it was rather chilly at that time). The problem I encountered going through my form was finding sufficient space. Nothing worked inside and the only available space outside was the street corner. It had a width and length that was conducive for the moves. As a street corner with a crossing light, however, there was constant foot traffic. I appreciated the people giving me wide berth while I slowly moved. The Londoners didn't seem to pay attention to me (or maybe I just wasn't paying attention to them). Apparently the students saw me doing this and were perplexed at why I would do something that was potentially embarrassing. They must have decided that I truly was from a different planet or maybe from a generation with different values. They weren't sure what to say when I told them that it didn't matter to me one bit what people saw or believed. The coat made some of the moves cumbersome, but the exercise was essential for my chronic back pain.

When I offered the basic aging course at Canisius, I required the students to make an oral presentation of their histories of the people they interviewed. Additionally, I required them to work in small groups to reach some conclusions about what they learned and how it related to the course's material. The last class would include an explanation about qualitative research and how they had participated in a qualitatively oriented research project. Each group would present its conclusions and we would then reach class wide agreement on observations and results. Unfortunately I wasn't able to do this step with the students in London, but I did share with them some of the results from other courses in our last class session. What I found over the years was that this technique worked very well at dispelling some of the more common stereotypes that college students had about older people – one of my course goals.

One of the primary stereotypes to be broken was the belief that older people are pretty homogeneous. Don't they all look and act alike? During the interviews, the students began to see the older people as individuals and not as members of a group. Some students interviewed older relatives or neighbors and were quite surprised to learn about their histories, ups and downs, loves and heartbreaks, etc. As we began to discuss this observation, I mentioned to them the fact that older people are probably far more diverse than younger populations. People become more themselves as they age, which means their individuality comes to the forefront. We talked about the outside view and inside view in this regard. From the outside older people may start blurring together if you don't pay attention to them. During this assignment instead of just seeing wrinkles, students began to see and hear about the landscape of their life and how aging etches very distinctive patterns on one's heart, soul, body and mind. These etchings reveal very unique personalities as the personal stories began to unfold. We talked about how health was a primary factor in their lives. Alzheimer's and dementia in general are game changers. A person's uniqueness begins to fade away as memories become lost and interaction becomes more problematic.

"You can't teach an old dog new tricks" also became redefined. Habits may be hard to break at any age. We talked about addictions that the students or their peers may be dealing with and how addictions create habits that may be quite destructive and impossible to break. We also discussed how much of their behavior was really habitual. As they saw the lives of the older people unfolding, they began to see exactly how much change and adaptation was a part of their life. Learning how to deal with physical limitations, experiencing the death of loved ones, moving to warmer climates, traveling more, having to adjust to different rhythms in retirement are just some of the changes the students heard. Another corollary to the changes in their lives was how active and vital the older people were. The stereotypes of the nursing home patient or senile old grouch were replaced with a vitality and love for life that was unexpected. One of the older men being interviewed by a female student dressed up for the interview and got out his saxophone to play for her. He wanted her to include his playing on the tape that she was required to make. Sharing pictures of travels or experiences in war were eye-opening for the students.

There were emotional moments for many of the students. They were surprised at how wrapped up they became in the person's story and how painful experiences were still on the surface of their emotions, even 50 or 60 years later. Some of the students confessed that they too became emotional. I had told the students to take tissues with them and be prepared to gently offer it when necessary. They were taken aback when they needed the tissue for themselves. There were teachable moments when some of the male students confessed that they needed some too. This little detour in addressing gender stereotypes and gender-identified behaviors was a bonus lesson. One of the questions I required them to ask was about the person's ethnic heritage and about their religion. Again students were sometimes shocked at the answers. Living in Buffalo it is not difficult to meet older Italians, Poles or Germans. Many of them had spent their lives with customs, meals, and ceremonies that came from the Mother Country (even if they were many generations from the family's immigration). There was an interesting contrast one semester. One student interviewed an older Italian woman who was immersed in her heritage making cookies for weddings and serving a St. Joseph's Day Table every year. Another student said that her older Italian woman said that she couldn't be bothered with ethnic customs and wouldn't attend the Italian Festival "even if they paid me."

Students expected that all older people would be religious, pray often, go to church and have conservative religious views. Buffalo has a large Roman Catholic population and many of Canisius' students are Roman Catholic. Again stereotypes were replaced with a wide variety of responses. The common consensus was that we could make no generalizations about religion or religious practices. There were atheists, agnostics, devoted practitioners, as well as those who thought the rules of their religion were silly or should just be ignored. Not all the interviewees were Roman Catholic and hearing about other religious traditions added real flavor to the discussions. We talked about why we pigeon hole older people and their religious beliefs and practices, yet expect that younger people will experiment, reject or continue to embrace the religion of their childhood. Why do we not see older people as having been young before? Why don't we recognize how life may deeply affect them? Many students ended up having prolonged conversations with their interviewees about the difference between religion and spirituality. They smiled because those were conversations they had been having in other classes at the college.

One of the primary purposes of this exercise is to humanize the topic of aging and to examine the life course. The Decisions game was one way to help students understand some of the dynamics in life. These interviews and the process of doing some qualitative research was another. Much of Social Science research works on trying to be as quantitative as possible. My project was an alternative type of research that tried to help students connect their outside view of older people with the inside view of older people themselves. The conclusions we reached were inductive and qualitative. I was not trying to prepare them for publication or a research career in Gerontology. Most of the students were majoring in Psychology or Sociology and would receive quantitative training in other courses. My aim was to address the ignorance that social stereotypes perpetuated about aging and older people. The students received instant feedback from the people who were interviewed. In almost all cases the older interviewee really appreciated the conversations and was very interested in the students and their lives. The intergenerational dialogue was a way for older people to address their own stereotypes about younger people too. The comments from the students indicated that they too began to humanize older people and not just lump them together. One example that assured me that what I was doing was important came after our daughter died. We had received hundreds of sympathy cards. One of them was from a former student who wrote:

"As a part of a project for your gerontology class, I had interviewed my maternal grandmother about her life experiences. She passed away two weeks ago at the age of 92, and I cannot express to you how grateful I am to have the audio tape from that interview. She had spoken freely and at length, and I learned so much about her in that hour or so. Listening to that tape helped me to write her eulogy, and I made copies for my sister and cousins. It was one of the most important projects I've completed in my years at Canisius."

Before I began studying and thinking about aging, I accepted and believed the common ageist stereotypes in our society. As a college student in the '60s I was a part of the "authentic" generation. Older people were superficial. My parents didn't like my musical tastes and said that everything sounded the same to them. Of course this made no sense to me since their music was homogeneous and boring; mine was meaningful and authentic. My relatives in Kentucky were different and in my mind's eye didn't belong to an older population or generation. They were individuals whom I loved and my parents were, well, just my parents. There is nothing quite like youthful assurance of understanding life and the short-comings of the ignorant older generations. Of course this attitude changes the day you find yourself uttering words to your children that echo your parents' directives or warnings.

When I ponder the ageism I have experienced and seen in my life, I see how applicable the sources for ageism are with other prejudices and stereotypes. There are common elements in all prejudicial attitudes and behaviors regardless of the subject of our ism. Ignorance, family upbringing, and societal attitudes, for example, affect the formation of all of our prejudices. Our openness to learning about others and our personal experiences are key factors in understanding our prejudices and discriminatory behaviors. Understanding ageism is a vehicle for understanding any other ism in our life. Thinking about my own aging has also given me a sense of what lessons I have learned and how they apply to other areas of my life. So far this book has outlined my walk through the ignorance, isms, interrelationships and insights in the areas of race, religion, gender and generations. Part V will focus upon life and death experiences, grieving and how I have evolved in my understanding of what meaningful and balanced grieving is. In addition, Part VI will provide my basic answer for addressing bigotry, hatred, and interpersonal conflicts. Respect: for the natural world, for people and places; and Love: for family and friends. Respect has opened me up to love the world, my family, my friends, and those who have walked upon my stage.

PART V:

ON GRIEVING

CHAPTER 9
THE JOURNEY BEGINS - LEARNING
FROM IGNORANCE

But grief still has to be worked through.
It is like walking through water.
Sometimes there are little waves lapping about my feet.
Sometimes there is an enormous breaker that knocks me down.
Sometimes there is a sudden and fierce squall.
But I know that many waters cannot quench love,
neither can the floods drown it.

Madeline L'Engle

There are three routes we usually take from our home in Tonawanda, a northern suburb of Buffalo, to Niagara Falls, my hometown. Each one is saturated with memories, the most poignant being the one I drove on Christmas Eve, 1986. Before telling that story, let me paint a picture of these different routes. One route is Niagara Falls Boulevard, which is a commercial corridor that can also take us to the cemetery that has become a part of our life (more of that later). This route runs through the eastern part of North Tonawanda, a city quite different from our Town of Tonawanda. They are in two different counties and have different cultures. The Boulevard, as locals call it, is a direct route to one of my homes when I was growing up - the Love Canal area, which became famous as a toxic waste dump. After my mom and her second husband (I refuse to refer to him as a step-father for far too many reasons than can be listed here) moved from the Canal, they lived in a trailer park whose entrance was on The Boulevard. Avoiding commercial traffic and taking a more scenic drive takes us on the second route, which goes through the west side of North Tonawanda and along the Niagara River. The memories are less dense this way - only triggering benign recollections, a calmer drive, and an access to an Expressway through the LaSalle section of Niagara Falls.

When we moved out to the Love Canal area when I was going into fifth grade, my dad's drive to work became almost five minutes longer. Smitty was known for his punctuality and precise habits (e.g. arriving home from work at 4:52; sitting down to eat dinner at 5:00; sitting on the toilet at 5:15). He carpooled with a man he had done so before and a new neighbor who lived two houses away from us. This second man became an unusual part of my growing up. When I was 14, I started babysitting for his children. Two memories stick in my mind. He subscribed to *Playboy* and I saw some of those issues when I was there. It was rather sinful for me to look at them, I believed, but for a 14-year-old boy, the temptation was just far too great to ignore. The second memory was during my senior year of high school. One day my dad said that Mr. F and his wife wanted to see me. I walked the 75 feet to their house with real concern that my misdeeds while babysitting had been discovered somehow (despite my meticulous care in returning the dirty magazines in the exact location and precise position as they were discovered). When I sat at their dining room table he began: "Your dad tells me that you are near the top of your class at Bishop Duffy and that you are very involved at school. He also said that you are very religious and know about Catholicism." I wasn't sure where this was leading, and I was a little shocked to hear that my dad had praised me in any way. He continued: "We are Catholics and need to know what the Church's teachings on birth control are. Your dad said that you wrote something about it."

Another startling revelation: how did dad know? I'm not sure how much they observed about the dropping of my jaw or the incredible tremor that seemed to course through my veins. One of the traits that I had been cultivating (since my brother, Paul, told me that it was essential for success in life) was to always pretend you know what you are talking about. I was hoping this attitude would come to my rescue. I mustered up some confidence and hoped they might actually believe me. Of course it is always better if you actually know what you're talking about, but this was not one of those moments. I summoned my meager knowledge of the subject (heightened by that essay assignment) and talked my way through a discourse on the Church's absolute requirement of abstinence or use of the rhythm method. Sexual relations (I wasn't very clear about the details of what that might really entail in marriage or even outside of it for that matter) were solely for the purpose of having children. These doctrines became my opening salvo and default position. It was the church's teaching and thus what they had to follow. Period. They asked about forms of birth control that were foreign territory for me. I kept deflecting and returning to the "party line": abstinence and rhythm (another concept I knew was the right answer but had no real idea what it meant). Ah yes, this was the same genius who had read *The Scarlet Letter* that year and didn't know what the scarlet A really meant. At the time I was too lazy to check a dictionary and didn't think that understanding what the A meant was all that important for the plot anyway. Besides was it really so hard to read the book without understanding A? I didn't think so. I know I did well in that course, but I have no recollection about a grade for my assignment on that book. There is nothing like the self-righteousness of a teenager who thinks he knows more than he really does. Isn't that a dangerous conceit we all may share: thinking we know more than we really do and actually impacting the lives of others through our ignorance and shallow beliefs?

After about an hour (which felt like three years), they seemed a little disheartened. I hoped it wasn't me that was the disappointment. They thanked me very much. Now I look back on that conversation with considerable amusement. Why would they believe a 17-year-old who obviously was over his head? They were looking for some leeway, I'm sure. I now assume that they were in the Catholic bind of wanting to have an active sex life without the consequences of children while also not wanting to sin or go against Catholic teaching. The only reason I could discern for coming to me was that a priest didn't give them the answer they wanted. Or maybe they didn't want to talk to a priest because they were sure his answer would be unsatisfactory. I have no idea what they did or what happened to their sex life. I do remember that they had no more children.

Now back to my dad's carpool. He only drove once every three days because of the rotation but was always looking for ways to cut costs. He was a draftsman who worked with angles, numbers, and connecting dots. He grumbled his whole life that there should have been a connecting highway from our area to his place of work and to the Falls. Most of that happened after he had died. The LaSalle Expressway now connects parts of the LaSalle suburban area with the city of Niagara Falls. The exits and entrances to get my dad from our home to his place of work would probably have added time (maybe a couple of minutes more) than if he and his co-drivers just continued to use the route they did each day. I'm glad he didn't have to experience the frustration of it all. Today this route along River Road easily connects to this Expressway and makes the drive to the Falls very benign and calm (light traffic and the tranquil feel of driving along the river are key factors).

My drive on that fateful Christmas Eve day, however, was over Grand Island, the last of the routes. Going over the Island meant that you blitzed along the Thruway that connected the south and north bridges of the Island. The exits on the Island were fingers into areas of varying neighborhoods, churches, commercial areas, golf courses and a beach. As I drove to the hospital to visit my mom, memories started flooding my consciousness even before I was on the southern bridge (the first for me in that direction).

One of my best friends from high school lived on the Island. Jerry and I played football for three years, worked on the yearbook our senior year, hung out (not the phrase we used back then), and ended up at the seminary together. We were even in the school's choir our senior year (he because he could sing and me because I was on the football team). He stayed in the seminary longer than I did, but there was a bond between us that ran deep in our souls. I hadn't seen him for over a decade, but I thought about our friendship and our kindred way of looking at life. Twenty-five years later I would visit him in Montana and confirm our kinship in life and in the depth of deaths in our lives. As long as I can remember, Jerry loved his guitar and fishing. Montana became a real escape into a world that matched these loves. He began working for a bamboo fly fishing maker who only hired musicians to complete his creations. Fly fishing was a naturalistic religion for my friend and his employer. They believed that the primary tool for creating authentic fly rods required touching a deeper side of life than a simple manufacturing of poles. When I visited, I saw the passion in his description of his art and left with two of his books about fishing - it would be a real disservice to his writings to believe they are about fishing. They are about life and about one man's journey that includes streams, fish, the world, man's place in it, and the path to finding meaning. He told me of his wife, her illness and death as well as the sadness he had for the death of both of his parents. Years before we reconnected and after our daughter Heidi died, he contacted me and said that he had practiced a Native American tradition after a loved one passes. He took rose petals and laid them in a stream. He gave them up to her spirit and to the Great Spirit. Diane and I were very touched and smiled with his use of rose petals, since the rose had become a symbol for Heidi during her illness. My visit in Montana was all too short but so very reaffirming. He has now moved east, to Baltimore, and we reconnected through email. Eventually we had a reunion just for the two of us in Ithaca in 2017. We shared laughs and tears, frustrations and achievements - the webs of friendship. That event, however, would come decades after my drive over The Island in '86.

On that transformative day, as I headed to the northern bridge, I glanced at the Hooker Chemical building and smiled at one of the real positive memories I have of my dad. As a draftsman for Hooker, he specialized in heating and plumping. When they were building that facility, he was the leader of the drafting group and would go to inspect the building's progress. One Saturday when no one was working there, he took me for an adventure. I was 8 or 9 and was relieved of my chores to go with him. We actually talked - mostly him - about the building and what he was doing. I have no recollection of anything he said, just that we seemed to be doing something together that didn't involve drinking, chores, or criticism of what I was doing. He didn't call me a knucklehead that day. He gave me free rein when we entered. That building became a fortress (both to defend and attack as I changed allegiances and shifted war scenarios). The lights were dim so the eerie feeling was an asset for my imagination. Dad took me into other areas of the facility, and they too became hideouts for the outlaws that my posse would smoke out. When we walked around outside, I had to lead a countercharge against an attacking foe who had overwhelming forces. My heroism saved the day. On the way home I remember thanking my dad and I saw him smile with a satisfaction I had never seen before.

That recollection faded as I crossed the north bridge and passed by my high school. The memory floodgates opened again and I made it to the hospital on a cavalcade of people and events from my past. Over my four years in high school I changed dramatically, starting as a shy freshman with little school participation to a fully engaged senior. I was easy pickings for the priests in recruiting me into the seminary even though I was going steady during my senior year. All of those people and events crunched into a wispy recollection as I exited the highway and headed for Niagara Falls Memorial Hospital.

I always tried to avoid paying for parking, often making my family walk farther than necessary. Today was no exception. I didn't like the parking garage anyway, and there was a perfect place on the street. The slush on the sidewalk soaked my feet because I had reverted to my non-work practice of wearing sneakers regardless of the weather. They were my trademark footwear in college and are still my preferred outdoor wear (when I'm not barefoot). I heard that a number of family and friends were betting on whether I would wear sneakers with my tux for my wedding. My fashion trend was way ahead of its time. Looking up at the building to my right brought another avalanche of memories. Of course I don't remember my birth there, but I can recall having my tonsils out when I was 30 (a procedure I fervently regretted a year later when a bout of viral pneumonia triggered my latent asthma).

My junior year of high school was a breakout period in my life. I was starting on the football team and that spring I was given the lead in the school's play *No Time for Sergeants*. The play was a success and I was coming out of my shell (something that thrilled my mom). But that was also the year that my dad had part of one lung removed because of cancer. Months later my mom was hospitalized with pneumonia and a couple of months after that my brother, Bill, was also hospitalized with pneumonia. My folks took care of Bill, but I had real responsibilities when Mom was hospitalized. People drove us to the hospital to see my dad, but that didn't occur as often for my mom, something that surprised me. Friends were interested in driving Mom to see Dad, but less willing to visit her (unless they did so without letting me know). My dad was still recuperating, and I didn't have my license yet. I remember walking from the high school (about four miles) to visit Mom, then walking home (about seven miles). Walking miles was easy for me then. In grammar school I walked about a mile and in high school I walked three miles one way every day. I visited Mom alone a couple of times. On the first visit, Mom sent me to the drugstore across the street for some feminine products and toothpaste. She had a wry smile on her face for the first request, and later in life I figured that was her attempt to educate me about women. We never talked about such stuff, which proved to be a real disadvantage when I got married and had four daughters. I'm not sure my dad thought such a talk was ever necessary. I do know that no such conversation occurred with either one of them. Getting her toothpaste was just another example of my lifelong incompetence for shopping. At the store I sheepishly showed a female employee my mom's list and pointed to the product I needed. No words were exchanged; she merely smiled and walked me to the proper aisle and handed me a package that was far too large to hide under my arm. Sigh. I proudly handed mom the items and she moaned.

"Charlie, you got me Colgate shaving cream, not Colgate toothpaste!" Ugh. Toothpaste. That word became part of the humor we shared on this Christmas Eve 23 years later.

When I entered Mom's room, I had to shift away from the dread and sadness that hung around me as I took the elevator and walked down that green hallway smelling of cleaning liquids. At the door I paused, took a breath, and burst into the room with my required smile and jovial demeanor. It was <u>Showtime</u> and for the next three hours I played the role exactly as I knew my mom hoped and expected to experience. She had trained me in subtle and in some not so subtle ways since childhood. She was immobile that afternoon and the nurses had propped her up for my visit. There were machines and the dreaded bedpan. I have had a love/hate relationship with bedpans. I hated what they represented, yet I used the one dad had at home for his long illness. That bedpan was a perfect receptacle for oil when I used to do my own oil changes. It was still in regular use at the time of this visit, and I glanced at the more antiseptically acceptable one in mom's room. She smiled and I walked over to kiss her forehead and touch her hand. The dullness in her eyes was one of the many signs that this illness was not only robbing her of her body, but was also affecting her soul.

For a number of years the doctors had said she had Parkinson's, but some of her symptoms were atypical. A few years earlier I had gone with her husband and her on a fruitless visit to the Cleveland Clinic. They had no answer for her atypical symptoms. We were surprised a year later when her diagnosis was finalized by a researcher in Buffalo. She had a rare form of Parkinson's: Shy-Drager (today it is called Multiple System Atrophy - MSA). Although we were told of the disease's progression, its reality felt somewhat different and its impacts were far more profound. MSA is irreversible and death occurs usually within 7-9 years. I don't remember ever hearing a doctor say this to us. We don't really know when mom's symptoms started (probably in her mid 50s), and I was too busy to try and research her illness (being a father of four, a husband, a dean, an active deacon in our church, and someone who tried to fix the myriad of glitches that a house provides). Mom's second husband, Chet, was her primary caretaker, and I willingly ceded that role to him. Maybe I shouldn't have. As time went along, her eyes became more glazed; she went from having balance problems to a wheelchair to immobility in bed; her vocal cords became paralyzed and her speech left her; she went from a vibrant bowler, housekeeper, dancer, and life of the party to someone who could not feed herself, brush her teeth or attend to normal toilet activities. As I smiled at her, she became a blend of the woman I had loved as a child, the one who had loved and cared for me and the patient I now visited as an adult.

The plan was for me to spend the afternoon with her alone; Bill and Chet would visit at night; and I would bring my whole family up for Christmas Day. Funny how plans are illusions that don't always match up with reality. As mom started losing her ability to speak soon after the final diagnosis, we bought her a child's magnetic board with letters. We jovially kidded about her return to childhood and began to agree on the meaning of particular letters so she didn't have to spell out entire words. As her muscle control began to decline, she couldn't even manipulate this simple communication device. At the hospital I relied on a lifetime of stories, shared memories, and humor triggers to help me keep the conversation light and continuous. I was not there to sit with her; I was there to be the son she loved and trained. I regaled her with stories so she could laugh and smile. Some of the references were directed at my dad.

Mom and I definitely had an unhealthy relationship directed at my dad. It reached its apex one night when they came back from drinking. I was 14 or 15 at the time. Dad fell into the closet and I had to help him into bed. When he was settled into the bed, Mom said she wanted to talk. Bill (age eight or nine) stayed in his room for the whole time (a common form of his avoidance of those experiences, besides it was late and he was young). Mom was a happy drunk; Dad was nasty. That night she talked about the difficulties of living with Dad, most of which we had discussed endlessly before. However, she added a story I had never heard. Mom started slowly with her eyes looking at her cup of coffee, a common drink when she returned home from a night at the bar(s).

"Charlie, I have something you need to hear." I was tired but that line caused an immediate surge of adrenaline - I was now fully awake.

"Soon after your dad and I were married we were living in an apartment. Did you know that?" I screwed up my brow and slowly shook my head. I thought Mom and Dad had always lived in the house on Whitkop where I spent my early childhood.

"Well we did. It was there when your dad and I adopted Paul." My look of shock must have caught her attention.

"You didn't know, did you?" This time my indication of "no" was not subtle or slow. She did not tell me that night that Dad had been married before and that Dad's first wife, Marie, and he had adopted Paul. Nor did she let me know that his first wife had died suddenly; that he had left Paul with his sister, Martha; and that he lived in Alaska with a woman. I knew he had worked in Alaska before going to Oak Ridge, Tennessee during the Second World War. That's where Mom and Dad met. I had no idea about any of these other details. I have just learned from Paul all these decades later that my dad joined the army when Marie died and was stationed in Alaska with the Corps of Engineers. Dad was distraught and needed to get out of Chicago and all the memories of Marie. I have never seen a picture of any of these events. These stories came to me piecemeal and much later in life. My dad has always been a mystery to me partly because he never shared anything about his life, his heartaches, or his past. I wish I had known him before Marie had died; from all I have heard he was a very different man then. That night Mom just referred to adopting Paul.

"Paul was a handful in those days and your dad was a difficult man. He and his friends made fun of me. 'Did you ever wear shoes in Kentucky?' they would say before laughing at what they thought was funny." Mom had never had a Southern drawl like her relatives. I never asked and never knew when she had lost it, but I'm sure getting rid of it was a defense mechanism. I could see real sadness in her eyes. Then she continued.

"We had to send him to Father Baker's in Buffalo for a while." Her eyes were sad and I could see the regret in her face. (Paul has recently told me that he was sent to the Buffalo orphanage because the next door neighbor and he tried to burn down their school. No school would enroll him, so he was sent away for awhile.) She paused for a moment and I struggled about whether I should say anything, but I honestly was rather speechless. My muteness would only increase over the next few minutes.

"I was so homesick. Niagara Falls and the people here seemed hateful and I had not made any real friends at that time. Of course later I certainly did with Jane and then Pat." (Jane was my friend Donny's mother and Pat was a neighbor who became a lifelong friend to Mom. I know Mom and Pat shared their trials and tribulations. They drank coffee almost daily, but they and their husbands rarely got together as couples.)

"I decided I had to go back home and stay with my family: permanently." At first the implication of "permanently" flew by me. Mom continued, "While there, I talked to grandma and my family and they said they would support anything I decided to do." I assumed Mom was staying with Aunt Myrtle and Uncle Oral, since that was her home growing up. As she paused to gather her thoughts I began to wonder where she was going with this story and was a little surprised at her reference to talking to her mother. I knew my mom was very close with her brothers and somewhat so with Myrtle, but never really saw much of a close relationship between mom and grandma. She then startled me when she continued.

"I wasn't feeling well and James made me go to a doctor who told me I was pregnant. That was you." She looked up and smiled faintly. I was now speechless.

"I had no idea that was what was wrong with me. So after talking with my family some more, I decided I had to come back to your dad: I wasn't going to try and raise you without a father. When you were born, I knew I had made the right decision. A boy needs a father. You were far more important than my happiness." She stopped and I finally had enough time to make a feeble reply.

"Have you ever been happy? Has this been so awful?"

"Oh, Charlie, you and your brothers … why … you are the lights of my life. You boys have made me very proud and happy. Over the years I've had many friends; I've learned to enjoy the neighborhood parties, my bowling, and the people and good times in the bars. When I came home and told your dad that I was staying I demanded that he take me home every year. We have gone almost every summer, as you know. I am so happy that you love my family and the farms down there."

She seemed to have run out of steam. There was so much I didn't know about my parents. And I rarely ever asked any probing questions. It may not have been just me, though. My sense is that there were not a lot of personal details shared among the generations in those days. None of my Kentucky family ever talked about Mom's saga; in fact, that night was the only time the topic was ever broached by either Mom or me. I'm sure telling me all of this was difficult for her. It struck me in that lull that I was the reason for my mother's unhappiness in her marriage. For decades after,

I hated my birthday. This conversation sealed our bond and irrevocably placed a barrier between my dad and me. It was difficult not to see him in a different light. Mom's confession created a psychological rift I had with my dad until he became a pathetic figure in the last years of his life. For his last five years he sat in his chair and watched TV. He had emphysema, was still smoking, and his water bottle was laced with whiskey. The oxygen tank was behind the ashtray, and he kept a booklet to record scores on the game shows he watched. Often he would not bother shuffling down the hall to the bathroom; rather he used the urine bottle nestled next to the newspapers that were under the ashtray. My dad was about 58 when he surrendered to his chair. He died five years later.

Mom and I didn't go into these stories that day in the hospital, but they were part of the context that surrounded our time together. All of us had made fun of Dad's driving style, and I mimicked his posture so mom would giggle. My Dad had a habit of leaning forward and keeping two hands at the top of the steering wheel while resting his elbows on the bottom of it. It reminded me of the way he would lean on shopping carts with his elbows bent and his forearms resting on the cart. I refuse to assume that pose whenever I'm shopping. We also chuckled at Dad's rules about mowing the lawn and how he would watch me out the windows on Saturdays when I'd manicure the grass. It was a source of ongoing irritation for me and amusement for mom. I also reminded her of the time our new next door neighbor was regaling me with some inane story about weeds while mom was standing behind her. Mom made faces and tried to make me laugh inappropriately at the neighbor. She loved hearing that one. Then I drifted our conversation (actually my monologue and mom's nodding or laughter) to Kentucky. It was always a rich source of stories and family folklore. I grimaced appropriately while detailing the awfulness of Aunt Myrtle's cooking; smiled while regaling the stories of her brothers' teasing; and reminisced about the relatives who had already passed. I teased mom about the silliness of thinking her mother never knew she smoked.

"Mom, don't you know that smokers smell?" I held my nose and she laughed.

Of course I told stories about our girls (15, 13, 12 and 5 at the time) and shared things Diane and I were doing. I recounted battles I was having at work and told her about a sermon I had given. She seemed weak but completely attentive. As I left, I kissed her good-bye and said we would all be up on Christmas. When we were growing up, we never hugged or kissed. Those gestures came to me after I married. It felt right to kiss her, and she seemed to have enjoyed that shift toward showing signs of affection for one another. Growing up it was taboo to be demonstrative or as we used to say "acting mushy or goofy." I don't recall my folks ever holding hands or even giving a good-bye or hello kiss. Dad once goosed mom in front of me, which brought an immediate wave of nausea over me. I don't recall the last words that I spoke to her for sure but I like to think I said that I loved her and would see her the next day. I do remember turning at the door and waving good-bye. She didn't, actually couldn't, respond with any physical gesture but I felt her smile internally. I felt a touch of sadness when I closed the door, but I was glad that I had had so much alone time with her before continuing my Christmas activities. I was surprised how weary I felt.

As I was driving home, my focus shifted away from my past as I was launched almost immediately into my present (and immediate future). Diane is sometimes amused, sometimes perplexed with my almost constant planning and rehearsing of what is about to happen (or working through future details that sometimes actually become realized). That day my mind went to the upcoming Christmas Eve rituals with our girls. Final gift wrapping; the girls and I writing silly poems for Diane to trek around the house to find her big present from me; going to church; gathering at Diane's sister's home for an extended family time of eating and gift exchange; then returning to see if Santa had visited our home. That night is somewhat of a blur. I'm sure we wrote the poems and finished wrapping presents; without a doubt we went to church; I don't remember if I was deacon at our service, however. I do know that after church we gathered at Diane's sisters' home. Gifts were given out, I believe. If so, Laurie (my brother-in-law who had been an usher at our wedding and a close college friend) and I would have handed out the presents with our usual corny jokes and constant searching for the presents that had to be handed out in tandem.

Then the phone rang.

It was my brother Bill.

"Mom's dead."

No prep for me. No lead up. Just a declaration.

"What?"

"Yeah, she's gone."

"How, when, wait I'll be right there."

"Don't bother. Chet has already sent her to be cremated."

I was stunned. How could she have slipped away? I had just spent the afternoon with her and it was only about 9ish. I knew she was dying, but this was a shock. Intellectually I knew death was coming, but emotionally I wasn't ready. Then it struck me. Chet had done what? I stammered something back to Bill and he repeated that mom wasn't there anymore and there was no reason for me to come up. I said that I would be up tomorrow to work out funeral arrangements. He said don't bother. Chet had decided to have her cremated; there would be no viewing; and he would work out a memorial service later. Of course I would give the eulogy; mom had been emphatic to him about that. Even more stunned, I just said,

"Uh. Um. Talk to you later."

I hung up, stumbled over to a chair in the living room, sat down and cried. The whole house had become silent; everyone had guessed from my side of the conversation what had happened. When I told them what Bill said, everyone was just as perplexed and shocked as I had been. Diane and our girls, Diane's folks, her aunt and uncle, Donna and Laurie, their kids

- all of them not sure what to say or what to do. Then we did all that was left to do: we hugged and shared our tears.

Everything changed.

Usually when we get back to our house, Santa had arrived and we stayed up late into the night opening presents and finally sending Diane on her tour. I don't recall what happened that night. Grief that I didn't really understand at that time had crept into my consciousness and was ripping memory traces away. I only remember the phone call and a deep sense of loss I had never experienced before.

A few months before Mom's death, she had told me that she wanted me to give the eulogy at her funeral and she wanted me to write her obituary. Both of which I was to read to her as soon as I had written them (an indirect order to get it done). Mom wanted me to know that things would be different for her than they were for my dad 13 years earlier. He had rejected his Catholic upbringing when no priest visited him in the hospital or at home after his surgery. He never went to church after that and may have severed any psychological ties that had remained: to a church, to a religion, and maybe even to his God. So when he died, my brothers and I held a quasi service at the funeral home. I picked out a couple of Bible readings, we said a prayer or two and the three of us took turns giving a scattered eulogy. Bill had the most difficulty (not being a public speaker and the youngest), while Paul was in his element even though the audience was small.

The three of us had actually experienced a different father, even though it was the same person. Paul is 8 1/2 years older than me, and Bill is 6 1/2 years younger. We grew up in different generations and our dad was different in physical abilities for each of us. He also drastically changed psychologically over time. For Paul he was vibrant; they had spent a summer without the rest of us and remodeled the house on Witkop; they shared fixing cars and using their hands; Paul respected the discipline my father provided. Bill experienced an alcoholic who was immobile and indifferent to people and life. For me, Dad was a blend. I had seen him have fun at neighborhood parties, but I did not share his interest in using my hands. Going to the bars and dealing with his drinking were on-going barriers between the two of us. Additionally, my mother had shifted the way I looked at him. I missed my dad after he died, but to be honest I was actually more relieved for my mom when he was gone. She had had a difficult marriage, as I've noted, and the last 10 years of dad's life were bound up in medical problems, hospital stays, ignoring doctors' orders, deepening alcoholism, and withdrawing himself even more from society than he had before. The burden of care-giving for my mom was exacerbated by her inability to drive and her loss of the routine bar social life that my dad's drinking had provided. A friend of the family did take mom out periodically so she didn't go completely stir crazy. So my grieving was mixed and confused when mom died.

As a philosophy major, I had read a lot about death and dying and over the years I did research, then taught about aging and dying from a wide variety of disciplines. I taught in a wide variety of departments and programs for 35 years (principally Psychology, Sociology, Philosophy, Anthropology, English, Gerontology, Communication Studies, Sports Administration and Women's Studies). I had read Kubla Ross and her stages of grief, and I had delved into philosophical discussions and theories about the meaning of life, of death, of dying and of grieving. When my father died, it was easy to move on as Freud had suggested and I didn't even need to go through Kubla Ross' stages to return to my family (Diane was pregnant with our second daughter at the time) and my job as a grant writer for the college. I look back now and realize that I knew nothing of grieving and was one of those who live within society's narrow meaning of grief - a meaning that I believe creates something I call Societal Griefism: the overt and covert prejudices, biases, discriminatory practices, and ignorance about healthy, balanced and meaningful grieving.

I remember reading Mom's obituary to her before she went into the hospital for the last time. She was propped up and sitting in a chair in her mobile home. Her eyes were dull and rather blank. She could still nod her head and bring some glow to her face with a faint smile. As I read her obit she seemed to brighten and nodded and smiled her approval. It never got printed in the paper because it did not follow the style or format that paper notices required. But Mom had heard it, and that was what was important. She approved! Although her eyes appeared dull, I could see underneath them: she was content with my twists and turns that covered her walk through life. Even though I was reading her obit to her and I knew that her illness was terminal, it never dawned on me that she was actually going to die. The contradiction (or paradox) that was the source of my grieving in those days was the strange notion that my existential experience of death and grief were actually only ideas. My emotions were surface experiences and the depths I touched were intellectual and cerebral. The friends, my dad, and other relatives who had died were not gut wrenching experiences that stopped me in my tracks. The one exception was Marsha, the woman who had introduced Diane and me. She was in her thirties, a mother of three, a deep and close friend of Diane's and someone I considered to be a close friend. Her death rattled all of us, and I did spend time with my friend, Ron, her husband while she was fighting her cancer, then after her death. At the time I found that I really didn't grieve her loss as much as I was saddened for Diane and Ron. My role was to support them, listen to their pain, and be there. My grief for her was channeled in their direction and suppressed into deep recesses of my consciousness.

Death and grieving were still more abstract than real because I had thought long and hard for years about one's meaning in life, the tragedy of death, the horrors of war, etc. Camus' question about whether suicide was the first and most fundamental issue a person ever faced in his/her life preoccupied my thoughts in college, maybe too much so. I did not really go into my heart, but rather followed the shallow dictates of society's ideas about death and grieving. Besides, I was a male and we were supposed to control our emotions and not have to deal with them directly.

Giving the eulogy at Mom's memorial was my first real excursion into genuine grief. Family and friends had gathered at St. James Methodist church near the golf course in Niagara Falls. I had never been there before but Chet had followed what Mom had wanted, or at least that's what he told us was true. The bulletin was simple and included a picture of Mom, of course smiling before the illness ravaged her, and the lyrics to "Green, Green Grass of Home." Since this was a favorite of Mom's, I made sure that I referenced the lyrics as I spoke. Additionally, I included the three typical topics for any eulogy: mom's life story, a few attempts at humor, and a closing that wrapped up what she meant to her family and me. Her three sons were the light of her life, yet each one of us provided real challenges for her. Paul and Mom clashed when he was growing up, but as I said in the eulogy:

"Over time the mutual love and respect that Paul and Mom had has been seen and felt by all who dared to notice. Family folklore tells of the time that the two of them went out one evening while Dad was working in Michigan. Upon his return, some friends informed dad that his wife was seen with a tall, dark (and someone even said, handsome), young man. These friends were quite perplexed at Dad's laughter and Mom's glee. You all can picture her magical smile and gleam at being caught."

Mom's challenge with Bill and me were more medical in nature. She had gained 70 pounds during her pregnancy with me, and I was a breach birth. Grandma Pearl came up to take care of Paul before I was born and she stayed to take care of both of us until mom had recovered. Mom was hospitalized for quite some time and was told never to have another child. Her doctor prescribed she start smoking to calm her nerves. She thought it would be safe to just smoke two packs of filtered cigarettes, since my Dad was smoking three packs of unfiltered Camels each day. Bill was born 6 1/2 years later; he had severe asthma and required shots, medical attention and a restrictive diet and lifestyle. It was a difficult time for Mom trying to care for him. For example, one day I was along for his monthly allergy shot. The drive was about 10 minutes from our house, and we had to wait 20 minutes after the shot to see if he had a reaction. After our wait, Mom and Dad were chatting in the front seat as we drove home. About half way there I noticed that Billy was starting to droop sideways. Just as we were getting home, he slumped all the way and looked purplish. I screamed, "He's dying!" My folks turned around, saw his state and we made it back to the doctor's in less than half the time. He received the antidote but all of us were scared. My worry eventually turned to annoyance as we had to be more careful with him than ever before. He sensed what was going on and used it to his advantage. Mom never really caught on to his ruse; but I did.

Mom's boys teased her, loved her, and treated her like one of their own. She loved the attention, but I'm sure that she would have liked to have been treated with a little more understanding and tenderness. Paul was the best at being attentive. The tragedy for me was that Mom's second husband took her away from us in a very real way. I noticed the distance from the beginning of their relationship but really didn't try to do anything to change the dynamic. I don't know if it was an excuse to avoid conflict or just a resignation that yielded to support Mom's wishes. I vividly remember when she asked me to speak at her wedding. She sensed that Chet and I would never get along, which we didn't. Proclaiming my support for their marriage verged on hypocrisy - but that's what you do when a loved one asks.

At the memorial I was standing in the pulpit and looking out at those who were listening to me. As I spoke, my body remained in the pulpit while my mind seemed to shift places. It was a strange contortion and relationship of mind and body for me. Usually my mind is the center of thought, reason and evidence; the body the source of drives, impulses, emotions and confusion. That day a reversal took place: my mind harbored my feelings while my body delivered the eulogy. There were a couple of moments when they merged and I began to choke up; however, for the most part they took their separate ways and adopted alien characteristics. I had the sense that I was and was not present, and there were times when I watched myself speak. I almost always prepare remarks, sermons, monologs or papers and write the whole presentation (although sometimes it is just an outline). I still have the eulogy as it was written, but not as it was delivered. I have spoken in a wide range of venues, on a plethora of subjects, and to very diverse groups of people. In all cases I diverge from the written text, so in reality I don't know what I actually said at the eulogy. Having the script only reflects parts of what I might have said.

As I left the pulpit, my grief overwhelmed me, and I cried while my insides seemed to lurch across time and bump into memory after memory. My studies had taught me that there were stages to my grief; society urged everyone to move on and get back into the swing of things (that's what our loved ones want); and that we should seek closure so we wouldn't be burdened with grief for too long. With my mom (and even on that day) these dictates seemed reasonable but difficult to achieve. At the reception afterward, I played the role of congenial host and received the appropriate acclamations and condolences. All of that was swept away when Paul, Bill and I had a drink with Chet after everyone had left.

The proceeds from selling our house in the Love Canal were used to purchase the trailer that Mom and Chet had moved into when the Canal area became somewhat deserted and a dangerous place in which to live. The agreement we had with Chet, at Mom's request, was that he would live in the trailer until his death or until he wanted to move elsewhere. The trailer would then revert to the three of us and Chet's grandson. As we sat around the table at the Sportsman's Club, the room was empty, the cooks and servers were finished and the bartender was cleaning up. Chet looked at us and told his story. One of his daughter's was impregnated by a man Chet did not like. The man wasn't going to marry his daughter so Chet hired a hit man and had the offender taken care of: permanently. He looked at me, Mom's Executor and the one who had been with the two of them when they drew up their wills, with steely eyes. Message received: don't mess with him.

After telling this story to Diane, we became a bit paranoid, and I did some sleuthing with the trailer management office. I got a copy of their agreement for the trailer and the copy that I had. Chet had forged Mom's signature turning over the trailer to him. When I talked to a lawyer who was a high school classmate and showed him the evidence, he said that the money for the trailer would probably not even cover the cost of litigation. Given the not so subtle threat and the financial realities of the situation, I decided to follow the Chinese principle of *Wu Wei*: do nothing. All of this activity diverted me from dealing with the emotional loss of Mom and helped me follow the dictates of grieving that are far too prevalent in our society. I believed that I didn't need to follow the stages of grief to any great degree because I was strong enough to move on and return to my normal life as husband, father, friend, dean and deacon. I never really denied Mom's death (check); my anger was directed at Chet (check); there was no need to bargain (check); any depressed feelings were fleeting (check); and acceptance seemed completed at the Club that night (final check). Thus, my grief stages were checked off.

I didn't realize then how easily I bought into society's version of grieving and how little I understood about meaningful, balanced and healthy grieving. Overcoming my prejudices and understanding the dynamics of the human condition has been a lifelong process, whether it was dealing with race, gender, generation, religion, or grieving. The deeply engrained feelings and ideas that were a part of my culture and emblazoned upon my personality held a sway over me that was deep and profound. The challenge for me in addressing or minimizing their effects has always required "aha" moments or experiences that revealed the subtle, sometimes not so subtle, characteristics of my prejudices, biases and misunderstandings. There have been overt and covert elements in my life that leave me saddened and remorseful. When it comes to grieving, I have become intellectually militant against the very insidious ignorance in our society about healthy and meaningful grieving: Societal Griefism. While my mother's death led to my first true experience with grief, my daughter's battle with leukemia and her death truly transformed by beliefs, ideas, feelings, and understanding of life, death and grieving.

CHAPTER 10
HEIDI CHANGES EVERYTHING

When faced with a dark fear, she reveled in past comforts
and beauty of the future. She wanted a symbol ...
To focus her fear she pondered many choices.
None fit. Until ... The rosebud was suggested.
It was comfort.
An avid rose lover, it brought together past, present ...
and future for the girl.
You see, her first doll was named "Rosebud."
Aptly so, with the rosebud pattern on her dress.
Precious remembrances of a simple rag doll, a simple time.
A rosebud brings a promise. A promise a future.
The rosebud has an untainted beauty, but as it grows,
it will develop a unique soul and become a rose.
She felt the strength of its promise:
The promise of her future.

Heidi Schmidtke

Aug. 23, 2000: a date etched into our consciousness. It was a sunny, Wednesday afternoon and our close friends, Joe and Audrey, were with Diane and me planning an outing for the day. We had had wonderful experiences with them over the years. That day we had no idea that in less than three years we would share another bond: grieving parents. Diane was a bit lame which would limit some of our adventure. She had gone to NYC with some college friends and had gotten her foot twisted on a curb. She was hobbling when she returned and when we went to see a doctor, the diagnosis was a "Jones fracture" of her foot. She had become rather proficient with the crutches for short distances. Our so-called adventure that day was driving around Buffalo to see the buffaloes that had been decorated and displayed around the city. It was a phenomenon around the country to adopt an animal and decorate them for a whole variety of causes. The decorated buffaloes were scattered around Western New York and we had a map and brief description of each. Our plan was to navigate around the different locations and see as many as we could. One strange twist was the Composition Book.

The week before our planned adventure I was shopping with Diane (crutches and all) at a favorite grocery store (actually a supermarket but for some reason the old name of grocery store sounds better to me here). As we were headed for check out I saw the Composition Books on display. For some unknown reason I picked one up leading Diane to ask why in the world should we buy it. My enlightened response: "I have no idea."

So on that Wednesday the reason came to me: we could use the book to write down our observations and have some running commentary for our touring. We had never done that before; the closest equivalent would be the notebooks we often write when we travel. I fudged the idea and said this would be a good idea. As I recall, Diane's response was a shrug, maybe even a rolling of the eyes at something that was even silly for me, but I did want a purpose for the Composition Book – just not what it eventually came to be.

As we were getting ready to take off, the phone rang. Diane answered and I didn't like her side of the conversation. "Oh, hi. ... Um ... hmm." Diane's face became grey and she looked at me with frightened eyes. "Are you sure? ... So you're not sure. ... Ok, thanks." Context matters so let me back up a few days. On the previous Friday I had taken Heidi to an emergency room after Diane and I found her in tears on her bed with back pain. She had just returned from being a hostess at a popular pancake house. I mistakenly believed it was comparable to my back problems, so Diane urged me to take her to the local hospital. While Heidi and I were waiting in the ER, we talked about her future. She was home for the summer after completing her freshman year at the Theater Program at C.W. Post/Long Island University. She was frustrated with her program at Post and wanted to strike out and start auditioning in NYC. We made no decisions then but I kept an open mind to her pleas. Today I wistfully look back on this conversation – how I wish we could have seen her make the difficult choice to follow her dream of auditioning and finding roles in the competitive theater world. Instead, her life was about to follow a completely unforeseen course. When the attending doctor saw Heidi, he said that the X-rays of her back were negative, but she looked anemic and should have her blood tested. So on the following Monday, Heidi had blood work done.

When Diane hung up the phone that Wednesday, I braced myself. She looked scared and stunned. She turned to me with frightened eyes and told us "That was Carol" (a former friend of ours who was a nurse at the doctor's office that ordered the blood work). "She said the blood work came back and the diagnosis is bad. They think it might be leukemia. We have to get Heidi to the doctor's office immediately."

Heidi and her boyfriend were out shopping and didn't have a cell phone with them. I rushed to a nearby shopping mall and scoured the lot for his car. No good. I went home and fretted with the others. Heidi unexpectedly dropped by on their way to who knows where. All of our lives changed as we told her we had to go to the doctor's office immediately. We didn't tell her then what our friend had said. As we sat in the doctor's office his news stunned us (denial was clearly at play after the phone call) and we rushed her to the cancer hospital in the city. A room was already waiting for her. The actual diagnosis of Acute Lymphoblastic Leukemia (ALL) came later that night.

Heidi was 18 when she was diagnosed with ALL. She died at home 2 1/2 years later. Her journey was a family one. From the start we (Diane, her sisters, their husbands, and I) were there. Kris provided her bone marrow for Heidi's first transplant, and Tara her stem cells for the second one. Both were perfect matches. Katie was not a match but was an oncology nurse at Sloan Kettering Memorial Hospital and became our resident expert. Even if Diane or I had accurate information about a medication, procedure, or treatment, Heidi often needed Katie's imprimatur. How can I capture these 2 1/2 years so you can grasp my message? They were the most terrifying and most enriching days and months of our lives. Yes, in a sense, "they were the best of times and the worst of times." It took me a few years after her death to realize the perverse blessing and gift the entire experience provided. Hopefully you will see what this means in what follows.

After being told that she would immediately undergo chemotherapy, be hospitalized for a month, and would need a bone marrow transplant in 6-7 months, Heidi's attitude was remarkable and inspirational. I have heard Diane telling many people about a conversation she and Heidi had when Heidi was about 14. They were having a typical mother/daughter moment. Diane doesn't remember what the conversation was all about but she does remember Heidi being a bit difficult and "teenage-ish". The conversation was light and at one point Diane's retort was "Heidi, some day you'll regret this because I'll be gone." Diane was not angry just trying to make a point that she didn't particularly care for Heidi's attitude. All of a sudden Heidi's demeanor changed and she became very serious.

"Mom, that's not going to happen; I'm going to die before you."

Diane didn't shift to a serious mode and replied "Oh, Heid, don't be silly. Of course I'll die before you."

On another occasion Heidi informed Diane that she would get cancer someday. In hindsight we wonder if she really was prescient. She seemed to slip into her role as cancer patient *par excellence* almost effortlessly. Her mission during every stay at the hospital was to spread cheer and bring smiles to everyone she encountered. She seemed to embrace what she had already known and dealt with the illness in ways that we considered heroic and wise. It seemed as if the diagnosis had stripped her of her teen and young adult persona (with its self-centeredness and condescending attitude) and replaced it with someone who would look after others and sincerely try to make the world a better place because she was in it.

These are just some of the memorable pronouncements Heidi made during her 2 ½ year ordeal:

"If I'm pleasant to everyone, then won't they treat me well?"

"This is the best thing that ever happened to me. I was living a very vanilla life and this will give me more depth for my acting career."

"My biggest disappointment this time in the hospital was not getting that boy in the adjacent room to smile."

"I didn't do anything to cause this; so let's do whatever we need to do to cure it."

"I shall wear my baldness proudly."

"OK, what are we going to play now; Yahtzee or Castle?"

"What blessings will we discover today?"

"I'd love to plan a party for you and the neighbors. What theme do you want?"

During Heidi's initial hospitalization, she made everyone who visited her draw a picture so we could hang it on the walls. Her room was a miniature art gallery with the offerings becoming a reflection of the personality of the artist. I felt that Heidi wanted to see her friends and family at night and in those lonely moments when a person gets wrapped up in her/his own thoughts. From that first stay one of us would spend each night with her so she would not be physically alone. We also had a role in making sure meds and procedures were followed properly during the overnight shifts. On the first night of her admittance, I realized that we were far more ignorant of this disease and what it entailed than we ever knew. We had known others who suffered and died from some form of leukemia. They were friends so the impact was muted compared to the waves of emotions that buffeted us with Heidi. It also became very clear to me that we needed to keep a log of what happened each day (for medical, psychological, and personal reasons). Thus, that Composition Book took on the life my subconscious ordained it to become. It was the first of two such daily journals we kept. Leukemia never defined Heidi, even though it was her greatest challenge and ultimate executioner.

Heidi loved the theater and was dedicated to restoring Audrey Hepburn's class and style to the stage. She loved Gene Kelly, Walter Matthau and musicals both old and new. She was a blonde who had a beauty in a Hepburn way. Heidi's blue eyes were captivating, yet could be very penetrating when she needed them to be. An admirer during her senior year of high school took a close up photograph of Heidi's eyes. She was shocked and indignant when that picture graced the cover of the high school year book. I never believed her proclaimed indignation; deep down I think she was touched/ flattered/thrilled. (This memory became the inspiration for this book's cover. The book is about the "I's" in my life but the real inspiration for my adult insights have come from Diane and my daughters. Their eyes reflect my "I's" on the cover.) Although Heidi loved the theater, people needed to be careful that they didn't underestimate her analytic and deductive abilities. After her second transplant, she began to entertain the possibility of becoming a Theater Critic. We all feared for those who would have been the subjects of her keen eye and intellectual analysis. Her first stab at being such a critic came when she was 10. We took her to Toronto to see *The Phantom of the Opera* with Colm Wilkinson playing the character of the Phantom. He was famously known for his portrayal of Jean Valjean in *Les Mis* and was receiving great reviews for his current role. As we were walking away from the theater I asked her what she thought.

"Well he doesn't pronounce his 'esses' properly and he makes up for his weak acting with strong singing." All I could do was smile. Her artistic flare for life and her passion for the theater were her persona to the world, but beware her critically acute mind. All of my daughters have intensely developed abilities at critical thinking; Heidi was no exception.

Her path to the first transplant was scary and bumpy: chemo, infections, late night emergency trips to the hospital, fatigue, worry, dealing with the unknowns, fevers of unknown origin, a port first inserted in her neck, then in her chest, setbacks, radiation, far too many spinal taps, etc. On the day of her transplant her sisters, Diane and I crowded into her room and tried to have a mini-party as the life-changing drip ran its course. Since we never let her spend a night in the hospital alone, Katie got the first night stay after the transplant and got to enjoy the cream corn smell that emanated from Heidi. The first 100 days following a transplant are the most critical; we anxiously watched for evidence that the transplant had taken hold and rejoiced as her counts started to rebound. Her new bone marrow wasn't rejecting her! After 100 days, the complications were all under control, and she was proclaimed to be cancer free. So we had a party. The Victory Party included family, friends, neighbors and church members. I watched Heidi, now sporting black, spiky hair (the color changed when it returned after the chemo and transplant) give a heartfelt thank you to everyone attending a celebration that was far too short lived. Heidi was asked by the transplant team to write advice for other patients. She did so, and we still have her sage words included in a brochure that we periodically give to someone we know who is confronting cancer.

The Victory Party was in August and Heidi said she may go back to Post for the spring semester. She still needed monitoring and minor treatments for a few months in the fall. If she did go back to Post, she was looking into transferring to a better theater program for the following year. She was also entertaining her dream of just going to NYC and auditioning for both on and off Broadway productions. As a preparation for her transition from patient to theatre geek we talked about her starting to re-engage in school and social activities. On the Sunday after 9/11, for example, she sang a solo of "Amazing Grace" at the end of our worship service as a way to honor the victims in New York, at the Pentagon and in Pennsylvania. There were very few dry eyes when she finished. That fall semester I was teaching an Honors course I thought might interest her and Heidi agreed to audit the class so she could reengage in coursework and meet some people of her own age. She didn't want a grade, but I did demand that she participate in the group project assignment. She smiled assent. Heidi was getting her life back on track.

And then one morning as Heidi and I were preparing to go to class, Diane and I heard a scream from the bathroom. Diane rushed in to see what was wrong. When Diane and Heidi emerged, I learned that Heidi had found a lump on her breast. They were concerned that the radiation and/or chemo may have caused a cancerous tumor to develop: a common enough possibility. I had read the material the doctor had given us about her experimental bone marrow transplant. Without going into any detail, there was the possibility that a hard mass may emerge somewhere in her body within the first couple of years. I blithely assumed that that was the issue -- again, denial reared its head.

After testing the mass, her leukemia specialist pronounced our dreaded fear: Heidi had relapsed. Dr. Wetzler said that he had never seen leukemia, a blood cancer, return in the form of a lump in the breast. He explained that he had expected that it was a mass formed by the experimental treatment and was shocked when he heard the results. He had believed that Heidi was going to be one of his best success stories. That, however, is not what happened. He said they had a room prepared for her and she would be immediately admitted so treatments could begin.

"No," Heidi said politely. "I'm going home and will return tomorrow. I hope you don't mind."

It was a statement, not a question. Dr. Wetzler was taken aback but offered no resistance. When we got into the car Heidi announced that she was hungry and wanted to stop for some lunch. By now Diane and I were in no condition to respond, think, or do anything other than what she wanted. When we had ordered some food and drinks she calmly said, "Let's have a party tonight. Last time I didn't have time to have one. That's why I wasn't going to be admitted now. We can keep the gathering simple and just invite a few friends and family over. We'll play some games. But there will be two rules. 1. No one can cry. 2. No one can talk about my condition."

And so with that proclamation we had a party, played games (the men beat the women in Outburst), laughed and wrapped each other in a communal bond of love that was unspoken but whose tendrils encircled all of us. Everyone followed her rules (although there was some whispering between people when they were out of Heidi's line of vision and hearing). How could she respond to relapsing by wanting a party? How typical that she thought of others and didn't want sympathy for herself. Here's a story that illustrates Heidi's tenacity.

By the age of seven Heidi had already been in the high school's production of *Hello Dolly* and was intent upon auditioning for a part in their production of *South Pacific*. The director wanted two elementary school students to be the plantation owner's children. Diane took Heidi to the audition and all of us were concerned about her response to rejection. She had not yet become fashion conscious and wore old yellow sweat pants and a sweat shirt. The audition consisted of groups of children singing together on stage along with the director. As they exited the stage the director stopped each one and asked the child to sing what she had just sung (part of a scale). On the way home, afterwards, Diane tried to prepare Heidi,

"Did you see all those other kids trying out?" And "you're so blonde and fair; they're looking for somebody who looks Polynesian."

Heidi just smiled.

Diane asked, "Wasn't it fun to just audition?"

Heidi just sat in the car and nodded with a satisfied smile on her face. When they arrived home, a message from the director awaited them: Heidi had the part, if she wanted it.

Diane immediately called the director. "Are you sure you have the correct girl?" she asked.

The director laughed. "Heidi has perfect pitch. We can easily remedy her blonde hair and fair complexion with temporary dye and make-up."

Heidi was thrilled but not overly surprised. She enjoyed the rehearsals, something she did throughout her life. Performing was great, but rehearsing was also special. For Heidi the whole experience (reading, blocking, rehearsing, make-up, costuming, miscues, incorrect lines, props/wrong props, etc.) were the elements that made her soul dance. The whole experience put her in contact with a deep-seated love for being on stage and experiencing the magic of being someone else. She smelled the sawdust. Heidi was sick the day before the dress rehearsal with chicken pox. The pox marks were beginning to show, and she had a fever. When we tried to console her about missing the opportunity to perform, she looked at us as if we were aliens from another planet.

"What are you talking about?" she said with her wide-eyed intensity. "The show must go on!"

There was no question in her mind that she was going to be on that stage and be the best Polynesian girl she could be. The director agreed to let her light up that stage and sing her part. Heidi not only made it to the dress rehearsal, but also to each performance. She never complained and never missed a line or a note. Many people didn't even know she was sick, including some members of the cast. She looked for no sympathy. She relished in her moments on the stage. "The show must go on," became her trademark and mantra. We now have that phrase on her grave marker and the bench next to her plot. She lived that refrain all too often in her shortened life.

It would take an entire volume to describe the ups and downs, the hopes and worries leading to the second transplant. I'm not sure whether our experiences of the previous year were a help or a barrier as we waded into a repetition of the spinal taps, chemo, radiation, fevers of unknown origin, fatigue, complications, worry, shots, administering drugs and saline at home, changing her dressings, getting reacquainted with hospital staff, and finding the stamina to do it all again. Heidi led the way. We continued to organize our work schedules so someone was available to assist her and again she never spent a night in the hospital alone.

Transplant day #2 was May 2, 2002. Again I have to back up a few days to set the scene. Heidi was hospitalized in preparation for the transplant and undergoing what was to be her last round of chemo. On April 30 she exclaimed: "This is my last chemo treatment EVER!" In our journal for Heidi I characterized the previous 4-5 days before the last treatment as "a little off" and thought we had entered a type of twilight zone. The first example occurred on April 25th. Heidi was scheduled to have a line put in her hand to take care of blood draws and for administering drugs and a dye for transplant day. They had a difficult time putting it in because Heidi's veins were rather compromised by all the treatments and problems she had experienced. An hour later she was told they had put the line in the wrong hand and they had to repeat the dreaded procedure again. Then she received an order to have a repeat of an Echo test. This puzzle was solved when her doctor showed up later and explained the problem. Her testing had been inconclusive and again she was faced with upsetting possibilities. The results could be either: an inflammation that would resolve itself over time; an infection which would not be resolved by the transplant treatments and would have to be addressed later; or her leukemia may have returned. The doctor asked Heidi if she wanted to proceed with the transplant or to undergo a biopsy to determine whether it was an infection or leukemia. Hesitantly Heidi decided to skip the biopsy and proceed as planned.

April 26th was an example of finding ourselves in a surreal landscape. Heidi was given a prescription that Katie said was being taken off the market. Her breakfast wasn't delivered (they were always rather regular before). Heidi needed an unscheduled transfusion of two units of blood because there were small traces of blood in her urine. She also had to have a respiratory treatment, again unscheduled. She was groggy for much of the day. When the psychologist came to see her, she slept and I talked. The PT lady came, then just turned around and didn't try to rouse Heidi. As I said, just a little off. As I've said before whenever Heidi was hospitalized someone spent the night with her. Not just to be supportive but also to insure that treatment during the night was consistent with what was prescribed for her. Over the 2 1/2 years this practice proved to be quite helpful, both in bolstering Heidi's spirit but also in providing a check on what the professionals were doing. That night we had the nurse recheck a medication that didn't seem correct. It wasn't. On the 27th her doctor came in to discuss the transplant. He indicated that he was going to send her home the day after the transplant - something rather unusual.

"You and your family are well-equipped to handle the basic care. Your mom changes the dressings and your dad and sister can administer medications and shots. What do you think", he said with his wry smile. Heidi didn't even have to respond. Her smile was answer enough.

"Of course you'll be making almost daily visits for check-ups. But that's nothing new for you", was something he really didn't have to add.

Tara was getting shots (by Katie, me or her husband) before the harvesting. The shots were boosting her blood cell count to insure that her stem cells would be rich. Although Transplant Day was May 2, Tara had to go into the hospital for the first of two draws the day before the transplant. They wanted to insure that they had enough of her stem cells to insure a successful transplant. Originally we thought she would only have to undergo the draw on the 1st but the transplant director wanted to be extra cautious, especially given the fact this was Heidi's second transplant.

The day was very long for Tara: she couldn't move for over 6 hours. Doing crosswords with her husband didn't make the experience any easier. The next day was a return to the Twilight Zone. No one really knew how to feel this time around. We were so sure that the first transplant had been successful: we had done everything right and still Heidi relapsed. What would the results be for this day's transplant? In the morning Tara was again connected to the machine that extracts stem cells to be transfused into Heidi. On the 2nd she only had to experience 6 cycles instead of the 8 she had the day before. However, it was still almost a 5 hour ordeal of lying on her back and not being able to move. Again it was long and very uncomfortable. Tara was sore but didn't experience any of the complications that had plagued Kris (explained in Chapter 14). For her first transplant all six of us were in the room with Heidi as they hung the bags with Kris' bone marrow. We talked, joked and tried to have a party in the room while the separated marrow was administered at two different times. This time around the girls decided that we would handle the day quite differently. Tara and Joe were busy downstairs with the extra session for harvesting. Kris and Katie sent Diane and me out to breakfast and when we returned they went shopping. Just as the previous day I floated between Heidi and Tara while Diane stayed with Heidi. Diane had spent the previous night with Heidi and was exhausted. She went home with Tara and Joe and I stayed with Heidi and played cards. Kris and Katie brought birthday presents home for Heidi. Transplant days are often referred to as birthdays because of their transformative nature. When she went home the next day she told Tara that she, Heidi, could go out and kill someone knowing that Tara's DNA would be on the murder weapon! We all have watched too many "Law and Order" episodes.

After the transplant the road became rather bumpy and quite strained. One of the most important issues following a stem cell (or bone marrow) transplant for a leukemia patient relates to GVHD (Graft versus Host Disease). In simple terms a leukemia transplant is different from a lung or heart transplant. For those procedures the post operation problem is whether the patient will reject the new organ. Something from the outside is seen as alien and the body's immune system kicks in and may reject the invader. It's the opposite for leukemia. The transplant is trying to change a person's immune system. So the problem here is that the new blood (the new stem cells) becomes the immune system and it may start rejecting the recipient's (host's) body. It is typical, for example, to get hives or rashes as the new immune system sees the body itself as a foreign, unwanted organism. The medical staff monitors the body's reaction and tries to adjust medications accordingly. A little GVHS is desirable. After her first transplant Heidi experienced minimal problems with GVHD which led to the feelings of success by her physician and those who were attending to her. Heidi's body started to take a beating from the second procedure. It included rashes and scratchy, dry eyes. Her joints became inflamed. Those were acceptable rejections of her body. The respiratory complications she experienced sealed her fate. As her breathing became more compromised she needed constant oxygen. At home we had a machine with a very long tube so she could keep the canula in her nose while moving around the first floor of the house (living room, kitchen, dining room, bathroom and her bedroom. We were also supplied with portable oxygen tanks whenever she left the house. She started a part-time job at a local Import/Export business thanks to a connection with a neighbor. She answered the phones and acted as if everything was under control. Other than the oxygen tank her fellow employees didn't realize how compromised she really was. She even attended their Christmas party at a local restaurant. We drove her there and waited at a neighboring restaurant until she called to tell us she was ready to go home. I can still see her dressed with such class and walking so elegantly into that party.

Even though Christmas Eve had become psychologically redefined after my Mom died, we kept our traditions alive even throughout Heidi's illness. One of the cuter traditions we had related to Susie dolls. Each of our daughters received one when she was very young. At Christmas time, Santa's elves would steal into the house and abscond the doll, only to have it returned with repairs and new clothes on Christmas Eve. Heidi's last Christmas Eve was a worrisome time. Her respiratory system was becoming severely compromised and her recuperation was difficult and fraught with anxiety. I had read that respiratory complications after a transplant were fatal -- maybe not imminently, but it was irreversible. I never let that knowledge sink into my consciousness, never talked to anyone about it, and proceeded to live as if Heidi was not facing a death sentence. (Yes. Denial.) All of us, however, had learned to grasp each moment with her as precious. So that Christmas, with our daughters aged 31, 29, 28 and 21, we decided to repair their Susie dolls and place them under the tree. The husbands found their wives' dolls and we secreted Heidi's from her room. We cleaned and dressed them. When we returned from Diane's sister's house, the girls discovered the dolls under the Christmas tree and beamed with glee. They were giddy and we saw the thrill of an adult regaining a touch of her childhood. A more profound experience awaited all of them.

We had kept memorabilia for all of our girls in file cabinets in our basement: drawings, letters, awards, school activities, and a wide array of papers that reflected moments in each of their lives. The previous September we suggested to Heidi that she could have these files and make scrapbooks for her sisters. This idea was one of the best ones we had throughout her entire struggle. She was struggling and needed a mission or project. This was it. She threw herself into scrap booking as if it were a spiritual calling. She planned and organized, using her analytic, left-brain skills. She bought materials, stickers, and borders that followed the creative juices of her artistic, right brain. Each sister received over a month of concentrated effort and devotion. The end products were masterpieces, each scrapbook capturing the heart and soul of each sister with a singular flare. Heidi was thrilled with her creations and was excited about giving them out on Christmas Eve. She loved her sisters dearly and felt indebted to them for all of their sacrifices throughout her struggle. The bond of love that we have seen and continue to see in our daughters is a blessing that fills Diane and me with a sense of fulfillment and joy. The three older daughters had taken Heidi away to a resort to celebrate her 21st birthday the previous October. It was a memorable trip for all of them. In Heidi's honor, our daughters still get together each year in September or October to celebrate "Sisters' Weekend."

On December 23 Heidi had been unexpectedly hospitalized. Her doctor, with whom she had a deep and abiding friendship, informed her that she would have to stay for five days. In uncharacteristic sharpness she informed him that she was going home the next day and that he had nothing to say about it. Taken aback he grudgingly agreed and Heidi was home for our traditions and celebrations. We celebrated her last Christmas with the beauty of a family's love. Although other gifts were exchanged that night, I remember most vividly the scrapbooks. Diane and I saw all the love Heidi had poured into them, and all the hardship she endured while creating them. The GVHD symptoms were becoming even more problematic: using her hands was painful; she was having difficulty breathing; her back and joints were inflamed; and her eyes were scratchy. So that evening Heidi carefully watched the faces of each of her sisters with delight, pride and love as they, their own eyes gleaming with tears, paged through the masterpieces. The house echoed with their delighted exclamations and laughter.

"Remember these dresses Grandma made for us?"

"Look at my hair!"

"Oh my gosh, listen to this!"

"Heid, I's so interesting to see my life through your eyes."

"What a treasure this is."

"How did you do all of this?"

"Where did you find all of this?"

As Tara, Kris, and Katie continued to examine their scrapbooks and share with their husbands the stories that accompanied each picture, each memento, each page, Heidi grew quieter. She smiled at the collective memory being explored and continued to watch carefully the expressions on her sisters' faces. I remember wondering what she was thinking and how she must have felt handing over the projects that had consumed her for four months. She sat so proper and erect (maybe using the admonitions of correct posture for the stage). Did she pick the red bandana that night because it was the best choice for a Christmas accessory? I thought I saw a flicker of sadness settle into her eyes, but I wonder now if it was my own sadness that I was projecting. For a brief time the sounds faded and I retreated into that quiet place in my soul, the place of awe with a touch of serenity, the place where I can watch my loved ones as if I am no longer there. Was Heidi's smile and gaze a signal that she too had this spiritual retreat? Was she savoring these sounds of joy and locking them away for future reminiscences? The memory of that Christmas Eve blends with the one that brought my mom's death. Yes, Christmas Eve is a transformed part of my life.

[The following pages borrow material from *Riding the Subway with Heidi: A Father's Journey of Grieving* – my book published in 2012.]

January was a long month of worry, hospital visits, and Heidi's slow decline. I'm not sure I noticed the differences on a daily basis. Every once in awhile I would take stock and see that she was worse this month than last. Early in February, 2003 we started feeling that there was some promising developments in her condition but those hopes were dashed. The days leading up to Heidi's last hospital visit are quite a blur. Some days stick out when I spend a lot of time concentrating on what we did. Without that concentration everything blended into days that felt like I was walking through molasses. On Friday January 31 Heidi and I had had a long visit to the hospital. The day started with a painful blood draw (her veins were collapsed by then) and an EKG which showed irregularities in blood flow pattern. Her doctor was hopeful that Heidi's respiratory problems were caused by cardiac complications and not as the result of complications from her stem cell transplant.

Hoping for cardiac problems just seemed so surreal. One major problem that we also had to address that day was whether Heidi wanted to have an access port placed either in her neck or hand. Pam, the PA, told Heidi:

"We could try it on your hand although the neck would be the most effective."

"I really don't think I can handle one in my neck right now. Do I really have to have one?" Heidi responded with tears welling up. Pam said that it was Heidi's decision and she would be back in a few minutes so we could talk in private.

Although I started to convince Heidi that a PIC line would be useful, I could see that she needed me to just be there for her and to stop trying to fix a situation that was really beyond me.

"I'm getting tired. I'm not going to have a neck IV. I wish they would just put in a port. The PIC is a real pain." Heidi's breathing was deteriorating and the physical strain of daily living was very sad to see. Her reputation at the hospital and among all the staff was almost story book. If you've seen "Hello Dolly", then you would understand that Heidi's presence at Roswell was akin to Dolly's entrance into *Harmonia Gardens*. Today, however, she was tired and discouraged instead of her usual smiling, cheerfully greeting others. Her reputation was enhanced among the staff when she wrote an op. ed. letter to the local paper praising the heroes of the hospital: first the patients, then the skilled professionals who provided such life giving care. It was always magical for me to see Heidi's charisma spreading to any and everyone she encountered at the hospital. A good example occurred one day a year and a half before when the two of us got on an elevator with a woman we had never really noticed before. She turned to Heidi and said:

"I was a nurse before becoming a patient. I've noticed you before and admire that you wear your baldness with great pride. Your bandanas are so well chosen. But what I really wanted to say was how important your article really was. It is a real morale boost for all the people here, especially the support staff. You'll never know how much it has meant to so many. Thank you." Life connects people in strange and unexpected ways. We both smiled and thanked her.

On that January day as I pushed Heidi out of the elevator I thought about how many people Heidi had impacted in her life and thought back to that conversation on the elevator. Did Heidi realize the impact she had? In fact, how much impact did she have that I would never know? She did leave her mark on so many people's hearts and souls. We recently have gone through the thousands of cards she received while she was struggling and the hundreds of cards and letters we received after she died. They tell the story of her impact – she truly did touch so many people in so many different ways.

So I slipped out of the room telling Heidi I had to go to the restroom (a white lie we all tell in life). Instead, I talked to the PA in the hall and told her

"Pam, I think you need to know a couple of things. Heidi is quite fragile right now. She's tired and afraid of going through these procedures again. Her long-term boyfriend left for Kuwait today. She's becoming overwhelmed and is really struggling to be the perfect patient. She does not want anyone here to see her sick or selfish or depressed. She wants you to only see her with a smile. To see the obedient patient who does whatever she is asked to do. This may surprise you, but she's concerned that the staff might yell at her because she was doing something wrong."

Both Pam and the nurse we knew so well shook their heads. I could see that both of them were choking up. Pam returned to the room, walked over to Heidi, knelt in front of her, held her hand and said

"Listen, Heidi, if anyone and I mean anyone, yells at you for any reason, I'm going to slap that person silly. You are the hero here. Our job is to take care of you – you don't have to worry about us."

The smile on Heidi's face was priceless. Her shoulders relaxed as much as they were capable of doing. She was ready for the news from her physician. Before he arrived a cardiologist who was totally arrogant the last time we encountered him came into the room. Today he has gentle and kind. He informed us that Heidi did not have a heart attack and did not have heart disease. I remember thinking that it was bizarre for me to be very disappointed in hearing that. Along with her doctor I was rooting for heart problems. Her doctor followed shortly afterward and offered Heidi an experimental regimen used at Johns Hopkins for kidney transplant patients.

"As strange as it seems it might be helpful. You need to know that the drug is very dangerous and we'll have to monitor your condition carefully." His eyes were gentle. "We can administer the drug today."

I never asked Pam but wondered if she may have told him about Heidi's mental attitude; on the other hand he seemed attuned to her most of the time over the past 2 ½ years. Heidi's eyebrows shot up.

"Today?" Oh, how one word can capture hope and relief. We spent over six hours that day with most of the time devoted to cards and Yahtzee. So the following Monday we drove to Roswell and encountered a rather benign visit. Heidi had baked cookies for the staff and their smiles of appreciation were deep and genuine. When her doctor stopped by he indicated that it was too early to tell what effect the regimen would have. We needed to return on Friday. While we were there Heidi no longer could go to the bathroom by herself. A new ritual was introduced into our lives – my lifting her and holding her while she went. I can still feel her frail arms draped over mine and how carefully I tried to move her since movements were becoming painful – even the simplest motions. Pam ordered a potty chair which arrived at home very quickly.

On Thursday, February 6, I came home and saw Heidi at her usual perch in the living room (sitting on the couch and looking out our picture window. I put down my briefcase, sat down and asked how she was doing.

"Dad, I've written something" she said rather seriously.

"Ok. Can I read it?"

"Yes but my writing isn't very good."

"Do you want me to type it up for you?" I am a touch typist and have played the role of secretary for a number of people throughout my life. In college I was the guy who could type up a paper for a friend the night before the due date. I also helped Diane during the semester we were engaged. So typing something for Heidi would be easy – or so I thought.

"That would be great, but Dad," her words just hung in the air.

"What is it?" was my puzzled response.

"You can't show this to anybody else. You know, like putting it in the church newsletter or anything. It's personal".

"Is it OK for me to read it?"

"Yeah. I want you and mom to see it. And my sisters. But that's all."

As I began to type my eyes began to well up and deciphering her writing became a bit of a challenge. Heidi never had great penmanship but her writing that day can best be described as chicken scratches. Her story was beautiful, personal, and filled me with such deep hope and comfort. Without betraying her admonition I can say that she wrote about purpose, meaning, God and her life. It was beautiful. I handed the finished copy to her; she looked and smiled. "I'm ready to go to my room now." I clearly remember holding her very thin arm and helping her across the living room, around the hall way and into her bedroom. That was the last time she ever sat on the couch and looked out to the real and imaginary world on the other side of the window.

The next day became momentous. Heidi was sitting beside me in the car with the oxygen canula in her nose and intently staring ahead. She seemed deep in thought and I wondered where her mind was taking her.

"Hey, Heid, look, the Mega jackpot is now at $28 million. Do we need the money or should we let someone else have it?" was my attempt at seeing where she was. She turned, smiled and said, "Let's keep the dollar so someone else can get the jackpot." We continued with some banter then

I turned our conversation to a more focused topic: "It's amazing how every time we go to Roswell, something unexpected happens. Who would have predicted last Friday, for example".

"That's what makes life so interesting, isn't it? It's fun to enjoy those unexpected blessings", she replied.

As we arrived at the hospital I dropped Heidi at the front door and a volunteer helped her into a wheelchair as I parked the car. Our routine was rather automatic by then. We'd head to the elevators and Heidi would greet people as we went along. Her stays in the hospital were on the 5th floor while her post transplant visits took us to the 6th floor. We knew to proceed to the scales for weigh in and the nurse would go over routine questions, blood pressure, etc. We knew all the nurses well and the Physician's Assistant had become an integral part of both of Heidi's post transplant journeys. As Heidi was being weighed, Pam (the PA) motioned me to the nurses' station. In hushed tones she whispered:

"Meir wants to meet you in my room." The first of many feelings and moments of panic slammed into my heart. My immediate thoughts:

"This is not good. He never meets me alone. What went wrong? Oh no." I nodded assent and turned to join Heidi and take her to the assigned room. One of our favorite nurses was on duty and she whispered to me that she would make an excuse for me when the doctor was ready. It wasn't too long before she came into the room and announced:

"Ah, I need to talk to Heidi, why don't you wait outside?"

"OK!" This was not atypical and I didn't see any change in Heidi's demeanor or eyes. I left them and walked with purpose to Pam's office. As I walked into the room a picture that I shall never forget met me. The canvass was glum and there was a sadness that pervaded everything. Pam was sitting very quietly and leaning forward in her swivel chair. But it was the look on Meir's face that told me I did not want to be here and I did not want to hear what he was going to say. He sat with his head slightly bowed, hands folded in his lap. As I entered he slowly raised his head and looked at me with strangely blank eyes. I feebly sat on the cushioned chair strategically placed across from him. The room was small so our knees almost touched. His eyes went to the floor. He began to review the regimen we had started the previous Friday and then abruptly finished the preliminaries. He was always thorough with me because from the start I asked many questions, probably more than Heidi wanted to hear. His preambles, however, were now over.

"The tests from the regimen were negative" was his transition to the gut wrenching statement.

"Could it just be too early to tell?" Time to grasp onto some element of hope.

He shook his head. "No. There should have been immediate, positive effects. In fact, we expected results by last Monday. The best we can do now is manage her symptoms for a very brief period of time." He paused and let the "very brief time" sink in. His eyes met mine with empathy and sadness. He quietly dropped the bombshell: "It's time to call her Sisters home. Is Diane available to meet with us today?" My response is lost in the tangled memories of fear and disbelief. All I know is that other words were exchanged and I did go to the restroom to recompose myself and then to call Diane. Pam, Meir and I had all cried; that I do remember. What do I tell Diane? I was afraid of telling her the truth because I didn't want her driving to the hospital with this yoke falling so surprisingly on her.

"Hi Hon."

"Hi, what's the problem?" There was no anticipated reason for me to call so I tried to lie in such a way that it might make some sense.

"The results are going to take longer to get than expected." Not an unusual occurrence throughout the previous 2 ½ years. "Would you bring a lunch up for Heidi, she really needs to eat something?"

This gambit worked only in the sense that Diane did not ask me to explain and did bring Heidi a lunch. She now was with us. After she arrived Meir walked into the room, pulled up a chair and talked to the three of us.

Again some memory traces are murky for me. I do know that he **never** said that Heidi was going to die. He **did** say that the experimental procedure had failed. I remember asking, almost pleading, if it just needed a little more time, even though I knew the answer already.

"No, she should have responded by now. Your condition will not improve. You need to make sure that your advanced directive expresses exactly what you want." Pow! All three of us were speechless for a moment. Diane and Heidi were more startled looking than I was.

The silence was broken when Heidi quietly asked: "What does this mean?" Looking at Heidi he said,

"We could put you on a ventilator in an induced coma. If we do, you may never regain consciousness." He seemed to understand that our battle had been a family one. Heidi needed to be home with us, not end her heroic struggle in an institution.

"What do you think I should do?" she whispered.

"Whatever you want, Heid," I said immediately.

Diane tried a reassuring smile but her eyes were dripping with pain. "Don't think about us," she said. "Do whatever you want for yourself."

Shock and numbness seemed to be the best descriptors for our initial responses. Meir did say that there was one other drug that he could give but he did not believe it would do any good. Heidi opted to take the medication so we remained in the room for awhile. Again, those moments were the transition that led to a weekend of our family's vigil for Heidi. Our daughters and their husbands dropped everything and immediately returned home when we called:

"Meir says it's time for you to come home."

The weekend was a strange blend of routine and chunks of singular experiences. We had the port-o-potty in her room and I would hold her up while others would pull her pants down. Often I would stay to make sure she could sit OK; other times that task fell to Diane or one of her sisters. Her medications continued, especially those being administered to control her pain. We played games. We joked. We recalled family stories. Saturday night brought a wonderful dinner prepared by Anthony with assistance I'm sure. We watched TV. We poked gentle fun at one another. We listened to music. The family also dove into cookie making as one of those singular moments of the weekend. Heidi had created two cookie recipes: "Snow Mountain Caps" and "Chocolate Coconut Decadence". She was delighted with the results of the baking but even more by the gushing compliments from everyone. Even though Heidi had never lost her dreams of performing on the stage, she had started pursuing other options as well. In the past year, she had watched many cooking shows, inquired into a culinary school, created lavish menus, and, most recently, had created her cookie recipes. We laughed heartily when she announced, "I want to enter them into this contest I read about and want to win third place."

Swallowing an amused chuckle, one of her sisters asked, "Why third and not first or even second?"

"Because I want to win the standing mixer. I've always wanted one. That's the third place prize."

"Only you, Heid, would want to WIN third place!" Everyone laughed again. Beneath the surface lightheartedness, however, was the growing realization that Heidi was getting worse more quickly than we had imagined. On Monday, Feb. 10 the final vigil played itself out. I couldn't sleep so I secreted down to the small rocking chair next to Heidi's bed so I could be close. Kris was in bed with Heidi and her eyes were closed but she didn't seem to be asleep. I quietly watched Heidi struggling to breathe as she slept. I remember thinking how much closer our family had become since her initial diagnosis. Somehow Heidi's illness had brought out the best in everybody as we all assumed roles we had never anticipated: caretaker, friend, game player, debate contestant, reminiscent partner, trivia test taker, TV critic, cooking companion, medication dispenser. Vragil was on her bed and nestled under her legs as she bridged them to minimize the joint pain.

At 6:00 a.m. Heidi awakened the household with shouts of pain. Everyone hurried to her room dreading what would be found. Her pain quickly subsided and she sat back in her bed. The room is not large, but we were gathered to continue to care for her and squeeze out every second we could. As she relaxed the men drifted out of the room and I went upstairs to shave. Heidi did have another appointment that day and I was going to take her. While I was upstairs Heidi looked at Katie, who was sitting next to her. "Am I going to die?" she asked, saying those dreaded words for the first time.

"Yes, honey. You are."

The girls told me that Heidi looked a little surprised before saying, "Do I at least have a few days?"

"Yes, there's some time."

"Is it okay to be scared?" she asked.

"Yes," her sisters replied.

"Well, then, I'm a little scared." Heidi paused. "I'm a lot scared."

"We all love you."

The women told me that they had a frank discussion among all of them. The upshot was that Heidi finally realized that no measures existed that would cure her. A respirator may prolong her life, but she would still die. At the end of the discussion, Heidi made it clear that she no longer wanted the option of a respirator. One of her sisters then asked, "Heid, have you given any thought about how we're going to get you to the hospital today? It's so painful for you to move."

Katie continued "we could just call Meir and tell him you're not coming in. We could have nurses come to the house. They could bring a wet oxygen mask."

"We can do that?"

"Heid, we can do anything you want."

"They won't be mad?"

"No, we promise."

301

"This isn't giving up?"

"No, honey."

"Okay, you can all cry now."

Diane came upstairs and told me that I wasn't taking Heidi to the hospital. At first I was taken aback but then she told me about what happened in Heidi's room. "It would just be too tough for her," she said, quietly. I nodded. Maybe it was at that moment that the vigil actually began. I called Meir a couple of times during the day. He increased her Ativan and called in Hospice. During one conversation I said that she had deteriorated noticeably over the weekend. "I don't know whether she will last for days or weeks in this condition."

"It won't be weeks," he replied, a slight catch in his normally calm voice. I then knew that he would never see her alive again.

Throughout the day, Heidi slipped in and out of coherence. At one point she asked her sisters to be sure to enter her recipes in the contests she had talked about earlier. When someone suggested that we tell some jokes Heidi replied, "Don't bother, we're not a very funny family." She would settle into a sort of stupor, and then, suddenly, shout something out. "Skaneateles!" she blurted out once. Her sisters looked startled, tears creeping into their eyes. "Yes, Heid, we took you there for your 21st birthday. Didn't we have a great time?" Her sisters reminisced a bit about the trip before realizing Heidi was no longer tracking their conversation.

As the day wore on, Heidi became more and more fixated with her clogged nose. We would ask her if she needed something, and she'd cry out. "A decongestant. All I want is a decongestant!" She didn't seem to understand that a decongestant would not help her any longer. Katie suggested that she take the nose piece from her breathing machine and place it in her mouth, since she wasn't really capable of breathing through her nose anyhow. There were times when her gasping for breath was very frightening. By the afternoon Hospice had succeeded in sending us a mask for her.

It helped for a little while, but it was not going to provide the breath of life for very long.

For the last couple of hours of Heidi's life, Diane was lying in bed with her, stroking her hair and placing a comforting arm around her shoulders. "Find the light, Heid," she kept whispering. "Find the light." I was standing next to Heidi. "It's okay to relax, sweetie," I repeatedly said in a hushed tone. "Find peace. You don't have to fight any longer." Toward the end I, too, stroked her hair and patted her head. I just needed to touch my little girl, keep her close to me. The other girls and their husbands also crowded into her room, alternately joining Diane and Heidi on the bed, or crouching on the floor. She kept struggling to breathe and straining to stay awake. Just as she would start to doze, she would snap her head up and open her eyes, as if she were arousing herself to continue the struggle. "Relax, Sweetie. It's okay to go to sleep," I would say. Sometimes she would respond with a soft, sweet "Okay" that was almost melodious. I had heard that same "okay" so often in the past few years as she faced so many difficult situations. I can still hear it echo today.

Although we knew Heidi was going to die, I did not believe it was going to be that night. I had hoped Heidi would go to sleep and have another day with us. But, I also had the conflicted feeling that by telling her to relax I was giving her permission to die, to find the peace that would come after struggling for so long and so hard. Was her last "okay" her way of telling us that she was through; she was going to find the light; and she was no longer going to fight the losing battle? I remember praying: "Either give my baby peace or miraculously start repairing her lungs and give her the life she should have." God picked the wrong option.

Heidi's eyelids were getting heavier and heavier and were staying closed for longer periods of time. We would think she was asleep and then her eyelids would flutter and she'd look blankly around. There were choruses of "We love you"; "We're all here"; "You're such a good girl." Finally, Heidi looked around, made eye contact with us, and said, "Good night."

She looked at me again. "Good night," she repeated and finally fell into sleep. Her sisters and husbands went into the kitchen to make some coffee, knowing it was going to be a long night. Diane continued cradling her. Slowly her breathing changed from staccato and strained to regular and peace. "Girls!" Diane shouted. "Come quickly!" My other three daughters vaulted into the room. Kris and Katie threw themselves on the bed, while Tara hovered by Heidi's side next to me. The gaps between Heidi's breaths got longer. Then, in the flash of a moment that has implanted itself indelibly in my consciousness, Heidi stopped breathing.

There are no words to describe the next couple of hours. Family and some close friends came to see her and say "Good night." Heidi's sisters and cousins cleaned her body; Katie dug the clots out of her nose; they dressed her in her pink silk rose pajamas. We prayed. We started to share some Heidi stories. We cried. We even laughed a little. When the funeral director carried her out of the house for the last time, we all unconsciously formed a line from her room, through the living room, and out the door. We surrounded her with our presence, our energy, our love. We watched her leave and numbness settled over me.

Riding the Subway with Heidi: A Father's Journey of Grieving is the book I wrote a few years after her death. It provides many of my views about grieving, most of which I am not duplicating in this book. However, there are some salient issues that I have learned since then and want to share with you. These issues relate to my experiences of stereotyping and the ignorance I had of healthy and meaningful grieving. I have continued examining what grieving means to me since writing that book. Putting grieving into a book about my isms makes sense. The back cover of my book about Heidi explains what that book was all about:

"When my daughter Heidi died at the age of 21, I discovered that I was abysmally unprepared for the grief that consumed me. Despite my academic training in death, dying, spirituality and cultural values, I struggled with finding the meaning in her death and understanding what it means to grieve. This book is the culmination of my thoughts and experiences about Heidi, my personal grieving journey, the American cultural expectations of grief, and the emotional and existential dimensions of life and grieving. *Riding the Subway with Heidi* provides a new perspective on what it means to grieve, debunks cultural myths that actually hinder grieving, and shows how to integrate the process of grieving into your new grief-filled life. With a focus on finding balance, health, and meaning in life rather than chasing "closure," "moving on," or "going through stages," this book makes sense of the grieving process. It is both Heidi's story and mine". These words are still true, but in the years since the book was published, I have continued to learn more about myself and society. I am still coming to terms with my ignorance about death, dying and grieving. In like manner I'm also trying to understand society's ill-conceived relationship with death and grieving and how this Societal Griefism has affected me.

Death affects us directly when we have a true personal connection. The depth of that connection defines our behavior and the attitude that others will have toward us. I am struck by the common question or comment: "Was he/she close to you?" If the answer is yes, then appropriate sympathy is in order; if no, then no one needs to spend too much time on the issue. I am also struck by the superficial attitude that seems to be so prevalent in America: we judge a person's grieving by the display of tears that he or she exhibits. "How is she doing?" is a common enough question. The answer usually is determined by whether or not she is displaying her emotions or is considered to not be in control of her life. She is doing well if she doesn't cry too much or seems to behave the way normal people expect. Crying, of course, is to be expected, but loss of control is another matter. There seems to be an unwritten social rule dictating the amount of crying that is permissible. We may not be able to identify what this social rule is, but we apply it unwittingly. I remember early in our marriage when I went to a funeral of a friend of my in-laws and Diane couldn't go. She asked how Norm was doing. My reply: "Not well. He was inconsolable at church. You know how dependent he was on Marge." I went on to explain how his outward expression of grief did not assuage anyone's concern that he wasn't dealing well with his grief. Our own concern for him and his crying wasn't wrong, but its underlying assumptions and messages now concern me. These are subtle, covert signs of Societal Griefism

While everyone processes, or should process, grief differently, society appears to have a uniform approach to death. People think there is a right way and a wrong way. Our prejudices, biases, discomfort, and ignorance have led to unhealthy patterns, superficial gestures, unrealistic expectations, and real hindrances to live with and experience grief effectively. I coined the term "Societal Griefism" to illustrate the prejudicial and often harmful approach society and its rituals impart on those who are grieving.

Each death includes an intermingling web of connections, relationships, and meanings. These webs are not disconnected with death -- they are transformed. Ignoring the transforming effects or trying to disentangle from the web is not healthy, regardless of society's attempts to extricate us from the downer of dying or having to cope with the depths of grieving. I am concerned with society's perpetuating the superficial ideas that once a person goes through the expected stages of grief and finds closure or moves on that that person is somehow no longer emotionally or psychologically connected with his or her loved one. The common belief seems to say that grieving is something to be fixed; it is not to be continued for too long. Beware of someone who is not grieving properly; stay away lest you catch their disease. This chapter is dedicated to shifting our societal beliefs and trying to help redefine the relationship all of us have with death, dying and grieving in our lives. Heidi's illness and death has transformed me in ways that excises the superficial and corroding approaches that our society condones and perpetuates. I shudder every time I hear a reporter claim that "now the family can find closure because ..." - fill in the blank about what provides the closure. Grieving isn't a broken bone that can be put back in place and heal completely. It isn't an interruption in a person's life that has a time period to return to normal. We don't fix it or put it on a shelf to be lost and ignored.

I have learned that my grief for my father was selfish and superficial. It was far more for the loss of what I wanted a father to be rather than grief for the man my dad really was. Isn't this a type of misplaced grief: feeling sorry for myself rather than honoring this man's troubled life? I have used Tolstoy's *The Death of Ivan Ilyich* in an English class to address the very superficial way friends, acquaintances and even family members may deal with grief. One scene, in particular, exemplifies the social problems of not knowing what to do or how to act. A fellow employee of Ivan's displays his social incompetence while attending Ivan's wake. His awkwardness and tongue-tied demeanor readily resonates with my classes. The false belief is that if we go through the expected rituals, then we can put away having to deal with the discomfort that dying and death introduce into our life. Not knowing what to say or how to act around those who are grieving, especially acquaintances, is a familiar experience for all of us. Our friend's Marsha's death gave me an opportunity to look outward and care for others in their grief -- Diane and Ron. This step may have helped pave the way for me to recognize that grieving requires a connection with others. When it is healthy, it allows the individual's death to become a part of our life - not dismissed as an inconvenient intrusion. Mom's death started to shift my thinking; it was important to take my emotions and feelings into account. Societal Griefism still dominated my thinking and attitude, but that began to change slightly when my boyhood friend, Don, died.

I have shared some of my boyhood experiences with Don. We reconnected when I was responsible for a significant government grant in the mid-seventies. My position required me to go to Washington, D. C. a few times each year. Don was then living in Manassas, Virginia. I stayed with him a couple of times, and we rekindled our friendship. He was one of those people with whom it takes about one nanosecond to get back into interpersonal synchronicity despite our outwardly incompatible lifestyles.

He had divorced and sometimes had his children living with him; sometimes he had female friends sharing his space. By the mid-seventies, Don had already resigned his commission in the Air Force and was a Federal Marshall stationed in D. C. He was a Vietnam Vet, but we never talked about his service. He did tell me once that he was one of the intelligence officials who debriefed a pilot who defected from North Korea.

He also told me about how he experienced a wonderful sense of pay back. Around 1970 he was working on his Master's degree. A professor was advising him for his thesis and gave him a poor recommendation based on a blistering critique of his thesis. His evaluation and grade almost derailed Don from receiving his degree. A year later, Don saw that the faculty member had used Don's thesis as a theme for a professional paper he had published. Don was incensed. But justice came to him a few years later. While he was working as a Federal Marshall, Don had the responsibility for overseeing grant activity and possible misuse of funds for a particular federal department. Lo and behold this faculty member's name appeared as someone deserving investigation. Don beamed and volunteered to take the case. It shouldn't come as a surprise that the faculty member lost the grant and became black balled for future grants. Don told me this story with a glint in his eye and his distinctive smile. Later Don began to work with the Department of Energy, eventually becoming a director. In 1991 he was one of the inspectors to go to Iraq after the Persian Gulf War to determine Iraq's nuclear capability.

On one visit to D. C. in the late 70s I had a free Saturday, and he asked if I wanted to go rock climbing with him. This sounded like a way to restore the adventuresome spirit we had as children and when I had visited him in South Carolina. We drove for a while and he found the perfect place. It was along the Potomac and had a cliff face about 50-60 feet high. Our first task was to rappel down. He hooked us up with his climbing gear, and we took turns spotting, then rappelling down the face. It was exhilarating -- I hadn't rappelled for years. Next he showed me how to rock climb. He guided me by telling me where to place my feet and where I could grab onto a protrusion or fissure to help lift myself up. It took me awhile, but I began to see a path to take and succeeded in the climb. Afterward we went to his place and had a couple of beers and talked about our futures. I saw myself in academia for the rest of my life, and he was going to make a career in government. He also said that he was seriously thinking about getting into mountain climbing - rock climbing over the Potomac was too mundane and unchallenging. We clearly were kindred spirits with totally different views of life, family relationships and risk taking.

In the early 80s, he contacted me and said that he had become involved in real mountain climbing and wanted me to join him in the Himalayas. By then my asthma had surfaced, my family had grown, and I was not willing to risk such an adventure. I harkened back to the thrill of adventure I had had with him, as a child, in South Carolina and along the Potomac. My practical side overruled my risk taking side and I said no. I wished I had had the time and lung capacity at the time to throw care to the wind and have one more adventure with him. My rational mind won the internal battle and to this day I realize I made the correct decision. I do regret, however, that I didn't reconnect with him - ever. Later on I heard that Don had remarried, moved to New Mexico, and climbed mountains throughout the world. He provided pictures of a climb in the Andes for National Geographic and ascended the north peak of Mt. Everest. I mentioned to Diane that I needed to reconnect with him, but I never seemed to find or make the time. There were occasional Christmas cards that were totally unsatisfying. Why did I use his distant location as a reason to take his presence in my life for granted?

Then, in 1997, I came home one day from being out of town and instead of her usual warm welcome, Diane just told me to sit down. I knew the news was not good, but I had no idea what was coming.

I'm not sure how Diane prefaced her remarks, I only remember: "Don has died in a mountain climbing accident on Mt. Rainier."

Her words punched me both physically and psychologically. How could this be? Why didn't I try to get together with him? What do I do with these feelings? After the initial shock, I honestly do not remember what I did or how I managed my grief. I suspect I continued to follow the stereotypic American approach for men by putting my sadness into a mental container so I could move along with my life. Our oldest daughter, Tara, was going to be married soon and that took precedence over anything else I may be feeling. My grief became compartmentalized and tucked away for another day. Again I succumbed to Societal Griefism.

When an important chapter in life closes, there will always be residual feelings that will resurface over the years that follow. This truism belies the idea that grieving is something that men, especially, can successfully ignore. Just move on; find closure; get through the stages; and life will be fine. This myth needs repeating and reemphasis in this part of the book because it is so false and unhealthy. With Don there are stories to tell my grandchildren, wonderful memories, and a wellspring of regret. Society may push us to move on or find closure, but even with Don I became conscious that those sentiments and approaches were insufficient. It took my experience with Heidi to crystallize the discomfort that I felt about Don -- Murgy/Donny, my kindred, non-blood brother.

I mentioned earlier that on the day we received the news about Heidi's diagnosis we were planning an outing with two of our friends. Tragedy struck them a couple of months after Heidi died. Their son passed away in California and the four of us now shared another dimension in our friendship – one we never anticipated and one we never wanted. Our friendship with them would shift in other ways over the years and now Joe is gone. I connect with Audrey when I have a role at the church she continues to attend, while Diane does see her occasionally socially. Grief and death were not the only obstacles for us, but they sure made a huge difference in our shared social lives. Lost were the parties, gatherings, traveling and outings we had shared with them over the decades.

All of these stories provide a context for understanding my journey of grieving. Contextual influences pervade the meaning of a person's death and how loved ones will address their own grief. There is significant difference for those who experience the death of a spouse, a friend, a relative, or a child. The feelings and experiences make the context unique in each person's death (which is singular) and every person's journey of grieving (which is individualistic). Understanding the contextual elements helps people to empathize and share the person's pain. There are real differences when parents experience the death of a child who is killed in a car accident, or one who dies by suicide, or one that overdoses, or one that is murdered, or one that dies after a long (or short) illness, or one that is killed while on duty in the armed forces, in law enforcement or fighting a fire or one that is stillborn or miscarried. Those who understand that it is the context that makes the death and grieving unique are also equipped to share the meaning and significance of the tragedy with others. In the grief groups Diane and I attend, it is very clear that each one of us has a singular story to tell and a unique journey to live. However, we can share the meaning, the tears, and the story of our loved one because we all can relate to our own core of grief. I have told friends and family that I do not know how I would be able to live without the love of Diane and my family. The relationship that parents have with one another and with other members of the family creates the context for their journey of grieving. Part of the work of grieving is coming to terms with what these relationships mean and how they will continue to unfold in the months and years that follow a loved one's death. Context sets the conditions and significance for death, but it's the particulars, the unique character of each death that gives the context its full meaning. I find it tragic when couples split or divorce after the death of their child. It's not necessarily that the death or grieving causes the splits - it is usually something else. Their grieving may become the catalyst that brings out the rifts and tears in the relationship.

Trying to cope with Heidi's death was quite overwhelming. There was a core at the pit of my stomach that made her death not just emotional, psychological and spiritual, but also physical. It crept into every part of my being; the grief I had experienced before was swept away as trite and missing the point. Until that time I was swayed by Societal Griefism and followed the prejudices and dictates of our common culture. Societal Griefism includes society's stereotypes, values, and beliefs about what is normal and acceptable for grief or grieving. It entails ideas, attitudes, and expectations about how people are supposed to grieve and can involve implicit or explicit sanctioning for those who deviate from its norms. It includes forms of discrimination, and I began to see them after Heidi's death: seeing a neighbor in the supermarket who avoided eye contact and scooted to the next aisle; recognizing the pitying looks at gatherings; having to endure the head tilts of unstated sympathy; seeing the utter shock when someone asks how many daughters we have and what are they doing; or being told that Heidi was now in a better place. These were subtle forms of discrimination or ignorance, and I'm sure that I had been on the other side in years past. Society teaches us that someone who is grieving is set aside until he or she has gotten over it or has been able to return to normal living, working, and behaving "the way the dead person would want." Getting through the stages of grief may be difficult but that is what is expected of all of us.

Societal Griefism also has language cues at its disposal: "He's completed his purpose in life"; "She wouldn't want you to feel so sad"; "It's time to get back to normal"; "I know he would want you to ..." (fill in the blank); "It's not your fault she committed suicide"; "Once the court case is over you'll have closure and be able to move on with your life"; and the list goes on. These sentiments may be well intentioned, but they are still based on ignorance. Priests, rabbis, imams, ministers and lay church leaders are not exempt from the ignorance surrounding what healthy grieving should be. In like manner health care professionals and many in the psychological fields continue to buy into Freud's (move on) and Kubla-Ross' (go through the stages) mistaken contentions. I have heard about some awful statements spouted by clergy and laity of all faiths. "Since your child isn't Catholic, she can't go to heaven - maybe she is in Purgatory." "Since the baby wasn't baptized, you won't see her in heaven – she'll be in Limbo." "Suicide is a mortal sin, so your son cannot be buried in our cemetery." "Since she was a lesbian, we won't allow a funeral service here." "We don't allow eulogies anymore, so I will be the only one saying anything at the service." You get the picture.

I've come to learn that no one "commits" suicide; someone may die by suicide, he/she doesn't commit it. The distinction matters. Saying someone commits suicide assumes a rational decision was reached or an irrational compulsion overtook the person. It also seems to assume that mental problems or medication issues are part of the equation. "No one in his right mind would do such a thing!" This sentiment judges the one who has died with outside standards and misses the reality of the person who has died. Outside judging of a person's inside motives or intentions is a sure way of perpetuating ignorance. And although well-intentioned, telling someone that his or her loved one is in a better place or is part of God's plan, slips the conversation away from being healthy and into a so-cially prescribed way of ignoring the depths of the human condition. Is it really wise to tell a grieving mother that her drug addicted son is in a better place and no longer has any problems? Respect the depth of grief and do not deny or ignore its reality and presence in everyone's life.

We all change, certainly I have. These chapters reflect the changes in my attitudes, beliefs, and actions. We will all experience grief in our lives and it will come expectedly and unexpectedly. We often continue to stumble in our understanding of what is happening with us. There are no universal truths or stages of grieving. My reflections do not provide a guidebook for successfully grieving (whatever that might mean). What my experiences have taught me is that we need to respect the individuality and singularity of dying and grieving. Society seems to be trying to set standards of language and behavior that is not in harmony with what individuals need when they openly and honestly grapple with grief. A balanced understanding of what is meaningful and important should replace the stale social crutch of prescribing stages that fix the pain and return you to your normal life. What have been called stages (anger, denial, acceptance, bargaining, and depression) really become characteristics of grief that move like waves into and out of our lives. We may suppress their appearance; we may deny their existence; and we may pretend we are in complete control. I have done all of those things. Heidi taught me to stop lying to myself and accept what I had learned in my doctoral studies: change is a continual dimension in all of life. Understanding what that means has been a preoccupying theme in my thoughts and musings. Societal Griefism casts all of us into a web of imbalance and disharmony with our psychological and emotional selves. Again, I am calling for everyone to move away from societal extremes and find the middle between: becoming immobilized emotionally or ignoring the pain; spiraling into a never ending self-pity or compartmentalizing emotions out of one's mind; running away from social interaction or jumping back into society without any need for self reflection; pining helplessly for what can no longer be or finding a superficial closure that denies reality and truth. Through my own journey with grieving, I have allowed myself to transform my attitudes and question society's expectations. Today I understand that silence, hugs, and listening are more meaningful than Societal Griefism.

CHAPTER 11
OUR JOURNEY CONTINUES

Have you ever lost someone you love and wanted one more conversation,
one more chance to make up for the time when you thought they
would be here forever? If so, then you know you can go your
whole life collecting days, and none will outweigh the
one you wish you had back.

Mitch Albom

Everyone can master a grief but he that has it.

William Shakespeare

In my doctoral thesis one of my premises asserted that life is continuous and ever changing. "No one can step into the same river twice." This paraphrase from the Greek Philosopher, Heraclitus, was a simple summary of my belief that nature is a continually, ever creative force. Our life certainly reflected this belief for the 18 months following Heidi's funeral (February 15, 2003). The world really didn't care what had happened to us; it just kept rolling along. Family, friends and our church often swept us up in their currents. Society, furthermore, continued to churn along its merry way seeming only to stop a beat when a national catastrophe occurred, a major event happened, or when a national, sports or entertainment figure passed away. Those interruptions are rather brief because society's attention span is short. America has an insatiable need to keep a fast pace to life and is continually driven by forces that reinforce that drive.

So it was with our life after her death. Even though our grieving was deep and raw we found ourselves re-engaging with family and friends in a wide variety of events and requiring extensive traveling. Additionally my professional responsibilities called me to start teaching again while also attending to other activities beyond Canisius. I remember feeling out of sync in so many ways in those early days of being grieving parents. For example, a month after Heidi's funeral, we felt obligated to travel to Toronto with very close friends to go to a Hindu wedding. Our friends (the ones who were with us the day we found out about Heidi's diagnosis) had housed refugees from around the world as they were seeking asylum from torturous experiences in their native countries. One man had been living with them for awhile and was now getting married in Toronto because Canada had granted his wife and him asylum and eventual citizenship. A Hindu wedding was a new experience for us and we were unfamiliar with expectations for guests. We were used to the norms of being on time for the wedding ceremony; sitting in pews or chairs depending on the venue; keeping food in a separate area; and remaining quiet except for secreted whispers. As we entered the hall we found seats and dutifully sat in them (not in the front row). For the next few hours people roamed in and out of the ceremony, often continuing conversations. We couldn't really tell when or even if there was a ceremony that had a beginning and end. Our friend showed up and after awhile proceeded to sit with someone we believed was the Official (or whatever should be the proper Hindu word). His bride entered in beautiful Indian garb and then a ceremony seemed to occur. The bride, groom, official, musicians and a couple of others sat surrounded by a rich display of food. At one point a man introduced himself to me as an uncle. He asked if I had any questions – silly question to ask me. I got up and sat next to him during a part of the ceremony and we discussed the role of arranged marriages and its benefits in their Hindu community. It was rather surreal to be having a conversation (among many others) when our friend may have been exchanging vows. Diane and I were taken aback when we were asked to take off our shoes, go up to the bride, pour rice over her head and congratulate our friend. We weren't sure when the ceremony ended because the roaming and talking continued after the bride left the room. She returned later in another exquisite dress with beautiful Indian accessories. More words were said and soon after that the food that was prepared for all of us began being served in the back of the hall. We guessed that was the beginning of the reception. Although the experience was very different for us and something that would normally have been very intriguing, it really wasn't a diversion. The unfamiliarity with the ceremonies and rituals and being immersed with a large number of strangers compounded our unease. It was more of an intrusion that was based on obligations that arise within friendships.

I also found myself out of sync in April. I was asked to preside at the funeral of a young man who died in our parish. As a Conference Deacon in the Evangelical Lutheran Church of America, I am authorized to lead worship and preach when a pastor is not available. Over the years since Heidi's death, I have done so at 13 different parishes around Western New York. On this April day I was filling in for our pastor because he was attending his brother's wedding in another city. Although I knew the deceased, I made sure I met with his family and his young son beforehand. I went through the proper routine of asking questions, getting some anecdotes, and preparing a eulogy, since no one in the family cared to do so. As I stood at the lectern to begin my comments, I heeded Heidi's voice. She told me that this was about Brian, not me. It was his family's grief that was central today, not mine. All of this was a performance for me. My amateur acting skills serve me well when I have obligations that cannot truly engage my mind or heart. The performances are not insincere. I do care. That day I did care for Brian and his family. The truth of the matter was that my heart was elsewhere, and I felt my words were rather hollow.

I tried to deliver them in a way that did not show these feelings. Living in grief requires performances. There is also a self-centeredness to grieving. I hurt, can't you see? My life has changed, don't you understand? My world is upside down, can't you help? It is important to restore a balance in life and not stay trapped in a self-centered world. That is not easy; there are no cookbook methods; finding synchronicity is difficult and halting. Re-engaging with society, friends and family has no timetable and will not be linear. Life will ebb and flow and learning how to navigate through the currents and rocks can be tricky and tedious.

In a strange way I was out of sync the following October for one of our niece's wedding in Washington, DC. Tara was driving with Diane and me to New Jersey. Katie would join us for the overnight stay for the wedding. The day before we were to leave I came down with one of my rather often reoccurring respiratory infections. My stubbornness drove me to get in the car and go to Katie's. We were only spending one night with Anthony and Katie before heading to the wedding. My body told me that it was in charge and so I would not be making the drive to D.C., rather it demanded that I retire to the couch and withdraw from life until Diane, Tara and Katie returned. Thus this possibility of connecting with extended family was taken away and in a sad way I was very relieved of the responsibility of connecting.

The feelings of being out of sync were very pronounced for me in my professional responsibilities too. Heidi's voice was important for me so I could cope with the onslaught of society's expectations. Heidi was buried on Saturday, Feb. 15: a cold and relentless day. The following Monday and Tuesday were Presidents' Day holidays for the college. Feb. 19, Wednesday, was the next day for classes. I had missed classes during the funeral week, but now I went to teach. No one at the college seemed to notice my presence; only a very few may have even noticed my absence the week before; even fewer had anything to say to me. I have come to learn that avoidance of those in pain is rather common and relates to our social call for pain free living. Besides, what can anyone say to someone in deep grief? I knew people cared as was attested to by the hundreds of cards we had received (many from the faculty and staff at Canisius). So, feeling out of sync began with my return to the campus. I avoided areas where people congregated to socialize and hurried to and from my office. As I went to my first class, my mind was rather foggy and dense. That first class was three hours long and was located in the college's Old Main building. My classroom was on the third floor and its podium looked out large windows at a cemetery across the street from the campus. As I finished organizing my notes (which I always had but rarely used) I looked up. Across the street a funeral procession was entering the cemetery. "OK Heidi, I don't find that very funny. Find some other way to help me get over myself and do my job well." **I didn't** teach my classes that day, the rest of the week and the whole semester because of some noble heart or Germanic sense of duty. **I did** it because of Heidi. During her illness, Diane and I had organized our schedules so someone could be with her (at the hospital or home) when she needed us (or when we thought she needed us). She was adamant however about my teaching.

"Dad, don't miss a class because of me. They are depending on you."

These words rang in my consciousness throughout her illness and very loudly on that day. They lingered for the rest of the semester, and I went through the motions relying on body consciousness and deep familiarity with course material. I did perform characters toward the end of the semester in each course, but those too remain foggy in my memory. That was the semester I started giving out Heidi's advice on the last day of class and telling her story to my students. That class material was probably the best lesson plan I had for the remainder of my teaching at Canisius. My students were her peers, and they could learn from her attitude and the discomfort her friends showed toward the end. Her friends were all too absent; even her boyfriend had escaped with the military overseas. He later told me he didn't have to go, but just needed to get away. He said it was too difficult for him to be around. That was my message to the students. Another's illness or death is not about your discomfort. Get over your self-pity and be a presence for those who are confronting the loneliest times of their lives. I was very impressed with some of the students in the Honors class Heidi had audited for almost two months before her relapse. Some of them wrote to her, sent cards and a couple even visited her. One male came out to the house a couple of times. They had learned my lesson before I had even given it. All of my activity was another form of performance because I was not completely present.

There were two other professional activities that reinforced my feelings of disconnectedness. The first one was wrapped in feelings of connectedness with our family yet the professional part of the trip created an ambiguous blending of emotions. In late February, 2004 I was driving to the annual meeting of the Association for Gerontology in Higher Education (AGHE). That was the organization in which I had been extremely active for about 15 years before Heidi was diagnosed. Immediately after her diagnosis I curtailed all of my professional travel and resigned my AGHE committee memberships to be with her and the family through her journey. So it was in 2004 I was going to try and re-engage with people with whom I had been friends and colleagues before my life changed forever. Throughout Heidi's illness and when she died, many of these people kept in touch (calls, emails, letters, and cards). I really wasn't sure what this trip would bring and didn't know if I could really reconnect. A few of my friends were not going to attend, so this added to my concern about synchronizing. The conference was being held in Richmond and I used that location as an excuse to drive rather than fly. My route would take me to New Jersey so I could visit with Katie and Anthony. As I headed to their home I received a call from Anthony informing me that Katie was going into labor sooner than expected. (Details about what happened will be included at the end of this chapter.) Since I spent two nights in New Jersey instead of one, my arrival at the conference missed the opening night session and reception. The conference format had continued with my re-design of programming so that social interaction remained a primary goal. So I engaged in group discussions, a luncheon with mostly strangers, and informal chatter and conversations. I was there and I wasn't. My friends were welcoming and as was true in this conference, acquaintances became friends and strangers quickly became acquaintances. The context should have led me to feeling reconnected with people and an organization with whom I had built long and abiding friendships. None of that seemed to matter. I felt so much like a stranger that I went by myself for dinner one night. While sitting alone in an outdoor restaurant bustling with people I realized that my feelings of disconnectedness were totally coming from my pain and grief. I didn't belong not because I wasn't being embraced or welcomed, but because I just couldn't feel any synchronicity. As you will hear later this entire experience was wrapped in a wonderful gift and bless-ing. The jarring feelings of connectedness and disconnectedness were deep.

At the conference one of my friends asked me to meet him for a chat and drink. As we chatted he turned the conversation to a proposal for me. He was organizing a weeklong professional worship in Tallahassee. He wanted me to teach and run a session each day. I had run such professional programs before but not since Heidi. Although I was hesitant, I agreed. This occurred early in the conference and I wonder if I would have been so agreeable at the end. So I prepared the material and made the trip. I did not know any of the participants and most of them didn't belong to AGHE. The program was designed to train professionals and to use the professional expertise from AGHE's leaders. I felt completely disconnected from the time I set foot on the Florida State campus until the time I checked out. The people were friendly and quite receptive to my presentations and dis-cussion sessions. There were many friendly exchanges throughout each day. It didn't seem to matter. Again I was there and I wasn't.

Part of the reason for this strange disconnected/connected feeling may have been due to a strange confluence of family events that preceded this

June 21 - 25, 2004 conference: June 5 putting our dog to sleep; June 8 my Aunt Lona dying; June 12 sponsoring the first Heidi's day; June 14-18 going to my aunt's funeral and attending to her estate. We had been planning Heidi's Day for a long time and had been advertising the event to family, friends, church members, and neighbors. The Day was intended to honor Heidi, to bring people together to celebrate her life, and raise funds for The Heidi Leukemia Research Fund. When Heidi died I contacted the hospital and said that I wanted a separate account with her name so friends and family could feel they were doing something specifically for her. I had worked in fundraising at Canisius for the first few years I was in administration. I learned that organizations prefer to put donations into the general fund to help their annual budget. I didn't want donations for Heidi to get lost in a general pot to pay for electricity and heating. Furthermore, we wanted to directly support her attending physician in his research. We held the day at the Casino in Elliott Creek (see Chapter 12 for some details about this park's role in our life). People brought food; we raffled gift baskets; and celebrated our daughter's impact on others. The day started with bike rides of various distances. Each rider was responsible for getting sponsors to donate to our fund. Another idea that originated with Kris was to sell "Heidi Hats." The hats were designed by a neighbor and included an artistic swirling of two Hs and a comedy/tragedy mask in Van Gogh colors (blue and orange). People purchased the hats and we would then give them to Roswell to distribute to patients who had cancer. The monies we collected went into her Fund. We put a removable label on the hat to tell the recipient who had donated it. Hundreds of these hats are now sprinkled around Western New York. We still have a couple of dozen hats left that we give to people we hear who have cancer. We include Heidi's advice brochure whenever we do so. The Casino is an old stone building that houses some very useful facilities for running an event such as Heidi's Day. There is a large kitchen, rest rooms, two large gathering rooms for eating and housing our raffle. The day went extremely well and we increased

Heidi's fund to over $20,000. Today the fund continues as an endowment in Heidi's name and has over $50,000, even after funding is withdrawn to support research every year.

I need to say something about Heidi's physician. He rode his bike and stayed the entire day. He loved Heidi and took her death very personally. I can still remember seeing him carefully looking at the pictures of Heidi on display at her wake. He attended each Heidi's Day (we had three over a four year period). Diane and I were invited to tour his research facilities and find the paver with Heidi's name. We spent some time talking to him before the tour and reconnecting with a man that was so important in our life. During the summer of 2003 I created Heidi's Garden in the area behind our house. Friends and neighbors donated perennials as well as annuals to grace the garden. This garden truly reflects the premise that life is ever changing. Over the years this space has evolved in so many different ways. Flowers have died, some never renewed, and new ones filled the empty areas. One year a squirrel or bird had planted a cherry tomato plant that grew in the basement's window well located in the garden. We were blessed with some very delicious tomatoes without any effort on our part. Recently it has changed dramatically again as the new air conditioning unit now has a permanent place in that area. It's amazing how practical concerns can intrude and sometimes even dominate a situation. Heidi's doctor contributed to this garden the summer after she died. He sent us Irises that were a deep, beautiful black. He said their elegance reminded him of Heidi. The following letter reflects so much about the man and his relationship with her.

"Last week I set out west to ride the 100-mile bike for the Leukemia and Lymphoma Society of America. I prepared for this ride since January of this year. Part of the preparation included fund-raising and the other part included rigorous training to conquer the path around Lake Tahoe. We were a total of 9 members from the Buffalo area.

We left Buffalo on Thursday 5/29/03 as planned and arrived on time to Lake Tahoe. On Friday we assembled our bikes and went out for a short ride to get used to the altitude but not to exhaust ourselves. On Saturday I woke up very early and felt elated. The sun was shining and everything seemed so bright and clear. I decided to have a quick ride before everybody else woke up. I don't know if you have ever been out there. The scenery is amazing. The lake is bright blue and the mountains are still covered with snow at this time of the year. I enjoyed the beauty and didn't notice a hole in the road and fell with my bike. I hurt my left hip and initially couldn't stand up. When I finally stood up on my right leg, I wasn't able to walk. I was out in the middle of nowhere with my bike. That was when Heidi came to my help.

I remembered how she showed up to the clinic before Christmas. She was dressed up in a cream-colored suit, with make-up and all the accessories. She was visibly short of breath and suffering. We talked about her condition and how serious it was. She started crying, reached behind her chair and handed me a big bag. She said: 'here is your damn present for the holidays!' And we all laughed.

I mounted my bike and rode back to the hotel. Only upon reaching my room did I realize that during my fall I had hurt my left elbow and face. The rest of the day was obviously 20 minutes ice on and off. But would I be able to ride on Sunday, the day of the ride?

Again, Heidi's memory was there to help me. If she was able to fight all that she had against her, I should be able to accomplish this mission too. I limped downstairs with the bike and tried the impossible: mounting the bike. After several attempts I was able to stand on my injured leg and raised the other leg to mount the bike. From there on it seemed much easier: you have to ride the bike. Thank God that we have different muscle systems to ride a bike than those we use for walking. However, one cannot ride 100 miles without stopping. I needed a lot of help to get off and then on again to accomplish this mission.

Heidi was there to support me through the whole 100 miles.

Thank you, Meir"

This letter was a blessing for us in our grief. He was a significant part of Heidi's journey and did everything he could. We believe he helped give us precious time with our little girl. The relationship he and Heidi shared was a blessing and a reason why we created the research fund to support his work. He was someone with whom we felt a connectedness, even after Heidi died. Although he could not grieve the way a parent who's experienced the death of a child, he did understand Heidi's journey to her death. He understood her experience in ways we could not and he felt deeply for our loss (and his). Tragedy struck in June 2015 when he died after a skiing accident. I went to his memorial at the hospital and appreciated the widespread outpouring of grief from colleagues (other physicians, nurses, and the other wide array of health care personnel), patients, their families, and friends. Of course my grief for him was wrapped with Heidi. I felt as if another chapter in her life had also come to an end. This grief illustrated the reality that grieving is like a wave, never linear. In fact water imagery seems to apply to so much in life since "we can't step into the same river twice." I feel that water imagery comes to me as soft ripples on the edge of a river, or the waves from the wake of a passing boat, or the raging and crashing of the Rapids before heading over Niagara Falls, or the gentle flow of a calm stream. Grieving ebbs and flows; it crashes and benignly drifts along; it dangles in still water and tumbles over rocks. It never leaves, just drifts into the background sometimes. Hearing of Meir's death and going to the memorial illustrated to me what I had learned over a decade before: Heidi's life and death would remain a significant dimension in my life. Healthy grieving recognizes that it is not a process to fear or run away from. Grasping it and rolling with its waves is much healthier than denying its continuing existence and pretending to put it behind you forever.

That first Heidi's Day was bookended by two powerful sources of further grieving. One week before Heidi's Day we were at the Veterinarian having our dog, Vragil, put to sleep. The connections with Heidi were deep. Our girls had asked for years to get a dog. I had allergies to cats and dogs from the late 70s through the 80s. However, they seemed to abate by 1988 and we investigated dogs with hair, not fur and that were non-allergenic. Heidi was 7 and so eager to have a puppy. So in early December we picked out a Shih Tzu and brought him home. He was part of a litter and seemed to be left out when we looked at them. Diane picked him up and it was love at first sight. Shih Tzu's have a tendency to bond with the first one who holds them and so it was with Diane. He was her puppy. Over time he became mine too and became my male buddy in the family (at least until he was neutered). We allowed Heidi to name him - Vragil. We weren't sure at first what she was saying but then it occurred to us that she meant Virgil, the name of a chimpanzee in a recent movie we had watched. We loved the unusual name and pronunciation and Vrag became an integral part of our family (especially as the older daughters made their way into a world beyond our home). Heidi was thrilled but then taken aback over the years as he tended to ignore her pleadings or attempts at closeness. Shih Tzu's were bred as elitist and can be considered snobbish (except by the owners).

There were only three incidents that I can recall when Vragil paid Heidi any attention. On August 22, 2000 Vrag went downstairs after Diane, Heidi, and I had all gone to bed. The dog slept with Diane and me almost from the day we brought him home. At first we thought about imposing some rules: caging, no sitting on furniture, no lying in our bed, etc. They were all shattered rather quickly as he conquered our love seat in the living room and our bed at night. But on that August night he was going to deign to sleep with Heidi. She was thrilled. I mention that night because it was the night before Heidi received her diagnosis and her first day in her revolving door with the hospital. Did Vrag know? The second incident occurred the day Heidi died. He came down the night before wanting to spend the night with her. He stayed with her the entire day she lay in her bed for the last time. Did Vrag know? The last direct incident was after Heidi was gone. He was in her room and Diane went in to talk to him. When she was reaching to pick him up a very loud rattling sound suddenly pervaded the bedroom. Diane finally realized it was coming from a drawer in the end table that Heidi used. Diane opened it up and discovered a hand massager was running and had been mysteriously turned on by an unseen hand. Heidi had been given it as a way for getting some relief for her pain. Was Heidi saying "Hi" to Vrag? For those who are grieving, they will recognize that these questions make sense. They are signs. I hope others will not dismiss the intent of the question or the belief in signs out of hand. The intent is the need to continue to connect with a loved one. Signs become a connector and a source for hope. Life just continues and so does our desire to remain connected to our loved one.

The other bookend to that inaugural Heidi's Day was the death of my Aunt Lona. Three days after Vragil was put to sleep, I received a call from the Nursing Home that my aunt had passed away. As her Executor and "son" I was responsible for all decisions and insuring that my aunt's wishes were addressed. I had worked with the funeral home when my Uncle James died so I was familiar with their approach and the arrangements my aunt had made with them. Because Heidi's Day was scheduled for the 12th I delayed Aunt Lona's wake until the following week. So after completing the preparations, sponsoring the event, cleaning up and counting the donations, I took the trip to Kentucky with a heart swirling with emotions and memories. Instead of making the 1600 mile round trip by car, I flew to Nashville and rented one. I was no longer able to stay in my aunt's home/farm (a long and angering story) so I booked a room at a Holiday Inn on Rte. 68 in Draffenville. My relatives' farms were located on Rte. 68 and Draffenville had some quirky links to the past. Draffenville is really a stop on a highway built in the late 60s. No one really lives on the main road; there are just a couple of gas stations, places to eat, bank branches, and a grocery/hardware store. My first reason for staying there emerged from a memory of my uncle years earlier. He came into the living room one evening when Aunt Lona, Diane, Heidi and I were sitting together. He started railing on about one of the gas stations. He rarely railed on anything but that day he was incensed as he told us how that gas station was selling "Lot-tree" tickets. His deep Southern Baptist roots condemned any type of gambling and my uncle was a man of high integrity. He lived exactly as he believed.

Another reason to stay in Draffenville came from memories just about Aunt Lona. Even before my aunt was admitted to the nursing home, she started to take me (and Diane when she was with me) to eateries in Draffenville. The two more popular places for her included a buffet at one and the other was behind one of the gas stations. It wasn't the usual display found in gas stations along interstate highways because it had a small dining room that served broasted chicken (something I had never heard of before). Each body part that came our way was uncooked and sported blood dripping along the bones. Whatever else appeared on the plate did not help make that chicken any easier to look at, much less eat. The buffet was just plain horrible. I couldn't even manage downing the plain side dish of corn. I do not know how they managed to make even those staples inedible. These memories may sound rather trivial and boring. To me they recall the simple farm life cast in feelings of Camelot. My kin were from the earth and cherished life in what was direct and simple.

The first day there I started to attend to the banking and clean out Aunt Lona's room at Oakview Nursing Home. There was not much to gather from her room - the only really important item was her bible (well-worn and filled with notations). At the bank I withdrew her remaining CDs, including two in my name. One was part of the 10 CDs she had before entering the Nursing Home. I paid for her stay by surrendering one CD at a time. She had given me the order for surrendering them with the last on the list being for me. The other CD was the proceeds from selling the farm. I wondered if Aunt Lona was attuned enough with her banking toward the end so her expenses didn't eat into the CDs for me. I thought that she might have even though it had been years since she ever looked at her bank book or statement. Life's synchronicities may be quite surprising at times. Was this one of them? After her stroke a neighbor kept her finances, but at the urging of her niece I took over for the last few years of her life. I would let her checkbook balance get below $4000 before redeeming the next CD. She died when there was about $8000 left in her account before I had to redeem the last one: mine. I drove up the highway to drive by her farm and stop at my Aunt Myrtle's (5 miles up the way). The memories were vivid in both places and were now surrounded by people who were all gone. I was thrown back into the pit of grief created when Heidi died. Life continued but so did grieving.

The next day was her wake, funeral and burial. Very few people appeared although a couple of folks had signed the book before I showed up. None of her nieces or nephew showed up or signed the register. It was common practice at the funeral home to allow callers to come before the family arrived for viewing. I was disappointed that so few people came to show their respects. The preacher was not one Aunt Lona had requested, rather he was the funeral home's fill-in preacher when the need arose. He did not know my aunt and didn't bother trying to find out anything about her. His preaching was totally sterile and perfunctory. When he started describing the exact room that my aunt had in heaven I could feel my anger rising. How dare he use his canned message for my aunt! This experience was infuriating because my uncle and aunt had been devoted to their churches (Mount Mariah Primitive Baptist, then Zion's Cause). My aunt made sure that 10% of her assets were committed to the church and I know they tithed their entire lives. I felt no comfort in his words. The drive from the funeral home in Benton to the cemetery (tucked away on a rural road off the Symsonia Road) was memorable because of all the cars that stopped on both sides of the road as we drove along. This type of respect pleased me as a touch of kindness that strangers can bestow on others. I waited until the grounds men finished covering my aunt's casket (abiding by my uncle's custom). I had called my aunt's attorney when she died and arranged to go over her estate while I was there for the funeral. He also had arranged for a judge to provide probate proceedings while I was in town. The next day was the probate hearing in the morning with no other commitments until my flight back 24 hours later. So I headed to the Land-Between-the-Lakes and spent the rest of the day in familiar territory and living with memories cascading from almost six decades of experience. Now this place is haunted with the voices and experiences from days gone by. Another disconnect from a place of deep connectedness. I returned home with this dichotomy banging around in my head and heart.

Amid the events I've already recounted Diane and I did try to eke out some time for us. These experiences seemed to illustrate a truth we came to learn over the years: there is no cookbook to follow for successful grieving. In fact, I've come to believe that the idea of successful grieving is a red herring and a fool's errand. Trying to identify standards for judging success seems to me to be rather shallow. If you have experienced the death of a child (or maybe any loved one), judging successful grieving always remains a moot point. Grief remains; there are no stages to complete; there is no way to make it go away; there is merely learning how to make your journey meaningful, healthy and balanced. So over the summer of 2003 we made a number of trips that buffeted us in ways we did not expect. In May we visited Katie and went into the city to see Brian Stokes Mitchell perform in *Man of LaMancha*. We followed that profoundly moving experience two months later with a trip to Italy with our friends, Peter and Tiny. It was wonderful and awful. Our grief permeated everything and changed the colors and shapes that we experienced. Our friends planned a great retreat for the four of us as we stayed and toured Tuscany, with stops in Heidelberg (my request), Verona for the opera and Venice for a day. Both of these travels will be developed more fully in Chapter 13. Our Italy trip happened after I had returned from visiting my aunt the summer before she died (the last time I saw her alive). We didn't know how we felt for our trip to Italy; we certainly didn't know how other people may have thought we should feel. Our friends were attentive, empathetic and caring. Their embrace was beautiful, yet the depth of our pain created a jumble of feelings.

A month after returning from Europe we decided that we needed to go away in order to deal with the important dates of August 23 (Heidi's diagnosis) and August 24 (our anniversary and Tara's birthday). Our daughters had given us a two night get-a-way at an exclusive Manor in the Finger Lakes region, so off we went. We walked Watkins Glen, attended a Mennonite market, toured wineries and sat overlooking a beautiful landscape from the porch of the Manor. The grief clung to us. We wandered through these activities and began to learn that Heidi's death would become a defining trait of our life's journey. A year later, August 23 - 25, 2004, I planned another short get-away over those anniversaries and learned that they will always shadow us for the rest of our lives. I surprised Diane by getting a two night stay in Frankenmuth. We had not yet explored Germany and this seemed a place I wanted to try. It is hard to know if a visit before Heidi would have made a difference for us. This trip was all too disappointing. It just seemed all too pointless and superficial. We had changed - dramatically so. We no longer were who we were before Heidi's death. What may have seemed interesting or entertaining before her illness began to pale and recede in entertainment value. Synchronizing with such venues just didn't seem to work. Yet another consequence of us changing and becoming new and different people. Perceptive people in our lives know this is true; others may just be fooled by how well we perform sometimes. The depth of the performance has itself changed over time. The more we engaged in life the more natural our new selves began to adapt and come closer into sync with others. In a sense life is less difficult (the pain is less raw) and the feelings of carrying a weight on our shoulders have lessened over the years but they do not go away.

Life continued to march along with other family activities that brought new wrinkles and challenges. In mid-May, 2003 Diane and I visited family in Minnesota, spending a couple of days in Minneapolis with her uncles and then in Rochester to visit our daughter, Kris. We were at Panera with our son-in-law and Kris when we received a call that Diane's mother had fallen down the stairs backwards. She had been watching our dog and had fallen when she was getting him in from the backyard. Diagnosis: broken neck. We returned home a couple of days after she fell and immediately went to see her. The hospital was a large complex, but entering the room was torturous. Seeing her mom lying there was a terrible punch in the solar plexus for both of us. She was immobilized and hooked up to machines. Both of us shuddered to see those all too familiar connectors to meds and fluids. I focused on the tubing and beeps and could feel the times I had connected Heidi at home to our machine for her. It was a real struggle to focus attention upon her mom. On other visits we had to contend with Diane's Aunt Charlotte, who was a drama queen and very hard of hearing. Her dad had also hearing problems, so the decibel level of even our own speech was annoying to both of us. On that first visit, Diane's mom was lying flat on her back with a neck brace immobilizing her. She had always been a fighter, stubborn, and active. She was having a deep-seated mental challenge of remaining still. I talked to her about *Wu Wei* the Daoist principle of doing nothing. The idea is that the best way to deal with pain, physical or mental, was to stop struggling. There are times when it is wisest to just let the waves of life wash over you and stop fighting the current. Some problems are best left alone for awhile so a proper solution may emerge when the time is more conducive for one. I told Mom to stop fighting, that her job now was *Wu Wei* - work hard at doing nothing (for someone like me this does not sound like an oxymoron). Mom understood and would repeat the words to me whenever we visited. It is a principle that has become more prevalent in my life. I began listening to myself and learned to let the waves of life and grief carry me through minutes, hours and days when the world kept lobbing its demands and expectations my way.

The swirls of life brought some beautiful gifts our way too. On October 22 our first granddaughter was born: Collette Heidi. Kris had found out she was pregnant while we were gathered together for Heidi's funeral. Kris told Diane, "I now know how much you have always loved me." Another gift! Diane and I decided that we would go separately to help Kris acclimate to the new world and role of motherhood. We now were entering one of the greatest roles in life: grandparent. My relationship with all of my grandchildren is deep and special. It started with our first and has only grown over the years with all of them. (It is only fitting that I dedicated this book to them: my Munchkins.) Diane immediately left and stayed for 10 days; I followed a couple of weeks later for a long weekend, since classes were in session and Heidi's dictum of not missing classes still rang rather loudly in my conscience.

The following February (2004) was when I was driving to the conference on aging held in Richmond. I remember being in the Catskills and receiving the unexpected call from my son-in-law, Anthony, who told me Katie was in labor. My original plan was to spend the night with them, go to the conference and possibly stop by on the way home. Oh how humans plan and God laughs. Not only did I spend that night at their apartment, I stayed the next day and night so I wouldn't miss Isabella's birth (changing my reservations for the conference). The next day another sweetheart came into our world and life just kept moving along. I remember standing at the maturity window with Anthony's mom to welcome Isabella into the world. I drove home from the conference a little early and stopped for a night. Then I drove home to pick up Diane and drive her back to N. J. so she could help the new parents and both of us could enjoy our newest addition. I returned to go to my classes and Diane flew home a week later. The following July after returning from Aunt Lona's funeral and the professional program in Tallahassee Diane and I drove down to the N. J. shore. Bella's

Christening was being held down there and we would stay with Anthony's family at their shore house, a beautiful, large home into which Anthony's father, mother and whole family had poured so much effort and love.

Then it was Tara's turn. She was due in December, 2004 but was hospitalized in September. On the 30th she delivered twins at 29 weeks. Her hospitalization and seeing her little ones in the NICU were emotional rides fraught with worry and wonder. Alexandra Park and Jonah Charles (the first male in my line of the family tree) were gifts that have continued to bring us joy. They were born in Erie, PA because that city is closer than Buffalo to Mayville, N. Y. their hometown. So our drives to Erie became rather regular for some time. Four more grandchildren entered our lives over the next two and a half years. Kris also had twins, Fiona and Liam while Tara added a singleton, Eliot. Our youngest joined Isabella in New Jersey; her name is Elizabeth Hope. Eight grandchildren who would never see Heidi but who would all, in their own ways, experience her presence through the love of our family had burst into our lives. It was becoming very clear to me through these gifts that the idea of stages of grief was superficial and inaccurate. Life was not linear and I never went through stages: there was no denial, anger, bargaining, depression nor acceptance. These feelings rolled in and out of our lives. They never stayed so long that we could not re-engage with our family or friends but they have become conditional elements of our life riding along with us. There is so much more to say about the births and our travels to all of our daughters, but their stories are not mine to tell. To start sharing my stories of my Munchkins would be a book itself. Each one brings me a sense of wonder and awe. How beautiful life can be. I have learned how precious each life is and I try to cherish every moment with each one of them.

Our daughters and we have been very open about Heidi's life and presence with the Munchkins. One Christmas I made a special gift for each family. I had found audio tapes of Heidi practicing for a wide variety of shows. We also had videotapes of some of her performances. I listened to the tapes and selected those performances that connected to stories about the song she was singing. I wrote a booklet to go along with the performance telling the Munchkins the story of "Aunt Heidi Sings". I did it secretly so Diane didn't know what I was doing. Tears flowed freely some days, especially when I discovered Heidi singing the song "Papa Can You Hear Me?" We have learned that it is foolish to live in a world of avoidance. If we always avoid what is painful, we are living in a false world with a false sense of security. There is a myth that if we avoid talking about death, maybe we can prevent its inevitability. I found it much healthier and comforting to have open conversations with my Kentucky relatives about their deaths, rather than listening to people refuse to have such conversations. This avoidance can become very painful for those who may be facing their own deaths. Loved ones or friends who do not want to listen to those who are dying talk about their death or funeral arrangements create a real dissonance. One example of this insensitivity reveals itself in the statement: "Oh, don't talk that way; you'll be fine". Saying this is a horrible response to someone who needs to share his or her feelings, fears, and thoughts. Think how isolating that statement is for the person who needs to talk. It shuts down any meaningful conversation. As I told my students: when you are confronted with the uncomfortable conversation that a loved one wants to have, remember the discussion is not about you or your discomfort, it is about supporting your loved one with your attentiveness, care and empathy.

Avoidance and self-pity are extremes that deny a healthy attitude from developing for anyone who is grieving. Any loss, especially grieving the death of a loved one, can bring emotional immobility and a depression that locks someone into an all-consuming ennui. Not caring about others or oneself becomes an inevitable stop along the way. None of these feelings are unrealistic; they may not even be avoidable. The issue is: how do we learn to take a step out of that pit; how do we step away from these extremes that can consume us and destroy our ability to re-engage in life.

I have talked above about how I began to re-engage in life. I did not like hearing "well that's what she would want." Even if that is true, I didn't want to hear it. As I have been reflecting upon the deaths in my life I have become very sensitive to my feelings (and the feelings of others who are grieving). There is a sense of self-centeredness with grieving. We expect the world to understand and accommodate our feelings and moods. When we do not feel the empathy we expect or we hear phrases that irritate us, we become impatient, sometimes judgmental, and always inward looking. Trying to restore a sense of balance and harmony with others is an on-going task in any healthy grieving. But there are limits to what we may find acceptable. Those limits are very individualistic and can morph or change over time. The phrase "well that's what she would want" uttered to encourage me to re-engage in my previous activities is not one of those phrases that has morphed or changed. It irritated me at the funeral home, shortly after the funeral, and over the months and years that have passed. It still irritates me to hear it directed at others. How can anyone really know what Heidi wants for me? How could I ever know? Would I even accept what she would want anyhow? In addition to those questions I am also struck by the person's failure of recognizing how radically my life has changed. I have come to realize that this statement is almost always uttered by well-intentioned people. It is their attempt to assist, or console, or to support. The question and intention themselves are not the real problem here. It is me. It seems as if the people saying these things are oblivious to the way I feel. I would much rather they rethink what they're saying to me. All too often people resort to clichés or the superficial statements created by Societal Griefism.

If we all were to reflect on our lives, our language, and our experiences about our own grieving and the grieving of our friends, family, fellow church members or neighbors, we could better learn how to walk with grief. I know the prescriptions involved with the stages of grief or psychiatric manuals provide tools for helping patients move on (maybe even get over) their grief or sense of loss. I do not espouse these techniques as genuine cures. Some may have limited value, but I would be very cautious about believing that your grieving can be cured by such tools. The one truth I firmly believe is that each person's journey is truly unique. Trying to compress one's feelings into some recipe for successful reengagement or trying to prescribe behaviors or actions that supposedly complete one's journey is just plain wrong. Societal Griefism provides a series of actions that reaffirm a socially acceptable way of behaving and a socially prescribed set of norms that should govern death, dying and loss. I have held many of those attitudes and beliefs in my life and I am sorry for all the well-intentioned but misguided efforts and advice I have given along the way. I can only justify my words and actions by claiming that I was just oblivious and steeped in my ignorance. This book is my attempt to share my reflections on these inadequacies in my life and to share what I have learned. Who knows, maybe there are little kernels of wisdom to be found in these pages.

I started this part of the book with the story about my mom's death. I also described the three routes we take to get to Niagara Falls. The first one, the commercial route, is named Niagara Falls Boulevard. Driving "up" the Boulevard takes us to North Tonawanda, which used to be the home of a musical venue, Melody Fair, which holds a significant place in my family's memories. Melody Fair hosted musicals and concerts. When our daughters were young, we took them to a couple of musicals there as well as to a Peter, Paul, and Mary concert. It was also the site of a Judy Collins concert that I attended with Diane a few years after Heidi died. That visit was especially poignant since Diane had had some contact with Judy Collins because she too experienced the death of a child. Melody Fair was also the site of the date Heidi and I had when we went to see the Righteous Brothers.

She had just graduated from high school and The Righteous Brothers were giving a concert there. Throughout their lives I have taken my daughters out on dates. In fact, Tara just took me out on a date a few months before I drafted this chapter: we went on a pub crawl. Diane and I had done a good job of corrupting our girls to enjoy our music and a beverage. Of course, they also had their own generational favorites, but we regaled them with tapes of folk music and the sounds of the 60s as we drove around the country on our family vacations. Heidi and I shared a real love for the Righteous Brothers. So it made sense that we would make a night of it. We went out to dinner first, which turned out to be disappointing. But the concert was magical. Before it started and during intermission we spent time outside the tented venue making up stories about the people around us.

"They're cheating on their spouses."

"He is definitely a spy."

"Have those men come out publicly or did they meet here; they keep looking around suspiciously?"

"She runs that marriage."

You get the picture. When The Righteous Brothers sang *Unchained Melody*, I felt a warmth and love for Heidi that has never left me. It certainly wasn't the words (they don't apply); it was the feel and sense about the piece, about the venue, about sitting next to my youngest, and about the deep seated connectedness of father and daughter. Each of my older daughters picked a very special song for us to dance at her wedding. Each song touched our relationship in a beautiful and profound way. One of the many difficulties I have experienced since Heidi's death has been watching father's dance with their daughters at a wedding. I will never have that opportunity with Heidi. I am convinced that *Unchained Melody* would have been her selection. A couple of years after she died we were invited to a wedding along the shores of one of New York's Finger Lakes. It was a beautiful setting. When our friend danced with his daughter, the tears choked me up but I remained seated: as Heidi had always told me - it was their day and it was about them, not about me. Later on when *Unchained Melody* began to play, my ability to stay in that room had vanished. Diane understood. We slipped out of the hall, held hands, and sat on a park bench overlooking the lake. I don't remember what we said to one another, maybe nothing. Her presence was soothing, but the pain was visceral. I hate the phrase "time heals all wounds." Time itself is not a causal agent for healing. Healing of any kind, on the other hand, requires a temporal process. The process only provides a context within which healing may or may not take place. I'll refer to this concept in the next chapter. One of my strategies for healing over time has involved me working on shifting the pain of that song to a feeling of a cherished memory. It brings me into a safe place now; one that is enriching (although a tear or two can crop up unexpectedly).

My phrase for such work is that while we are grieving there are times when we have to go to the pain but we must avoid the torture. In order to create some healing and meaning in our life, we must connect with people, events, and contexts that are challenging, uncomfortable, or down-right painful. But we cannot go to the torture. Understanding our limits is important in grieving (as well as in any facet of life). Failure to grasp our limits, whether physical, mental, etc., may be one of the leading causes of our setbacks in life or increasing our stress level. In this sense, Heidi's death has been a gift because I have become more aware of my limits: life is not just about fixing problems or helping others solve their challenges in life. Instead, a healthy lifestyle recognizes the boundaries to our abilities and the supportive nature of human interrelationships. *Unchained Melody* helps me feel my love for Heidi, despite the pain of her physical absence in my life. I just heard it today (the day I'm drafting this section) and realized I had to include this story. That song will always transform the moments it is playing to the feelings I had on that date: my enduring love for my daughter.

Now, however, going "up" the Boulevard to North Tonawanda is not about going to Niagara Falls or Melody Fair. It is about visiting Heidi. As we make the curve leading out of Erie County into Niagara County, we make the turn that leads us to Acacia, the cemetery that is home to Heidi, Diane's mom, dad, aunt, and uncle, her grandparents and a growing list of friends. The ride to entertainment and visits to the Falls now represents a turn to Heidi's gravesite. Her bench has her saying: "Smile: the show must go on." That saying was so cute when she was in *South Pacific* as a chicken pox victim who would not be deterred. Now, there is a painfulness that lingers. There are many ways of dealing with this pain, and I would like to share one more memory now.

A couple of years ago Diane and I were going to find an area to view the night sky without radiant light. A meteor shower was supposed to produce hundreds of shooting stars and we had not had success in the past in our back yard. We headed to the Niagara River and a park we thought might be ideal. We had gone there with Heidi years ago when she was 10 or 11. It was a fruitless trip but provided grist for humor about such things. When we got there one of the entrances was closed, and it was too dark to see the other one. So we kept driving until one of us said we should go and watch with Heidi; maybe this time would be more successful. The cemetery doesn't close its gates so we drove to our normal parking on the roadway near her grave. We said "Hi" to Heidi, unfolded the chairs, got out the blankets, and started to gaze into the sky. We only saw a few shooting stars that night, but we spent an evening with some chuckles and enjoyment of our relationship. It was a good night and made the cemetery site welcoming rather than oppressive. We touched Heidi, just not in the way we wished we could. We went to some pain, but there was no torture.

PART VI:

IT'S ALL ABOUT LOVE AND RESPECT

CHAPTER 12
FOR THE NATURAL WORLD

Keep close to Nature's heart ... and break clear away, once in awhile,
and climb a mountain or spend a week in the woods.
Wash your spirit clean.

John Muir

Without feelings of respect, what is there to distinguish
men from beasts.

Confucius.

There was a chill in the air, but that brisk July morning seemed ideal for a swim in Lake Ontario. The night before this adventure I had camped with a girl friend, her parents, and seven of her brothers and sisters. We had had the usual campfire with stories and laughter. Before I bundled myself into a sleeping bag, nestled between two of her brothers, my girl friend asked me if I wanted to get up early and go for a swim. My 20 year old risk-taking self responded, "of course," even though I have never been a great swimmer. From fifth grade through twelfth I had attended schools without pools. My only real swimming time as a child or youth was the summer in South Carolina. Donny, my childhood soul-mate, not only taught me the Jim Crow Laws, but also helped me learn how to swim and dive. My center of gravity must be in an unusual location because I can't even float in salt water. I've tried it a number of times when we went to the

Gulf Coast while living in New Orleans and in the Pacific, the Caribbean, and the Atlantic at various times throughout my life. Each time I would sink, or at least my legs and lower torso would. Trying to float on my back is a certain means for cleansing the sinuses as I quickly sink in a V-formation below the water line.

That morning we walked to the water's edge, and she ran into the water with abandon. Not to be outdone, I followed.

"Race you to the buoy!" she challenged. The buoy wasn't too far, but it turned out to be far enough. I did make it while lagging well behind a more advanced swimmer. She waited at the buoy then repeated the challenge. This time the goal was the shore, "first foot on the sand wins!" So off we went. About 15 yards from the buoy, both of my legs began to cramp. I remembered it was the calves that seemed to stop working. They became dead weights that ended up perpendicular to the water's surface. I could not move them and they felt like lead pipes attached to my knees. There is a different quality and quantity to cramping in water as compared with being on land. Before this experience the worst leg cramping I'd experienced was during football practice in high school. I thought that was painful - in comparison, it wasn't. This time there was no way for me to bend up my toes or grab my foot with my hand. There was no way for me to wait out the pain. This time the pain and cramping were taking me into a frightening depth. Cramping in water that may be at least 15 - 20+ feet deep is not the best way to navigate back to shore. My legs began to sink and my body followed suit. It happened quite slowly but inexorably. There was nothing I could do. Flailing my arms did no good. I tried kicking my feet, but my cramped calves prevented any movement. My lack of buoyancy was another impediment. I grabbed at my girlfriend's foot but thankfully missed. My desperation would have been very dangerous for her. I learned this lesson the hard way years later when Diane, our three oldest daughters and I shared a cabin with the couple who introduced us at their wedding.

We had rented a cabin in a little town called North Java. One of the features was a good sized pond with a swimming area, row boat and pier going into the water about 15 feet. All of us were gathered at the campsite when we heard screams coming from the pond. Ron and I bolted to the pond; he used calm and reason, I used an unbridled "save the day" mentality. He remained on the pier looking for something floatable or a pole to reach out to the flailing swimmers. Without any thought at all I, on the other hand, ran down the pier and dove into the water (sneakers and all). Two teens (both very heavy) were thrashing about in the water. Later we found out that the rowboat had a leak and had caused them to sink. I guess I had a residual unconscious memory of the time I was drowning in Lake Ontario and I wanted to save these girls from the same experience. As I have mentioned I am not an expert swimmer and have never done any life saving activities in my life. When I reached the girls they lunged at my neck to grab on - we all began to sink. My first reaction was to take one girl at a time, grab them and hurl them toward the shore. That's what I immediately began to do. In time, I threw each one of them to a place where her feet could touch the ground. They ran away without saying a word. Later on we took a walk and I saw one of them peering out a living room window while partially hiding behind a curtain. I used this experience in an Introduction to Human Services course I taught. I would ask my students why they wanted to work in social or human services. If they said they wanted to help people, I would challenge them by asking if they wanted to do so because they wanted their appreciation. My message was this reason was too weak to be a long-lasting motivation. Serving others does NOT necessarily mean there will ever be expressions of gratitude or appreciation. I told the students to be prepared for strange, sometimes even hostile responses even when they have done everything right and genuinely helped their clients.

As the water rose around me, on that memorable swim, I had a sense of complete helplessness. There was nothing I could do to save myself:

Mother Nature and an ill-considered swim had won. Grabbing at my girlfriend's leg was an act of desperation, not one that would work or be safe for her or me. Of course, if there were any rational thoughts at that moment, I would have realized that my dead weight would drag her down too. Reflecting on that action, I have always marveled at the power of instinct and self-preservation over personal values and rational decision-making. There was no flash of my life going before me, only the darkness of the water. I kept holding my breath, wanting to prolong the inevitable; humanity's desire for survival is primordial and profound. That lesson was very clear as I was enveloped by an unforgiving lake. The cold temperatures seemed appropriate for my body which seemed frozen and sinking. Suddenly a hand grabbed my upward stretched arms and lifted me toward the surface, toward air and survival. A lifeguard was blessedly on duty and fully aware of my plight. He lifted me with great agility onto his board. I was gasping to breathe when he asked whether or not I could kick. I told him about the cramps and the uselessness of my legs in between gulping air.

"No problem," he said. We got to the shore and I thanked him profusely. He rubbed my calves until the cramping subsided, and my girlfriend and I were able to return to the campsite. That is the last time I ever tried to swim out to a buoy anywhere.

Twenty-five years later water and I did not seem in sync again; this time Diane was the victim. I was going to a conference in San Antonio and Diane met me on the last day of sessions for the conference. We explored the Alamo and the Riverwalk and enjoyed the ambiance and dining. Always a bit venturesome, we headed north to a German area which boasted some of the best water rafting or tubing in Texas. We were going to raft on a rubberized canoe. It was in the spring so the river was running a bit higher and faster than usual.

"Are there any hazards along the way?" Diane prudently asked.

"Not really. There is a little white water in the middle of the journey. You'll be going over a small dam," replied the woman who was taking our money. She was in the small shelter where our journey would begin. She was young and may have been reassuring Diane so we would buy tickets.

"How high is the dam?" There was now some concern in Diane's voice.

"Not high. Maybe six or seven feet."

"Seven feet?" More concern.

"Actually there is no problem. Just head straight over the dam and you'll have the thrill of a lifetime."

"That sounds very doable," I eagerly added; to me, the ride seemed idyllic. She grudgingly decided to go along. We put our valuables in the trunk of the rental and boarded the bus that took us upstream. The rental canoe was new and looked sturdy and safe. We began our trip realizing that we were not as prepared as others. There were tubers and other rafters. Many had coolers for drinks and refreshments. Some had snacks and I even heard music from one group of canoers. The stream cut into heavily wooded areas. The starter told us to avoid going on the banks and exploring because there were snakes in the woods. We didn't see any snakes swimming along the way. There was a family on a larger raft when we started which reassured Diane. We floated along enjoying the scenery and each other's company. The water flow began to increase, and we saw the white water and the dam area. There were tubers who cut ahead of us and wanted to head over the dam as a group. I remember trying to back paddle to avoid the tubers, but the flow of the stream caught us. I saw some people on the shore (on-lookers who enjoyed the scene of rafters and tubers heading over the dam). A couple of them were waving their arms at us, and I understood that the tubers were not clear of our descent. I could not stop nor slow our canoe. I did manage to square it to the dam, so we would be heading straight over it and not crooked which would have added another complication to our excitement. We headed over, as straight as I could get the canoe, and then it happened. One of the tubers was caught in the back waters just under the dam. As our canoe came down on him, he pushed up and flipped us over. Diane and I tumbled out of the safety of our boat. I grabbed the seat by hooking my arm around it; the other hand held onto one of our oars. I went under water with the boat above me, for how long I wasn't sure. The speed of the water rushed me away from the dam. At first I was trapped, feeling entombed in a rubberized cave, but I was able to flip the canoe over and hold onto it while I was gasping for air. I didn't see Diane. She had been flipped free and crashed her knee and arm as the current had buffeted her over rocks. She was on the shore in shallow water and felt quite battered and sore. When I found her, I swam with the canoe and oar over to her.

"Are you okay?" My voice sounded out-of-breath and saturated with worry.

"No. I'm hurt."

"Where?"

"My knee and shoulder."

"What can I do?"

"Nothing." Her curt answer told me that she was in pain.

"Can you get back into the boat to head back to our car?"

"No," she tearfully groaned . She was very hurt. We checked to make sure that she hadn't broken anything. We talked about our options. "I could finish the course; get the car; and drive back to pick you up," was our first option. Unfortunately the banks at that area were not conducive for resting or waiting or even scaling. The admonition about snakes put a real damper on this option.

"We can't go back to the dam area because the current is too fast and other tubers and rafters are going over the dam," was the next option. Diane didn't say much; she was hurting and disoriented. She finally and very reluctantly got back into the canoe. Our third option was to finish the course, drop off the canoe where we had started, and get her back to the hotel. She had lost her oar but was in no shape to help anyhow. The rest of the trip was calm, but the beauty had gone away. There was one area where the water level was so low that the bottom of the boat was touching the rocks. I asked Diane if she could get out and walk along until the water was a little deeper. Her response was a clear and decisive "No". So I got in front of the canoe and pulled it over the rocks. As would be expected she was very sore that night. We applied ice but didn't seek any real medical assistance. She will never white water raft ever again. This experience was another example of my deep respect for the natural world and the unexpected turns that nature can provide - especially if and when humans are involved. No matter how prepared I may be and no matter how much I believe I am in control or know how to handle a situation, life and nature can always send twists and turns. Nature and life are in charge -- not us.

A year later I was on Oahu taking a cross cultural course at the University of Hawaii with faculty members from 30 different countries. It was a great experience and helped me in the design of two courses that I routinely offered for 18 years. One Sunday a Maori from New Zealand asked if I had a car. When I said yes, he said we should go surfing. I told him I had never done so and wasn't a good swimmer. He said "no problem, just bring a towel and your suit." So we headed for a swim on the North Shore, famous for its waves and surfing. The waves were rolling in, and he asked if I had ever body surfed. I had not but decided it was well worth trying. It was. There was something quite different about swimming that day in the warm Oahu waters as compared to the chilly waters of Lake Ontario many years before, or even the rafting experience I had recently encountered. I started rather cautiously at first, catching the waves after they were breaking, and I could still touch the bottom with my feet. After a while I became more confident and began to swim out a little farther, bobbing in waters now over my head. I began catching the waves as they were just breaking. I knew I could never really surf and found that using my body instead of a board for riding the waves was an existentially superior experience. I vividly remember waiting for a wave as I was bobbing in the ocean and looking around at the beauty that the North Shore provided. It struck me how majestic our world can be and how magnificent creation truly was. I felt quite humbled in the face of God. I felt a surge of grace fill my consciousness and realized that that grace was and is always available to me. Maybe it is the basis for my capacity to love, especially Diane, my daughters and now my Munchkins. Sometimes it takes unexpected moments to realize this truth of my faith. In both of the swimming instances and the rafting experience, I found a profound respect for Mother Nature and for God's creation. In one instance this respect was intertwined with fear and trembling, in the second it was enmeshed with worry and remorse for hurting Diane, while in the last it was wrapped in awe and wonder. In all cases, respect became a common denominator. This word, respect, was a word I often heard while growing up. My father always demanded respect: for him and for Mom. It was a mantra I heard over and over again. I have recounted some of my difficulties with my dad over the years, but I have learned that his mantra was true and right on the money: respect is the essence of human relationships. I certainly didn't feel that way toward him when I was growing up. As a youth and teen I found it impossible to respect a man who was drunk so much. How do you respect someone who falls into a linen closet or our coat closet and needs to be helped to his bed? How do you respect a man who in the middle of the night confused your bed for the toilet and almost relieved himself in your face? How can you respect a drunken driver for crashing the car into a snow bank, causing my mom to trudge home in the snow while helping him along? How do you respect a man for demanding that we respect mom but who didn't seem to follow his own advice? How do you respect a smoker who refused to give up his habit even after having part of a lung removed? However, as I have reflected upon my life, I have come to conclude that Dad was right. It **is** all about respect. I wish I could tell him that; I never did when he was alive. But don't we all have regrets about what we have said or did not say to someone else in our lives, including "I love you"? This last part of my book will examine the importance of respect and love in my life and how they may be the primary values and attitudes we should espouse and develop in all areas of our lives. Respect and love should be the basis for our relationships with nature (this chapter), with people and places (the next chapter) and with family and friends (the last three chapters).

Awe and wonder produce experiences that elicit a response that is respectful. Diane and I have traveled throughout the United States, Canada, the Caribbean and Europe. We have camped in Rocky Mountain National Park, the Tetons and Yellowstone with our family. We also have rented cabins in Allegany State Park, Robert Tremaine State Park and taken a pop-up camper to the Adirondacks, Prince Edward Island (twice), Fort Wilderness in Disney, and a campsite in Pennsylvania Amish country. Our journeys have included stays and visits to Bryce Canyon, Zion, the north and south rims of the Grand Canyon, Olympic National Park, return visits to the Tetons and Yellowstone, a day drive through Glacier National and explorations of Jasper, Banff, and Kootaney in Canada with our friends from Holland. Our European adventures have included drives through the Alps and Pyrenees, exploring Greek Islands, the Peloponnesus, Tuscany, and the country sides of Holland, France, Belgium, Austria, Italy, Spain, Germany and the Czech Republic. We've explored the Blue Ridge Mountains and water and swamp habitats such as Shark Valley in southern Florida. Hikes, nights under the stars, skipping stones on lakes (large and small), campfire stories and the search for wildlife large and small have become family adventures which have provided rich memories for all of us. My respect for Mother Nature goes well beyond the experiences I had in Lake Ontario, in Texas and in the Pacific. The respect that continues to unfold in my life for the natural world is very deep and profound. When I was growing up that was not necessarily so evident.

When I was about 9 or 10, my dad took us to Muskegon, Michigan. Paul didn't go with us. Dad had been working at the Hooker plant in Muskegon providing drafting for new facilities that were being built. He had been commuting, coming home on the weekends. One week, however, we went back with him. My only recollection of that trip was my slingshot. Paul had helped me build this weapon that all young boys "should" have. He taught me how to pick the correct size stone, how to aim and how to propel the projectile to the desired target. One afternoon I ventured into a wooded area near the motel. I was determined to become a proficient hunter and the woods would be the perfect place for me to practice my new found skill. I searched for the right size stones and packed them into my pocket. I took aim at some knots in trees and even made a direct hit on one of them. Then I saw a goldfinch flying around a nearby bush. Aha, time to go after a living target. I loaded the slingshot, aimed and let the stone sail directly at the bird. It was a direct hit. Success: until I went over to see what I really had done. The goldfinch was lying still at my feet. I didn't feel nauseous, but I did have a tsunami of regret wash over my mind, body and soul. How could I be so brutal and ruthless? What did this beautiful creature ever do to me? I didn't know what to do and felt too ashamed to even give the little creature a burial. I just turned and walked away. I went to my room and experienced one of those transformational moments in a child's life. I would never hunt again. I would never kill another animal ever again. This was just cruel and wrong.

The next day my dad asked if I wanted to take my slingshot out and go for a walk with him. I shrugged and just walked next to him. The slingshot had already been packed away and would never be used again. This lesson has led me to forego any hunting in my life. I could never bring myself to destroy something living for my own pleasure. Killing animals just for the fun of it is antithetical to my genuine sense of respect for God's creation. I have not made the leap to become a vegetarian because we humans are omnivores and eating meat is one gift of nature I fully embrace. I have been impressed with Native Americans who have realized the necessity of killing animals for food and clothing. But that necessity does not preclude their deep respect for their prey. Words of honor or signs of thanksgiving often accompany a hunt. Traditionally such events were wrapped in ritual. There are even some tribes who have asked the ground for forgiveness when they till the soil. We can learn a lot from people who have such a deep respect for the world in which we live. We do not own the world and the living creatures within it: we share the world and should respect all of our co-inhabitants.

My desire to never kill an animal has only been challenged by roaches, ants and mosquitoes. I consider them justifiable exceptions. There were, however, two ignominious moments when I did not follow my goal of doing no harm. The first occurred sometime in the late 1970s. I was headed home from a conference in the Catskills. As I drove along the highway along southern New York State I saw a blur and felt a terrible impact. The hoof of the deer flew in front of my face. I pulled over and a nearby farmer rushed to me. I was visibly shaken and horrified at what had happened. Such a beautiful animal and I was the reason it lay dead along the side of the road. The man asked if my car was okay. The front was smashed but the radiator seemed intact and I saw nothing leaking. He brought out some wire that held the hood down so I could drive the remaining 250 miles home. His next question took me out of the fog.

"Do you want the deer?"

"Um, uh, of course not," I feebly replied.

"Can I have it?"

"Sure".

He quickly said good-bye and proceeded to drag the poor animal to his farm. As I drove home, I thought long and hard about different priorities and perspectives in life. At first I was a bit repulsed by the farmer's request and what I thought was a disrespectful display of dragging the corpse away. When I became a little more reasonable in my thinking, I realized that hunting for food is engraved into humanity's DNA. We are omnivores, and hunting has been our means of sustenance for hundreds of thousands if not millions of years. The farmer was actually being sensible and probably respectful. How awful would it be to leave the poor animal on the side of the road to rot and decay? The kinder way of treating the animal was to do exactly as he had done. I felt guilty for killing the deer, but that is the nature of accidents. Life is sometimes just beyond our control. That is a lesson that keeps being drummed into my head. Again I was facing an experience that was upsetting and seemed to confirm the dictum that life is not inherently fair or just. I'm not sure how I feel about hunting deer not for the sake of food, but for thinning the herd in suburban areas. That is a moral dilemma for me. Dilemmas, by definition, do not have an acceptable answer or resolution. A decision or action must be taken but no truly positive results will occur from a true dilemma. Is killing animals to protect gardens really justified? Not sure.

My second unintended assault on the animal kingdom occurred the day a squirrel was in our house. Heidi and Diane were traumatized and headed across the street to a neighbor's to await my attempts to deal with the frightened creature. This was the one and only squirrel to get into our house (ever). After prying a side door open and trying to chase the speedy little guy out, I realized that I had to try something else. In my folly of believing I have quick hands, I donned a baseball glove on my left hand and put one of my hockey gloves on the right hand. I didn't want the frightened beast biting me. We had camped with friends years before and the young boy was snapped at by a raccoon when he was trying to bait it. So I thought I was being very clever. I did manage to corral him in Katie's bedroom. I slammed the door and we were now *mano a mano*. He jutted and I lunged. He ran and I darted. This dance occurred for a few minutes when my hockey hand grabbed his tail. Aha, I have him. Little did I know that squirrel tails can rip apart quite easily. Instead of picking him up by the tail to take him outside, he scampered away while I was holding a portion of the tail. I quickly discarded it into the wastebasket and continued my futile efforts. Finally I called animal control, and a professional came and did what I was ill equipped to do. There were two consequences to my ineptness. First we found out that they had to kill the animal and test it for rabies because it had bitten my baseball glove. I saw I wasn't bitten but that isn't the regulation, I guess. The second surprise happened when we heard a blood-curling scream come from Katie. I forgot about the tail in her wastebasket and when she went to throw something away, she was confronted with a furry remnant of the afternoon. So if I really want to respect nature and animals, I need to understand my place. What is really doable and respectful; what is foolish and harmful. I'm trying to follow my own advice these days.

Sometimes I find myself taking people and places for granted. Whenever I become aware of doing so, I try to shift my attitude and act in ways that are more caring and attentive. I guess I've learned that lesson in many different ways in my life. Two clear lessons came from friends. When Diane's friend, Marsha, died, I spent a lot of time talking with Ron. One of his laments was the fact that he had spent so much time working hard to make money so he and Marsha could enjoy life with financial ease in the future that he didn't take time to be with her in the present. He **knew** he had a lifetime ahead to do so. That regret was very painful for him, and I learned that looking at life quantitatively rather than qualitatively was not wise. I've also mentioned my regret about not contacting my friend, Donny, after he had moved to New Mexico. I took our friendship for granted, only to learn of his death and the subsequent loss of his presence in my life completely. As I have been reflecting on the wonderful experiences I have had around the country and in Canada, Europe, Israel and Asia, I have realized that I have taken a local gift for granted. I'm not talking about Niagara Falls because I am one of the residents of the Falls who has always loved to go and see its majesty. No, I've never taken that majesty for granted. I still stand in awe at the power and beauty of the Falls including the recurrent rainbows and perpetual misty feel. Recently Diane and I took our granddaughter, Collette, down to the Cave of the Winds. After donning flip flops and a skimpy poncho provided on the tour, we walked through the tunnel out to the walkways that head toward the American and Bridal Veil Falls. Ascending the Hurricane platform and feeling the power and force of nature instills a profound sense of the secondary place in life that humans really possess. We aren't in charge. Anyone who has lived through tornadoes, blizzards, tsunamis or hurricanes know of which I speak. I also took my grandson, Eliot, on this tour. He relished in the experience and saw it as a thrill. It was great to see both of them leave the experience with the sense of awe and respect that I had hoped would occur. That was truly our intent. However, I'm not talking about taking the Falls for granted. No. It is Ellicott Creek Park.

We live two blocks south of this 165 acre park. Ellicott Creek provides the southern boundary while Tonawanda Creek provides the northern boundary for the park. There is a road that splits it into two portions - more of that in a moment. There is also a road that transverses the southern portion. There are two walk bridges from our neighborhood to the Park, one is conducive for riding a bike. Heading east from the bridge Ellicott Creek Bike Path heads along the creek with many natural areas, although it does go through the northern part of the North campus of the University of Buffalo and ends at a golf course. The ubiquitous ducks and geese abound along the way. It is not uncommon to see a Blue Heron, along with cardinals, blue jays, wrens, black birds, orioles, crows, goldfinches, and other varieties that I still have not learned to identify. Usually the woodpeckers can only be heard, but there are a couple of trees that have revealed their diners. That bike path has been a route for me for decades. My daughters have occasionally gone with me. Diane and I usually bike another path altogether. I can also head west in the park and follow a bike path that follows Tonawanda Creek to the Niagara River. The path runs all the way to downtown Buffalo. I have yet to take the 50 mile round trip but have plans to do so once my body cooperates. The path east is shorter and usually I decide which route to take by the direction of the wind. I prefer heading into the wind on my journey out so the wind can help my weary legs and asthmatic lungs on the return. Ellicott Creek itself is 45 miles long and begins as a tributary of Tonawanda Creek. They follow their separate paths until they reunite about 1/2 mile from the Niagara River.

The park itself has been far more important in our lives than just a starting place for riding on bike paths. There is a small hill along the road that bisects the main park area. Our girls in their childhoods had used the hill for winter sledding (using old runner sleds or saucers). For years the county made an outdoor skating rink on the west end of the park. We would take our girls, with skates and shovels to enjoy one of the few winter sports I could or would attempt. My skating skills are minimal but we wanted to expose our girls to another way of dealing with Buffalo winters. Sometimes we only shoveled paths for skating; sometimes we shoveled larger areas for more freeform skating. Later in life I tried rollerblading along the bike paths. It was not a pretty picture. Tara tried to help me with this means of alleged enjoyment. Unfortunately my right leg is not normally aligned and my right foot naturally moves at a distinct angle. (I have heard "quack quack" more than once in my life.). Tara has shown the folly of my attempts to others by using her hands and extending the left in a straight line and her right hand jutting to the right. Looking at that demonstration it was easy for me to see why I crashed while going down a slight incline on the path. My German determination to conquer such an easy looking means of movement led to a number of bumps and bruises (especially to my ego). Finally I surrendered my skates and admitted utter defeat.

I really respect those who skate well and use this talent in such a variety of ways. The Olympics are always an amazing display of skill, grace and determination. My only attempt at hockey on an on-going basis was an indoor, floor version in a gym. My brother-in-law and I distinguished ourselves over two seasons. The one time I tried ice hockey was when I was in the Seminary. There was a rink in an area near our living quarters. A group of us took the skates that were made available to any who dared. We choose up teams and I quickly began to slide my way through the game, attempting to stay upright on the figure skates which were two sizes too big. Trying to make cuts to stay with an opponent is not so easily done with figure skates, especially for a poor skater like I was/am. Unfortunately for me some of the players on the other team played high school hockey. Even with proper skates I didn't stand a chance. My knees saw more ice time than the skates. When the pain got to be too much I opted to play goalie. That was another jolt to the ego. The next couple of weeks were torture as my bloodied and scraped knees were not conducive to comfortable kneeing at meditation or Mass times. My injuries were no excuse to sit; no, they were merely a means to really feel the depth of my faith: I never thought to ask for an exemption from kneeling.

Our family has not picnicked in the park very often, although we have taken our girls and even our grandchildren, when they were young, to the playground areas. There is a walking/bike path through the southern part of the park, which crosses the road and continues along Tonawanda Creek to the Island at the northernmost point of the park. I have walked and biked this 2+ mile path by crossing over one of the walk bridges. It is my longer walk through the park; the shorter versions include crossing into the park from one of the bridges, walking along Ellicott Creek, then returning to the neighborhood across the other bridge. Sometimes I become adventuresome and go off the path and meander near the more wooded and reedy sections. The Island has had a checkered past. I would only bike it during the daytime - having no qualms about doing so with Diane or any of our girls. Evenings and nighttimes brought out some of the more seedy behaviors in our town, thus precluding any desire to see those sights. Today the Island is a dog park which means I no longer enter - trying to zigzag around running canines is not my choice of rides. Often my walks include wearing the ipod my girls gave me years ago. I have managed to import much of my music, including the grief discs I created as my "sharing time with Heidi" music. These walks are for heart, soul and body.

The park's tennis courts are conveniently located, so I have played tennis there with a couple of people, most notably my brother Bill. One instance remains vivid in my memory – not for our tennis playing but for our encounter with teenage thieves. My brother and I had just finished playing a match, something we have not done often enough over the past decade due to surgeries and other limitations. On this particular morning, however, I had ridden by bicycle over and met Bill at the courts. At the time the park was charging to enter, so he parked near one of the foot bridges and walked to the courts. They were only charging cars to enter; walkers and bikers had continued free access. When we had finished our attempts at glory, we meandered to his car. As we chatted, we heard a splash and looked down the creek. About 100 yards away, we saw three teen-age boys stomping on the bumper of a car in order to submerge it into the creek. I tossed the keys to my home to Bill, told him to drive to the house and call the police; I would follow the teens on my bike. He took off. I continued watching the teens, but kept my distance. After a while they noticed that I was paying attention to them, and they began throwing rocks at me. They climbed up onto a railroad track and started walking down the tracks that crossed over the creek and toward our neighborhood area. I hustled back to the bridge, and as I started heading up the road to the tracks, a police car screeched to a halt. He asked me if I was involved in the call, and as soon as I nodded, he yelled for me to get into the car. I left my bike on the side of the road, jumped into the cruiser and directed him to the railroad tracks. He made a hard left and started driving down the tracks. That was by far the bumpiest ride I've ever had in a car. When the teens saw the pursuit, they ran into our neighborhood. The policeman got on his radio and gave directions to the other cars that were involved in the pursuit. Within 10 or 15 minutes, all three teens were in custody. Of course the policeman wanted me to identify them. I had a request.

"I have four daughters. If these guys are in their school, I don't want them to see me." The policeman nodded.

We slowly drove by the teens as they were seated in another police cruiser. I said they were the ones who pushed the car into the creek. The policeman thanked me and drove me home; my brother had recovered my bike. The policeman asked me to come to the station to give a formal, written statement later. When I did, I asked him if he could tell me why they did what they did. He explained that I didn't have to worry about my daughters - a real relief. The teens had escaped from a teen detention facility in Pennsylvania. They stole the car in Erie, along with robbing a store and getting cigarettes and alcohol. I asked what would happen to them. He said they probably wouldn't be prosecuted for these offenses because they were all under the age of 16; they'd just be sent back to Detention and add some bad time to their incarceration. As I talked with the policeman we agreed that their recidivism would be a problem, maybe throughout their lives. Without some positive intervention, they had already adopted an antisocial and criminal mindset. It was sad to see. I thanked him for the way he handled the case and for helping me to protect my girls. He thanked me for not turning a blind eye.

Other parts of the park have woven themselves into my life in very, very different ways. One is a stone building that stands between the two walk bridges abutting the Creek. It is called the Casino. My first encounter with this facility was in 8th grade. Our teacher, Mother John Edward, a strict but fair woman, announced one day that we would have a field trip to Erie County. That was a big deal for all of us. We lived in Niagara County and it was a rare occurrence to venture that far south in my childhood. I only remember crossing the county line to go to stock cars races a couple of times and this outing with my school. Even in high school the only sojourns to this neighboring county were for football games and an acting competition. This 8th grade trip seems to capture a bit of my life in elementary and middle school. I started at Prince of Peace in 5th grade and quickly became part of the class, both in school and out (including dance parties in 7th and 8th grades at someone's home). By 8th grade I think there were only about 18 kids in the class. Our lives were rather interconnected (I can still remember each one of them) and I don't remember any inner circle. I do remember one girl who didn't seem to fit in and one boy who was awkward but became one of my best friends, especially in high school. He had scarlet fever in 9th grade and I took his homework to him and helped him keep up. By our senior year he was the class valedictorian, a tackle on the football team and one of the co-editors with me on the yearbook. He was the one who ended up handing out programs while I worked the lights during the concert for the girls and boys joint choir performance. He was also with me in the seminary. He and I were close in those days.

The bus ride to the park seemed rather uneventful. The nuns certainly made sure of it. Although we were headed to the park for playing and picnicking, my recollection was that we were still required to wear our school uniforms: dresses for the girls and shirts and ties for the boys. The green and yellow colors were not a fashion statement, although I would not have realized that back in those days. At the park I really only remember one series of events - they overshadowed anything else. Our picnic was at the Casino, which in those days included rentals of canoes or rowboats. Many of us were immediately drawn to the adventure of it all. Of course we were given strict instructions. Boys and girls could not be in the same rowboat (canoes seemed too risky). Also no splashing or swimming would be permitted. Any breach of these rules would be immediate grounding. I'm not sure how many of us ventured into the boats nor how many there were, maybe three or four rowboats. Someone who pretended he knew everything about rowing headed us all on an easterly course along the creek and away from the prying eyes of our authorities. Once we had crossed under Niagara Falls Boulevard and clear of the rule enforcers, the oars began to splash. Squeals of delight or surprise rang out. Someone suggested we dive into the water. The water did not look that tempting and I couldn't imagine going into water without a bathing suit. (Later in life when I was watching the movie *Stand By Me* the scene of the boys ending up with leeches on their bodies was an instant recall to the waters of the Creek. Even when it is not covered with algae, it still has all of the appeal of that movie's creepy scene.) The suggestion for us to jump into the water seemed totally unreasonable to me. Besides it was against the rules! No one took up his call and he gave up by swinging his oar in a grand arc that sprayed everyone. We cheered and laughed. I have a faint recollection that a couple of the girls were horrified and I have to honestly confess that I was not one to splash. I may have pretended to but I do know that no one got wet from anything I did. I didn't begrudge anyone else doing so, I just didn't want to disobey. I look back with some sadness at that rigidness.

When we returned the rowboats our uniforms were rather wet. Mother John Edward was not pleased, to say the least. We were gathered for an interrogation. This moment brought back a vivid experience in 6th grade when someone misfired and the spitball intended for a classmate hit our teacher. She lined us up and demanded a confession. No one stepped forward so we were all punished. I didn't see the perpetrator, although we all had a pretty good idea who was behind this dastardly deed. That mass punishment seemed unfair to me and remains as a childhood experience that began my adult understanding that life is not fair and we cannot expect people to behave in just and honorable ways. As we stood at that picnic, I had visions of wholesale punishments. I'm not sure who spoke because I kept my eyes fixed straight forward and only listened to the wind blowing through my ears.

"Mother, we're all inexperienced. We couldn't help but make some mistakes."

It was a male voice and he was compounding the disobedience by lying. We all knew it and said nothing. Then came a moment that shocked me. Mother John Edward told us to go and enjoy the rest of the day but we couldn't go on the rowboats anymore. Would miracles never cease?

Years later the Casino and bike paths became integral parts of two of our Heidi's Day celebrations which I described in the last chapter. The Casino was an ideal facility for picnics for large families or groups. A decade after the last Heidi's Day I was the coordinator of a Task Force of five Lutheran churches that were working together to have joint activities. One major event we sponsored was a picnic for all members of all the churches. A wonderful woman volunteered to organize the day. Entering the Casino for that church event was very bittersweet. Those who attended thought it was a great day and we repeated the event the next year. For me (and Diane) it was difficult to be in that facility with new faces and without any attention being given to Heidi. It was truly a selfish feeling, but it was deep and real.

The last story about Ellicott Creek Park does not include the Casino. There is a senior center building in the northern section along Tonawanda Creek. It is a facility that has a kitchen, tables, and rest rooms indoors. Outside are picnic tables and grills. I rented the facility for two summers. Each June while I was a Dean at Canisius, I had an Advisory Council meeting and held the gathering off-campus. I was the Dean of Continuing Studies and was responsible for a wide variety of programs. I asked faculty from across the campus to serve on the Council which only met once per year (the day-long session was after classes were finished and before many faculty scattered for the summer). There were faculty with whom I had worked closely on projects, some were personal friends away from campus, and two were even former teachers. We had representatives from business, education, including physical education, the natural sciences, the social sciences and the humanities. Those who attended agreed that it was the only time anyone provided an opportunity for such cross disciplinary activity to occur at the college. Each year I gave a report and asked people to break into work sessions. Members of my staff had worked to provide agendas for each of the groups although it was very common for faculty members to divert the conversations and head in very different directions.

I'm not sure how many of those attending would remember any of our conversations nor of the conclusions we reached at the end of those sessions, even though we advanced programmatic efforts in a multitude of ways across the campus. I do believe, however, everyone would remember one incident that occurred to me. There are a couple of attendees who still remind me of the event when we run into each other.

After we had goodies and coffee for breakfast I gathered everyone together (usually about 50 people) for an overview of the day and my expectations for addressing issues I believed were critical for our programs and the school. One year we gathered outside using the tables and chairs to form a large circle. The weather was perfect and being outside was always preferable to inside. As I began my remarks I suddenly noticed a distinctly different look on the faces of those who were looking at me. The looks ranged from amusement to surprise. Then I felt the reason for their changed countenances. The webbed feet of a park duck brushed my head. The interloper continued his flight pattern out across the Creek and into the wooded area on the other side. The laughter was infectious and many wanted to tell me their view of the matter. Apparently the duck was flying a bit low and was headed directly to our assemblage. About 100 yards or so away he lowered his flight path so he could aim directly for my head. I'm not bald, so I have no idea what his fascination was. I refer to the duck as male because I couldn't imagine a female being that hostile to me! Besides I saw his bright plumage as he gracefully swooped away. (By the way, I neither felt nor found any elimination product on me. Whew.)

As I reflect upon the importance of respect in human relationships I am struck by a realization that it may need to start with a respect for nature and the world within which we live. Respect needs to recognize humanity's place in creation. The world has beauty that should strike us with awe and wonder. There is also power and the unexpected that can cause destruction and elicit fear and dread. The Daoist symbol of Yin Yang comes to mind: weak and strong, female and male, dual forces of life that necessitate balance and harmony. These forces are not just for nature, they also apply to humanity. So it makes sense to me that I should reflect upon how my feelings of wonder and awe for nature can relate to the people in our world. My reminiscences of nature are a first building block in my world view of life:

We should not degrade the world around us.

We are co-inhibitors on earth, not its owner.

We should respect all of life that surrounds us.

Global warming is our responsibility and requires immediate human action.

We have a moral imperative to support all efforts to protect our world and environment.

Lastly, we need to be careful that we do not take this world for granted.

CHAPTER 13
FOR PEOPLE AND PLACES

When you are content to be simply yourself
and don't compare or compete, everybody will respect you.

Lao Tzu

Love has no gender - compassion no religion – character has no race.

Abhijit Naskar

Throughout my childhood our family made frequent visits to a bar named Fritz's. Fritz was the owner when I was younger. My dad liked him and the way he ran his business. I have no idea what these norms or standards were. We often went there on Fridays for the traditional Western New York Fish Fry. In those days Catholics were not supposed to eat meat on Fridays. My dad complied with that rule, although other inconvenient rules he was ready to ignore (e.g. confession before communion). When I was younger (between 3 and 7), I had the run of the place. I would go behind the bar so the bartender could lavish me with cherries from the HUGE jar tucked away near the washing bin. The kitchen staff were wonderful. If I sat and talked with them, they would reward me with all the French fries I wanted. I don't remember singing for quarters or sitting on men's laps when they played Euchre when I was very young, but mom told me that is exactly what I did. In one corner of the bar was a bowling machine (the kind with the metal puck to slide over the sandy surface to hit spring loaded pins). Experts who played the game knew exactly how much sand to administer to the surface. They had a stool for kids like me to play when I was young. I was thrilled when my dad was willing to part with the change to play. Of course I had observed many adults playing the game and wanted to use the shaker to get the surface perfect. Unfortunately I was too small to reach all the way down the alley. That shortcoming never seemed to cross my mind. I was able to play an adult game at a bar and I thought I was pretty special. As I got older, the machine had less interest; in fact, going to the bars became less interesting. Observing people and watching their behavior, especially those who were sitting on the stools, were ways to pass the time away. Unfortunately almost-teens and teenagers don't try to hustle French fries in the kitchen or sneak cherries from the bartender, so that pastime slowly ebbed away. After we ate our meal, mom would work the crowd and dad would retire to a stool. Being stuck with my younger brother was never a peak experience in those days. One spring day when I was 14 my mom gleefully introduced me to the new bartender's son. He was my age and my mom's hope for a quick friendship was blatantly obvious. Mom always wanted people to be happy, and she loved her sons completely. I knew her thinking: if Charlie has someone to play with while we're here, then he will be happy too. I'll call the other teenager X. After awkward hellos X asked if I wanted to play the bowling machine. He saw that I was hesitant and quickly figured out the reason.

"Don't worry, I can play for free."

So we spent the rest of my dad's beer and shot time bowling and chatting a little bit. He, his mom and stepdad had moved from another city and they lived in rooms above the bar. I had been coming to this bar all my life and never bothered trying to figure out what was on the second floor. Oh, well, so much for my being oblivious to my surroundings. This period of time included my dad also venturing to a bar a couple of buildings down from Fritz's, so I didn't see X every time the family went out. During the summer X and I left the bar a couple of times to venture outside and wander over to Cayuga Creek that was just across the street. He talked about how much he loved the water and couldn't wait until his stepdad bought him a boat. I learned that his mother was his biological mom, but he was now living with his stepdad (the bartender). X did not like this man. He was a disciplinarian and gave X a lot of grief – a common enough grievance for a teen. We commiserated about fathers who were too strict and thanked God for understanding mothers. X and I never saw or talked to each other except when I was at the bar with my folks. That would only be on Fridays because the other 3-4 nights my folks went out to drink I stayed home to watch my brother. One evening we were having our dinner at home. Dad had already spent the six minutes that he allotted for the meal before retiring to the bathroom. Mom answered the phone and called dad.

"Smitty, Y is on the phone and has something important to talk about."

"#%* sakes".

He still hadn't fully zipped himself up when he took the receiver. Mom looked a bit worried since Y had never called before. Dad didn't say a word but grunted and groaned at what I believed were appropriate times. When dad hung up the phone his initial comment was "well I'll be damned." He took mom into another room and Bill and I heard gasps and comments of disbelief. I couldn't hear and was told to go back to the kitchen when I tried sneaking within earshot. Finally they reemerged. Mom said that she and dad had decided that I should know what's going on. They sent Bill to his room. (Of course, I told him later, but it didn't matter to him and he has never recalled this incident.) Apparently X had asked his mother for a boat. She had said yes and told X that he and his step father could go shopping for it very soon. When X approached his stepfather about when they could go, he put X off. After awhile the step father finally told X that he would never buy him a boat. That X was too young and irresponsible to be rewarded with having a boat. This rejection was more than X could handle. He went to his stepfather's closet, got out the shot gun, and loaded it. When his stepfather was in the bathroom shaving, X opened the door and shot him in the face. Later I heard the scene was bloody and gruesome. I never saw X nor his mother again. As time went on, we did hear that his mother was doing everything she could to keep her son out of any detention or prison facility. I vividly remember hearing my dad, mom and other people at the bar talking about how terrible the incident was and how irresponsible the mother was in trying to prevent her son from ever experiencing any consequences for his behavior. Spoiled children became a common theme in this bar for quite some time. I learned then that consequences matter, especially when someone makes terrible decisions or behaves in a horrible way. I also learned that when someone doesn't respect another person, terrible things can happen.

Many times in my life I have done something and realized, then, or later, that I should have done something else. Why did I not practice my own mantra in those instances? Why didn't I always behave in ways that made relationships grounded in respect? When I was in South Carolina and went with Donny and his gang into the woods and threw those bricks at the shanties, I even realized then that what I was doing was wrong. Yet I did it. There are other times when we behave in a way that we don't realize that we are doing something we shouldn't. These actions are based on ignorance or gut reactions. Certainly the time I tied the neighborhood girl to the telephone pole is an illustration of the disconnect between what I did and what I should have done. I'm not sure that I could have done anything to prevent X from doing what he did. I do know that I never bothered talking about respecting my dad. I was a teen and just complained to X even though, deep down, I always had an abiding respect for dad. He had taught me how important that was but I never thought to share that lesson with X. I really don't feel guilty about not doing so. It is just one of those subtle regrets about wishing I had done something differently. Besides, why should I think that I would have any impact on X or his behavior?

Decades later and a continent away I saw how total disrespect and hatred worked their ugly ways into Europe and cascaded the world into chaos, war, and the suspension of human decency in so many ways. I also saw how respect and trust could produce beauty and human understanding. The incredible diversity of human achievements and destruction were on display for us. To explain this point I guess I should begin with the volcanic eruption of *Eyjafjallajokull* in Iceland. Diane and I had planned to spend a week in Malaga, Spain with our Dutch friends, Peter and Tiny. The trip was to tour Andalusia, then go through Valencia and Barcelona before touring small towns and villages through central France. I had studied French and France's culture; we had visited Paris with our friends years earlier, but I wanted to get a feel of the French people in the towns and rural areas of the country. Touring Europe with our Dutch friends gives us a sense of belonging; we don't feel completely like American tourists – almost as if we too belonged. We wanted to finish with a stay in Normandy to pay our respects to all the fallen in WWII and to see the beginning of Diane's dad's war experience. Although he was not involved on D-Day, his entry into the war was on the beaches of Normandy. We would end up in Purmerend, our friends' hometown, which is north of Amsterdam. Again, I must repeat: man plans and God laughs.

That Icelandic volcano disrupted traffic to and from Europe for days. Our flight was included as one of the casualties. We debated whether we should cancel our trip and reschedule, but the logistics were too difficult. So we curtailed our stay in Malaga while our friends toured for the five days we were delayed. We did get to go to Cordoba to visit the *Mezquita* and to Granada to tour *Al Hombra*. Lessons of respect became very obvious. These towns are in Andalusia, a southern region of Spain that was controlled by the Moors from the 8th to the 15th century. During that time there was a period when the Moors established a wonderful climate of peace and cooperation among Muslims, Jews and Christians. Art, literature, science and philosophy flourished, and thinkers, artists, scientists and physicians from all the Abrahamic religions worked together. It was a time of peace and reciprocal respect. *Al Hombra* is an exquisite architectural masterpiece of Moorish design. After the conquest of Andalusia by the Catholics, the palace was used by Ferdinand and Isabella. The current gardens and buildings also include Christian influences. As we walked around and admired the details in the woodwork, the stunning views, the pools and the gardens, I tried wondering about the ideas and feelings that first inspired the builders and renovators of the complex and those that drove the conquerors to do what they had done.

My ideas that day were influenced by the preceding day's visit to the *Mezquita*. It is also referred to originally as the Mosque of Cordoba. It includes 856 columns made from jasper, onyx, marble, granite and porphyry. I pictured the faithful coming to pray, to learn, and to discuss life and important matters. I wondered if the Muslims knew about the great Mosque in Medina and Mohammad's Charter that established laws and rules fostering peace and respect among the Abrahamic faiths. I wonder what the world would be like if Mohammad's Charter that was based on reciprocal respect had succeeded him and had become the blueprint for interfaith relationships. As we stood in awe of the beauty and genius of the Mosque, I became disturbed with the Catholic Cathedral that sits within the Mosque itself. We were told that the Cathedral was built inside the Mosque as a way to demonstrate Christianity's power and control over the conquered Moors. As I noted earlier on the part about religion, prejudice and hatred have sometimes replaced the values of love and respect when religions clash. Walking in this beautiful building I saw a clear example of religious art and architecture being suborned by political hatred and discrimination. The *Mezquita* seems to be an example of overt religious prejudice on display. However, six days later I saw what hatred on a grander scale can cause.

After we toured Valencia and Barcelona, we drove over the snowy mountains into France. Our first night was in Carcasoone. The medieval city surrounded by a moat and castle still remain. Our hotel was in the new city but we spent most of the day exploring life of centuries gone by. One particular experience touched us very much. We wandered into the old town's church and immediately heard beautiful harmony coming from four singers. Instead of moving on, we sat down to enjoy the concert. We later learned that they were students from Russia. I thought about the wonder of life that would create such a moment of serendipity. Here were two people from the Netherlands, two people from the U. S., and four students from Russia, in a small church in the remote city of Carcasoone, France. The world can be truly small and connected. We loved their singing and realized that beauty, grace and human accomplishments can be shared in small and enriching ways. The next day we drove and stayed on a farm in *L'Auberge des Mathres*. I was getting a sense of the rural side of the country. We loved the fields rich in vibrant yellow flowers and the hills and countryside that were not so different from areas we have seen in other countries. The people on the farm didn't speak English so our friends again were our means of communicating. This farm was not like the ones of western Kentucky. The barns and animal enclosures had a different layout and feel to them. Was this cultural or just the result of different personalities? Earlier we had stopped at a village on market day. The sights and sounds were familiar, yet not quite the same for me. The cheeses and breads were more abundant and meat was less conspicuous. The following day was rainy and chilly - the type of day when it is impossible to get warm while being outside. After breakfast our friends took us to *Oradur-Sur-Glane*. We were not prepared for what we experienced.

In the quiet rolling farmlands of France, dotted by towns and villages, we entered a truly horrific memorial. The parking lot was hidden by bushes and trees. As we emerged along the path we entered a building that was the information center. Along the walls were photographs and details of the slaughter that had occurred on June 10, 1944. We didn't stop to peruse the information; we did so on our way out. It made more sense to do so then.

As we left the building spread out in front of us was a town that has been stopped in time. We walked back to 1944. Nothing has changed from that gruesome day. Only charred stone buildings remained standing. Anything that was made of wood was gone. Doorways were perpetually open and windows were hollowed out rectangles on the sides of homes. A burnt out bicycle frame was leaning against one of the homes. Dotted around the village were a couple of burnt out cars resting on wheels without tires and devoid of seats. We learned that the German unit that was responsible for this atrocity was heading north to fight against the allied forces that had landed in Normandy. They had heard that a German officer had been captured by the resistance movement in a nearby town. The Germans believed this village also had members of the resistance. As it turned out, most of the men of the village were gone that day tending to their fields (or maybe helping with the resistance). The Germans gathered everyone else in the village into the town square to check their identity papers. Women and children were taken to the village church. The men (generally old, sick, or injured) were taken to barns at the edge of town. Machine guns had been placed at kneecap level along the sides of the barns. When the men were gathered inside the machine guns opened fire. When the men were immobilized the soldiers doused them with gasoline, then, set them ablaze. After completing that task, the SS men next proceeded to the church and placed an incendiary device beside it. When it was ignited, women and children tried to escape through the doors and windows, only to be met with machine-gun fire. The only survivor was 47-year-old Marguerite Rouffanche. She escaped through a rear sacristy window, followed by a young woman and child. All three were shot, two of them fatally. Rouffanche crawled to some pea bushes and remained hidden overnight until she was found and rescued the next morning. Before leaving, the Germans set fire to the village and took all the edible animals with them.

The wind, rain and cold temperatures made our chilling experience one that was physically and emotionally draining. We could find no warmth.

As we walked toward the cemetery that was built at the edge of town the rain began to come down a little harder, adding to my mood of disbelief and shock. We wandered through the cemetery and read headstones of individuals and of whole families. Most of them had the same day of death: that awful day - June 10, 1944. As we walked back through town Diane saw yellow flowers growing in the crevices of a wall. She remembered a poem about flowers in a crannied wall. She gently picked one and walked over to a window sill. Here she placed a memorial to all those who had so tragically died: 642 in all. So many families lost; so many children sent to an early grave. The poem spoke to her that day:

Flower in the crannied wall,

I pluck you out of the crannies,

I hold you here, root and all, in my hand,

Little flower - but if I could understand

What you are, root and all, all in all,

I should know what God and man is.

Alfred Lord Tennyson

We must never forget; we must always remain hopeful. Humanity is capable of the greatest atrocities and of the greatest beauty. Did the Nazis' hatred of the Jews and the drive for political supremacy just start with individuals harboring overt bigotry and prejudice? Did Hitler plug into these fears and prejudices to stoke a nation into a collective acceptance of hatred? What happened to basic human decency and basic respect for others? These and many more questions swirled in my head that day. Maybe in order to combat the social hatreds we see among supremacists and those espousing bigotry and prejudice, we need to start with ourselves and with individuals in our own life. It is justified to condemn the horrors of the Holocaust, but we should not overlook the daily, even subtle, covert prejudices we hold and that can unwittingly build into the hatred of a whole class of people. I have often wondered what I would have done if I was born in Germany in 1920. Do social circumstances cause us to lose our own beliefs or are they so influenced by the context of our time that it is only by chance that we have not also become the moral monsters who killed all those innocent men, women and children of *Oradour-Sur-Glane*?

In a sense this space has become sacred. It is a living memorial to people so unjustly slaughtered in the cause of hatred and power.

Twenty-two years earlier we had travelled to Europe with our four daughters (three teens and a seven year-old). First we had toured England and Scotland for eight days, then flew to be with our Dutch friends. We had a wonderful time exploring a country that was new to all of us. One afternoon sticks out as memorable for reasons other than sharing a great experience with dear friends. We were walking along one of the many canals of Amsterdam. Our friends had educated us about the homes in Amsterdam and the basic architecture. We walked into one home and even through the front door we could sense that there was something special that was about to happen. We walked to The Door that led upstairs to the sanctuary for the Frank family. As we ascended the creaking stairs I began to feel as if I was entering sacred space. By the time we reached the loft, I knew that my feeling was on the mark. There were only brief hushed whispers by anyone who shared this space with us. Each of us retreated into our own thoughts and feelings. Each of us had had different introductions into Anne Frank's life and diary. I'm not sure how many of my daughters had read it before entering the Frank's hide-away. I remember hearing the church bells and thinking that in some strange way I was sharing a moment with that tragic family. Unlike Oradour this was a singular, small sacred space. The context of the war may have been the same, but the feel and experience was so profoundly different. This was one family and one young girl: there but for the grace of God, this could have been my family's fate. The day was warm, but the chills I felt were still real. Both of these experiences have had a profound impact on the way I look at the need for love, trust and respect between and among human beings. Look what happens when bigotry and hatred overtake respect and acceptance.

A few days after we left *Oradour-Sur-Glane*, we were driving to Normandy. I felt as if Diane and I were on a pilgrimage for her father. Of course we were seeing the sights and sounds without the anxiety, fear and dread that must have pervaded so many of those who fought and survived, as well as those who died. As we walked Omaha Beach, <u>Les Braves</u> rose up from the sand. It is a stainless steel statue, which the sculptor says has three elements. The first was the Wings of Hope. As I looked at this element, I was struck that despite the slaughter and death the beach saw on that June day, the invasion brought hope, not just to the French, but to the whole world. Humanity could correct itself. Good could confront evil and triumph. My thoughts continued along that vein when I read that the second element was Rise Freedom. Isn't that what the world celebrated on V-E day? There was still fighting in Asia, but freedom had overcome the tyranny of the Nazis and the Fascists. For France, the dark days of oppression were at an end. Italy too was rescued. Again, out of death and destruction had come hope and a renewed sense of respect for one another. The last element is the Wings of Fraternity. I believe this is a hope and dream for all who work and pray for a world populated by those who have mutual respect for one another. Fraternity for the French harkens back to their Revolution and the hopes and dreams the idealists had in overthrowing the tyranny of the 18th century (as well as centuries gone by).

After walking the beach we climbed up the dunes to view the scene from the German vantage points. I spent some time in one of the pillboxes to see what the German defenders saw. What were they thinking? Did they suffer from a sense of invulnerability? Did their overconfidence erode into incredulous fear and dread? Never having been in combat I could only project what I supposed these men may have felt. My military training was far too superficial to capture the reality of battle. The memorial and cemetery at *Colleville-Sur-Mer* also provided a false sense of serenity to the horrors of what had occurred. There are about 10,000 white crosses and a much smaller number of stars of David to mark the graves of Americans who died. Walking through the cemetery was too peaceful and serene. There was a deceptive sense of beauty. As a memorial, it is wonderful. The deception is turning the tragedy of death into a place of peace and quiet. Maybe that is as is should be. Isn't that how we should honor those who have died for us? Isn't that how we pay our respect? Each cross or Star of David represents a life full of stories, family members and friends. It is so important for the survivors to keep the stories alive. I applaud all the efforts to undertake oral histories for our veterans. Their stories are important; their lives have been so important. We have a tape of Diane's dad's oral history which remains a part of our family lore. Years ago in another family, a nephew wanted to learn about his uncle's service in WWII. He contacted the men in his uncle's unit. My father-in-law was one of those men. My father-in-law remembered Lt. Lee well. That contact began an on-going connectedness between families. There were visits, letters, emails and sharing memories that were powerful for Lt. Lee's family as well as for Diane's dad, mom, and even Diane. Since both of her parents are now gone, Diane has sustained the connection. That is a story of Fraternity: human interconnectedness and a shared sense of humanity, respect and caring.

After Normandy we made two stops that gave us snapshots of very important life lessons. The first came while we spent time in the *Cathedral de Notre Dame* in Amiens. The magnificence of the building was stunning, but it was a small statue inside that caught our fascination. It was the statue of the "Weeping Angel." Its story touched us on so many levels. Nicolas Blasset sculpted it in 1636 to honor his son, Jean-Baptiste, who had died at the age of 8. During the 17th century children died often during childbirth. They were called little angels and families felt as if youth and death were inextricably linked. The angel's right hand is set on an hourglass symbolizing the brevity of life. As for his left elbow, it rests on the skull of a skeleton, a symbol of death. He is seated and bent over. His sad face and slouched demeanor gave me a sense of sorrow with a look of sadness.

Life and death are part of the same coin. The statue became famous during WWI. After the battle of the Somme, a truly gruesome conflict, surviving soldiers began to send postcards of the Weeping Angel to family, friends and fiancées to tell of their survival. For them this small statue showed the connection between life and death and how fragile anyone's life really is. Sending these postcards lasted throughout the rest of the war and was taken up by American soldiers when our country jumped into the combat. The Weeping Angel struck us as a symbol for our grieving for Heidi. We had survived; she hadn't. Youth and death were wrapped into her life and passing. Viewing this angel created a sacred space for me. The Cathedral may be considered by many believers to be sacred because it is a cathedral and their faith may posit that all such places of worship are sacred. I find that churches become sacred when there are moments, experiences, and/or people who create the sacredness for me. The church or cathedral building itself may be a masterpiece in architecture, but that's not what bestows sacredness upon it. This little angel conferred sacredness onto the large cathedral that housed it. For some strange reason, I felt more connected to the hopefulness of the surviving soldiers than I did to the father who sculpted it. Maybe I was too deeply impressed with the beauty of the memorials in Normandy. The beaches were now quiet and the cemetery was peaceful. These perceptions may have had more of an impact on my overall mood than what I knew about the horrors that Normandy represents. My emotions were probably overriding my thoughts, and I was allowing my feelings to dictate the moment. It may also be the case that I felt the effects of the other stop that had occurred the day before.

Impressionistic art is my favorite form of painting. Since my collegiate days and my studies of Bergson, the impressionists represented a way of looking at life and the world that spoke to me. We live in continuing flux and change. What we see as being so solid and constant is a bit of an illusion. Energy is the basis for life; atoms are in continual motion and are predominantly empty space. We are not as solid as we believe; we are not as changeless as we may hope. The impressionists captured this theme in a visual way that has fascinated me for decades. Another surprise for us was visiting *Giverny*, Claude Monet's home. We walked over the small bridge, saw the row boat in the famous pond and strolled through the gardens. The whole experience was surreal. We felt as if we had walked into an impressionistic world and saw Monet's canvasses open up in living colors. We were actually in a painting. The beauty of the moment was deep and brought me a sense of hopefulness.

As I indicated in the previous chapter, nature deserves our respect. It is our world, yet we are mere tenants within it. Monet's world showed me a way to capture beauty, respect and goodness. It is up to us to sustain what nature provides us. Maybe it was this mood that carried over to the Cathedral and influenced me to see the Weeping Angel the way I did. Every experience is contextual. These experiences in Europe are clear illustrations of the contextual richness that brings out deeper meanings in all that we saw and felt. Seeing those meanings enrich life provided us with an opportunity to gain insight, maybe even some wisdom. Experience itself is not the teacher. It is a context that occurs within space and time. Experience gives us the opportunity to learn - to be taught. We also need insight, thoughtfulness, or someone to enlighten us to these meanings. The contextual framework for all experiences or situations provides the background or backdrop for discovering meaning and purpose. If we only pay attention to the situation or experience itself, and disregard the context within which it occurs, we may continue to foster misunderstanding and damaging stereotypes. Prejudices, discrimination and ignorance miss the broader pictures of life or of people or of groups. Ignorance often refuses or just doesn't bother to look at the context and see a broader picture. Keeping our blinders on helps to protect us from having to confront our prejudices, hatreds and insecurities. Travel and education are important tools for taking people out of their narrow world views and understanding the need to respect others. Just as experience itself is not a teacher, so too is travel and education. Going to another city or country only provides a context within which we can open our minds. Being in a classroom is never sufficient for genuine learning to occur. A closed or indifferent mind may garner information, but it will never process what has been given and convert the experience into genuine knowledge or the next step, wisdom. Just looking at the Weeping Angel may not produce any profound lesson; another element is necessary to convert the gaze into a real moment of respect and awe.

A situation or experience involves the elements of the event in question, that is, the people, place, action and possibly consequences of the activity. The context for the situation is much deeper. It involves the cultural background of the people, place and event. That cultural background can be seen in the blending of race, ethnicity, gender, generation, religion and geography. These cultural elements mold the layers of cause(s) included in the action, as well as the mood, mindset, knowledge and understanding of those involved. An understanding of our cultural contexts will illustrate options, stereotypes, prejudices, and discriminatory behaviors of those involved. In a sense all of the stories in this book are ways for me to provide a context for understanding why I think the way I do and what I believe I have learned about my prejudices and my ignorance of the human condition in my life's journey.

One example to illustrate the distinction between a situation or experience and its context involves a meeting I had in Indianapolis in 2006.

The Situation/experience: In February 2006 I was attending the national conference for AGHE (Association for Gerontology in Higher Education). I went to dinner alone at the Ram Brewery on the last full day of the conference and wrote some notes at the table. On my way back to the hotel I was strolling on the walkway through the RCA Dome that connected the hotel and the shopping/dining area where I had had dinner. A friend of mine who was the incoming President for GSA (Gerontological Society of America) and I bumped into each other and he asked me to meet him the next morning about an idea he had. We met and he asked me if I could do one of my performances at the GSA national meeting in Dallas the following November. I agreed and he said he would take care of getting me set up for a room and a place on the program.

Those details of my experience fail to tell the story.

The Context. During the 1980s I had given a variety of papers and presentations at both organizations (GSA and AGHE). Although I had become somewhat involved in GSA's Humanities section, I found involvement in AGHE to be much more fulfilling. GSA is the larger organization and it focuses upon research, predominantly in the areas of Biological Sciences and Social Sciences. The Humanities section had lesser status during my tenure with them. AGHE was devoted to helping institutions, predominantly colleges and universities, in sharing ideas and programs that focused upon education and educational services for our aging population. By the 1990s I had become involved in Faculty Development programming at the national conferences and later became an active member on the Executive Committee. I continued to present papers in the 1990s. By 1995 the in-coming President for AGHE asked me to revolutionize the format for the national convention that would be held in Boston in 1996. He was a national figure in Aging in the United States and I was eager to work with him (personally and professionally). I formed a task force with people from around the country and we rethought the format for the conference. Instead of focusing on paper presentations, we introduced a variety of different formats within the conference. First we had a working lunch with assigned topics and a discussion leader at different tables. People could then select what topic interested them and could share ideas and email/phone number information with colleagues from around the country who shared their intellectual interests. We then had round table discussion periods. Each table had a discussion leader who would talk about a particular topic for 30 minutes. After 30 minutes a bell would sound and people could move to another table. This format allowed for discussions and gave people the opportunity of selecting different topics that interested them within one time slot of the conference. We kept paper presentations for students only and started having poster sessions where experts could display their research, programs or ideas on poster boards and conventioneers could move around and talk to as many presenters as they wanted. We expanded symposiums and discussion periods with strict time limits for the panel members so they would not speak too long. The intent for the whole format was to enhance interaction among the attendees and insure that people could share ideas and information while also enhancing the normal opportunities for networking. We believed that creating networks of professionals would be invaluable in furthering the educational programming in aging in America. The changes were ushered in at the meeting in Boston and their success led to my being selected or suckered into being the program chairman for a second year in a row for the next year's meeting in Philadelphia. This is the context for my jumbled feelings of connectedness and disconnectedness that I experienced in 2004 as noted in Chapter 11.

After I finished my terms on the Executive Committee I remained involved in AGHE and decided to provide some alternative programming of my own. One such offering occurred in 1998 when I gave my performance of Marius from _Les Miserables_ as a special program at the AGHE conference in Winston-Salem. Attendees had not seen a dramatic performance used as a teaching tool in a classroom. My performance was comparable to that which I gave in London when I was orienting Canisius students to the city. As with my performance for my classes I had the lyrics to the music available for those who attended. I also provided a précis of the musical for those who may be unfamiliar with the theme and characters. I asked the national leader who had recruited me years earlier to revamp the convention experience to introduce the character. I felt as if I needed someone with a national reputation to give a semblance of respectability for such an unusual offering at a national conference on aging. I was worried about the response from anyone who attended the session and found that I was more nervous than usual. Actors do need nerves and some anxiety before a performance in order to enhance the quality of delivery and believability of the character. The room was surprisingly full and I wondered about the sterility of a conference room for delivering a dramatic presentation.

There was no possibility of using the room to enhance the feeling or emotion of the music or lines. At times during the 45-50 minute performance I wondered whether I would stay for the whole thing if I was an attendee. When I concluded I was taken aback by the warmth of the applause and the affirming faces throughout the room. During the Q&A session people were interested in student response. I shared some of the responses they had given over the years in their letters they were required to write to Marius. The attendees were also interested in how I went about incorporating this activity into a course, and my reaction to the experiences I had had. The man I met in 2006 was at this performance. Between my performance and our chance encounter in 2006 my life had changed dramatically, especially due to Heidi's illness and death. During that period I became inactive with the organizations. My interest in attending national conferences diminished, and I found that I was withdrawing from many professional interactions. Heidi's death re-oriented my priorities, and my ability to interact with other people waned considerably (especially with the strangers and acquaintances that attend conferences). In order to understand the contextual elements for my friend's request and my actual performance the following year, it is important to digress further. As I have indicated in other sections, understanding context is like peeling an onion. There are so many layers. You may know that layers exist, but you may not know what they look like or what is involved in each one of them. So I need to return to Heidi's funeral to start uncovering another layer.

Our friends from the Netherlands flew to Toronto, rented a car, and drove to our home to attend Heidi's funeral. They had planned on visiting us, especially Heidi, in January but Peter's mother became quite ill and she needed their attention. They felt badly that they had not had the opportunity to see Heidi before she died. After the funeral, Tiny and I were chatting in our home about the trips the four of us had had over the years. She offered to have us come to visit them. I mentioned Diane's desire to go to Tuscany. Usually we provide each other with ideas about where we want to go, and the hosts work out the details. Diane and I told them that we were in no shape to plan anything; they would be responsible for taking care of us. My only request was to stop in Heidelberg on our drive to Italy. They were gracious and planned a wonderful tour: stopping in both directions at different cities: attending an opera in the coliseum in Verona; having a day tour of Venice; lunch in Innsbruck; and staying in New Ulm and, of course, Heidelberg. We stayed in a villa in Tuscany for a week. Each day we toured throughout the region. It was wonderful and awful. Our friends made our days filled with wonderful things to see and do. The nights were very difficult. Once we went to our own rooms, the sadness hit us. We would never see Heidi again. Many times I felt as if I was dream walking and watching myself tour, eat and chat with our friends. During our grieving we began to find pennies which Diane dubbed "pennies from heaven," meaning from Heidi. We have had many very contextually significant penny stories since she died. It is not that Heidi literally places the penny in our path; rather the context of finding the penny connects us in a meaningful way with her. (But who knows, maybe she does place some of them in unique places for us!)

Our villa was not glamorous, but it was very functional. We were the only occupants during the week, and it was located a few miles outside of the small village of *Colle de val d'estra*. On one side was a grassy area with an arbor about 20 feet from the building. Each morning I did my Tai Chi in this area. Each evening we would play cards in the area by taking out a small table. We would have our large meal in the early afternoon and snack on bread, cheeses, wine and beer in the evening. Ever since we met in New Orleans in 1970, the four of us have enjoyed playing cards and so we continued that practice in the quietness of the nights of our solitary villa. A few days into our stay I bent over to pick up a wayward card and saw a penny at my feet. It was an American coin. Quite a surprise. We had left all of our American currency at our friends' home in Purmerend since there was no need for any of it on our travels. There had been no other Americans staying with us or even before we had come. In our loneliness (yes it is possible to feel lonely when you are with your spouse and your dear friends) finding this penny was a sign from Heidi. It spoke to our souls and said that she was sharing our adventures.

One way we coped during the evenings was to read. I brought Cervantes' Don Quixote. It seemed fitting enough for some reason. As I worked through the novel, I became inspired to create a new character for performances: Sancho. I would project him as an old arthritic man who had honored his master by learning how to read and write. The performance would focus upon his adventures with Don Quixote and what he had learned from the man. The music would be taken from the musical.

When we returned home, I began writing the character by blending the portrayals in the musical *The Man of La Mancha* (which is based on Don Quioxte) with those written in Cervantes' masterpiece. This whole project was permeated with Heidi's spirit. She was Quixotic in her life and espoused the theme of the novel:

"When life itself seems lunatic, who knows where madness lies? Perhaps to be too practical is madness. To surrender dreams — this may be madness. Too much sanity may be madness — and maddest of all: to see life as it is, and not as it should be!"

This theme became the focus for my performance, and my character, Sancho, echoed these words and what they meant for him. My intent was to articulate the beauty and power of idealism while illustrating the challenges that such a belief would encounter. One of my central points was to talk about the word real or reality. Why are these words restricted to negative or skeptical connotations? Being realistic usually means that one sees the challenges, barriers, or impracticality of an action, belief, or project. Sancho is unwilling to accept this meaning.

My first performance was at our church near the first anniversary of Heidi's death. (This was another significant event in that 18 months after Heidi died that I discussed in Chapter 11.) Diane helped me organize the dinner/theater offering. Friends, neighbors and members of the congregation attended. They had known Heidi and most had attended other performances I had had before. I dedicated my performance that night to Heidi. It was very difficult to prepare for being my new character, and I broke down afterward in the sacristy. During the performance, however, I felt transformed and slipped almost seamlessly into being Sancho. During the middle of the performance, I was sitting while we all listened to one of the songs being sung by the cast of the revival of the musical running on Broadway. There was a soft tap on my shoulder and whether this was real or imaginary was irrelevant. I felt Heidi's presence.

During Heidi's illness Diane had contacted some famous actors and a writer that were important to Heidi. Mr. Rogers wrote a long letter and sent a shirt; Angela Landsbury, Melissa Gilbert, James Earl Jones and Mandy Patinkin sent signed pictures; Madalene L'Engle also wrote a letter. However, it was Brian Stokes Mitchell who became part of our journey. We had taken Heidi to see him in *Ragtime* when it was playing in Toronto. Heidi fell in love immediately (which was sealed as we drove away from the theater and saw him walking his dog after the performance). During her recovery phases she did manage to make a trip to visit Katie in New Jersey. They went to see Brian Stokes Mitchell in *Kiss Me Kate* on Broadway. After Heidi's relapse, she and Diane were watching an interview with him. Heidi turned to Diane and said that she just knew he was genuine. He began a run of *Man of LaMancha* on Broadway and Heidi wanted desperately to attend. It was a perfect combination: Brian Stokes Mitchell in the lead and a musical that represented Heidi's ideal of following dreams rather than succumbing to the negative realities and roadblocks that the world used to crush an idealist's drive to improve life. After her death Diane and I agreed to finish some of Heidi's bucket list. So we got tickets to the musical. Just as she did not let me know that she had written to actors during Heidi's illness, Diane had kept me in the dark about her letter to Brian Stokes Mitchell. She told him about our impending attendance and he wrote back to her. That's when I learned that he would he honored to see us after the show.

Going into the theater seemed to be a sacred calling. Heidi's presence felt real and powerful - she was sitting with us hearing the dialogue and the music. She too was being swept away by the emotions that almost crushed my heart. "Impossible Dream" was overpowering and has remained a sacred song to me. My knees were a bit wobbly as we found our way to the Stage Door. We showed the guard the actor's letter and he said to wait. A few minutes later we were led into a darkened back stage area. Brian Stokes Mitchell's attendant talked to us about the show and said we would be meeting him in his dressing room. As we entered the room, Brian Stokes had a beaming smile and warm welcome - just as Heidi had said he would. As we talked he mentioned that he had dedicated this performance to Heidi and he had put the picture Diane had sent on his mirror. I gave him a copy of the advice Heidi had written for the hospital. Brian Stokes was gracious, friendly, and his smile made the emotions of the evening seem healing rather than painful. We will both remember the hug he gave each one of us when it was time to leave. His attendant walked us out to the door and explained that Brian Stokes really was genuine and authentic. There was no acting in who he was.

Included in understanding the context for these stories is the sabbatical I had in 2006. My primary focus was writing my book *Riding the Subway with Heidi*. As I was working on it I was in Indiana for the AGHE conference that year. As I mentioned, I was withdrawing psychologically from other professionals and that conference was no exception. One night I went to the Ram Brewery alone and carried a clipboard with me. (It was the same one I was given in high school and the same one I still use today.) My concluding chapter's theme claims that a healthy attitude is an essential characteristic for grieving people to possess. Healthy grieving should try to find balance and a renewed purpose or meaning for living. I was stuck writing this chapter because just saying that it's all about attitude is fine and good, but what does it mean? What suggestions could I give to others about bringing a healthy attitude into their lives? I had and have totally rejected the ideas of going through stages, moving on or finding closure as operative in healthy and meaningful grieving. I felt a bit stumped and hoped that somehow Heidi would touch my mind and give me some inspiration on this topic. I began to jot down a few items at the table but felt quite unsatisfied.

The restaurant was part of a complex that was connected to the hotel by a walkway through the RCA dome. As I was walking from the restaurant/stores area, I was on an enclosed walkway over the street below. Suddenly I stopped and lifted my clipboard. I wrote furiously with idea after idea spilling out of my mind. I filled page after page. I'm not sure how long I was standing there and writing. I have no recollection of whether anyone else used that walkway while I was there. The world around me had become a cloudy background - the ideas for my last chapter were flooding my consciousness. It was exhilarating, and my spirit had been rejuvenated. I wasn't going to seek out anyone I knew, but I was not going to avoid talking to anyone either. As I walked through the door and entered the upper level of the domed building, I saw a long table that still had the white tablecloth that had probably been used as part of a display. As I walked by the table, I glanced at it and saw one and only one object on it: a shiny penny. Heidi was telling me that my ideas were acceptable for her book. As I continued on my way I ran into the in-coming president of GSA. We embraced and he said he was glad he ran into me. He wanted to meet with me the next morning.

When we met he recalled the performance I had given years before (my character of Marius). He said that he had admired the way I had helped refashion the format of AGHE's national convention. GSA, as I have mentioned, is research oriented. My friend said that he wanted to change things in a small way. He wanted me to give a performance at the upcoming GSA meeting in Dallas the following fall. I talked to him about my new character of Sancho and gave him some of the background. He had tears as I talked about Heidi and my first performance. He said Sancho would be perfect. The following fall I went to the GSA meeting and found myself feeling completely alienated from the conference. It was a large gathering and my withdrawal from professional contacts had narrowed the number of people I knew or even recognized. How was my performance going to impact anyone at a conference dedicated to research and populated by PhDs and MDs from around the United States and Canada? Since the late 1990s I always tried to have someone introduce my character regardless of whether it was for any of my courses, in churches, or any other venue. For that special program at GSA, I had asked the man who had first asked me to revise the format for AGHE in the 1990s and who had introduced me as Marius years before. He was a renowned author and professor in the field and a prominent figure in this organization. As before I figured having his name in the program might interest people in coming to hear Sancho speak or at least it would sanction the session as respectable or even acceptable.

The day of the performance was a difficult one for me emotionally. Should I share such a personal character and interpretation to a group of professional strangers? The room was packed, which was the first pleasant surprise. I had begun to perform in venues more conducive to dramatic portrayals. At Canisius I no longer performed in classrooms but ended up having my characters tell their stories to my students in a wide variety of venues or stages throughout the campus. However, at this conference Sancho had to use a normal podium, a boom box managed by my friend for the music, and stand on one side of a convention breakout room: not overly conducive to a drama trying to elicit emotional responses to some of the deeply felt experiences of Don Quixote and Sancho Panza. When I finished, I was surprised to get a prolonged ovation. There was a short Q&A session, which proved to be unexpectedly supportive and interested in why and how I brought drama into a course. Afterward the positive feedback took me aback. It was not the response I had expected at this convention. It was even more surprising and gratifying than what I had experienced with my Marius character. My stereotypic image of those attending the conference was of professionals so wrapped up in their research that this type of offering would be thought of as frivolous or nonacademic or just a waste of time. The people were warm and encouraging of what I was doing. That one chance meeting of my colleague and friend had led to this wonderful experience for me in my grieving

Even though this story may be a bit lengthy and include a wide variety of details, it actually does not peel off all the onion layers for explaining the context for my experience and the consequences of that meeting in Indianapolis. It strikes me that stereotyping and our ignorance of others may find many of their roots in only dealing with situations and not trying to unearth the contexts. When we see someone we may make snap judgments without understanding what that person has experienced or is undergoing. We see a stereotype and not an individual. Respect should take us beyond just situations and wake us up to the importance of context. We have all had the experience of coming into a room in the middle of a conversation. It may be comic to say something that seems appropriate but is totally out of context. Quoting from books, newspapers or the bible and taking the words out of context can radically change the intended meaning or story. Context matters. Deeply and importantly so.

CHAPTER 14
FOR FAMILY AND FRIENDS
LIFE'S CHALLENGES AND TRAGEDIES

You should respect each other and refrain from disputes;
you should not, like water and oil, repel each other, but should,
like milk and water, mingle together.

The Buddha

We live in an interconnected world; humans are inherently interdependent. Martin Luther King, Jr., said it so well: "We are caught in an inescapable network of mutuality, tied in a single garment of destiny. Whatever affects one directly affects all indirectly." We may tend to think that when we are alone and reading, doing drugs, listening to music or exercising that we cannot possibly be affecting anyone else. However, we are directly or indirectly doing so. The impacts may be small, but nonetheless they do exist. It is wise to recognize this underlying characteristic of what it means to be a human being. Likewise the importance of respect for others (and for ourself) is a fundamental value in our relationships. I learned this lesson when I was five.

My dad had taken me to a drug store about four blocks from our house. I asked if I could bring my wagon along and he said why not. We were walking because Dad didn't want to waste gas since he only needed to buy some cigarettes. The irony of exercising to get his smokes brings a smile to me now. So we headed for the store, and I left my wagon by the store's door. In those days we didn't even lock our doors of the house or of the car; cats and dogs went without leashes; bikes didn't need locks. It was a time of false security because things were stolen and homes were invaded. We went into the store and I saw a glider that had a rubber band propeller. It was love at first sight. I had a balsa glider without a propeller and it invariably collided with the ground within ten feet of my mighty toss. It just was unacceptable and I knew intuitively that the motorized version would enhance my flights of fancy immeasurably. So I pleaded with my father to buy it for me - only 50 cents as compared to his cigarettes. My dad gave me the usual refrain that he worked hard for the money we needed to run the house. I wasn't going to get that plane. Dad turned back to the store owner, and they continued to talk about whatever was the topic of their conversation before I interrupted. I saw my chance.

They were too busy to notice a little kid slip one of the planes off the rack and stick it under the stuff I had in my wagon. I hadn't planned on stealing anything that day and felt that I was quite lucky to bring the wagon along. (Did that reduce my guilt from 1st to 2nd degree theft?). I slipped back into the store to quiet any suspicion that my absence might cause. I have no recollection of anything my dad and I talked about on our walk either way. We may not have said anything. When we returned home, I waited until I was alone before I unwrapped the plane, slid the wings into the middle and back and then gloriously wound the rubber band into place. I twirled it until it was as taut as it could be and went into the back yard. Five years olds have a tendency to think that the rest of the world is quite irrelevant or may not even exist. When parents show up or call our name, it is an intrusion that can be quite startling. I once read that this type of interruption is as jarring as intruding upon a couple making love (strange phrase if you think about it). That day in my youth may be an anecdotal verification. As I was retrieving the plane from a successful flight, I was jerked into reality by the angry shout of my dad.

"CHARLES RAYMOND!" I sensed impending doom. "Where in the hell did you get that?"

I stuttered an answer that wasn't one at all.

"Did you steal that this morning?" He pointed at the contraband lying on the ground.

I sheepishly had to confess.

"Well, young man, put it back into its package. We're headed back to the store."

Fear gripped me. I picked up my trophy that was no longer a part of my toy arsenal; repackaged as best I could; and walked back to the store with my tail between my legs. I know for sure that nothing was said on this return trip. I kept grousing to myself, "He had a lot of these on his rack. Why would he miss this one?"

At an early age I was already adopting an adult rationalization for doing what I really knew was wrong. When we entered the store we went up to the counter, and my father merely said, "He has something to say".

I didn't know that I did. I had expected that my dad would explain everything and I would be yelled at by the store owner.

Instead I had to muster my courage and quietly squeak out, "Um – Uh – I'm sorry. I shouldn't a, um, taken this."

I handed the plane back to the man. He seemed quite tall, but at five every adult was tall. He looked between my dad and me. His response was quite different from what I had expected.

"Your dad's punishment will be worse than mine. Never do this again. In any store!" He shook my father's hand and patted me on the shoulder.

I have never stolen anything from a store after that. I can't remember my dad's punishment because for the rest of the day my mind was a blank. How could I have committed such a sin and how could I have been so careless as to have flown the plane in our back yard? Sinfulness and carelessness were lumped together in a lesson that has stayed with me all of my life. I do remember part of my dad's sermon that he gave when we got home. "You must respect what I say. I told you that you could not have that plane. Never disobey me. I demand respect. And don't you realize that that storeowner makes a living by selling what is in his store? You stole from him. How could you be so disrespectful?"

I had no answer. Apologizing again wasn't enough. I'm sure I was grounded and maybe even television was taken away for awhile. As I said I don't remember the punishment, but I do remember the lesson. Maybe it is true that we learn everything we need for life in Kindergarten. Respect our parents; respect store owners; and respect the fact that you may think you are alone, but you aren't.

Later that summer we traveled to Kentucky. This was a refuge to restore my sense of value and importance in the world. At that time my favorite cousin was James Holt. He was married to Aunt Myrtle and Uncle Oral's daughter, Myra Ellis (pronounced as one word - Mar/ALIS). He was a large man, with big hands and a bigger smile. Everyone loved him because he was ideal for life in McCracken and Marshall Counties. He was building his own home (almost adjacent to the county line) on a farm that he was working; helped his in-laws and his parents with their farms; had a country charm driven by a sense of humor that was known throughout both counties. I loved going to his farm - a short walk through the fields from Aunt Myrtle and Uncle Oral's. One day our family was visiting James and Myra. As he was showing us their garden he offered me a banana pepper because I loved the sweet variety. This time he made sure it was a hot one.

"It's real good, Char-le-RAY. Take a really big bite and taste its flavor," James said with a sly grin I did not notice at the time. When I went running to the house for water, he laughed and told me that I needed to learn how to tell the difference. It was impossible to keep a grudge against him (even if it included setting fire to your mouth). I remember riding on his shoulder (he could easily lift me onto one shoulder and balance me with one arm). We would stride through the fields that connected his farm to my uncle and aunt's. I can recall feeling free of any snakes that may be on the ground and being taller than anyone I had ever met. It was a joyful experience. I was genuinely shocked when I not only learned about his death ten years later, but even more so about the circumstances surrounding it.

We had had a short visit to Kentucky in the summer of 1962. We were there for a quick visit because we were driving to New Iberia, Louisiana for my brother Paul's wing ceremony. He was becoming a Navy pilot, a boyhood dream come true. We didn't see James that visit, but that did not surprise me because the stay was so short. When I found out that we wouldn't have been able to see him even if we wanted to disturbed me even more. Myra had become involved with a tent religion whose beliefs shocked me: they used snakes to determine who had sinned; swore off the use of any medications or doctors; believed the government was Satan's army; and acted in every way as a cult. James had come down with some form of cancer, but it would/could never be diagnosed and never treated. The leader of the group was a man named Rex, and he and a few others of the group moved into James and Myra's home. My other relatives judged that it was to take over the property and wait for James to die. In fact, my relatives told me that James had lost well over 100 pounds by the time he passed away. He died a few months after our trip to New Iberia.

The story that I heard was that those who were living in his home could not or would not help him do anything, regardless of his condition. Apparently he died in the bathtub because he was too weak to get out of it. To this day I do not know exactly what they believed or what really happened on that farm and to James. My Uncle James and Aunt Lona condemned the behavior and were quite unwilling to forgive Myra's behavior and treatment (non-treatment) of her husband.

Six years after his death, Diane and I were visiting during our honeymoon. We stopped to see my Aunt Myrtle, and Myra was there with her son, Keith. We visited and chatted but nothing was ever said about James. In fact, Myra and I never spoke about it at any time for the rest of her life. James' death was the elephant in the room. It was a taboo topic and forgiveness was an unspoken expectation for me. Of course, I forgave her; but I have never forgotten. That seems reasonable. Respect does not require amnesia. Forgiveness requires an acceptance of the other person, as a person, as an individual. I did not and have not condoned her behavior; but there were two reasons why forgiveness was necessary. She was a family member who was very close to my mother and, thus, forgiveness seemed expected. The second reason was that I really did not know what happened; I only had heard what other family members had said. Ignorance is never really bliss and should never be an excuse for how one treats another human being. I have been amazed at the capacity for forgiveness in humans.

My dad's demand for respect framed my childhood. He expected that this respect be given to those he indicated deserved my respect - family and friends most notably. My religious upbringing demanded that the Ten Commandments be a central code in life. As I reflect on the values in my life, the commandment of honoring one's parents may be the cornerstone for my values that define human interrelationships. Depending on whether you use the book of Exodus or use Deuteronomy, the commandment to honor one's parents is placed 4th or 5th in the list given to Moses by God. Respect, trust and love were commingled in my childhood. I feared I had lost my dad's trust when I stole that glider plane. Parental love is unconditional but it is not immune from breaches of trust.

When I served on a delegation to China, I studied Confucian philosophy and his moral norms. For Confucius, the basis for all human relationships and the centerpiece for a just society was filial piety. The child owes honor and respect to his/her parents; they brought the child into the world and there is no greater debt in one's life. Confucius established a hierarchical society based on filial piety. I have tried to blend the good from religions and philosophies I have studied throughout my life. This blending has given me an amalgam of views and values. The importance of balance and harmony from Eastern thought mixes well with my sense of respect, trust and love. Confucius said that we should not do unto others what we would not want them to do unto us. I prefer Christ's positively stated version of this belief. All of the Abrahamic faiths emphasize the importance of honoring one's parents. The prophet Mohammad emphasized the command to love one's parents and the obligation to show utmost respect, kindness and obedience. My dad's expectation of respect had a profound basis in the great religions and philosophies of the world. Respect is not just for the living. We talk about showing respect when someone dies. I have attended far more funerals than I wish I had to; I've also presided at funerals for fellow church members, as well as family. Some of these experiences have taught me some important lessons.

It was April 1, 1958. My sixth grade class was going through a routine set of lessons. I looked up from my work and saw my brother, Paul, talking to the teacher. My first reaction was, "Oh my god what prank is he trying to play on this teacher?" Paul has always been a jokester and the life of a party. Why he would be trying to do something in my class was a little befuddling. He was living at Niagara University and his semester was far from being over. The teacher called me up, and I sheepishly went to her desk, knowing that every eye in the class was on my back and flittering between my brother and me.

"Get your bike; we'll throw it into the trunk. The car's outside," Paul said without a smile. This uncharacteristically serious command surprised me. As we hurried outside and tumbled into the car, he explained that my paternal grandma, Nana, was dying and we were headed straight to Chicago. I was stunned. Nana and Pops were not as much a part of my life as my maternal relatives. My only real memory of Nana was playing Canasta with her and Pops when I was very young. The car ride was very long because no one really had very much to say. We arrived at my Aunt Babe's (her name was Martha, and she was dad's sister). Her husband was Uncle Pete, and he was always lively and seemed to me to be far too irreverent for my youthful sensibilities. Much of the stay and trip are blurry in my memory but two experiences stand out. We were sitting in Aunt Babe's; she insisted we have something to eat and drink before Dad went to the hospital. Paul would have been allowed to go up but Bill and I were too young to do so. He was five and I was twelve. As we sat and the adults chatted (Paul may have joined in because of his close relationship with our paternal family). Bill and I had nothing to contribute. Paul had been raised by Aunt Babe when my dad left for Alaska after his first wife died. She cared for him until she had to place him into an orphanage when she was expecting her third child. Paul has always remained close with the cousins; I have not. It started with the funeral.

The ceremony was a real blur. I was assigned to ride with one of my cousins. At the time Bill, Peter and Liz were Paul's age - late teens to 20ish. My brother, Bill, was probably with Mom and Dad, while Paul and I went with the others in the car processional from the church to the cemetery. The reception was going to take place back in the church basement, which was only a few houses down the street from Aunt Babe's house. When the cousins, Paul and I got into the two cars, I heard a challenge extended from one sibling to another: "Beat you back to the house!" I was horrified to see the cars speed through the streets to be the first one back to the house. How disrespectful was all I could think. My shock and disgust, however, were intensified a little while later. We sat in tables that had been moved together to form a couple of long rows. I don't remember the meal but do recall that it was in the church's basement and was a buffet style arrangement. I saw drinks being served and noticed that my cousins were going to the bar almost as much as my dad. The next scene for me was when I was walking with Pops back to the house. He had already begun using a cane to assist him. I never knew why he needed the assistance and my unfamiliarity with this side of the family seemed to tie my tongue. There have always been far too many questions left unanswered for me with these kin. When we approached Aunt Babe's house Peter and Bill were wrestling on the ground. I never knew what started the fight, I just saw them wrapped around each other and rolling back and forth. Pops was furious and waved his cane at them: "Can't you show your grandmother any respect?" he screamed. The next thing I knew, he was on the ground. The wrestling brothers had knocked him down with a flailing foot. I was appalled, not realizing then that this spill may have been unintentional. For a very serious 12 year old, it broke the commandment and we had just been to a funeral mass that morning.

This image of Pops on the ground has stuck in my mind my whole life. I don't remember ever talking to either one of my cousins again. I didn't reconnect with my Aunt Babe or cousin, Liz, until over five decades later. For me a time for paying respect was shattered by combative, maybe drunken, teens. Dad's estrangement from his sister began with the dispersal of Nana's effects. My mom was supposed to get Nana's horse collection. I remember hearing Dad fuming about how his sister kept the most expensive horses and only sent the cheap ones to Mom. There had to have been close to 100 horses involved and Mom certainly received a large number of them, some of which were displayed at our home. The estrangement became a complete and final break six years later when Pops died. Dad was convinced that he was ripped off by his sister. Her son-in-law was the lawyer for the estate, and his dad was the probate judge. Dad never talked to his sister again. As I think back, I know I didn't attend Pops' funeral; I'm not sure if Dad went. Thus as I was growing up, I saw the destructive forces that can ripple throughout a family. Wills, money and property can become tremendous wedges that sow seeds of mistrust, disrespect and a breaking of the bond of love that may have existed before. My dad and I never spoke of any of these matters. I have no idea if there were other factors or causal influences that were involved. Maybe this silence and unwillingness or inability to share one's thoughts and one's feelings can become the context wherein trust and respect are lost. Once gone, can loss of a loving bond be far behind?

Now shifting gears to an alternative funeral experience, 51 years after Nana's death, my brother-in-law, Laurie, and I were heading to the D. C. area to attend the military funeral of our friend and my former college roommate, Boo. The contrast between the two funerals could not have been more pronounced. Of course, the contexts intensify the differences. My relationship with Nana and my Chicago relatives was rather superficial, even for a twelve year old. The subsequent experiences and estrangements made the sense of loss of my grandmother rather muted. My friend's funeral had a very deep impact, especially because of our history and relationship. I had talked Boo into joining the drill team, which eventually led to his commissioning and subsequent posting at Fort Myer in Arlington. The post changed its name in 2005 when this post that housed the Army's honor guard for Arlington Cemetery merged with a Marine post. Boo and I were almost inseparable for the two years we attended Canisius together. When I began dating Diane, we did not spend as much time together as before, but we were roommates and remained very close. We shared our hopes, dreams, worries, and joys. We had many risky adventures, some of which I've already shared with you (jumping trains, scaling the dome at the college, working on trick moves for the drill team to name a few). One more may illustrate how we played to each other's juvenile selves.

It was a common practice for us to go to the large city park near the campus at night. We would walk or even Indian wrestle on the fairways of the golf course late at night. One such night we decided to wander over to the zoo. The walls were too tempting and we managed to secret ourselves onto the premises. As we wandered, we saw the mountain exhibit that provided the backdrop for the polar bears. We scaled the rocks and stood on a ledge overlooking the bear area. We were about 10 feet or so above the bears. We decided to call to one of them and caught his or her attention. We never realized how tall nor how far a polar bear can reach. The giant paw came within about a foot of our position. We decided that now was the time to exercise some discretion so we hustled down the other side of the rock formation. We were now looking for an exit. We saw one trench that was separating some animals from visitors. On the other side of the animal exhibit was a fence we could scale to get out. We didn't see any animals; we figured whoever were in the area were asleep in the shelter to the left. We jumped the divide and proceeded to leisurely walk to the fence. This pace proved to be quite inadequate when we first heard, then saw, a herd of llamas running toward us. Instead of waiting to see what would happen if we stayed and tried to talk to them, we bolted for a nearby tree and scurried up to a sturdy branch that put us out of reach of possible harm. We chatted with the residents for a minute and, then, decided it was time to shimmy along the branch to a position just on the other side of the fence. After jumping to safety we decided that would be our only visit to the zoo.

I visited Boo a few times after he graduated. He also visited Diane and me in New Orleans when he was stationed at Fort Benning in Georgia. There were two memorable visits with him and his wife Maryanne when he was stationed at Ft. Myer. One time we were there when another friend was in town with his Ukrainian parents. We all gathered at Boo's house for a meal to be followed by watching the interview of Aleksandr Solzhenitsyn. He was going to reveal the horrors of the Russian gulags, and the Ukrainians had a vested interest in hearing what he had to say. They resented the USSR and especially the Russians. We were stunned at the atrocities Solzhenitsyn described. When he was done talking, the Ukrainian parents exploded. They were incensed at his whitewashing of the gulag experience. It was difficult to understand their anger. Our ears heard how terrible conditions were; how horrible the Russian treatment was of those imprisoned. The Ukrainian ears heard the same words but interpreted them in a very different way. Such is the human condition. On another occasion, I visited Boo without Diane. I was visiting federal officials with whom I was working because of a grant that I was coordinating. Boo was on duty the night I was with them. After he left for his assignment, his wife asked if I wanted to visit the Kennedy gravesite.

I was surprised. "Isn't the cemetery closed after dark?"

"Doesn't matter" she said. "We can jump the wall" (which was only a couple of feet high).

So a few minutes later we were hurrying through the cemetery and heading toward the gravesite. It was a truly marvelous site. D. C. was all aglow. We could look down one of the bridges to the monuments that were spread out before us. Behind us and up the hill the Custis-Lee Mansion itself was lit up. The eternal flame was near our feet. The view was breathtaking. The next day Boo informed me that we were intruders, and he was monitoring our activity. He told his duty Sergeant to ignore this breach of security. Oh well.

Boo was in our wedding and drove Diane and me from the church to the reception. Unbeknownst to me he decided to take a long detour so he could drive us through Forest Lawn Cemetery, which is across the street from the college campus but in the opposite direction from the church to the reception. The cemetery was a popular place for each of us individually, sometimes together, to go to walk, meditate and/or study. He thought it would be meaningful for him to take us through. I was nervous; Diane was furious. The detour made us rather late in arriving at the reception, something neither of us condoned. Diane's folks were, of course, worried. Boo remained unapologetic. As life went on, we became more distant. Boo became an alcoholic and heavy smoker. His young son begged me to change his father but nothing I said or asked made a difference. My daughters became uncomfortable with his overtures at Tara's wedding. His behavior came across as threatening. I never saw or talked to him again until he was dying of lung cancer. His brother and wife asked me to visit; I did. It was a horrible experience. I foolishly brought pictures, hoping that I could divert his attention and return to some connectedness. He was too preoccupied with his pain; he was unresponsive and dismissive. He died just before Thanksgiving 2008. A local funeral in a town about 20 miles south of Buffalo was going to take place on the Saturday after the holiday; the military funeral would not happen for another six months. I went to the cardiologist on the day before Thanksgiving to take a stress test, which I failed. The doctor wanted to put me into the hospital immediately to have an angiogram performed to determine what I needed. I refused, telling the doctor that my family was coming home for Thanksgiving and I had a funeral to attend on Saturday. He relented and put me on medication and a nitroglycerine patch. My procedure was scheduled for the following Monday. I had three stents inserted and was told that I had probably had a minor heart attack sometime before the stress test. But when I got home from the test I only told my family about the testing on Monday and not that the doctor wanted me to be admitted immediately. Obviously I survived, but I have promised Diane I would never be that stupid again.

Laurie drove me to that Saturday funeral and noted how gray I was looking (not a reference to my hair). It was a small and rural, Catholic affair attended mostly by family. The military funeral in April was with full honors. For two years while Boo was stationed at Ft. Myer he served as the officer in charge of the Honor Guard at scores of funerals (most notably Lyndon Johnson's). This unit was also responsible for the guards stationed at the Tomb of the Unknown Soldier. His family and friends gathered in Arlington's military chapel for a service. We then processed on foot for about a mile. In front of us was the caisson carrying his ashes along with the Honor Guard and Band. We walked in relative silence. Memories streamed through my mind. Friendship that is deep and profound carries throughout a person's life. I did not judge his behavior (although maybe I should have); I did not condemn his actions to him; I did respect my daughter's wishes and didn't meet with him until that deathbed visit. Laurie and I were visibly moved when the band played "Amazing Grace" at the gravesite. The repeat of the rifle salute sent a chill through me. What a striking way to signal the end. The contrast between Boo's funeral and my Nana's is striking. Yes context and depth of relationships matter. Sometimes friendships are deeper than family. My Nana was not a blood relative - she and her husband, Pops, had adopted my dad and we visited her only twice that I can remember. I felt respect for her but really had no emotional ties. That is sad in and of itself.

There have been many other funerals which have impacted me significantly. Paying one's respects is an accurate way of talking about the meaning of a funeral. It also relates to wakes or other forms of connecting with family or friends or even acquaintances during the initial grieving process. Of course it's the shared life and experiences that set the context for our grieving. Family and friends are an integral part of our lives. This book has been filled with the impact so many people have had in my life. I have not included all of the wonderful people who have walked across my stage - at work, in churches, at retreats, in the neighborhoods, on delegations or at professional meetings, and all the other venues where relationships begin, flourish and recede. So many people have walked into my life and have enriched who I am. They have taught me so much. I wish to thank each one of them for the love and respect I have experienced.

CHAPTER 15
FOR FAMILY
BEING WRAPPED IN LOVE

In family life, love is the oil that eases friction,
the cement that binds closer together and the
music that brings harmony.

Friedrich Nietzsche

How many times have I been bored with route 71? How many times have I caught this route south of Cleveland and headed toward Cincinnati – sometimes as a final destination, sometimes on my way to Kentucky? Just how many times have I traveled this straight, flat, uninteresting stretch of road? Of course the perennial question has been whether to take the by-passes around Columbus and Cincinnati. I never thought of the Cincy by-pass until the summer our family was headed to my relatives. We became trapped in the travel heading to a Reds' home game. Who doesn't hate losing time while sitting in traffic that is just in your way? The route through Ohio to Louisville goes by the stadium and over the bridge connecting the two states. That experience prompted me to always check the Reds' schedule when traveling through. Columbus was a different story. Once the by-pass was made, I heard my dad's voice: "Always take a by-pass. That's why they're built." So once the by-pass was completed, around Columbus we would go. One summer as we sped our way to Columbus we passed a "vehicle" traveling no more than 45 miles per hour. I call it a vehicle because it was a hybrid bus-carrier-artistically-designed-moving-conglomerate of furniture sticking out in various directions. After we took the long by-pass around the western hemisphere of the city, lo and behold about 10 miles south of Columbus I see this vehicle puttering along as before. Never again did I take that by-pass. This description is a good metaphor to the delays we often take in conversations to avoid or put off discussing something very painful. As it will be with this chapter; the story of focus is the trip to Cincinnati in July 1995 that started with Katie, Diane and I driving there in our red and white van. This van proved to be one of those purchases that was the right one at the right time. It was terrific for pulling our pop up camper to Prince Edward Island twice, to Fort Wilderness in Disney World, to Pennsylvania Dutch country for a week of camping, and to Kentucky a number of times. I loved to pick up my teenage daughters at school in this "bus of embarrassment," as they were wont to view it.

But before I continue with this Cincinnati trip, I must delay my story even further. This drive and subsequent stay has so many layers that I must digress and try to fill in some of the contours that brought our family together in a powerful, family-changing set of experiences. To do these transformative events real justice I would have to write a novel about each of my daughters and the relationships they had and have with one another and with Diane and me. I feel quite ill-equipped to write such things. Besides those stories are for them to tell. Instead I will try to highlight significant moments with which I was involved and which may shed some light upon the dynamics for our family. Certainly all the contextual dynamics of family life were in full force before, during and after the experience.

One arbitrary place to start is December 1988. Tara and I were headed to Marquette University in Wisconsin. There were a wide variety of reasons why I chose to stay at Canisius for 35 years instead of venturing out on some of the offers I had received to go to another college or university.

One of those reasons was because Canisius is part of the Jesuit College and University system - 28 schools of varying sizes, traditions, and reputations. The schools offered an exchange program so children of faculty and administrative staff would not have to pay tuition at a participating institution. I was still Dean in 1988 and each year the Deans of Continuing Studies met for a few days to share ideas and strategies for improving programming and offerings at our schools. These gatherings created friendships from around the country. The dean at Marquette and I had worked together on a mission statement to be adopted by all the Jesuit schools that offered adult, part-time and/or evening or alternative style or off-campus programs. Bob and I enjoyed completing this project together, and found that we had a lot in common. When Tara was a senior in high school and interested in colleges, I was encouraging her (and her sisters later on) to go away from Buffalo to study and live away from us. Diane went to school in Buffalo and stayed home during her college years, while I had gone to the Seminary and then lived in the dorms at Canisius. We agreed that going away would be an important learning and life-lesson experience for all of them. Bob's daughter was going to Marquette, and he said that she would be more than happy for Tara to spend a night on campus with her to get a sense of the university. I could stay with Bob. The night I stayed with him, Marquette was playing a home basketball game, so my evening was very pleasant. On the ride home I learned that this was the first disastrous experience in a series of such events while trying to select a college with my daughters. Tara hated the experience. She did not give me details, but the message was abundantly clear that she never wanted to step foot on the Marquette campus again. As we drove, I flipped back to an unpleasant experience I had had so many years before while I was in high school.

My high school football coach had arranged for the star running back and offensive captain of our team and for me, the defensive captain, to be taken to Columbia for interviews about receiving a scholarship to the school. An alumnus and his wife drove us and dropped us off at a dorm that had accommodations for those of us who were potential football recruits. We went to some classes, which illustrated that college would be significantly different from high school. One of the teachers at our high school told me that if we made it to Times Square that we would meet someone we knew. I thought that was a silly thing to say until lo and behold as Joe and I were walking along, a Duffy grad saw us and said hello. Well I'll be! The whole experience turned 180 degrees when we went to a party for team members and possible recruits. This gathering seemed to be occurring in another galaxy. It was the most uncomfortable experience I had ever had up until then. I didn't fit in; I didn't like anything I saw or heard; I didn't drink or do any of the things I heard were going on. Joe and I did not stay long. As I was tossing and turning that night, I began to realize the truth that America is not homogeneous in any sense of the word. There were worlds, lives, attitudes and behaviors far beyond my limited experiences. Even though I shared a love of football with those I visited, that superficial bond was not enough to overcome my total discomfort. Life continually presents us people and experiences that strain the bonds of acceptance, tolerance and respect. Yet I still believe that a person does not have to condone another person's life or attitude in order to respect the other person's humanity.

My values and attitudes toward life have evolved and shifted so much over the years. The one constant for me has been respect. As Tara and I drove through Chicago on the way home from Marquette, I wondered whether her experience was as upsetting to her as mine at Columbia was for me. I often wonder about sharing experiences. We process what we hear, taste, feel, smell and see through our own filters. How much does this filtering change what other people are trying to convey? I wonder about sharing memories, especially when people don't agree on details. How do we judge these differences? Most of all I wonder about sharing meaning. Grieving parents can share the meaning of a child's death, but can the listeners really understand what that death means? I love the conversation between Humpty Dumpty and Alice in "Through the Looking Glass". One of the issues they raised can be boiled down to: do people mean what they say or do they say what they mean? Basically, can we really know what meaning other people give to any experience? I am digressing to provide context and an appreciation for all that went into those few days and to try and share what all of that meant to me.

Tara, Kris and Katie all eventually enrolled in Jesuit schools: Tara at John Carroll University in Cleveland, Kris at Xavier University in Cincinnati, and Katie at Scranton University in Scranton, Pennsylvania. Heidi, of course, took another path. By the time Heidi was a senior in high school, she had dedicated her life and soul to the theater. She once told me that she would accept roles in television or the movies if she was forced to do so, but her passion was the stage. She was going to pursue her dream for the theater and the Jesuit system did not come close to meeting her needs. Before sharing the glitches in Heidi's collegiate auditioning, I'll turn to Kris' weekend nightmare, which followed Tara's unfortunate experience at Marquette.

Mount Union is not a Jesuit college, but it was a part of the exchange system. Usually I took the girls on the trips for scouting out schools and Diane stayed home. I thought I was being very clever by talking Diane into going with Kris and me. Kris would stay at the college overnight as part of their recruitment efforts. I had found a *Gone With the Wind* themed Bed-and-Breakfast about 45 minutes away from the campus. Planning a secret get-a-way and having Kris visit a campus was a real twofer. The girls helped me pack for Diane, and I secreted her clothes into the trunk of the car the day before we left. I hurriedly packed clothes for me. It was only for one night but included welcome wine and fruit, a beautiful room, an evening dinner served for all guests at a designated time, a luscious breakfast, and a tour of the estate the following morning. My attempts at a romantic getaway didn't quite materialize the way I planned. We had some delays in getting Kris to her visit and she was quiet and somewhat pale on the trip. We arrived at the B&B later than we should have. Instead of leisurely enjoying the fruit and wine while also having some time together before dinner, we had to hurriedly dress and walk through a waiting dining room filled with other guests not so patiently awaiting our entrance (no service would begin without everyone in attendance). That really wasn't the problem. All I had to tip the bellman were some quarters that I had in my pocket. Ugh. Then we started to get ready. Proudly I gave Diane the garment bag filled with what the girls knew she would be happy. Oops.

"Where's my slip"?

"Hmm. Uh. Isn't it there?"

"Oh my goodness. I found a slip lying on the driveway and couldn't figure out how it got there." Diane wasn't really amused at this revelation.

I looked at the garment bag and saw the hole that caused this mishap. As I was getting dressed, Diane realized that I hadn't run my combinations by our daughters. I don't remember the details, only the reality that tie, coat, trousers and shoes were not in harmony (apparently not very close either). Of course our table was in the back corner of the dining room, which required us to walk by everyone who was waiting for these tardy folks. Diane was far more self-conscious than I was; I guess her clinging dress didn't help. Wearing non-matching clothes has never bothered me. The get-away didn't start out well. The next morning it was raining and dreary so instead of a tour we were receiving a talk with a video about the estate. The proprietor came to us and asked us to step outside. We had a call from Mount Union because Kris was very sick. We hurried to get our poor daughter who had had an awful experience. When we got her home she was diagnosed with Strep Throat. She didn't want to spoil my surprise so she didn't tell us how sick she felt. The following year I held my breath when Katie and I went to visit Scranton but all went well. However, the cloud returned with Heidi in 1999. Heidi wanted to go directly to Broadway but agreed to go to college first (for a while at least). She only wanted to go to schools that offered Bachelors in Fine Arts degrees with recognized theater programs. So we planned one trip that would include auditioning at C.W. Post at Long Island University, visit Muhlenberg's program, then on to Carnegie Mellon for another audition. We left on our jaunt on Feb. 11 with a drive to New Jersey to spend a night with Katie. This trip came on the heels of a great deal of travel for me. From Jan. 20-31 I was participating in the University of North London program that I've discussed before. Diane and I met our friends from the Netherlands and stayed with them from Jan. 31 - Feb. 8. So just a few days later, I was on the road with my youngest who was only mildly interested in C. W. Post; had no desire to bother with Muhlenberg; and had her heart set on Carnegie Mellon. We enjoyed our evening with Katie and navigated ourselves across NYC and out onto Long Island. I found the driving a bit stressful and Heidi's attitude wasn't overly helpful. She graced the campus with her presence and seemed assured she would be given a slot in their program. In fact, that is where she attended school for her freshman year before her diagnosis. Onward we went to Muhlenberg which was done solely to placate a close friend of mine and V. P. at Canisius who was an alum. We spent a night in Mars, PA before heading to Carnegie Mellon. Heidi had been polite the day before at Muhlenberg but it was very clear that she had rejected the whole idea long before we went to visit. As we headed west the car had a major engine mishap. I was able to navigate it to a small town off the nearest exit from the highway. There was no way the garage in the small town we were forced to stop could fix the engine in time for us to make her audition. Many calls and pleas led to a rescheduling. Unfortunately when she went on her delayed audition she now was sick and knew she would never get accepted. She wasn't. Do fate and destiny really play transformative roles in our lives?

Despite these misadventures our three oldest daughters said they were going to the college that was her first choice. Deep down I'm not sure if that was completely true or if they convinced themselves that these were the best choices given the limitations I had placed upon them: go away to school and do so at a tuition exchange institution. I do know Katie had wanted to go to the nursing school at the University at Buffalo, but I felt that she and her sisters really needed to find their own paths away from us. Now that they live anywhere from 75 miles to 950 miles away I rue my insistence that they go away to school. Tara, (Cleveland), Kris, (Cincinnati), and Katie (Scranton) were never demanding about my driving them to or from their campuses. I wanted to do all I could to make their collegiate experiences wonderful and the one thing I could do was drive and be with them. In addition to the initial campus visits and helping the girls to move into their rooms, we attended most parents' weekends, or orientations and attended some other special events. I often picked them up for breaks throughout the year and brought them home at the end of the school year. The travel routes became routine fixtures of my life for years. The trips to Cleveland and Cincy were very familiar because of my travels to Kentucky. The trip to Scranton always went through Binghamton, NY a regular route for visiting Katie when she lived in Philadelphia and in N. J. Katie and I often smile at our belief that road construction in Binghamton is an annual part of the city's budget ever since 1991.

The collegiate experiences for each of the girls were incredibly different, including the day we took them to campus to move in for the first time. We packed up the red and white van with Tara's things and drove to campus. Diane and I helped her move into her room which was not as expected. There was an over enrollment that year and Tara was sharing a room with two other girls instead of one. The school had crammed a bunk bed in addition to the regular bed to accommodate the extra girl. My recollection was that Tara arrived third and was relegated to the top bunk. I thought back to my senior year in college when I petitioned to have a bunk bed in our room so we had more floor space. My roommate, Boo, was 2 years younger than me and I pulled rank and took the top bunk. I had no desire to be in the claustrophobic bottom bed. I know Tara didn't have the same positive vibes about her sleeping arrangement as I had had. My recollection was that her bed was overly tall and rather close to the ceiling. Falling out of that bed was not a great experience for her. As we left her to her new life I sensed some apprehension. Was she concerned about the uncertainty she was facing and the discomfort in the room or was I projecting my own feelings onto her? Aren't all experiences a combination? Could there ever be an experience that was totally objectively judged or understood?

Taking Kris to Xavier was a whole different event. Diane didn't go; instead Katie and I moved Kris into her new world. Xavier did things a little differently that year because they folded an orientation into initially moving on campus. Tara's orientation had taken place a month before her move. Katie and I got Kris settled into her room and the three of us proceeded to the orientation desk that was set up outside. I believe that is the last time Katie and I saw Kris. Off she ran to embrace her new life. We shrugged and I asked if she wanted to get away and go explore downtown Cincinnati. We grabbed a quick meal that was provided for the orientation and saw Kris' blond mane with other new friends. Kris has always been a magnet for people and friends accumulate almost effortlessly. I say this because that is how it looks from the outside. I know Kris would not see her life in such a way. As Katie and I left, probably with a quick good-by to Kris, we drove into the downtown area and saw that the Reds were playing. "Do you want to go?" "Sure" was her response. We ran into a scalper that I was going to ignore. When he said the tickets were only $6 I paid attention. I was even more surprised that it was $6 total for both seats. Neither Katie nor I had any interest in the game so cheap seats were very appealing. Our indifference led to us leaving early. But I thoroughly enjoyed the warm summer evening with her as we chatted our way through a game that was meaningless for both of us. It reminded me a bit of a game I attended at Camden Yards in Baltimore years earlier. I was with the Executive Committee for AGHE (the aging organization). Our hostess for the three days decided to take us on three outings: one was a tour of Annapolis; the second was a tour of the National Aquarium to see the venue for the national conference's cocktail reception; and the third was going to an Orioles game. I enjoy baseball, having played, coached and umpired throughout my lifetime. I am not an avid fan, but do check the Cub's and White Sox' (my apologies to those living in Chicago who believe such loyalty is tantamount to insanity) box scores every day and follow all the scores to keep up on the game. The playoffs and World Series are always of interest to me; but the year the Cubs FINALLY won was fantastic. I even won a bet from a long-time and cherished friend who is a devoted Indians fan. That level of interest was not present either in Baltimore or in Cincinnati. What was of interest were the people - the committee with whom I had developed some warm collegial friendships and, most of all, spending the evening with Katie.

Katie had been my traveling companion on a number of adventures related to her sisters. After the Cincinnati trip, we had quite a time of it when we tried to pick Tara up from John Carroll for her winter break one December. The trip was going quickly and without incident until we hit Ohio. For about an hour there had been some light snow and heavier snows were predicted over night. Katie and I left around 11 AM for the 3 hour trip. I figured we could quickly get Tara and her three friends into the van and head back early enough to avoid the snow and rush hour traffic in the area around the campus.. Again man plans and God laughs! We were starting to head down a rather long down-hill part of route 90 in Ohio. Ahead of us were hundreds of cars that were stopped. Some were off the road; some had collided; none at the bottom were moving; those of us heading to this mess were slipping and sliding. I could see that I had to apply the brakes with quick taps and glide the van just off the highway toward the median. We safely slid to a stop and I saw a huge tractor trailer headed in our direction. My nerves eased as he ended up adjacent rather than into us. Traffic slowly began to respond and after a time we continued our much slower trip to the campus. Instead of arriving around 2:00 we were piling the four collegians into the van around 4:00. Katie remained in the shot-gun seat and we tried to navigate our way home. The first hour didn't quite get us to the highway entrance that is normally a 10 minute ride. The snow and traffic were becoming much more hazardous and the enveloping darkness only added to our moods of worry. Later I heard that our passengers were on the verge of being terrified at times. For the next six hours we struggled to stay on Route 90 (highway in Ohio and Pennsylvania, Thruway in New York). Sometimes we had the tail lights of a semi ahead of us to provide me with some sense of where the road surface really was. The Defrost and windshield wipers were on full force, yet the snow and ice continued to accumulate on the windshield. I had brought a shovel and broom as a precaution (a normal addition for any winter driving when snow is predicted). On numerous occasions Katie had to open her window and reach around to try and clear the windshield. In fact, a couple of times I had to do so while trying to keep the van in motion. The snow was treacherous. The snow fall was heavy, dense and blowing. This was one of the worst drives I have ever had in the snow. That is quite a claim for someone who has spent over 70 years in Western New York. By the time we reached the New York Thruway, the storm had diminished enough for us to safely complete our trip home at normal speeds. I had given thought of trying to find a motel along the way, but doing so was not in my nature at that time. Plowing ahead and avoiding the expense were real factors in my thinking. As long as I felt I was not endangering anyone's life, especially two of my daughters, I felt the fear and concerns of the trip were quite manageable. We dropped off Tara's friends and made it home around midnight. Poor Diane was left to worry. There were no cell phones in those days. I think we gave a quick call before leaving John Carroll to alert her that we would be late. The usual 6 - 6 1/2 hour trip had taken about 13 hours (which included long portions of relatively normal driving conditions). The time was really not the real indicator of the nature of this adventure. We can talk about it now as an adventure, during the experience it was in a rather different category.

My daughters and I have spent a lot of time traveling together. Many of the trips have dotted the stories throughout this book. Travel has always been important to me. When I was in the Seminary I began to imagine that the world outside of that farm was vast and diverse. I have wanted to see and discover as much of it as I can. The Germans call it *Wunderlust*. Diane and I moved into our home in 1973, Tara was 2 and Kris was newborn. Over the years we have remodeled and remade our home. In 2003 we burned our $149/month mortgage payment. By staying in this one home we accomplished a number of goals: providing a stable home and environment for our girls; having a home where our grandchildren can share the same space their mothers had when they were growing up; remaining close to our parents (Diane's 7 miles away, mine 14 miles) for the remainder of each one of their lives; creating a care center for Heidi during her struggle with leukemia and a quiet, familiar place for her to pass from us; and finally, by staying in the same home we could afford to travel. One of the ways I tried to expand my daughters' view of people and the world was to have them have a diverse set of growing experiences. Travel gave us time to be together as a family or as parts of the family. Before they went to college, we travelled as a family at least once a year. The college years brought a great deal of travel to and from campuses and as you have seen with varying combinations of daughters. A couple of other examples illustrate the diverse range of these trips.

In September 1983, Tara (age: 12) and I went to Herndon, Virginia. A long-time friend of mine (the Indians fan who lost the World Series bet) asked me to be godfather for his daughter. Not only did we attend the ceremony, but we also headed further east to visit my Uncle Elmer and Aunt Marie who had moved from western Kentucky to Delaware in the 1950s. I entertained Tara with my sense of time and direction. Usually I am fastidious about looking at and using maps. This time I just headed on rural routes that were going to the ocean. When we hit Delaware near Dover, I called for specific directions. We hunted for punch bugs and Tara kept the tally in a small note pad. Periodically she would ask the time and I would blurt out a number. It was usually very close. I have never worn a watch, refusing to do so since I destroyed my Mickey Mouse watch when I was five.

On another trip, Kris and I went to Kentucky in July 1989 to attend my Aunt Myrtle's funeral. The following summer Kris, Katie, Heidi and I stopped at a horse farm in Georgetown, Kentucky before spending a few days with my relatives. In August 1993 the same foursome went to Washington, D. C. to tour and meet Diane who was attending a Lutheran women's conference in the capitol. Katie became my traveling companion when we drove Kris to Rehoboth Beach in the summer of 1992. Kris had completed her first year at Xavier and persuaded Diane and me (actually me because Diane had legitimate reservations) about going to Rehoboth and working as a waitress for the tourists. She and a girlfriend had planned the excursion and assured us that they would be staying in a house with other girls and she would make more money this way than staying home. As Katie and I saw with Kris' first day at Xavier, she wanted to be on her own. She was ready to be away from us. I understood this deep need in her. Tara was the stellar student in both high school and college. Kris had had to live in Tara's shadow, which was exacerbated in middle and high school with oblivious teachers who had the temerity to compare her with her older sister. Kris was vivacious, out-going and eager to experience life. She clearly forged a different path in high school. She was prone to be a part of a popular group of kids. We had to struggle to keep her on track academically. The distance among Kris and her sisters was noticeable. We tried to keep evening meals together a part of our lives and maintained holiday traditions. The relationships during those years were, to put it mildly, a bit bumpy. My goal was to remain supportive and available for anything each of them may have needed. People often use the phrase "mistakes were made." Doesn't that statement presume a set of norms to judge what happened? For the older daughters' high school years, I was no longer clear about what the norms were supposed to be. Interpersonal relationships involve a whole set of beliefs, values and norms that often go quite unnoticed or maybe even misunderstood.

At the time, then, I didn't want to be a roadblock to Kris as she struggled to learn about people and life. In fact, in March, 1992 during her Freshman year of college, Kris took a trip that will become central to the primary story of this part of the book. She was home for the spring break and said that a friend of hers suggested that they travel to Ann Arbor to visit some mutual friends attending the University of Michigan. Kris asked if she could go and borrow one of our cars. Diane was very reluctant. My daughters always knew that I was the easy trap for their plans. Diane and I talked about the venture, and I agreed with the proviso that she had to keep in touch with us so we knew where she was. The plan was for the two girls to drive to Ann Arbor on March 9th and return home on March 10th. I believe it was the night of the 9th that Kris called and said there was a change of plans. Her friend wasn't going back home but instead was going onto someplace in Ohio with other mutual friends. The weather forecast for the 10th was wintry. Was there any chance I could fly to Detroit? She would pick me up at the airport so I could drive home with her. That seemed like a reasonable request; the only glitch was my back. Since the 1980s I have suffered from back pain. Daily *Tai Chi* was and has been one of the strategies I've used to control the problem. Chiropractic adjustment and therapeutic massage have also helped. In 2013 I had the first of two surgeries to provide relief. Lower back and sciatica pain are still a part of my daily experience. The day Kris called was a bad day for my back. The flight to Detroit did not help the condition. Kris saw me hobbling to her. She apologized often, and I read her pale and worried look to be for my back. Three years later this trip would take on a completely different meaning than what I thought it meant. Our trip home through Canada was snowy and a bit slippery but paled in significance to the ordeal with Tara and Katie. I asked her about her stay and kept asking how she was doing. She deflected far more deftly than I ever knew. More of this later. I need to provide some more context first.

Katie was our practical daughter who didn't delay in getting at tasks. She was and still is very organized. She appears so calm and has the qualities to be the perfect nurse (which I believe she is). She has worked at the University of Pennsylvania Hospital and Sloan Kettering before and during Heidi's illness. When she had children, she stayed home for awhile but has been working part time as an oncology nurse at a treatment center not far from her home in Ho-Ho-Kus, New Jersey. When we took her to move into her dorm at Scranton in August, 1992 we knew she was prepared and ready. Scranton was the only campus she visited once she realized that the University of Buffalo was not a realistic option. Our visit the previous February seemed to satisfy whatever criteria she had. Diane came to this departure as she had for Tara. We did not expect what happened.

We had difficulty finding parking close enough to make the hauling of Katie's stuff somewhat reasonable. When we did find a spot and got out of the van, we were greeted with shouts from what I would loosely call males from across the street. They were indicating they were looking forward to meeting the "new meat" on campus. That was not reassuring for parents, especially a somewhat protective father. I always tried to appear calm and patient, but my family knows better. In this case I did reign in my administrative hat and father role and just helped Katie move into her room, rather than cross the street to confront those whom I had deemed Cro-Magnons. (No, I have not completely eliminated my stereotyping of people and their behaviors.) Katie and her first roommate did not last long together. Apparently they mutually decided to part company: Katie because she had nothing in common with the girl and found a soul mate with whom she spent the rest of her years at Scranton moving from dorm rooms to apartments. They remain close friends today. Katie's first roommate seemed to just want her privacy, having been shuffled from boarding school to boarding school throughout her life. After getting Katie settled and trying to make the round trip back home (circa 4 1/2 hours each way) at a reasonable time, we said that it was time to go. Katie looked sad and walked out to the Quad area with us. As we gave her our good-by hugs, she broke down in sobs, pleading loudly

"Please don't leave me here all alone!"

Diane and I were stunned; this was not the reaction we were expecting from our calm, undramatic daughter. The punch to the solar plexus was real. What had we done? Both of us gave her lame, reassuring comments and proceeded to leave her alone to face a new world all by herself. The unexpectedness of her plea crystallized the reality of the parent/child relationship. I have always valued the search for one's purpose and meaning in life. It is never an easy quest; in fact, it never really ever ends until death ... even then? We were doing what we believed was necessary and right; it didn't make it easy. Throughout my stories there are underlying lessons I've learned and truths I believe I have uncovered for myself and maybe for others. This moment was like so many that we all experience: sadness, growth, a hopeful assurance in doing what is right, and casting our children to the world without our complete protection and presence. It is a difficult lesson for a father and his daughters - maybe for all parents.

Katie's uncharacteristic distress at saying goodbye did not last long; she quickly adapted to dorm and college life. Kris was beginning her sophomore year at Xavier, and as the year progressed, even I began to sense that Kris' eating habits were not healthy. I kept dismissing the issue in a pattern of denial that I would learn to regret. Diane was clearly more attuned and perceptive than I. Tara graduated at the end of that year, and moved back to Buffalo. Kris began her junior year at Xavier a few months after Tara's graduation. By this time, she had a boy friend who lived in a suburban area of Cincinnati. We became friends with him and his family. In fact Diane, Heidi and I stayed with his parents a couple of times during our trips to Kentucky. The stops were pleasant and the company was truly enjoyable. The father and I are still friends and connect usually via email or Facebook (the older generations' attempt at being modern). Before her junior year Kris was now noticeably thin and overly preoccupied with food. That summer she and I did go to Cincinnati for a Jimmy Buffet party that her boy friend's parents held each year. I'm not a "parrothead" but enjoyed observing the insanity of middle-aged fans.

Kris did not return to Xavier for her senior year. She was far too compromised and we began acknowledging that she was anorexic and needed help. She grudgingly began to comply by going to counselors, psychiatrists, psychologists and nutritional therapists. We even had a family counseling session to start her work with one of the psychologists. Trust began to erode, certainly for us. We had learned how adept she had become at lying to us and how skilled she was in trying to deceive the counselors and therapists. For example, she placed some spare washers I kept in the basement in her socks to add weight. She enrolled at Canisius and eventually completed both a bachelor degree in psychology and years later a master degree in student personnel administration. She heavily relied on Heidi to be her friend and confidante. Her other sisters were loving but somewhat distant - Katie was at Scranton and Tara was going for her masters and working at Canisius. The high school years had created a pattern among them that placed them in loving and supportive ways, but not necessarily on trusting terms. Diane and I became totally alarmed. My response was a foreboding sense of helplessness. What had I done wrong? Why can't I help my little girl? I had been able to connect and relate to her all through her life, but now there seemed to be an invisible barrier that left me sad and impotent. In our desperation we found a month-long immersion therapy program in, of all places, Cincinnati. Kris agreed to attend. Before Diane and I drove her to the program, her boy friend and his parents came to visit us. Again I must digress.

When Heidi was still in elementary school she heard about a community theater company that was going to perform *Anne of Green Gables*. She saw this as a perfect opportunity for her to expand beyond what she would experience in her own school system. Over the years she was in the Show Choir in high school and performed in all of the school's musicals. She was the lead in the 8th grade play and was a part of any singing performance at the school. For three years during middle school and her freshman year she performed at a summer theater program at a high school in the city of Buffalo. She was an intern at Shakespeare in the Park after she graduated from high school. Her desire to audition for this community theater group certainly began a pattern that displayed her passion for the stage. During the community theater performance I noted to Diane that I could act as well as any of the males in the production. Thus began a period of time when Heidi, Diane, Kris and I performed in various productions of this company. I was in most of the plays after Heidi's debut in *Anne* (unfortunately for Heidi it was not the lead that time around). One of the strategies I employed during Kris' struggles was to encourage her to try out for a play. During the spring semester of her sophomore year at Xavier, Kris was one of the nuns in the school's performance of *Nunsense*. Heidi went with us when we attended that performance. Kris was so thin but I could hear her singing talent come through. I was becoming hopeful that by engaging in a school activity, Kris was breaking out of the cloud that had seemed to surround her.

I have always felt that theater or any social activity is essential for a person's well-being. Thus, Kris, Heidi and I were characters in *Murder at the Vicarage*. I was the Vicar while Kris ended up being cast as the murder victim. One of the most memorable moments during our performances was the night Diane's Aunt Charlotte attended. She was, well, Aunt Charlotte. Always well dressed. She also could get away with wearing loud colors and large earrings and accessories. During the murder scene, Kris' character is listening to other people in the room when her tea is spiked with poison.

As Kris brought the cup to her lips Aunt Charlotte screamed from the front row "Don't drink it Kris!" Not exactly the audience reaction you need in a murder drama. Kris' boyfriend and parents visited us so they could see the performance and get one of my tour options for Niagara Falls. I have a number of ways of showing off the natural wonder in our area. Almost all of the options include a drive past the Love Canal and regaling the visitors with tales I have about the area in which I grew up. By the time of their visit I believe that Kris was in a very critical stage of her anorexia. Their visit and her participation in the play were ways to try and return a sense of purpose and self-worth to her. A month after their visit, we drove Kris to the immersion program in Cincinnati. We left her with waves of uncertainty and foreboding. We knew she needed professionals, not us to restore her to health.

There are a couple more details to share before we return to Katie, Diane and me driving to Cincinnati in July, 1995. Heidi was beginning her first year at the summer theater program in Buffalo. She auditioned and received the lead role in *Meet Me in St. Louis*. The dress rehearsal was July 28th and the performances were July 29 and 30. Heidi immersed herself into the program with all of the passion a 13 year old could muster. She loved costuming, making the sets, rehearsing and blocking; she loved everything. During that summer Katie was working and preparing for her senior year while Tara was applying for high school teaching positions in English. She had an interview in a school district in eastern New York State. While she was away at the interview, she received a call from the principal of Mayville High School. Mayville is a beautiful small town situated on the northern part of Chautauqua Lake. It is also the town which boasts the famous Chautauqua Institution. When my daughters started going to college (maybe even during high school), I didn't make any plans for them without asking them first. On this occasion I made an exception and accepted the offer for Tara. He said great and he would be in touch regarding a time for the interview. When Tara got home, she thanked me but didn't seem to think very much of teaching in Mayville. Life has a way of creating confluences of events. July 26 through August 1st was such a confluence.

We received word a week earlier that the family was REQUIRED - all of us - to participate in Kris' program. We had to be there for 2 1/2 days, starting on the evening of July 26 and lasting all day on July 27 and 28. Heidi was incensed when she heard the news. She could NOT miss practices and the dress rehearsal. The director was noted for his strictness and Heidi's adamant response was borne both of her not wanting to miss what she loved doing and not wanting to approach the director who intimated her. I also believe she may have had some resentment of Kris intruding upon her dream. Nevertheless Diane, Heidi and I met the director one day after practice to explain the situation. Heidi was beside herself the first time we mentioned such a meeting. Her stress from the first word about the meeting until it actually occurred was palpable. He could not have been more supportive, flexible and understanding. We agreed that Heidi could attend practice on the 26th and would fly home on the 28th to be available for dress rehearsal. Tara's interview with Mayville was set for July 26 in the morning. As fate would have it, one of the interviewers is now her husband! That's another story for her to tell.

And now we're done with the digressions and can finally return to the story that began this chapter. July 26 Katie, Diane and I hopped into the van and headed for Cincinnati in order to arrive for the evening registration and to spend some time with Kris. While we were driving on the New York thruway heading west, we knew that Tara was driving east to go back home from her morning interview. She was going to accompany Heidi that evening on a flight to Cincinnati. That first evening remains rather fuzzy for me. I know we met some of the professionals in the program (two of whom we met when we dropped Kris off a couple of weeks earlier). I went to the airport to pick up Tara and Heidi. I think Tara told Diane that night there was a cute teacher with beautiful eyes who had interviewed her. That interview for Tara changed her life. She is still teaching in Mayville and her husband is now the Superintendent at Bemus Point a nearby school district.

So we were all gathered in an unfamiliar place and each of us with our own issues, concerns, and preoccupations. As a teacher I always started each semester by explaining my expectations for the students and going over the syllabus in some detail. I also had an open discussion to learn the students' names and I asked them to share what they expected from the course. As we gathered that night we had such diverse expectations - some of which we may have been aware, some which may have been very subconscious. There were a number of other families attending the sessions and we listened to their stories, just as they listened to Kris. The exercises and sharing sessions in the morning remain vague to me. I just remember the general sense of sharing backgrounds and becoming familiar with one another. The afternoon was transformational. Each girl in the program had to stand up in front of her family and address them by disclosing some terrible truths, feelings, hurts, etc. The rest of the gathering would sit in supportive silence. The intensity of emotions was quite overpowering at times. For example, my recollection for one of the girls was her confronting her father with a highly charged plea for him to admit to his sexual advances to her. None of the previous stories had the impact on us as the moment Kris began. The raw pain and shame she had been carrying was shocking to us. How could my little girl have had to bear such an awful experience in the loneliness of her own soul? Didn't she realize that we always have and always will love her unconditionally? Anorexia is not really about eating. It is about control and finding a way to be in charge of one's life when something has taken away one's self-worth, meaning in life, or so many other tragic feelings of inadequacy or hopelessness. One of the things we learned over those two days was that we were a perfect family to contribute to Kris' anorexia. We were all peace-makers and Kris needed more confrontation and challenges in high school. She needed more from us after her experience in Detroit. Our kindness and attempts at understanding actually seemed to have a counter effect for her. Her shame was exacerbated by them. That is as far as I'm going to go in sharing some analysis of the situation. The events and our response are the real story.

Kris had to stand up and tell us that she had lied about going to Detroit. She went alone. She lied because she knew not even I would have allowed her to take that trip by herself. She had been carrying the burden of that lie from the very time that I arrived at the airport. She perpetuated the lie whenever the topic arose. That lie was not her real burden; it only exacerbated the root cause for her need to turn to anorexia to regain some control in her life. While she was going to the university to be with her friends she stopped for gas. It was a self-serve station and she went to the outdoor pay station. The man opened the door, used a knife to force Kris into the station and raped her. That was her secret. That was the tragedy she had borne alone for the past few years. That was her shame. That was the root of her loneliness. That was the desperation she felt in needing to reconnect with her loved ones.

We were stunned into a moment of silence which erupted into hugs, tears, and words of solace. Of course there was no reason for her to blame herself for the awful abuse she had experienced. The lies were forgotten. I felt that Kris, the real Kris, was now ready to come back to us. Living with us for the previous couple of years were painful. Her obsession with food and its preparation was sad, sometimes irritating. She was distant, even in those times when we were having serious conversations. I have often steered conversations at home (during dinner, when traveling, or when just relaxing) to serious, deep discussions. The girls were well versed in me asking; "Tell me about your hopes and aspirations!" or "what were the best and worst experiences on the trip and why", etc. I have always reveled in asking other, more difficult questions or posing ethical dilemmas. After the rape and until this program, Kris was not really engaging in those conversations. She had always been more eager to do so in the past. In fact, since she has become a mother she may have replaced me as the instigator for such discussions at family gatherings. During those strained years, words may have been coming from her mouth, but they lacked her usual depth and intentionality. I felt that my little girl had been missing. Now I knew why. It is amazing how words and emotions can so physically drain a person. I believe we were all completely spent that evening. The next morning we returned to try and create a positive sense of how to move forward and restore the love, respect and trust that were so necessary for all of us. Kris now realized that she was loved and wasn't an outcast. Her feelings were her projections onto the history of our family and the different paths we all had been walking as the older girls graduated from high school and began to etch out their own way in the world.

That last day of the program was July 28. We took Heidi to the airport so she would be home in time for her dress rehearsal. Diane's folks picked her up and took care of her that night. After saying tearful good-byes to Kris, Tara, Katie, Diane and I headed back home. It was late in the day, but we decided that we needed to drive home, regardless of the hour, so we could attend Heidi's performances starting the next day. As we were heading from Cincinnati to Columbus and while going about 75 MPH, the van lurched and started swerving toward the medium. We had a flat tire. I was able to avoid any traffic and got the van pulled over to the right shoulder and safely off the highway. The spare tire was underneath the van and not easily accessible. Since it was getting dark and we were far from any civilization, I knew I had to try and fix it myself. As I assessed the damage I saw that the radial tire had wrapped itself around the wheel base. This was going to be very difficult. As I was under the van I saw headlights stop about 20 yards behind us. Three bearded men got out of their pickup and started toward us with a tire iron. One of the men stopped to relieve himself along the highway. I told the girls to get back into the van and prepared myself for the worst. I have never been in a fist fight in my life. Boxing in the backyard at age 9 was not the preparation I needed to protect my family. We had just left a completely emotionally draining experience where I left feeling so helpless in the face of my daughter's horrific experience. As a father when my daughters were growing up, I felt that the two worst tragedies a dad could experience with his girls would be rape or death. I had just learned that one of them had happened without me even knowing. Eight years later the second one hit. As I awaited what was going to happen with these strangers, another sense of helplessness overwhelmed me. Then it happened.

"Got a flat?" drawled one of the men.

"Uh, yeah" I feebly replied.

"Well, let's see what we got here."

For the next half hour or so I learned another lesson in the dangers of stereotyping. The men could not have been more pleasant, congenial or helpful. They worked to help me and chatted with the girls. We all were deeply appreciative as they ambled back to their truck and gave a toot as they sped on their way. Our conversation naturally turned to what had just happened and what we learned from the experience. As the miles rolled along we retreated to our own thoughts. Mine were worry. We had learned a great deal about anorexia those few days - far beyond anything we had read about before or had learned from our brief family counseling sessions in Buffalo. Kris had given us a bird's eye view of struggling with the addiction; but we were viewing everything from the outside and with our own worries and concerns clouding her ordeal. Kris was trapped in society's web of body image. I began to learn how terrible this societal curse really is. Projecting some mythical shape as the ideal form for the body is so unhealthy and imbalanced. I never really appreciated the effect this insidious influence had on all of the women of my life. Some females devote a great deal of time and energy into matching their body to the dictates of the body image myth. Others are far less affected. Kris was certainly taken in by this myth and strove to look pretty. She was rather successful. Since childhood she had heard the refrain of how pretty she was from family, friends, even strangers. The rape, however, was the trigger that sent her spiraling into anorexia. My belief is that body imaging was the context and sexual assault was the final causal agent that created her nightmare. We learned at the program that sexual assault or abuse of some kind is inevitably involved in eating order addictions. I had read something about this earlier but dismissed it as not being applicable to our daughter - how could that ever happen to her? So incredibly naive: one would think that with all that I had learned and experienced in life that I would not be so ill-informed or dense.

When we returned home, we quickly turned our attention in other directions. Heidi had her performances, which we attended. They did a wonderful job, and we were so thrilled that she was able to get to Cincinnati while also keeping her lead in the musical. I never really knew what lasting effects these few days had on Heidi. At the same time that Heidi was wrapped up in theater, Diane and I were preparing to travel to Europe. Long before we knew about the program and enrolled Kris in it, we had planned a trip to visit our friends in the Netherlands. This time we were headed to Brussels, Paris, the Hague, and by chance were there during the quadrennial Tall Ships event. Our friends took us to a rural spot along the Amstel River, and we wove our way down through tall grass to the river's edge. For hours we saw about 1000 vessels upon the water. The highlights of course were the tall ships with their sails and trimming spread out as peacocks on the seas. There were probably about 20-25 of these ships, but just as entertaining as watching them was observing all the variety of seaworthy craft that floated or motored by. There were yachts, row boats, canoes, fishing boats and trawlers, motor boats of all shapes and sizes, but the most entertaining one was the three men in a tub - yes, a bath tub. So we were traveling Europe while Kris finished her program and spent a few days at her boy friend's home before returning home. I recently asked her if she resented us leaving her for such a trip. Here is her response:

"And no ... absolutely no resentment. I was in such a surreal place and just felt emptied in the most positive sense. The whole experience was so deeply emotional and releasing. And I just remember feeling overwhelming love and gratitude for all of you. For holding my stories and still loving me. I had been carrying so much shame. And not that it completely evaporated but I felt reconnected to you all. I had felt so isolated (self imposed) and alone before that."

For me, trust had been restored; the love and respect had never been lost. These bonding agents make life so meaningful and valuable. Again, I return to the mantra that human relationships should begin with a mutuality of respect (akin to Confucius' notion of reciprocal respect). Love and trust provide deeper meaning to all relationships. When love, trust and respect merge, life can be positive, healthy and harmonious. As I was writing this passage, I was struck by three observations. First, it is tragic when we take family or friends for granted - when we do not invest the time or mental energy to connect with them in their times of need. How sad that Kris felt so isolated even while she lived with us. Loneliness can overwhelm us whether we are alone or in a small or even a large group. This mood can isolate us, undermine our sense of purpose or self worth, or separate our psyches from those we love. It can come upon us without our even being aware that it is creeping into our souls or minds. Everyone has moments of feeling alone or being lonely; when these moments extend into longer periods or become an on-going condition they can redefine who we are and how we relate to others. Loneliness is nothing to be ignored. I do not agree with a common approach of getting rid of loneliness by constantly having noise or people in one's life. The inability to be alone with oneself for reflection and away time is a real problem. We need harmony and balance in the sense that we need to be alone at times and we need to become comfortable with those times. We also need to relate to others and find relationships that provide love, trust and respect.

The second observation I had was the presence of our friends from the Netherlands in important moments in our lives. They stayed to be present when Tara was born. Now here we were being with them after the revelations in Cincinnati. We were with them so they could help us restore our hearts and minds. They came to Heidi's funeral, and we travelled to Tuscany the summer after she died. I have learned that life is so much more meaningful and rich with friends and family who respect me and my not so normal ways of thinking and acting.

The third observation was wonder and awe for my family. Such a challenge and having to confront our individual and collective fears and concerns can tear a family apart. The six of us could have spiraled with a centrifugal force that sent us on separate islands and paths. Instead the restoration of trust and respect solidified our bonds of love. The depth of the love that I felt pouring over Kris during the family sessions of the program was powerful. Meaning and purpose really do begin with the love of family and mushrooms with friends who share the bonds of respect, love and trust. I often wonder how I could be so blessed!

The power of familial love could not have been more evident throughout Heidi's struggle with leukemia. From the very beginning her sisters were by her side and changed their priorities in life. Tara had been married three years, Kris one, and Katie was just married three months before the diagnosis. Tara and Katie rushed home to be with Heidi and us during her first hospital stay (Kris was still living near us). They were all tested to see who, if any, would be matches for bone marrow or stem cell transplants. I don't know if they consciously postponed having children during those years but the first pregnancy wasn't confirmed until Heidi's funeral. They had suspended those plans too. Kris and Tara were complete matches; Katie, as I have said before, became the family medical consultant. Another confluence of family events that brought forth a profound surge of familial love came around my 55th birthday (January 5, 2001). My birthday was unimportant but the events surrounding it were not.

Of course, context is crucial for understanding the events in early January. Instead of again detailing the entire journey, I will highlight some experiences that are relevant to the points I am trying to make now. To do so, let's start with December 14, 2000 (a few months before Heidi's first transplant). Heidi went to the hospital for a routine procedure. However, the news we received was very scary. Her doctor informed us that her blood counts were off. He said: "There are two possibilities. The first is that you are no longer in remission," he paused to let this news settle. "If that is the case, we will have to change your protocol completely. Maybe have your transplant sooner, rather than in the spring."

Heidi had gone into remission with her chemotherapy treatments that started with her first hospital admission the previous August. Her initial genetic testing showed that she had what I think was called the Philadelphia gene. That diagnosis changed her treatment protocols. Her form of leukemia had high cure rates for children. She was 18, and considered on the cusp of that prognosis. Her chromosome indicators shifted the chances of success unless treatment also included a bone marrow or stem cell transplant. She decided to proceed with the transplant protocol, which required a series of chemotherapy treatments along with radiation sessions. Throughout her ordeal, she would have bone marrow biopsies, which required the doctor to inject a needle into her spine to extract fluid to be tested. The first night she was admitted to the hospital the physician said we could stay while he performed the procedure. I had to leave the room half way through the pounding I saw happening to my little girl. I almost fainted and had to make sure I didn't distract any of the professionals from doing their jobs. One nurse came out to check on me and I must have shown how embarrassed I was. "Don't feel ashamed. It's a horrible thing to see that being done to a loved one," she consolingly said. I just nodded sheepishly.

On that December 14th her doctor explained the second possibility. "Your marrow may just be tired". The marrow may not be replenishing your white cells in a normal time span after chemo treatments."

"What does that mean?" asked Heidi.

"You'll need a biopsy today to determine what we do next." His caring voice and gentle demeanor were slightly reassuring. "The results will be available in about four days."

Heidi's head sunk, and her chin touched her chest. She looked distraught. She had invested herself completely into the program, trying to be the perfect patient: smiling at others, remaining upbeat, reassuring us more than we were reassuring her, doing everything that the medical staff asked of her. Now this. A setback that was unforeseen. I could sense that she felt that life was being unfair, yet again.

"Are you ready for the biopsy?" Dr. Wetzler gently asked. Without a second's hesitation, she lifted up her head, sat straight up, smiled and said: "Sure, let's go."

We notified our daughters and the familial concern was apparent. Katie did some research with colleagues at Sloan Kettering and they indicated that tired marrow is rather common. When Katie told us her findings, she also said that it could just be that Heidi was being stubborn! Thankfully the diagnosis was tired marrow and we could proceed with the program as originally planned. The transplant team selected Kris for the first transplant. It was experimental. Instead of removing bone marrow from Kris and transfusing it directly into Heidi, Kris' bone marrow was harvested months before the transplant. Her marrow went through an experimental process that I do not fully understand. In layman's terms, Kris' marrow would be harvested, and then separated. On transplant day, Heidi would receive two transfusions. The first would create a net (like a catcher's mitt) for the marrow involved in the second transfusion. The theory is that this procedure would enhance the success of the transplant. Harvest Day was scheduled for January 4.

Heidi experienced some very difficult days during the remainder of that December. She had started radiation treatments before, during, and after Christmas that year. Of course life does not allow us to just proceed with attending to Heidi and trying to celebrate the holidays. The vagaries of home ownership do not give timeouts whenever we face challenges - they have their own schedules, plans, and intrusions into our daily existences. Our pipes froze, and one burst on Christmas day. My sons-in-law and I enjoyed an unusual time that day trying to deal with the mess and provide a temporary flow of water. We stuffed insulation in those areas too close to the outside cold and eventually got the water flowing again. We eventually decided to have all the pipes replaced for two reasons. One, so we didn't have to worry about other ruptures (especially since we had tiled ceilings in much of the basement). The second reason was even more important. After Heidi's transplant, we would have to be constantly vigilant about infections. We had decided to refurbish our kitchen during the transplant so we would have new cabinets, flooring and appliances as safeguards for her. So, new pipes would improve the quality of water being used for washing, drinking and showering.

On December 28, Heidi had a terrible day. In addition to a radiation treatment in the morning, she had to endure an Intrathecal in the afternoon without her physician this time. He had fractured a wrist (I think while skiing) and wasn't about to do the procedure one handed. She endured considerable spasms afterward and dry heaved on the way home. She was so exhausted her boyfriend had to carry her into her room where she slept for 15 hours. The only interruption was when I had to wake her to administer some chemo I had been trained to give. Subsequent radiation treatments went much more smoothly on the following days. On January 3rd, I talked to the nurse practitioner who was working with us and the transplant team. She indicated that Heidi was still clean (without any leukemia cells appearing in her blood tests). I entered the following into the journal we kept for Heidi: "It is difficult to accept the extra chromosome and the need for a transplant. Why can't we just say we've beaten this thing and let her get on with her life? She's now talking about moving to Toronto. It's close but still a major city with great theater."

January 4 was Harvest Day. The other details set the context for what was to happen over the next few days. Kris and her husband got to the hospital early and she was taken into surgery around 7:00 A. M. Diane, Heidi and I arrived around 8:00 and waited for her to come back from what was supposed to be a relatively routine procedure. Heidi had to undergo another Intrathecal. This time her physician did the procedure, and his gentleness helped prevent the complications she had endured the last time. How he managed with his wrist I don't know. He talked her through the procedure to try and minimize spasms. She concentrated on doing so and didn't even encounter the usual nausea. Diane stayed with Heidi while I drifted back and forth from her to Kris. Kris' procedure went well, and they harvested more marrow than they actually needed. When Kris returned to the room, her blood pressure was 63/37. We were immediately concerned. She was very groggy and said she felt as if horses had "beaten her on her back." Her blood pressure had increased somewhat by noon, but the doctors indicated she may have to stay in the hospital. When her blood pressure rose to 101/65, they released her. There are two bedrooms on the first floor of our house. We had converted one of them into a computer room. Joe, Tara's husband, and I had refurnished the other bedroom when Heidi was first diagnosed. We had converted it into a room just for her. Harvest night saw Heidi in her room recovering from her procedure while the computer room was turned into a recovery room for Kris. She slept on a bed while her husband slept on the floor under the piano. The next day was a nightmare.

January 5 happens to be my birthday; this year was not one to celebrate. Around 6:30 in the morning Kris vomited all the meds she had taken. When we called, they said to bring her into the hospital immediately. The usual 20 minute drive was much, much longer. We were encountering a major snow storm. The normal route was almost completely expressway traveling. Those roadways were impassable and too dangerous to take. Her husband and I took major street arteries, but the morning rush hour and blowing snow made the driving quite treacherous. Kris was asleep in the backseat - she almost looked as if she had passed out. We managed to get to the hospital going very slowly but without any major traffic incident. The extended time caused by the snow and the longer route made the experience feel as if we had driven across New York State. Kris' head was pounding so badly she couldn't keep her eyes open as she curled up in the backseat. The medical staff had a wide range of theories but no definitive diagnosis for her reaction to the harvesting. She remained relatively un-conscious with minimal response throughout the day. Her blood pressure had plunged to 80/40. They gave her fluids, an antibiotic drip and two units of blood. Kris' husband went to work, and Tara brought Heidi to the hospital for her radiation treatment. By late afternoon, Kris was admitted for an unknown period of time with an unknown diagnosis. This was another reason why I have not liked my birthday. Diane did take me out to dinner having previously made reservations for a restaurant we enjoyed. Being there seemed rather strange under the circumstances. Afterwards we went up to the hospital, the storm had abated and Buffalo's ability to quick-ly move past snowfalls made our travels relatively easy that night. When we arrived in her hospital room, we learned that Kris had eaten a little and was able to talk to us. All of us were very worried: Kris in the hospital; Diane and I visiting, then going home; Tara and Heidi going through radiation, then going home. Katie had the difficult task of being in New Jersey and having to work during this time.

The next day they released Kris in the afternoon with no definitive explanation. At home we had a very unusual series of events. I opened some birthday gifts while Kris' husband opened some Christmas gifts for him since he hadn't been with us during the holidays. In fact, that night he had to return to Indiana where he was working at the time. Kris and Heidi then watched the Miss World contest and had a slumber party. Diane and I retreated upstairs to our worry; she was becoming emotionally overwhelmed at what was happening to her loved ones. The next day Kris and I went back to the hospital. I won't go into the details of her symptoms nor the tests she took. The results were still inconclusive. The worry of not knowing can be more draining than dealing with a problem that is identified. Kris didn't sleep well that night and again we returned to the hospital the next day. Her pressure was 100/68 and the blood draw that day was much easier than on previous occasions. We had learned who to ask to do the draws because the abilities varied so widely among the friendly vampires. Diane brought Heidi up later for her radiation, and I quickly went to the college to prepare for the upcoming semester. When I returned we heard that they finally had an explanation for Kris' problems. Water had leaked into the cavity surrounding her lungs and into the abdominal area. This was causing the pressure problems and her shortness of breath. There was nothing to do about it - just let it naturally reabsorb into the body. We went home rather relieved and tried to return to normal living. On January 11 we went back to the hospital: Kris to have another CAT scan and Heidi another Intrathecal. Heidi's doctor came to talk to Kris and me. The water was gone from the cavity around Kris' lungs and was receding from the abdominal area. He shared a concern we did not know was a possibility. He indicated that he had worried about Kris' spleen during her ordeal. The CAT Scan had confirmed that the spleen was fine. Maybe in this case, ignorance was bliss. Usually Dr. Wetzler kept us completely informed of all possibilities; this time he chose to keep us in the dark until something definitive was determined. I remember thinking that I was perfectly okay with being kept in the dark this time - everyone has limits, especially emotional ones. I'm wondering how close to my emotional limit I would have been taken if we also had a ruptured spleen added to our list of worries.

The love and concern that surrounded us during those dark winter days was palpable. Saying I love you is important. Doing I love you even more so. We certainly felt it among ourselves, but extended family, neighbors, friends, physicians, hospital staff, church members, etc. uplifted us with prayers, food, visits, gifts, etc. We had put our trust into Heidi's doctor and the professionals surrounding him. Even during the deepest worry for both girls, I felt a deep trust for those surrounding them. I respected their judgment and in the end that trust and respect was well founded. In the chapter on grieving I talked about Heidi's last Christmas Eve. When she was looking at her sisters opening their scrap books, these winter days were a part of the reason for the depth of her love and gratitude.

CHAPTER 16
FOR FAMILY
WISDOM IN DEATH AND LOVE

Nothing is more important than empathy
for another human being's suffering.
Nothing.
Not career, not wealth, not intelligence, certainly not status.
We have to feel for one another
if we're going to survive with dignity.

Audrey Hepburn

Socrates and Plato once said that an unexamined life was not worth living. The context for their sentiment had many complex layers, but for my purposes here I want to simplify and reapply what Socrates meant. He was not talking about examining one's beliefs or actions to determine if someone's motivations were caused by prejudices or stereotyping. He was talking about using thought and reason to work through the ignorance with which we are all enmeshed in our lives. The importance of examining one's life arose at his trial, which eventually led to his death. His students, including Plato, understood that loving wisdom (philosophy: *philos* means love and *sophia* means wisdom) was essential for a good life. In the context of this book, Socrates would be telling us that we SHOULD examine our attitudes, beliefs and values in a thorough and thoughtful manner. Our actions may be caused by forces we do not understand or realize. This ignorance is not a justification for what we do nor how we feel nor what we may say. We may not like it, but we may need to change the meaning of our values or beliefs. It is important to ensure that our habits are just and fair. Pleading ignorance does not absolve anyone from the consequences of decisions or actions or inactions in our lives.

When I was in basic training at summer camp after my junior year in college, drill sergeants had the task of changing my habits and getting me to learn how to behave as a soldier. I would like to think they didn't have to go too far. I accepted military regimen based on my personality and my three years on the Drill Team in college. Sometimes we need to become our own drill sergeants. We have to change our ways of thinking and our behaviors in ways that are not easy, fun or enjoyable. We may want to resist, but maybe that's when we need to do pushups or run an extra mile. Those physical acts should not be taken literally. Do we cringe when we are alone and a large person of another race enters an elevator? Do we ridicule the slang or lingo of other people? Do we automatically judge someone with a heavy accent (especially when we are calling for assistance) as ignorant and someone that cannot possibly help us? If someone speaks like white trash or with an elitist, affected voice, do we dismiss him or her and fail to see his or her humanity and individuality? Do we see turbans or headscarves and automatically think of terrorists? Do we dismiss males who are effeminate as having no backbone or being weak? In fact, what does effeminate really mean anymore?

Openness to others rather than closed-minded thinking is a fundamental characteristic of respect. Sometimes humor crosses the line between being funny and being cruel or destructive. Most of us have probably felt the sting of humor gone awry with our friends or family (or especially strangers). The political persuasion or interpersonal relationship of the offender is not an excuse. Sharing a person's political views should not mean that you automatically condone when he or she crosses the line. More importantly, our daily lives may give us opportunities for reflecting on the way we think about and treat others. Maybe we need to stop and reflect rather than just continue to judge and behave the way we always have in the past. I am concerned about religions and groups that make condemning judgments about others and the impact that emerges from the power that that religion or group has upon its members. Writing this book has helped me examine my life and my judgments about myself and others. The simple conclusion for my journey through my prejudices and ignorance is I must continue to be open to the reality and humanity of others in my life. This openness must be grounded in respect and not diminished because of some self-righteous belief that I am right and anyone who disagrees with me must, therefore, be inherently wrong. Patience and tolerance are necessary tools for helping me be a better person; however, they do not come easily to me. Being a good person is difficult and trying to attend to one's prejudices, biases and discriminatory behavior is a challenge that really has no end-point. The task(s) will never be completed because our lives remain an open journey. A tragic life is one that ignores any call for personal development and which settles for accepting stereotypes of others as the final answer. Oftentimes our prejudices are deep seated and create a visceral response before our thinking can engage. Life, of course, is ambiguous. Even if we think through our prejudices and try to come to terms with our ignorance, we cannot be guaranteed to act the way we realize we should. There is no linear path from having prejudices to overcoming them or even of learning about their influence in our attitudes and activities and changing that which we know we need to change. The following stories are my reminders that intellect and reason are not the sole influences in my life.

Heidi, as I've mentioned, felt destined to perform on the stage. She said she would accept roles on television or the movies, but her passion was the stage. Having done some community theater, as well as my classroom, conference and church performances, I have a small reference point for understanding her passion. Responding to an audience without them

441

knowing you are doing so is empowering. Being able to portray some-one else and bring life to a script are ways to satisfy one's creative juices. Applause may not be the prime motivator, but it sure does warm one's heart and soul to hear the acclaim others give to your efforts. Like Heidi, I enjoyed rehearsals and the opportunity to work with others in changing locations on the set, interpreting lines, and figuring out how to get the most out of the props and the play itself. I loved the fact that no two live performances are ever the same. Lines are missed or added, positions are forgotten, props are in different places or even forgotten, etc. One time I was in a scene with a woman who skipped ahead a few pages in the script. It was a wonderful challenge to regain the story line without losing too much of the necessary background nor letting the audience sense a prob-lem. Heidi definitely wanted to go straight to Broadway after high school and launch her career. My practical, paternal instincts slowed that down a bit, and I encouraged her to go to college, get a degree and do so in a the-atre program. She relented. On that fateful day in August when I first took her to the emergency room, we talked about her future and I was not going to stand in her way. She wanted to leave C. W. Post but said that she had committed to a role in *Rocky Horror Picture Show* and felt she should honor that commitment. She only wanted to attend school for the semester.

I have talked about Heidi's auditions at colleges earlier; however, there is one more experience I wish to share. Her final audition occurred in early March 1999. It was at SUNY Purchase and turned out to be the school that Heidi really wanted to attend. Diane had not been with us on her first auditions, but had taken Heidi to Carnegie Mellon for her make-up tryout (since I was away at an AGHE conference). This last audition was near Katie's apartment, and the three of us decided to make a little trip, stay with Katie and go to the audition. So the morning of her big day, Katie, her boyfriend-now-husband, Anthony, Diane and I took our nervous daughter to the campus. On the way there, the women were in the back, Anthony drove, and I had the shot gun seat. I'm sure he and I were discussing the

NFL draft that was scheduled for the next month and were going over details that were utterly boring to the women. They had their own conversations, which I only intermittently joined. The five of us found our way to the audition area and discovered that we had to share a hallway with all the other prospective students. While we were waiting, Anthony and I were taken aback by some of the warm up routines of the male students. As we noted to one another, "their prancing is a bit disturbing." We were not ready to deal with the blatant choruses and movements of so many gay young men. As I stood there, I was surprised at my visceral feelings that made me quite uncomfortable. I thought I had finally overcome my homophobia, but I realized that intellectually addressing an issue of prejudice does not necessarily mean that a lifetime of latent, covert feelings is thereby overcome. I was a bit embarrassed but certainly said nothing and continued to roll my eyes at the antics of the gay men. I am less attuned to lesbians and have never really felt there was a problem with them. One of Diane's childhood friends in Minnesota was in a lesbian relationship, and I was always comfortable with her and her partner. I have come to realize that this deep-seated prejudice must be related to some sense of insecurity or feeling of being threatened somehow. I do not understand these feelings; I only know they are somehow deeply embedded in my sub-conscious and wrapped in a covert bastion of ignorance. I don't believe I have any of those visceral responses anymore, but that may just be wishful thinking.

After we left the audition, we spent time with Katie and Anthony, and then drove home the next day. Heidi was not accepted at SUNY Purchase, and Diane and I were relieved. Once Heidi received the rejection, a friend of ours told Diane of the over-the-top behavior exhibited at the school and specifically within the theater program. We were still being paternalistic and overly protective. I was still not ready to turn my little girl over to a world of *Rent*. (The drugs, the drag queens, abusive relationships, promiscuity and language in that play were about a world I had read about, but not one that was a part of my experience.)

April 2000 became a bit of a shock to my prudish way of life. C. W. Post had a policy in its theater program that no freshman would be cast in any of the school's productions. Instead in the spring all the freshmen would perform in a play devoted just for them. So we headed to see Heidi in a play entitled *Red, White and Blue*. It was written by one of the program's faculty members. The title was totally deceiving. Attending the performance were siblings, parents and even some grandparents of the freshmen. Katie and Anthony who would be married the following month joined Diane and me for the performance. All of us were taken aback. The language was worse than any R rated movie, and the themes were related to abusive relationships, prostitution, drug usage and destructive behaviors. Afterwards, before Heidi joined us, we all agreed that it was uncomfortable to attend. The content was questionable, and the writing seemed overdone and disconnected. Diane was especially concerned about the play's content for the younger siblings who were in the audience (to say nothing about the parents or grandparents). There was no nudity, but it was clear this was more than just R rated. When Heidi joined us, Diane and I lied as would be expected. Our only expressed critique was wondering aloud what the play was trying to say. Heidi complained about the audience's lack of support. She and the other actors could feel the audience wasn't with them. That feeling made it much more difficult to perform at the level that they had intended. As I think back on that experience, a number of questions keep rolling around in my head. Although I am a bit prudish in the way I live, I do enjoy some dirty jokes and have seen a lot of R rated movies in my life. Generally I don't find them offensive. What seemed to offend me about that play was that Heidi was involved. She was trying to bring to life a world I did not want her to embrace. The world of the theater is open to all dimensions within society and crosses so many of the boundaries that mainstream America does not understand. Was I uncomfortable with the play or with her role? Was the script really as bad as I thought? Were my covert prejudices dominating my feelings and overshadowing my thoughts?

Was I repulsed because of my bigotry and didn't even know that was happening? Was I unready to see my youngest daughter join an adult world with all its beauty and ugliness blending into the reality that awaits us all to some degree or other? Maybe it was all of these.

Now I am a bit clearer about my feelings and know that I still have a ways to go to understand all of the dimensions within my landscape of stereotyping. Overt prejudices are readily noticeable, if not by the person who displays such behavior, then at least by others who see and recognize the ism for what it is. This book has been more focused on the covert dimensions of my prejudices and ignorance. We all misunderstand others and ourselves. These misunderstandings may cause real pain and harm to ourselves and to others. My intent was to provide a mirror for you to examine your life, your interrelationships, your ignorance, stereotypes and prejudices. We may have different expressions or feelings of our prejudices and we may behave quite differently in comparable situations. I do believe very strongly that all of us have deep within us a wellspring of prejudices and biases that cloud our attitudes and affect our behaviors. Sharing my journey is a way to allow you to ask yourself about your stereotyping, about your prejudices and biases, about how you discriminate in overt or covert ways, and what role ignorance plays in your interrelationships. What insights have you recognized throughout your life that can help inform you?

Respect calls us to humanize and individualize others. Empathy should replace paternalism, and forgiveness should replace the desire for justifiable revenge. We can make the world more just and fair if we adopt a practical idealism; that is, an attitude that is open and honest and accepts each of our limitations and our covert biases. Blending trust, respect and love into my interpersonal relationships is my dream and goal. I would hope that these pillars of human connectedness would be the way all of us can begin to address the injustice and unfairness that we see in our lives. It was not easy to write about some of the stories in this book. Revealing an ugly underbelly of prejudices and discriminatory behaviors in my life was not always comforting. Sharing my ignorance and misunderstandings of others and of human interactions was humbling. Knowing that friends and loved ones might read these pages is a bit unsettling. Such is the way of revealing my truth and sharing it with others. Let me leave you with two more stories: the first is a strangely beautiful series of events and the second encapsulates the beauty I have experienced in my life.

On Dec. 13, 2017 Diane's mom fell while changing her bed. Apparently she got her feet tangled in the bedding on the floor, lost her balance and landed awkwardly. Again, I need to digress to provide some context for this event and why, in the end, it was beautiful. (Diane's mom was another mother to me. Ever since Diane and I got married, I called her mom and I know she loved me as a son. Thus, I will refer to her as mom throughout this story.)

My first encounter with Mom, Dad and Donna were at the wedding at which Diane and I met. Mom had a charm and grace that struck me immediately. There was a twinkle in her eye, which I was not able to interpret at first. Over the years that twinkle had many messages: glad you are here; do you have a story to share; naughty jokes are not unwelcome; I trust you to care for my daughter; and so much more. She had an ability to bring some peace into conversations and situations. She had deftly learned how to change the subject or divert a conversation away from an up-coming conflagration. Diane and I spent our wedding night at a local motel and were headed for New Orleans the next day. Mom and Dad came to the Lord Amherst Motor Lodge to send us on our way to a new world and new life. On the outside and to my untrained eyes, she was supportive, trusting and very happy for us. I'm sure those were only some of her feelings that day. For the next 49+ years she showered us with her heart and skills. She attended to little things as well as the big ones. She babysat our children and our dog; fed us; visited us in New Orleans; helped us with banking; taught our girls to sew; lavished Christmas gifts carefully coordinated for each person and family; made her famous scalloped potatoes on demand;

listened to our concerns and plans; showed complete interest in our pictures and slides from vacations; helped during Diane's pregnancies; and so, so much more.

At the time of her fall, Mom was 94 years old and living with Diane's sister, Donna. Diane's dad had died in 2009, and Mom initially continued to live in the house he had built for his family in the 1950s. She loved the ranch style home he had custom made. Moving out was sad on a variety of levels: saying goodbye to the home, knowing her independence was diminishing a little more and missing the comfort and familiarity of the rooms, appliances, furniture, etc. She had a car accident a couple of years before the move; so her daughters (and sons-in-law) convinced her that it was time for her to surrender her keys. She hated losing the independence that driving afforded her. That loss coupled with the need to depend on her daughters (sometimes her sons-in-law) for transport was hard to swallow. Her generational mantra was to remain independent and not become a burden to anyone. Any claims by us that it was no burden fell on deaf ears. No matter what we said, she still felt as if she was intruding upon our lives and was becoming a burden. One of the usual rituals when Diane and I both would drive with her was her insistence on sitting in the back seat so she wouldn't be getting between us. Sometimes we just ignored her claims, opened the shot gun seat and gently guided her into the seat she thought was so intrusive. After living alone in her home for a few years, it was becoming clear to everyone that a change was going to be needed. Donna offered to build a bedroom in a dining room area that was near a bathroom. Mom could live with them. Diane would become the principle chauffeur, and sometimes Mom would come to stay with us for short periods of time. I would take time to talk to her when we were alone. She talked to me about her qualms and feelings. My viewpoint was that she was providing her daughters with a wonderful opportunity to spend time with her. My mom died when she was 62, and I had seen very little of her in her last eleven years after she married her second husband. Diane's mom knew how much that bothered me, and I told her how much I wished I had had more time with my mom. I told her to be thankful that her daughters were receiving a gift I did not. I think that worked some of the time.

Mom was becoming especially compromised over the last few years of her life. Her eyesight was problematic, she had heart issues, and her walking had become very limited and worrisome for all of us. Medications were affecting her in many ways, e.g. she would fall asleep while sitting on the edge of her bed, or while sitting in a group, etc. She finally accepted that she needed a walker and in her usual German stubbornness tried to do without it as much as possible. It was difficult for her to surrender cooking and cleaning responsibilities. She continued to attend to her banking and would balance her checkbook exactly to the penny each month (her banking background never left her). Mom was born in Winona, Minnesota and met Diane's dad while he was stationed across the river in Wisconsin during WWII. They met in a bar and she hid her engagement ring from him. He was the one for her, more than the local man she had originally intended on marrying. They married and moved back to Dad's hometown of Buffalo after the war -- 1000 miles away from her small hometown. I guess that may be one reason why she didn't say a lot to Diane and me when we moved 1300 miles away when we got married. She raised her daughters and cared for her husband with deep respect. He suffered from PTSD (of course, as a WWII vet it went undiagnosed until very late in his life). He was loving, yet difficult at times. The psychic wounds of the war revealed themselves in ways that were often unanticipated. We all learned to accept him for his outbursts; yet they did cause some difficulties for everyone around him.

On that fateful day of Dec. 13th, Mom was trying to make her bed. She was fastidious in washing the sheets and blankets weekly while making the bed daily. Throughout her life she was always well-dressed (according to her tastes) and well-kept. Her Friday hair appointments were almost a religious commitment. As she became more compromised, she fought to maintain her dignity and independence. Diane helped her with social engagements: weekly church, hair appointment, weekly Home Bureau meetings, and monthly luncheons with women from church. Mom had numerous on-going doctors' visits and attended many of my adult education courses I offered at our church. I'm not sure how carefully she paid attention. My hunch is that she enjoyed the socialization and was proud of my teaching. In all cases she looked her best and took hours making sure that she was presentable. Of course her world was becoming more and more narrow (not an uncommon experience for older people dealing with health limits). During our talks over the last few years of her life, she asked me if praying to die was sinful. I was reminded of my talks with my father-in-law about his killing of German soldiers during the war. He wondered if that condemned him to hell. We had more than one conversation about his worries. When I assured Mom that her thoughts and prayers about dying were natural, her shoulders seemed to relax. I have always been a bit surprised at the moral authority Diane's parents seemed to bestow upon me. It was a role I cherished because it was a means for me to show them my love and respect. They loved and respected me. What a beautiful gift. There also was a profound trust I felt with each of them. It was a deep bond that I wish everyone could experience with his or her in-laws. I was not the sole recipient of their love and respect - it rippled throughout the family.

Donna called Diane and 911 when Mom fell. Mom spent too much time in the Emergency Room area before getting a private room. She had broken two vertebrae and was immobilized. Mom was wonderful over the years in preparing for her last days: completing arrangements with a funeral home, having health care proxy and powers of attorney, etc. Diane and Donna had been powers of attorney for years and were fully aware of her wishes with her Last Will and Testament. She had spoken openly to all of us about not wanting to have extraordinary measures taken if the end was inevitable. She didn't say it in so many words, but she was clear about her belief in the sanctity of the quality of life and not the artificial means for extending the quantity of life. Over the next few days, Diane and Donna had to enforce her beliefs. She was admitted to a Catholic-based hospital, which honors patient's wishes but which will extend life if not instructed otherwise. Those days were difficult for everyone. I could see the strains and stresses for Diane and Donna as they had to make decisions to withhold treatments, to refuse a feeding tube, and to authorize palliative care. Mom was highly medicated and often incoherent. Fortunately one day she was lucid enough to have phone conversations with her lone living brother in Minnesota and her grandchildren. They were able to tell her how much they loved her and she was able to reciprocate and tell them that too. Eventually she was taken to Hospice Buffalo; unfortunately it should have happened a couple of days earlier. Health care systems sometimes seem to overemphasize the system and underachieve in the health care department. She arrived at the Hospice facility in the late afternoon of Dec. 18 and passed away around 1:00 A.M. the next morning. We waited to have her wake and funeral until the following week because of the Christmas holidays and the 21 great-grandchildren that would be impacted. I have only shared some of the basic elements of the story; trying to capture the meaning of them is far too difficult. I won't try to capture what this experience meant to Diane, her sister, our daughters, etc. I really can only relate my experience, feelings and attitude. It would be far too presumptuous for me to try to speak for them.

When Mom was admitted to the hospital I was given strict instructions from Diane, Donna and Laurie that I was not to come to the hospital. For most of 2017 I dealt with on-going viral/respiratory infections, which finally became relieved to a certain degree with a surgery on my sinuses. The flu was rampant throughout Western New York and I was scheduled for rotator cuff surgery in January. My protective family wanted me to weather the month between mom's fall and my surgery without coming down with an impediment to the procedure. I did go to see Mom a couple of times in the hospital and for a brief time in the Hospice facility. My visits were authorized because I was either delivering food or clothes for Diane and Donna. As I sat in the rooms, I spent most of the time in my own reveries and reminiscences of Mom. It struck me that no one event screamed to be noted and remembered; no it was more of a steady stream of her presence, her smile, her gentle nature, and her stubbornness. The only event that I could not forget was her falling down the stairs after Heidi died and how that drastically changed her life and to a lesser degree, ours. (Details of this experience can be found in Chapter 11.)

Even at my first visit I could sense the emergence of a vigil and was swept back to Heidi's last week-end at home. Granddaughter and Grams were inextricably interwoven in my thoughts. Do grandparents receive the special care they need when a grandchild dies? Do they get overlooked as people turn to console parents and siblings? I pray I will never experience what she did. Thankfully she was open to sharing our stories and our sorrow. How difficult for her to see her daughter in so much pain? Now her daughter was going though the pain of her mother's dying. The contours of grief were swirling around us yet again. Dying beckons sadness, helplessness, and an inner pain that can creep into every cranny of one's heart and soul. All of that was present as I sat there and felt for Diane, for Donna, for the grandchildren, the great grandchildren and for Laurie and me. We had been dubbed "The Men who could do no wrong" in Mom's eyes. Her deference to us was almost uncomfortable at times; yet, I have to confess it touched me to know that I was so adored and loved by my Mom. Can any gift be more special?

This story, however, is not about sadness, loss, or pain. Yes that was present from the moment Mom fell. For me the overarching feeling was beauty, grace, and peace. We all became surrounded with her spirit and we were given to laughing, sharing tales, and being thankful for who she was. After Diane and Donna moved Mom to Hospice, they made arrangements for Donna to spend the first night, Diane the next. I took clothes up for Donna and sat with them while Mom lay on the bed, sleeping and unresponsive. When Diane came home late that night, she said that Donna had received a real surprise and gift. Her two daughters from Virginia had driven up to spend the night (one is a nurse). Donna also has another daughter who is a nurse who lived close to all of us. She decided to spend the night also. We received a call around 1:00 AM from our nieces - Mom was gone. Again, we were surprised -- even with the knowledge that the end was near and inevitable. There were seven of us gathered in Mom's room after we hurried to be with one another. The staff gave us the time and space we needed to say good night to her, to tell stories, to comfort one another, to know that her pain was now, after such a long, long battle, gone. Yes, maybe now her prayers had been answered. What a strange mixture of feelings; yet there was a grace and beauty that surrounded us: did it come from her spirit? I called the funeral home with whom we had entrusted many family members before and they arrived after we had smiled, laughed, cried, hugged and shared stories. The procession out of the Hospice facility was somber and punctuated at the door with a prayer, a reading and hugs from the staff on duty that night. A warm and fitting good night for Mom! Since Heidi died, we have come to deal with deaths and funerals with the belief that we are saying good night, not good bye. This sentiment arose from lyrics of a song by Beth Nielsen Chapman: "Say goodnight, not goodbye / You will never leave my heart behind / Like the path of a star / I'll be anywhere you are / Keep my light in your eyes / Say goodnight, not goodbye."

After Heidi died, Diane and I used music to spend some time with our daughter. Our musical selections were very different which reflected the reality that sometimes we deal with our grieving in different ways. I made a series of CDs which included the music that Heidi and I shared or enjoyed together. Many of the songs were from musicals, others from singers we both liked (Righteous Brothers, Simon and Garfunkel, Mandy Patinkin, e.g.). Diane turned to songs that spoke to her heart. She found singers who had written and performed music that dealt with death, pain and loss. Some of the musicians wrote of the death of a spouse, friend or child. Beth Nielsen Chapman was one of those artists. When I walk alone I always take my music that is now stored on an ipod. As I wander the neighborhood or Ellicott Creek Park, Heidi's music fills my space; it gives me a feeling of continued connectedness to her and doesn't have any sense of the bleakness of loss. I'll say good night to her when I'm finished; thus, it was more than fitting that we'd say Good Night to Mom.

My planning mode had kicked in a few days before as I started to make arrangements with a sense that dates may be shifted but the activities would go as planned. Our pastor was going away on Christmas day out to the northwest to be with his children and he gave his blessing for me to lead the services. I had contacted the funeral home to alert them to the inevitable and to have Mom's prearrangements ready. Laurie and I went later on the day she died to the funeral home to confirm and make final decisions for the arrangements. I began preparing the service by incorporating Mom's hymn requests. She had a poem in her file that we posted on the back of the bulletin. The eight days between her death and the wake were a bit surreal. There seemed to be so much time to make the calls, make arrangements, prepare readings, prayers and Words of Hope. In fact, however, when the day for the wake arrived, I was surprised at its quick appearance. We had a series of picture boards filled with the memories of her life, and Tara and Joe updated a zip drive of the pictures we had showing during her 90th birthday party we held at the church. The grandchildren celebrated Christmas with their families and then the pilgrimages began: Donna and Laurie's children/grandchildren descending on their home and ours coming home to us. Mom's only living brother, his wife and one of their daughters came in from Minneapolis. Calls, cards and notes began surrounding us with love and blessings from extended family, friends, and neighbors. I involved all of the grandchildren in the service: grandsons were pall bearers and granddaughters did readings with Tara giving the Eulogy. Again, the words of Ecclesiastes rang true: a time for laughter, a time for tears, a time for life, a time for death, a time for embracing and a time for letting go. Tara's Eulogy captured much of the spirit so beautifully. Here is part of what she said:

"Our grandmother was one of the great ones.

When my niece Collette was very young, she innocently coined the perfect name: Great Mama. Great Mama was great in the way that great used to mean -'the most important, the most worthy, the very best of the best.' A member of the greatest generation, she saw so many historical, technological and sociological changes over the course of her 94 years. Yet, she remained the same, steadfast - a woman filled with grace and class and beauty - both inner and outer - and wit and timeless charm and stubbornness and selflessness and generosity and pride and pinch of mischief. She didn't win a Nobel Prize or get on the cover of Time. There will be no national days of remembrance or moments of silence. But for those of us blessed enough to have her in our lives, Doris Nissen Fessel, Great Mama, is unforgettable.

Her greatness lay in how she lived her life. She modeled for us how to have grace under pressure, how to avoid conflict that had no solution; how to smile and be kind no matter the situation. The world is a better place simply because she was in it. If more of us could emulate her quiet strength and loving determination, how great our world could be.

She taught by example. She taught us to love selflessly and deeply thinking of others - her husband, her daughters, her sons-in-law, her sisters-in-law, her brothers, her sister, her grandchildren, their spouses, and great grandchildren - always before herself.

She showed us all how to live gracefully. How to hold tight to the memories and moments that were good and how to forget or ignore the ones that were bad. Her eyes would light up as she would relive the stories of her youth ... She showed us the power of love - meeting Grandpa during the war, writing him a letter every single night that he was overseas, leaving her beloved Winona to start a new life in Buffalo with him, giving birth to her two precious daughters. She taught me the power of remembering and the strength of narrative. She showed us the power of home. Through her stories and mere presence, she showed us how to live. She didn't lecture, admonish or yell. She just lived purely and simply and really

But, most importantly, Grams showed us how to cherish family. To be in her presence, was to feel loved.

Grams, your light will forever shine in our eyes, your presence forever in our hearts. You will be with us in the small moments. You will be with us in the big moments. And you will be with us in all the moments in between.

And, so, until we meet again, our beloved Great Mama, we say Good Night."

Mom's life and death, along with the beauty of Tara's Eulogy capture the essence of this chapter. Life truly should be all about a family connected with respect, trust and love. I ended the funeral service by inviting all of the Great Grandchildren to come and stand around Great Mama. I invited them to place a hand on the casket. As I stood in front of my family and friends, I could not help but feel mom's presence. Her spirit was emanating from each of those tender hands reaching out to his or her Great Mama. I paused so everyone could also share the beauty of this moment: a family Doing love. Then I shared the Irish Blessing:

May the road rise to meet you,

May the wind be ever at your back.

May the sun shine warm upon your face,

And the rains fall soft upon the fields.

And until we meet again,

May God hold you in the palm of His hand.

"Good Night, Sweet Lady, Good Night."

Nine months later our whole family (nuclear and extended) gathered again for a very different circumstance. Our daughters decided to have a surprise 50th anniversary party. Well, surprise is a bit of a stretch.

Logistically to coordinate a genuine surprise was daunting - maybe impossible. So they talked to us about having a party and working with us to set a date. After that we knew nothing. In fact we were finally told on the morning of the party when we were supposed to be ready to go. Of course, we didn't know the venue or what was going to be involved so Diane had the obvious question: "What do we wear?" That was certainly a more pressing concern for her than for me. One or more of the daughters used social code language to cue Diane as to what was appropriate. I call it social code language because I really have never bothered to figure out formal, casual, business, and all those other tags that let people who care about such things to know where to head to in his or her wardrobe. I obviously made some poor choices when I presented my selected items to Diane and Tara. The rejection was unequivocal. So, I enlisted the assistance and support of our son-in-law, Joe, to scarf through my side of the closet and select such items that would fit and be suitable. He was satisfied with his selections so I knew that I was presentable to whatever gathering awaited us. My initial selections were politely put back into the closet. The party was on the first Sunday of August (our real date is August 24th). Family began arriving on Friday. Kris came late in the morning with her three children, a man, Scott, whom she was seeing (whatever that means in today's culture) and his two sons. Later on that evening Tara and her family arrived, followed by Katie and her family. Our house was now brimming with 18 people. On Saturday the cousins reclaimed their connectedness with games they either invented or had taken from the world at large. The day was dedicated to tasks and activity by our children that were done in hushed tones or secret ventures to who knows where. For lunch we all headed out to a hot dog plus cafe to meet Donna, Laurie and their clan. By mid afternoon our garage became out of bounds for us. We furthered our delving into genuine Buffalo cuisine with orders of wings for dinner from our favorite place. Sunday morning was filled with more preparations and we were finally told that we'd be leaving around 12:30 and would be chauffeured by Joe and some of the munchkins.

As Joe began navigating his way, we could begin eliminating possible venues for the party. About 10 minutes out he said "I can let body memory get me the rest of the way there." I then knew we were headed to a popular brewery in downtown Buffalo. Over the years varying combinations of people have been part of my experience with the local favorite. Joe and I were a part of a foursome (Laurie and Fred, our pastor) heading to the Brewery during March Madness. Buffalo was hosting first round games on Thursday and Saturday. Canisius had a block of tickets at a discounted price, so I bought tickets for all of us. On Thursday there were two games in the afternoon and two at night. The college set up a buffet at the Brewery (a relatively short walk from the arena) for the in-between games refreshments and nourishment. So I guessed that Joe's "body memory" was connected with the brewery. Thus we arrived and proceeded to a private room on the 4th floor (the same one the college had used for the buffet). Before the event Tara had sent me a list of questions that related to Diane and me (e.g. what was the song I played to Diane when I first told her I loved her). On each table was a questionnaire to test how well the attendees really knew us. On the TV screen in the middle of the room was a looping series of pictures taken from a variety of different sources, times and people. Seeing our past and the people of our life pass by was touching and in some ways telling.

We didn't see the invitations that were sent out and assumed the usual "don't bring any gifts" was included. But people didn't obey the dictum and the table by the cake and cupcakes (made by Donna) was filled with cards and some very thoughtful gifts. I never made it to the food buffet but heard the selections were very good. It's a sin to go to a brewery and not have a beer so I made sure I made it to the bar (or hastened a willing gofer to get me a refill). Watching people from different walks and times of our life was a powerful reminder of the many venues of our lives and the diversity of people who have walked the stage with us: extended family, childhood and college friends, neighbors, members of both churches that have been an important part of our lives, colleagues from the college, and an assortment of people who entered our lives because of Heidi. There were also the feelings connected to those who were now gone: family and friends especially. As a child and throughout my college days I tended to withdraw psychologically when in crowds to observe and watch body language. There were a few moments about an hour into the celebration when I did so. So many collective memories: some for Diane, some for me, so many others that were ours. These memories stretched for decades and I saw in the distance my Munchkins interacting with Donna and Laurie's crew. Beautiful to see!

Tara and Kris spoke and brought tears to our eyes - we knew the words sprang from the love and respect that have woven themselves so tightly into all of our beings. It was oh so clear that they had embodied exactly the love and respect we had tried to provide for them. I spoke and told the story of body surfing in the Pacific: Diane interrupted and asked "when am I going to be mentioned?" I smiled and finished my comments with how the awe and respect I had that day on Oahu were now how I felt about her: in fact, the waves of love and respect we have had has transformed both of us. Our love was the most important gift we could give to our children and grandchildren. Learning how to Do Love and how to embed this love in reciprocal respect was the meaning of this day and of the marriage it was celebrating. Of all the people who have come into and out of my life, the one constant has been Diane - the source of love and respect in my life. We have journeyed through large challenges and tragedies in our life. "Tending to our knitting was important." I learned this phrase from an Academic Vice President with whom I had worked for over a decade in different capacities. He wisely urged me to do the little things well and tend to the details that can make or break the implementation of a new program and sustain a successful venture. We've heard of couples who have divorced after the death of a child. My belief is that they had not tended to the knitting before the death. It's the little things that solidify the foundation of any relationship. When they become strained or neglected, a large challenge or sadness can sweep in and wash away a weakened bond of love - sometimes respect has waned or trust has been eroded or broken. Love morphs when respect and trust are not providing the glue to sustain a relationship. I remember looking at Diane during the party and marveling in the life we have shared, the love that sustains us and the respect that remains unquestioned. And we continue to tend to the knitting through little things: sharing cocoa in the morning, holding hands, anticipating the needs of the other, playing Rummy-Q, reading books to one another and accepting the quirks and idiosyncrasies that we both exhibit.

Mom's death and funeral and our 50th anniversary party are the perfect conclusion for my journey through my "I's": my Isms, Ignorance, Interrelationships and Insights. Ecclesiastes has remained a view of life for me: there are times to rend and to bend, to laugh and to cry, to give birth and to say Good Night, to love and to hate. I've come to learn the hate in my life has been predicated on prejudices and ignorance. It saddens me that it exists at all in the world, yet even a pragmatic idealist like me must recognize the Yin and Yang, the opposites that frame the human condition. Deaths, marriages, divorces, new friendships, illnesses, challenges and opportunities have blessed my life in so many diverse and still not completely understood ways. Grace's amazing power has filled my heart throughout my life's journey. This grace is a beautiful gift that is always present for me - sometimes I forget that it's here. What I never forget is that Diane and my girls have become my guides and mentors; they have opened my eyes, touched my heart with grace and enriched my soul. I hope you have such love and respect in your life.

ABOUT THE AUTHOR

Charlie Schmidtke and his wife have four daughters and eight grand-children. This book is dedicated to his "Munchkins" and written so they may learn lessons from his life while also understanding some family history and folklore. His academic degrees are all in Philosophy: BA from Canisius College (in Buffalo, NY) and MA and PhD from Tulane University (in New Orleans). He is Professor Emeritus from Canisius where he served in different administrative positions for 17 years followed by 18 years of full-time teaching. His academic interests were interdisciplinary and diverse having taught courses in English, Psychology, Anthropology, Philosophy, Communication Studies, Sociology, Sports Administration, Lifelong Learning, Women's Studies and most notably Gerontology. A seasoned speaker, he has given over fifty professional papers and presentations, has had 18 academic publications and has received several prestigious awards, including the Canisius Dr. Martin Luther King, Jr. award and the Mildred M. Selzer Distinguished Service Award. He is a retired Army MP Captain who was born in Niagara Falls and currently lives in Tonawanda, NY.

For over 40 years he has been active within the Evangelical Lutheran Church in America both at the parish level, as well as working with the Synod. Activities and roles include Conference Deacon, Visioning Minister, Adult and Youth educator, grief and marriage counselor, member of the

Candidacy Committee and working with various parishes on conflict and healing. He has created over 13 biblical characters whom he has portrayed either in sermons or in full-length presentations at a variety of churches and community venues. Additionally, he has written and performed a number of dramatic personae for his courses as well as presenting them at a wide variety of settings and to a diverse group of audiences.

He has travelled extensively throughout the U. S. and Canada, Europe, Mexico, Panama, and the Caribbean. He has served on Medical Delegations to China, Israel, Russia, Ukraine, Czech Republic, and Germany. When he isn't traveling he enjoys gardening, reading, walking, golf, theater and daily Tai Chi. Another hobby was acting in a number of Community Theater performances.

His first book, *Riding the Subway with Heidi: A Father's Journey of Grieving*, was published in 2012.

ACKNOWLEDGEMENTS:

Diane has been my rock, my soul mate, my inspiration. Tara has been my editor and sounding board. This book was not possible without either one.

CPSIA information can be obtained
at www.ICGtesting.com
Printed in the USA
LVHW022230041021
699496LV00016B/671